The Elizabethan Pamphleteers

The Elizabethan Pamphleteers

Popular Moralistic Pamphlets 1580–1640

Sandra Clark

RUTHERFORD • MADISON • TEANECK
Fairleigh Dickinson University Press

© Sandra Clark 1983

Associated University Presses, Inc.
4 Cornwall Drive
East Brunswick, NJ 08816

Library of Congress Cataloging in Publication Data

Clark, Sandra, 1941–
   The Elizabethan pamphleteers.

   Bibliography: p.
   Includes index.
   1. English prose literature—Early modern, 1500–1700—
History and criticism. 2. Popular literature—Great
Britain. 3. Pamphlets. I. Title. II. Title: Moralistic
pamphlets, 1580–1640.
PR767.C57   828'.308'08   81-72064
ISBN 0-8386-3173-8   AACR2

Printed in the United States of America

Contents

Illustrations	7
Preface	9
Acknowledgments	15
Introduction: The Pamphleteers in their Context	17
1 Rogue and Prison Literature	40
2 News Pamphlets	86
3 Social Satire	121
4 Conventions of Subject Matter	164
5 Conventions of Style and Presentation	224
Notes	280
Bibliography	292
Index	312

Illustrations

1. Title-page of *Hic Mulier: Or, The Man-Woman* (1620). This woodcut, probably designed especially for this pamphlet, shows two 'masculine' women at the barber's shop. The woman standing seems just to have had her hair cut short and is considering her new style in a mirror. She is wearing the 'ruffianly broad-brim'd Hatte, and Wanton Feather' condemned in the pamphlet as unfeminine. The barber waits with his scissors at the ready to trim the seated woman. — 180

2. Title-page of *Haec-Vir: Or The Womanish-Man* (1620). This woodcut, also specially designed, shows a masculine woman and an effeminate man. The woman, whose appearance resembles the description given in the pamphlet (sig. A4), has short hair, and wears a broad-brimmed hat, boots and spurs, a dagger, and perhaps the whore's yellow ruff; she carries a pistol in her right hand, while the left rests on the pommel of a sword. The man wears more conventional clothing, but his effeminacy is signified by the battledore and shuttlecock he carries, tokens of a game associated particularly with women (*Haec-Vir*, sig. C1^v). — 181

3. Title-page of *Philocothonista, or, The Drunkard, Opened, Dissected, and Anatomized* (1635), by Thomas Heywood. This lively woodcut shows a party of revellers partially transformed into beasts in their drunkenness while a maidservant looks on in dismay. Some of the familiar stages of drunkenness, alluded to in the first chapter of the pamphlet, such as sheep-drunk, lion-drunk, and ape-drunk, are depicted here. Other vices traditionally associated with drunkenness are also referred to, such as quarrelling and smoking, lechery in the goat-headed man, and perhaps sloth or forgetfulness in the man with the ostrich's head. — 199

4. Table of contents for Dekker's *Lanthorne and Candle-light* (1608). — 234

Preface

Those who approach this book expecting to find a historical study of Elizabethan pamphlets devoted to religious or political controversy will be disappointed. The kinds of pamphlets which it discusses are primarily social, and they are treated from a literary point of view; the aim is to see them not as documents of social history but as an aspect of the range and variety of literature available to the Elizabethan reader.

My attention was first drawn to Elizabethan moralistic pamphlets as a particular class of writing by a passage from Nashe's *Christs Teares over Ierusalem:*

> It is not your pinches, your purles, your floury iaggings, superfluous enterlacings, and puffings vppe, that can any way offend God, but the puffings vppe of your soules, which therein you expresse. For as the byting of a bullet is not that which poysons the bullet, but the lying of the Gunpowder in the dint of the byting: so it is not the wearing of costly burnisht apparraile that shall be obiected vnto you for sinne, but the pryde of your harts, which (like the Moath) lyes closely shrouded amongst the thrids of that apparraile. Nothing els is garish apparraile, but Prydes vlcer broken forth. How will you attyre your selues, what gowne, what head-tyre will you put on, when you shall lyue in Hell amongst Hagges and deuils?
>
> As many iagges, blysters, and scarres, shall Toades, Cankers, and Serpents, make on your pure skinnes in the graue, as nowe you haue cuts, iagges, or raysings, vpon your garments. In the marrow of your bones snakes shall breede. Your morne-like christall countenaunces shall be netted ouer and (Masker-like) cawle-visarded with crawling venomous wormes. Your orient teeth Toades shall steale into theyr heads for pearle; Of the ielly of your decayed eyes shall they engender them young. In theyr hollowe Caues,(theyr transplendent iuyce so pollutionately employd,) shelly Snayles shall keepe house.[1]

It struck me then, and indeed still strikes me, as an extraordinary piece of prose, even though, as I was to discover, neither its style nor its feeling was unique or even peculiar to Nashe. This book came about through my efforts to piece together the literary context in which such writing was produced.

Elizabethan popular literature which cannot be categorized as fiction and discussed in relation to the development of the novel or some such familiar notion is something of an embarrassment to its modern critics and editors. For all the editions of *The Unfortunate Traveller,* people don't really like Elizabethan fiction much, but at least they know how to talk about it. But with *Pierce Penilesse,* for example, or *Nashes Lenten Stuffe,* or the pamphlets of Barnaby Rich or Nicholas Breton or Richard Brathwait, they are mostly very ill at ease. A few comments on Dekker, one of the most prolific of the pamphleteers, will illustrate this feeling. Saintsbury describes his pamphlets as belonging 'to a very curious division of English literature which has never since its own day been widely read, and which is not very easy to characterise briefly to those who have not read it.' He regrets that Dekker's prose was 'wasted on the ephemeral and barren fashion of composition which, as a hack writer, he probably had no choice but to adopt.'[2] Grosart, in the introduction to his edition of Dekker's non-dramatic works, has nothing at all to say of the form or genre of the pamphlets; the fact that they were produced 'for a piece of bread', as he puts it, seems to make them unworthy of consideration as literature. E.D. Pendry, however, one of Dekker's most recent editors, takes him to task for not being more self-conscious about form: 'There was no really settled form for the pamphlet, and Dekker was not farsighted enough to recognise that quasi-dramatic prose, which might have led him to the novel, was any more than one possibility amongst many.'[3] But it is not only the apparent lack of awareness of form that troubles critics; this is only part of a larger problem, quite basically that of not knowing what it is the pamphleteers were trying to *do*.

'What is to be said of the worth of this tract?' writes G.R. Price of Dekker's *The Seuen Deadly Sinnes of London.* 'Dekker lacks the power of Swift or Langland, of course, and no single, strong motif inspires the invective. But Dekker also has a more Christian wisdom than Swift. . . . And his sincerity is unquestionable.'[4] Price can find no terms or categories from which to formulate an assessment of Dekker's achievement; he looks in all directions for comparisons to help him, and in the end falls back on that most negative of literary qualities, sincerity. These difficulties are by no means peculiar to critics of Dekker, and they are multiplied to an extreme degree for anyone trying to consider the mass of moralistic prose pamphlets written over several decades.

Preface

I have organized the material of this book bearing in mind that my first task is to introduce the reader to the pamphlet genre by describing a number of its typical members and grouping them into categories before the more interesting job of defining the context and significance of the pamphlets within the whole area of better-known Elizabethan literature can be approached. It is certainly a difficulty that my primary sources are both very numerous and also largely unfamiliar, especially since part of my discussion is of matters of style which require detailed rather than general attention from the reader. On that account the central descriptive section of this book is longer than I would otherwise have wished, although even so I have dealt only with a representative selection of pamphlets. Chapter 1 describes pamphlets that form a recognizable group partly on account of their common subject-matter but also because the authors deliberately constructed relationships between them, by plagiarism and imitation, and by building on and extending the conventions derived from the works of the earliest writers. Chapter 2 deals with news pamphlets, a self-contained subdivision, apparently differing both in content and in function from other moralistic pamphlets; I must emphasize that those included here were chosen not for any intrinsic interest as news but because of the element of moralization to differing degrees integrated with the news. Chapter 3, social satire, includes a larger and more miscellaneous group of pamphlets; it could have been broken up into small subdivisions of pamphlets classified according to subjects or forms, but it seemed that such a method might overstress accidental differences between individual pamphlets and so lose sight of the essential important similarities between them. Chapters 4 and 5 form the heart of the book; they are analytical rather than descriptive. It is here that I have attempted a preliminary exploration of the whole nature of Elizabethan popular prose, first by considering the major objects of the pamphleteers' social criticism and also some of the undercurrents that run beneath the surface, and then by describing the style of the pamphlets in terms of the various influences and traditions that coalesced to create it.

I have all the time been uncomfortably aware not only that I have completely omitted large areas of Elizabethan prose that readers might have hoped to find considered here, but also that, by choosing this particular selection and arrangement of material, I have automatically excluded other versions of it which might have resulted in books with quite different emphases. I have not, for instance, discussed Elizabethan fiction, even though such works as *The Unfortunate Traveller* or the novels of Deloney might have been relevant to the rogue pamphlets; I have tried deliberately to exclude news pamphlets or short fictions which had little or no moralizing, belles-lettres, and sermons, though it has been difficult sometimes to establish boundaries, and very likely some pamphlets that do really belong to one or other of these borderline categories have crept in. What I regret most is that I have not been able to discuss the pamphleteers, in particular Greene, Nashe, Rich, and Dekker, individually; a study of the prose of any one of them would have much to reveal about popular writing and about moral attitudes in this period. But I have felt that although it would have been enjoyable, and in some ways no doubt easier, to concentrate on those few writers whose pamphlets contain most of the best popular writing, it would give a fairer picture of the moralistic pamphlet as a whole if I drew also on the work of the many lesser-known and often anonymous authors whose productions form the bulk of the genre. After all the typical and representative features of any literary kind can be more clearly seen and studied in the average examples than in those where talent or individuality has transformed their outlines into something stranger.

Where good modern editions of the pamphlets in old spelling exist I have taken my quotations from these; elsewhere, as with the works of Lodge or Dekker, I have preferred for the sake of consistency and also for the reader's convenience to use a uniform Victorian edition (those of Gosse and Grosart respectively) rather than individual modern editions of single pamphlets or of one or two odd works. Wherever possible, I have used old-spelling editions, since it seemed essential for what I have to say in Chapter 5 on style and presentation to stay as close to the originals as possible. I have not normalized spelling or punctuation.

Since I completed my manuscript in March 1980 two other books have appeared which I have been unable to consider in my text. They are Neil Rhodes's *Elizabethan Grotesque* (London, 1980) and Margaret Spufford's *Small Books and Pleasant Histories: Popular Fiction and its Readership in Seventeenth-century England* (London, 1981). *Elizabethan Grotesque* contains a particularly stimulating account of Nashe's comic prose, of his influence on other pamphleteers such as Lodge, Middleton, and Dekker, and of the ways in which grotesque imagery is transmuted into the new sensibility which informs Dekker's journalism of social concern. Rhodes's discussion of the hybrid mode of the grotesque, which he applies especially to Nashe, has much light to cast on the work of other pamphleteers, certainly on Greene's cony-catching pamphlets and probably also on the work of news-writers, with their interest in the strange and the fantastic. *Small Books and*

Pleasant Histories is a historian's survey of the kind of fictional reading matter available to humble or 'non-grammar school educated' readers in the later seventeenth century, based on the collection of chapbooks made by Pepys. It is much concerned with the facts of bookselling and distribution during this period, which I have barely touched on, and also with evidence for readership. Although Spufford admits that there is 'no direct evidence for the readership of the chapbooks' her survey of the chapbook trade supports her general view that many historians of literacy have been too conservative in their estimates of the spread of reading ability, with which I am very happy, in a less informed and much more impressionistic way, to concur. Her attitudes to the ways in which books can be used to illuminate the nature of the mental worlds of their readers are different from mine, partly, I think, because she concentrates her attention on the overt and obvious subject-matter of the chapbooks rather than considering how (and why) they were written. Her bias is rather towards the reading matter of countryfolk, whereas my own emphasis is mainly metropolitan. Both of these books encourage me in my belief that the study of popular writing in the later sixteenth and seventeenth centuries has much of interest and significance still to yield, both to historian and literary critic, as well as to anyone concerned with the culture of this period.

Acknowledgments

I should like to acknowledge the help of colleagues at Birkbeck College who made many constructive suggestions and also assisted in various practical ways. In addition, Sarah Pearsall has been meticulous and painstaking as a typist, and David Atkinson provided invaluable help with proofreading. My husband, David, has given constant cheer and encouragement over the long years during which this book has gone through several shapes to reach its final one. My thanks are also due to Birkbeck College Publications Fund for a grant to assist with the cost of the illustrations.

Introduction
The Pamphleteers in their Context

It was towards the end of the sixteenth century that the prose pamphlet began to appear in such numbers that observers of the contemporary scene became conscious of it as a literary novelty. Thomas Dekker, a spokesman for his time, scornfully characterized the period as 'this printing age of ours' and called the pamphleteers madmen who 'being free of *Wits Merchant-venturers,* do euery new moon (for gaine only) make 5. or 6. voiages to the *Presse,* and euery *Term-time* (vpon Booksellers Stalles) lay whole litters of blind inuention' (*Lanthorne and Candle-light,* 1608, *Non-Dramatic Works,* III, 178). That he was such a voyager himself is an irony typical of the pamphleteers' ambivalent attitude towards themselves, their work, and their public. Almost every writer who mentions pamphlets and pamphleteers does so only to carp and denigrate; and indeed it was at this time that the terms received the pejorative connotations they still possess. Nonetheless, pamphlets proliferated and established themselves as a distinct part, if a disreputable one, of the literary scene. The first writer to gain a contemporary reputation as a pamphleteer was the notorious and ill-fated Robert Greene, soon followed by his friend and defender Thomas Nashe. Thomas Dekker, Anthony Munday, Barnaby Rich, Henry Chettle, Thomas Kyd, Stephen Gosson, Thomas Lodge, Thomas Middleton, and Samuel Rowlands are among the best known writers of pamphlets in this period, though some of them are better known, at least to us, for other work. But the great majority of pamphlets produced in the period I am concerned with, which I may now define as extending from the days of University Wits and the early Shakespeare up to the outbreak of the Civil War, are either anonymous or pseudonymous, or else the productions of writers not otherwise known to us, and therefore readily invite treatment as a group. What I want to show is that the

Elizabethan prose pamphlet represented a new mode of writing which, although it set many precedents for the future, existed in this form only at this time, and therefore provides clues, not hitherto much scrutinized, to the habits of the Elizabethan mind.

Some types of pamphlet from this period have already been the object of scholarly, and to a lesser extent of literary-critical, attention: political, religious, or controversial pamphlets, for instance, or those by well-known writers such as Greene, Nashe, or Dekker, or those devoted to clearly defined subjects like cony-catching or the Martin Marprelate controversy. But the popular pamphlet as such has escaped attention; it is elusive and difficult to categorize, a literary chameleon, which fades now into the background of sociology, now into that of history, or else lurks in the obscure vegetation amongst 'other works' of authors better known for something else. I intend to isolate the creature by looking first at its habitat and shape; but its changing colours must be less directly observed, and will I hope, emerge gradually, in the course of other considerations.

To say that the popular pamphlet was the first kind of literature to cater on any wide scale for the new and increasing audience of middle-class readers would be one way of beginning, but it does beg certain questions. Now that 'middle-class' has become such a contentious term to use of any group of people in this period except one defined in strictly socio-economic terms[1] it is hard to know how to begin to demarcate that group for whom popular pamphlets were written; the warning that there is no direct connection between the social class of readers and the styles and genres of the books they read is salutary,[2] but it does not make things easier. Is it possible to say that these pamphlets were addressed primarily to those who were literate but not highly educated or sophisticated in their tastes, who wanted something both lively and instructive with which to occupy their minds, middle-brow readers, casual readers perhaps, but increasing steadily in their numbers, if the rise in the annual rate of book publication is anything to go by? Twentieth-century writers are often ready with assumptions about the readers of the past, but the evidence on the subject is both inconclusive and inconsistent. It is common to find references to 'the new, rising middle-class' and to 'the citizen and his wife' as typical readers of the mass of improving literature that began appearing at the end of the sixteenth century. E. L. Pearson in *Elizabethans at Home*[3], noting the growth of private libraries in upper-class homes at this time, and also the middle-class habit of keeping family Bibles, gives the impression that many books were available and literacy widespread. L. B. Wright in *Middle-Class Culture in Elizabethan England*[4] also suggests a vast potential readership, 'an enormous demand from the generality of citizens' (p. 83) for books of one kind or another. E. H. Miller in *The Professional Writer in Elizabethan England*[5] distinguishes between the tastes of 'the great masses of the middle class' and those of more select readers who preferred 'the classics' or Sidney, Spenser, and Daniel (p. 54). P. Sheavyn in *The Literary Profession in the Elizabethan Age,*[6] however, refers to 'large, lower-class audiences'. We should do well to remember, in this euphoric vision of reading Elizabethans, that by modern standards book production was very small; between 1500 and 1630 the number of new books and editions published annually rose from 45 to 460, in itself a large increase but as an absolute figure insignificant in comparison with 23,783, the corresponding number for 1960.[7]

Moreover, so basic a matter as the extent of literacy in the period is still in dispute. There has been a burst of interest recently in the whole subject of literacy in early modern England, and articles deducing the proportion of it amongst specific social or occupational groups or in different areas of the country, from evidence such as signatures on wills, bonds, and other legal depositions, or the ownership of books, are appearing all the time.[8] This kind of literacy is the only kind directly measurable,[9] but taken on its own it can tell us next to nothing about reading habits, though it does at least set boundaries to speculation. Historians are often offended by the practices of literary critics who take an impressionistic attitude towards historical and statistical evidence, yet make numerical judgements without any factual basis. But for all the evidence so far amassed, historians do not agree on a general view of literacy in Elizabethan society. Some feel that members of a highly literate society such as our own tend to minimize Elizabethan illiteracy, because they wrongly regard it as a stigma; others emphasize the 'astonishing expansion of education between 1560 and 1640' and see England in the early seventeenth century as 'at all levels the most literate society the world had ever known'.[10] Undoubtedly, the general level of literacy was higher in London than elsewhere in the country; it seems safe to assume that at this time at least half the adult male population of the city could read.

Literacy had certainly increased during the sixteenth century; many of the grammar schools destroyed under Henry VIII were refounded, and new ones established. William Harrison wrote in 1577:

> There are a great number of Grammar schooles through out the realme, and those verie liberallie indued, for the better reliefe of poore scholers, so that there are not manie corporat townes now under the queenes dominion, that hath not one Gramar schoole at the least, with a sufficient living for a maister and usher appointed to the same (*A Description of England*, ed. F. J. Furnivall, London, 1877–81, II, 83).

The period 1560–1600 was a most productive one for the founding of new schools,[11] and although literacy was probably generally commensurate with occupational requirements, it does seem to have been extending further down the social scale.[12] There is also evidence from the early part of the century for the existence of readers who had had no formal schooling.[13]

The pamphleteers themselves supply some suggestions about the identity of their readers, especially in prefaces, dedications, and asides, but they cannot always be taken at face value. Greene, for instance, addresses himself 'to the yong gentlemen' (*A Notable Discouery of Coosnage*, 1591, p. 7), 'to all the wanton youths of England' (*The Repentance of Robert Greene*, 1592, p. 5), and 'to all Gentlemen' (*A Disputation, Between a Hee Conny-Catcher and a Shee Conny-Catcher*, 1592, p. 3). Nashe, however, suggests that Greene's works were often to be found 'in serving mens pockets' (*Works*, I, 329), and Greene, like other writers of cony-catching pamphlets, elsewhere claimed to have cony-catchers themselves among his readers. In *The Overburian Characters* it is the chambermaid who 'reads *Greenes* works over and over', though her taste may have been more for Greene's romances. William Fennor addresses *The Compters Common-wealth* to 'all cashiered captains, or other their inferior officers, heedless and headless young gentlemen', calls it 'a book to instruct young heirs to keep out of books and bonds', and draws it to the attention of sergeants with the hope that it will not cause offence to those among them that are dutiful. Dekker appears to hope for a wide-ranging audience that includes both traditional educated readers and also the more newly literate for *The Bel-man of London* (1608), which is described on its title-page as 'Profitable for Gentlemen, Lawyers, Merchants, Citizens, Farmers, Masters of housholds, and all sorts of seruants, to marke, and delightfull for all men to reade'. Nashe concludes *The Anatomie of Absurditie* tactfully 'desiring of the learned pardon, and of Women patience' (*Works*, I, 49) but on the other hand he addresses *The Terrors of the Night* to 'Master or Goodman Reader, generally dispersed East or West', and refers slightly to the many who never read a pamphlet beyond the title-page. In *Nashes Lenten Stuffe*, 'to his Readers, hee cares not what they be', he mentions the likelihood of criticism from 'some scabbed scald squire' or 'John Dringle'. Lodge, however, directs *A Treatise of The Plague* specifically to the poor 'which having no supplies to satisfie the greedie desire of those that should attend them, are for the most part left desolate and die without relief' (sig. A2). The epistle to an anonymous collection of pseudo-Chaucerian fabliaux, *The Cobler of Canterburie* (1590), headed 'The Coblers Epistle to the Gentleman Readers' contains some interesting implications about the nature and variety of its potential readers:

> Here is a gallimaufrie of all sorts, the Gentlemen may find Salem, to sauour their eares with iests, and Clownes plaine Dunstable dogrell to make them laugh, while their leather buttens flie off. When the Farmer is set in his chaire turning (in a winters evening) the crabbe in the fire, here he may heare, how his sonne can read, and when he hath done, laugh while his bellie akes. The old wiues that wedded themselues to the profound histories of Robin Hood Clim of the Clough and Worthie Sir Isembras, may here learne a tale to tell their gosseps (sig. A3).

The author perhaps hoped for gentleman readers, but here he directs himself rather to the less educated. We may imagine the farmer's son, the first member of his family to be literate, reading aloud to a circle round the fire, and the old wives instinctively recording in their minds the new stories to pass on to their friends next day. Such claims as these, taken as a random sample, obviously call for special interpretation, and in themselves provide no reliable information about the readers, except that they seem likely not to have been altogether a homogeneous group, as we might anyway assume.

The pamphlets themselves vary widely in quality and appeal. Many news pamphlets, some cony-catching pamphlets, rogue biography, and comic books based on newsworthy events or characters, such as the dialogue between Banks' famous horse and his master, *Maroccus Extaticus. Or, Bankes Bay Horse in a Trance* (1595), by John Dando and Harrie Runt, or Oliver Oatmeale's *A Quest of Enquirie by women to know, whether the Tripe-Wife were trimmed by Doll yea or no* (1595), a pamphlet based on a topical scandal involving the remarriage of a widow[14] seem designed to appeal to the lower ranks of the literate. On the other hand there are a large number of pamphlets with different degrees of literary sophistication which presuppose an audience capable of recognising parody, burlesque, the use of rhetorical figures, who knew of Aristotle and Ramus, who appreciated, even if they could not necessarily understand, quotations in Latin and French, exempla, and marginal references to classical authorities.

If we take the division of the populace made by William Harrison in *A Description of England* (ed. Furnivall, II, 105–6) into four groups, 'gentlemen, citizens or burgesses, yeomen, and artificers or labourers' we can almost certainly say that artificers or labourers, Harrison's poorest section, could not have afforded to buy reading matter. On the other hand wills and diaries show us that it was not extraordinary for yeomen, the rural middle-class and often quite wealthy, to own and read books, and there are references in the pamphlets to the conservative tastes of farmers and to ignorant country people who buy books without being able to read them. Pamphlets were printed only in London, which was also the main centre of bookselling, but there were booksellers, some of them with fairly considerable stocks in most of the big towns,[15] and books and pamphlets were peddled at country fairs by itinerant chapmen.[16]

Gentlemen had traditionally constituted the audience for the poet or man of letters; to an extent the pamphleteers show themselves anxious to perpetuate this tradition. Title-pages and prefaces emphasize the writers' desire to be known as gentlemen or university graduates. Prefaces appeal to the readers as gentlemen and men of education, and offer insults to the less literate. Dekker is typical when he reviles any aspiring reader of *The Wonderfull Yeare* who has 'no more Gentilitie in him than Adam had (that was but a gardner) no more Civility than a Tartar, and no more Learning than the most errand Stinkard, that (except his owne name) could neuer finde anything in the Horne-booke (*The Plague Pamphlets of Thomas Dekker*, ed. F. P. Wilson, Oxford, 1925, p. 4). We can easily perceive the continued existence of a link between literature and the aristocracy, and of the concomitant ideal of the cultivated amateur for whom publication would be demeaning if not degrading.[17]

But it was not for high-brow tastes in reading that those little works on the vices of London, on cony-catchers and card-sharpers, witchcraft trials, monsters, and prodigies catered; rather, it was for those literary preferences we may reasonably ascribe to Harrison's middle groups, of citizens, burgesses and yeomen who do constitute a kind of middle class, though one differently composed from our own. This class was made up not of professional people such as teachers, lawyers, civil servants, and so on, but of tradesmen, merchants, bankers, shipowners, manufacturers, skilled craftsmen, and farmers, perhaps not self-aware or conscious of any group identity as are the middle-class today, but literate as they would not have been in the first half of the sixteenth century. The division between 'culture' and 'popular culture' has sometimes been seen as the product of conditions such as the growth of mass media which did not come into existence until the end of the eighteenth century.[18] L. B. Wright has been criticized for the way he uses the term 'middle-class' in his book *Middle-Class Culture in Elizabethan England*, but it cannot be denied that the huge mass of literature with which he deals, however it is described, testifies to the existence of tastes and values significantly different from those catered for by writers like Sidney and Spenser, tastes and values which appeared for the first time in this period.

New kinds of writing appeared, often designed to satisfy practical rather than aesthetic demands, and directed to readers who would have had neither the access to nor the education for the rare and costly handwritten books of the fifteenth century. Where the traditional reader might now choose sonnets and erotic narrative poems, this new reader would turn to chivalric romances, works of piety and moralizing, pamphlets, chapbooks, sermons. Evidence for the increasing importance of the new kind of literary taste can be seen in the popularity of didactic poetry in the period,[19] in the strength of puritan opposition both to classical learning[20] and to translations from the classics,[21] and in the fact that the best-selling fiction of the seventeenth century took the form either of religious allegory or of chivalric romance.[22]

The pamphlet constitutes a new form of writing for a new audience. Indeed, the word itself began at this time to take on an extra meaning. Hitherto it had meant only a small treatise or publication consisting of fewer pages than a book. Its modern sense of a small treatise 'on some subject or question of current or contemporary interest, personal, social, political, ecclesiastical, or controversial, on which the writer desires to appeal to the public' is first ascribed by the OED, from which this definition comes, to Harvey's *Foure Letters* of 1592 although in fact Nashe antedates him by three years in his *Preface to Greene's Menaphon (Works,* III, 312), and perhaps uses the derivative 'pamphleteer' for the first time also in the same piece. The distinction between 'book' and 'pamphlet' was not a clear or consistent one. 'Pamphlet' was often an unflattering term; a writer used it of his own productions in a spirit of humility or obsequiousness, of the work of others when he wished to scorn or belittle. 'S.R.' prefaces *Martin Mark-All, Beadle of Bridewell* (1610) ingratiatingly: 'Gentlemen, a Preface to a Pamphlet is as foolish as fancied . . . this I doe confesse, I shall bring upon this great Stage of fooles (for *omne sub sole vanitas*) a peece of folly' (sig. ¶ 2). He then spurns his rival, Dekker, as 'an upstart pamphletmaker and a most iniurious and Satiricall Libeller' and his works as 'malitious and iniurious Pamphlets'. The word is commonly taken to mean a publication shorter than a book, although the idea that 'book' was an honourable term affects Elizabethan usage. Joseph Swetnam, in the epistle to *The Araignment of Lewd, Idle, Froward, and unconstant women* (1615), calls his work a book, although we would undoubtedly refer to it as a pamphlet: 'Here I will conclude, lest thou hast cause to say, that my Epistles are longer than my booke, a Booke I hope I may call it without any offense: for the Collyer calls his Horse a Horse, & The Kings great Steed is but a Horse' (sig. A4^v). The modern idea of a pamphlet as a paper-bound booklet of half a dozen pages is often quite inappropriate to these works—for instance Dekker's *The Wonderfull Yeare* in a modern reprint runs to sixty-three pages, Fennor's *The Compters Common-Wealth* to sixty-five, and Nashe's *Christs Teares over Ierusalem* and *Haue with you to Saffron-Walden* to well over a hundred each. In Elizabethan times the term may also have referred to booklets sold unbound and therefore cheaper, or to the kind of work sold stitched sideways instead of through the middle.[23] The format of the pamphlet at this time is fairly standardized but not uniform. The length varies according to content; news reports, with the exception of witch trials where the material took sometimes months or years to collect, are generally not much longer than four signatures and sometimes as short as one; cony-catching pamphlets do not exceed seven signatures; general social satires may extend to great lengths, as with Lodge, Nashe, or Dekker, but most often they go to six or seven. The normal format is foolscap quarto, though some handbook type pamphlets, and those from later in the period which tend towards belles-lettres in forms such as the character or the essay, are produced in other sizes. In particular, manuals of instruction and information appear in octavos or smaller sizes.

Up to about 1620 popular pamphlets were generally printed in black-letter type, although roman had become standard in other kinds of publication since the 1590s. This fact in itself is significant as a further indication of the kind of reader aimed at. It is evident that in the late sixteenth century the main type-faces were fairly consistently distinguished; roman was the most common in books for the more scholarly or cultured reader, and black-letter for more popular or less exclusive publications such as ballads, fiction, plays, new pamphlets and proclamations. Poetry intended for gentlemen readers was ornamentally printed in roman and italic type, as were learned or technical works. Sentimental or heroic romances directed towards upper-class readers were printed in roman from the 1590s onwards, but chivalric romances and those designed for the less sophisticated continued to appear in black-letter until the 1700s. It is clear that the pamphleteers were aware of the possibilities in the variety of type-faces available to them; the different types served not only the printer's need for decoration and a suggestive appearance, but also authorial emphases, as Nashe's pamphlets, particularly *Haue with you to Saffron-Walden*, illustrate, yet black-letter persisted as the characteristic type-face for the pamphlet. On the one hand it probably implied cheapness, haste, and all the other qualities of catchpenny journalism, but on the other it must have come, through age and context, to be associated with a certain kind of old-fashioned and familiar writing. It was a reassuring guarantee that the reader's expectations would be satisfied.

Although pamphlets were among the cheapest publications available they were nonetheless too dear for all to afford. The price of books was high in relation to that of food and other necessities, and this ratio did not change very much during the period. In 1598 the Stationers' Company issued an 'ordinance against the excessive price of books' but even so it seems that twopence was the minimum price for a printed work, a sum which would also buy two visits to the theatre at the cheapest rate or a pound of beef. Almanacs sold for twopence, Greene's cony-catching pamphlets for threepence, as it seems from a reference in *The Defence of Conny-Catching*, and his *A Quip for an Upstart Courtier* probably for sixpence. At the rate of a halfpenny a sheet, a rather low estimate,[24] Dekker's *The Wonderfull Yeare* would have cost threepence, *The Bel-man of London* fourpence halfpenny, and the popular *Lanthorne and Candle-light* sixpence.

Such were the conditions of publication in this time that the authors themselves usually made very little from their work. Their only profits came from the fee paid to them by the stationer, or publisher, for their manuscripts, which might consist either of a sum of money up to £2, or of a smaller sum and the promise of a number of the printed copies, or simply of the copies without a fee.[25] They received neither royalties nor fees from reprints unless these included their own revisions, and they had no legal redress against anything that the publisher might choose to do to the manuscript. They were aware of their exploitation at the hands of the stationers; Dekker inveighs against the stationers' caprices:

> Go to one and offer a Copy, if it be merrie, the man likes no light Stuffe, if sad, it will not sell. Another meddles with nothing but what fits the time. I wold haue his ship stuft with nothing but proclamations, because he lyes i' the winde onely for the change of

weather (*Iests to make you merrie* (1606), *Non-Dramatic Works*, II, 271–72).

But they had no organization of their own with which to oppose the power of the Stationers' Company, only members of which were authorized to license books for publication. Greene was the most popular writer of his day; he could compose very fast, as Nashe relates: 'In a night & a day would he haue yarkt vp a Pamphlet as well as in seauen yeare' (*Works*, I, 287), and his very name was evidently enough to guarantee sales. In his short writing life he turned out a large number of works, some thirty-eight in twelve years. He may even have been paid more than the standard £2, but at any rate he died in the most wretched poverty. The complaint that the service of the muses, in however lowly a capacity, was a hard one sounded on all sides. Such was the hold the stationers had over the authors, and so great the difficulties of writing as a professional in an age not yet ready for them that writers were driven to all kinds of shifts, many of them humiliating, to achieve publication and to make ends meet. It was undignified but not unknown for an author to hawk his own work around; in *The Returne from Parnassus* Luxurio (Harvey) accuses Ingenioso (Nashe) of it:

> Were thy disapointed selfe possest with such a spirit as inhabiteth my face, thou wouldest neuer goe fidlinge thy pamphletes from doore to dore like a blinde harper from breade & cheese, presentinge thy poems like oulde broomes to euerie farmer (*The Three Parnassus Plays*, ed. J.B. Leishman, London, 1949, p. 155).

Some worked as hack writers for a printer such as John Wolfe or John Danter, as Anthony Munday, Nashe, and Harvey did. John Taylor collected subscriptions beforehand for most of the pamphlets he published, a method adopted on a wide scale later on in the century.

After considering whom the pamphlets were written for and read by, and what they themselves were like, it seems appropriate to say something more of the writers who in part stimulated and catered for the new tastes, with apparently such little benefit to themselves. That they had an ambivalent attitude towards their readers has already been suggested. The tones of studied humility and servile flattery that characterize some dedications may be a relic from a past age of aristocratic patrons and adoring authors, but yet they persist; alongside them are to be found mock dedications such as Dekker's of *Newes from Graues-end* to 'Syr Nicholas *Nemo*, alias Nobody' and Middleton's of *Father Hubburds Tales* to 'Sir Christopher Clutchfist', and abuse both of the ignorant patron ('a clown that knowes not how to use a scholar', Nashe, *Works,* I, 195) and of the humble reader. The pamphleteers both insulted their readers and vilified the class of writers to which they themselves belonged, as if assenting to the low reputation currently attached to their work. Barnaby Rich condemns 'our new writers of this age' along with their public: 'They doe well to sute the world with bookes according to the fashion; for rude limping lines, are best befitting a lame halting age: writers are not so vaine, but readers (for the most part) are iii times more foolish' (*Faultes faults, And nothing else but Faultes,* sig. L3^v). It is plain that the pamphleteers, though in search of a status and a place in the world, in no way tried to identify themselves with their readers. In fact, at this time, it was very hard for them to identify themselves with anybody, since writing for publication as a primary occupation was such a new form of livelihood.

While it was by no means the age of the professional writer, which was not to come for a century, there were for the first time men to whom writing for money, whether verse, prose or drama, was their main occupation, and whatever else they did to make a living a secondary one. An increase in book production in the second half of Elizabeth's reign[26] testifies, along with such other factors as the organization of writers who formed a close-knit community in London, and the establishment of what some have chosen to regard in its methods as an Elizabethan Grub Street, to the fact that, although printing was as yet a very young art and the conditions of publication could hardly have been less favourable to the professional, printed matter was becoming a commodity, and the demand-supply continuum between an expanding public and its reading matter was being set up. Those writers who turned, for only a short period in their careers, to pamphleteering, varied considerably in talent, literary status, and motives for writing, and it is difficult to generalize about their standing as professional writers. Pamphleteering was an occupation with a low status and a bad reputation. Many of those engaged in it, especially university graduates and others who regarded or presented themselves as gentlemen, either tried to claim superiority for their own work or deliberately demeaned what they were currently writing and boasted of better things to come. At one extreme of the spectrum was Nashe, among the earliest of the pamphleteers, who lived sometime with the family of one of his patrons, Sir George Carey, dedicating *The Terrors of the Night* (1594) to Carey's daughter and *Christs Teares over Ierusalem* (1593) to his wife. He was lavish in praise of their hospitality:

> Men that haue neuer tasted that full spring of his liberalitie . . . may rashly (at first sight) implead me of flatterie. . . . Through him my tender wainscot Studie doore is deliuered from much assault and battrie: through him I looke into, and am lookt on in the world (*Works*, I, 374–75).

But this comfort was merely temporary, and in 1596 Nashe was living with his publisher John Danter, and the allusion in *Haue with you to Saffron-Walden* (*Works*, III, 114–5) makes it sound as if this had been a long-standing arrangement.[27] in *The Returne from Parnassus*, Ingenioso, who represents Nashe, is shown as servilely dependent on Danter's kindness:

> I wante shiftes of shirtes, bandes, and all thinges els. yet I remain thrise humblie & most affectionatlie bounde to the right honorable printing house for my poore shiftes of apparell (*The Three Parnassus Plays*, p. 143).

Yet Nashe was a man proud of his learning from six years at Cambridge, and he scorned pamphleteers, moralists, ballad-mongers, and news-writers; nor did he fear to name names, for Barnaby Rich was among those he despised (*Works*, III, 16) and in *Strange Newes, Of the intercepting certaine Letters* (1592) he derisively exhorts other authors: 'Hough *Thomas Delone, Philip Stubs, Robert Armin,* &c Your father *Elderton* is abus'd.' He obviously aspired to better things than popular pamphleteering; he promised his readers 'something that shalbe better than nothinge' (*Works*, I, 333), '*something . . . beyond the common mediocritie*' (*Works*, II, 11), such as a history of the acting profession written in Latin (*Works*, I, 215) or an extensive eulogy of Lady Elizabeth Carey (*Works*, II, 10) but yet his literary sparring partner, Gabriel Harvey, accuses him of writing 'filthy rhymes' and he admits himself to a certain amount of literary prostitution:

> Thus farre Ile goe with you, that twise or thrise in a month, when *res est angusta domi*, the bottome of my purse is turnd downeward, & my conduit of incke will no longer flowe for want of reparations, I am fairne to let my plow stand still in the midst of a furrow, and follow some of these new fangled *Galiardos* and *Senior Fantasticos*, to whose amorous *Villanellas* and *Quipassas* I prostitute my pen in hope of gaine (*Works*, III, 30–31).

Ironically, it is from his slanging match with Harvey and from *Pierce Penilesse his Supplication to the Divell* (1592), that most moralistic and traditional of pamphlets, that he gained much of his reputation.

At the opposite extreme from Nashe are hack writers of the crudest kind who put together pamhlets out of other men's work, like Anthony Nixon,[28] Richard Johnson, the compiler of *A World of Wonders* (1614), and the authors of *Greenes Ghost Haunting Conie-catchers* (1602) and *The Art of Iugling* (1614), and the pseudonymous scribblers like Oliver Oatmeale, Adam Fouleweather, and Simon Smel-knave,[29] the anonymous reporters of winds and floods and prodigies, and the humble untalented like that 'most courteous unlearned louer of Poetry' Humfrey King, author of *An Halfe-penny-worth of Wit, in a Penny-worth of Paper. Or, The Hermites Tale* (c. 1599), in general, the 'riffe-raffe of the scribbling rascality' who, as Dekker puts it, 'out of a *Meere* and *Idle vaine-glory* will euer be Pamphleting' (*Lanthorne and Candle-light, Non-Dramatic Works*, III, 178). The proliferation of unlearned authors was a favourite subject for the reproof of their betters. Nashe writes scornfully: 'It fareth noe a daies with vnlearned Idiots as it doth with she Asses, who bring foorth all their life long; euen so these brainless Bussards, are euery quarter bigge wyth one Pamphlet or other' (*Works*, I, 9). Even Humfrey King finds an excuse for his own mediocrity in that it is not the lowest: 'I see my inferiours in the gifts of learning, wisdome, & vnderstanding, torment the Print daily with lighter trifles, and Iiggalorums, then my russet Hermit is, the which hath made me the bolder to shoulder in amongst thē' (*An Halfe-penny-worth of Wit*, sig. A2^v).

Between Nashe and this extreme stands a group of semi-professionals, like Thomas Churchyard, Anthony Munday, Barnaby Rich, Thomas Dekker, and John Taylor the Water Poet, all of them extremely prolific; the *Short-title Catalogue* lists forty-one titles for Churchyard, twenty-seven for Dekker excluding plays, and seventy-three for Taylor. None of these went to university, and all had some alternative means of livelihood. In varying degrees their talent was for what we may see as journalism, at any rate a type of writing for which there was as yet no formal outlet, and economic necessity often obliged them to experiment with forms for which they had no talent. Dekker for instance took up pamphleteering when the plague closed the theatres in 1603 and put a temporary stop to his chief source of income, and in twenty-nine years produced more than fifty works, including plays, despite an unproductive period in the King's Bench from 1613 to 1619. He wrote verse, a romance, anecdotes and short tales, entertainments, allegories, sensational reportage, rogue pamphlets, a mock behaviour book, dream visions, and even a mock almanac. He improvised and plagiarized, scribbled in haste and was constantly short of money; he tried almost every popular literary form of his day at least once, and on some occasions very successfully.

He constantly bewailed the wretched fortune of the writer who must flatter his ignorant reader 'with *Gentle Reader, Courteous Reader,* and *Learned Reader,* though he haue no more *Gentilitie* in him than *Adam* had' (*The Wonderfull Yeare,* p. 4), and face the uninformed censorship of 'those mad dogs (cald Booke-biters) that run barking vp and down Powles Church-yard, and bite the Muses by the shinnes' (*Newes from Graues-end,* p. 73). Like Nashe he did in his early days reject both 'empty-fisted Mecaen-Asses', ballad-singers, and popular writers, 'thin-headed fellowes that live vpon the scraps of inuention', although several of his slighter works are little better than those of the 'word-pirates' that he despised; like Nashe he won his audience from that class whose unsophisticated taste and uneducated response he affected—though always less vehemently than Nashe—to scorn. But his attitude to the reader contains an element of fear entirely lacking in Nashe: time after time he emphasizes the vulnerability of the writer with images and puns on the themes of torture and exposure:

> You (that are Readers) are the most desperate and fowlest players in the world, you will strike when a mans backe is towards you . . . where as we call *Lectores,* Readers, you turne your selues into *Lictores,* Executioners & tormenters (*The Seuen Deadly Sinnes of London,* 1606, *Non-Dramatic Works,* III, 5–6).

> To come to the presse is more dangerous, then to bee prest to death, for the payne of those Tortures, last but a few minutes, but he that lyes upon the rack in print, hath his flesh torne off by the teeth of Enuy, and Calumny euen when he meanes no body any hurt in his graue (*Newes from Hell,* 1606, *Non-Dramatic Works,* II, 84).[30]

Ultimately the pamphleteers could not afford to alienate any potential reader, however humble or undesirable, because pamphleteering was not a paying profession, and at this time the economic position of the author was uniquely precarious. They resented, yet hankered after the system of patronage. It still benefited the few, like Daniel and Jonson who could look for support to the reliable largesse of the Sidneys or Herberts, but it had nothing to offer the pamphleteers.

It is no wonder that in their prefaces and dedications they often call publication a hazardous undertaking to which they submit unwillingly. But at the same time they slander and insult the general public and its standards, claiming, as writers had done since shortly after the invention of printing that taste was on the decline. There seems to have existed a strong tension between what the popular writers felt they should do, and what they actually did, between their ideal conception of the writer's function and their practical awareness of what was demanded for success. The image of writer was still predominantly that of the amateur who did not write for money and therefore had no need to direct his work to a mass audience; popular taste was uncultivated, and for the writer who intended his work to satisfy it, there was little hope of prestige with popularity. Perhaps this is in part the explanation for the vehement scorn expressed by the more talented pamphleteers such as Nashe and Dekker for the ballad writers, their debased standards, their contemptible compositions, and their encouragement to idleness and dissolution.[31] Nashe is typical in his feeling that ballads lower the standards of taste: 'The cockscombes of our daies, like *Esops* Cock, had rather haue a Barly kernell wrapt vp in a Ballet then they wil dig for the welth of wit in any ground they know not' (*Works*, III, 329–30). Yet there is always a jealous insistence on their popularity. These 'babling Ballets' produced by 'euery red-nosed rimester' (*Martine Mar-sixtus, A second replie*, 1591, sig. A3ᵛ) were so far outside the pale of literary consideration that their authors, not obligated by guilt or hope of fame, had no need to apply standards other than those of popular appeal. The pamphleteers, despite high hopes and aspirations, were dogged by the need to compromise and make constant gestures towards respectability. Sadly for them they could never escape from being associated with a class of writers whom they despised and yet, for the success and popularity which came so much more easily to them, must have envied.

The milieu in which the pamphleteers lived and wrote was a small and intimate one. Writers of all kinds congregated in London, then a city of perhaps 160–180,000 people,[32] and their own world formed an integrated community within the larger one. Feuds and friendships between the literati might be publicly celebrated and personalities exposed for praise or defamation, in such a way that not only writers but readers too could appreciate the allusions. Nashe and Harvey maintained a literary feud for seven years until it was forcibly terminated by Whitgift, Archbishop of Canterbury, and Bancroft, Bishop of London, in 1599 in their prohibition against satirical works,[33] and all the publications of both writers were ordered to be called in. Whatever the real reason for this official action, it is clear that the battle had attained a certain importance. The issues at stake involved personal animosities and loyalties, and hurt pride, as well as literary principles. Nashe himself made light of the affair:

> Haruey and I (a couple of beggars) take upon us to bandie factions, and contend like the *Vrsini* and *Coloni* in *Roome* . . . when all the

controuersie is no more but this, he began with mee, and cannot tell how to make an end; and I would faine end or rid my hands of him, if he had not first begun (*Works*, III, 19).

There may also be some truth in the view taken by Middleton in *Father Hubburds Tales* that the whole thing was a mere literary flyting, even a kind of publicity campaign. What it does show is that Nashe, Harvey, and Greene who was also involved, had become public figures, whose habits, personalities, and private lives, like those of actors or film stars today, were in themselves newsworthy. Nashe and Harvey were not the only ones to jeer at each other in print. Harvey vilified Greene with his 'ruffianly haire, vnseemely apparell, and more vnseemelye Company', and Greene sneered at Shakespeare, the 'up-start Crow, beautified with our feathers'. Chettle, evidently embarrassed, apologized for Greene's attack on Shakespeare: 'my selfe haue seene his demeanor no less ciuill than he excelent in the qualitie he professes'. Nashe defended Greene, and Luke Hutton and Thomas Middleton praised him as a master of cony-catching writing. Jonson ridiculed Munday for his poor verses, and Dekker mocked at Jonson's pock-marked face. The Martin Marprelate controversy, though in essence a serious affair, thrived on the elements of personal gossip and scandal about the clerics involved. Thomas Heywood, in *The Hierarchy of the Blessed Angels* (1635), noticed how many famous writers, among others Greene, Marlowe, Nashe, Shakespeare, Jonson, and Middleton, were publicly known by familiar names. In such an atmosphere a conspicuously popular pamphlet, an assertive or controversial view, is readily followed up with a sequel or an answer. Nashe's *Pierce Penilesse* had three sequels. Joseph Swetnam's notorious *The Araignment of Lewd, Idle, Froward, and unconstant Women* (1617) brought immediate and angry answers from 'Constantia Munda', 'Rachel Speght', and 'Ester Sowernam'. *Hic-Mulier: Or, the Man-Woman* (1617) was rapidly succeeded by its counterpart *Haec-Vir: Or The Womanish-Man*, entered in the Stationers' Register a week later, and soon after by a sequel, *Muld Sacke: or The Apologie of Hic Mulier*. Dekker condemned the citizens of London for abandoning the city in plague time in *A Rod for Run-awayes* (1625), and 'B.V.' defended their action in *The run-awyaes Answer* a few months later. Thomas Heywood's *A Curtaine Lecture* (1637) was followed by Richard Brathwait's *Ar't asleepe Husband? A Boulster Lecture* (1640). Interrelations of this sort were an important element in the structure of the profession of popular literature; they acted as a guide to the vagaries of public taste for those whose business it was to assess it tendencies, and they indicate to us something of the relationships of writers amongst themselves and with their public. The centralization of the publishing business in London, with the result that all of those authors who wrote for print lived in London and directed their work towards a London audience, produced what has been called a fellowship of authors that cut across barriers of class and education. And this in turn has much to do with the kind of homogeneity that existed about the popular pamphlets of this time, and the impression, despite natural variations in talent and achievement, of the availability of a common fund of ideas and examples for all to draw on.

The vast amount of unacknowledged and uncensured plagiarism, not only in prose pamphlets but in literature of all kinds, may to a modern reader be one of the most pronounced and objectionable characteristics of writing in this period. But plainly, the Elizabethans, and the pamphleteers in particular, had a conception of literary borrowing that is not necessarily to be identified with stealing, and for this plagiarism is an inappropriate or misleading term. They had not yet developed the sense of exclusive rights that belongs to the professional attitude, and they seemed also to feel that using someone else's material, especially if it was older, would lend their own work an extra authority. Naturally, pamphlets constructed like patchwork entirely out of other men's writing, like those of Anthony Nixon, or the anonymous *Greenes Ghost Haunting Conie-Catchers* (1602), or S.R.'s *The Arte of Iugling* (1614), do their compositors no credit; but the most notable of the pamphleteers, Greene, Nashe, and Dekker, all silently took what they wanted from elsewhere and were not thought the less of for doing so.

So far, I have discussed very generally the mass of pamphlets produced over a period of about sixty years and the varieties of men who wrote them. It is high time to attempt to distinguish those particular pamphlets with which this study is concerned, best described by the forbidding epithet 'moralistic', a term with a slightly pejorative connotation which makes it exactly appropriate. Pamphlets properly called moralistic rather than moral or religious are those which not only treat events, situations, phenomena, and fashions as objects of moral reflection, but also subject all kinds of experience to moral judgement of a trite and limiting kind. They are in various ways less serious, less considerable than moral or religious pamphlets, more frivolous, more ephemeral, less far-reaching, and their context is restricted to a realm of easy judgement and fixed unquestioned standards. The term as used here relates both to the medieval habit of thought which regards all events as the manifestation of the interaction between God and man, and to the newer mentality that became very characteristic of the Elizabethan citizen in this period, which was concerned more with the human and less with the cosmic, and exalted the utilitarian virtues of honesty, thrift, and hard work in all walks of life. The implications of the word moralistic are important enough to justify a little more generalization, since it is through this that the claim of these pamphlets to be peculiarly representative of their times may best be seen.

The age itself is often described as a religious one; the great popularity of sermons and moral philosophy, the fact that the best-sellers of the time were works like the Sternhold-Hopkins Psalter (published in 1547 and in its forty-seventh edition by 1600) and John Norden's *The Pensive Man's Practice* (1584) (forty editions in as many years), so constant and great a demand for religious works that half of all books extant between 1583 and 1623 were theological, can all be adduced in support. Yet perhaps it would be truer to call it moralistic. Certainly the Elizabethans did not regard themselves as notably religious. Pamphleteers and moralists like Philip Stubbes deplored the fact that books 'full of all filthiness, scurility, baudry, dissolutenes, cosenage, conycatching and the like' were readily published and sold when the writer of a 'good book' might have to wait 'a quarter of a year . . . yea sometimes two or three years' to get it licensed (Stubbes, quoted in *Shakespeare's England* (Oxford, 1916, II, 222). They observed that Bibles and religious works were much in demand but often bought only to conform to the demands of fashion or respectability. The publishing history of Hooker's *Of Ecclesiastical Polity* shows that printers were very reluctant to take on the responsibility of this large profound work, and when John Windet eventually did so the first edition of 1000 copies did not sell out for thirteen years. Undeniably there was a strong popular taste for moralizing and for didactic writing, so long as it was not too weighty or demanding.

The current interest in education and the influence of Puritan ideology contributed to this taste. Learning was seen as a valuable asset, justified both on moral and religious grounds and for the social and economic advantages it could confer on its possessors. The Protestant insistence on individual study of the Bible combined, for many readers, with the demands of a more complex and urban society to enhance the prestige of education. The underlying implications of the idea that schooling could eliminate the disadvantages of poverty and low birth, and so enable a man to attain to the recognized good things of life in the shape of status and financial security, indicated a fundamental reorganization in morality from medieval times. Ambition, social mobility, and secular attitudes continued to be strongly reproved throughout the period, but there is no doubt that they were current as never before. There are abundant studies[34] to demonstrate that secularism in the form of usury flourished increasingly despite the almost universal condemnation that did not abate until well on in the seventeenth century. The Puritans, with their emphasis on vernacular religion, gave an impetus to education which more than offset the disruption caused by the suppression of religious foundations in the Reformation, and encouraged the spread of utilitarian learning as an ideal. Usefulness, an even more important criterion of value, explains the multiplication of conduct books which taught right living in terms both of morals and of manners; it is in part responsible also for the emphasis in popular literature on the instruction that is combined with entertainment. Prefaces and dedications to pamphlets reiterate the authors' claims that their work will be useful in all sorts of ways to the reader, warning him against temptation or delusion, providing him with models of exemplary behaviour, instructing him on the lessons to be learnt from God's will manifested in earthly prodigies. Often these assertions of moral or utilitarian value stand out as blatantly spurious justifications of pamphlets whose main interest and *raison d'être* are quite other; authors of sensational news pamphlets, for instance, make moralistic excuses for providing flagrantly unimproving anecdotes, and racy accounts of London low-life are similarly prefaced. The desire for entertainment alone explains the popularity of such forms as the romance and the jestbook, but it is always entertainment combined with instruction. Writers often make the point that the pleasurable parts are but sugar on the pill of moral profit: 'What I send you', wrote Dekker in the dedication of *Dekker his Dreame* (1620), 'may perhaps seeme bitter, yet is it wholesome; your best Physicke is not a Iulep; sweete sawces leaue rotten bodies'.

This strong and inescapable emphasis on moralizing does not tend to make the pamphlets an attractive prospect to a modern reader. It is possible to believe that the pamphleteers themselves would not have found this a matter for regret. They did not see their work quite as we do, but they had no illusions about its value, which they knew as well as anyone else lay in its topical appeal. Many of the pamphlets are not now easily available, and despite the modern trend towards facsimile reproductions and the perennial popularity, in their small way, of the cony-catchers, the interested reader must often have recourse to the large dusty Victorian editions of Grosart or Gosse, or, for the obscurer texts, to the slim black-letter first editions only to be found in scholarly libraries. Yet, for those who are prepared to take the trouble, the pamphlets as a collection of popular writing have much of unique value to offer. They can provide, as more self-conscious, more deliberately literary works cannot, evidence of ways of thinking common to the mass of people and so deeply ingrained, so completely a part of everyone's mental apparatus, that they are never explicitly formulated.

For instance, the innate conservatism of popular thought is illustrated in all sorts of ways from the lingering of Euphuism as a style until the end of the century, when it had died out in more aristocratic literature at least ten years earlier, to the increasing disquiet shown towards all manifestations of social change. We can trace the continuing domination of modes of thought inherited from the Middle Ages, particularly in the pamphlets devoted to social satire where both choice of subject and method of arrangement is dictated, often without the author's seeming to be consciously aware of it, by some such traditional structure as the seven deadly sins or the three estates. Conventional patterns and forms impose themselves readily; pamphlets which do not begin as dream visions although their subject matter is similar to dream vision material suddenly conclude with the narrator's awakening from a deep sleep; satirical denunciations of the follies of London citizens turn into processions led by a personified Avarice or Pride. Instinctive association of ideas often controls literary form to a greater extent than consciously made connections and preplanned structures. Recurrent subjects or preoccupations reveal themselves in the shape of a large basic notion built up from a complex of associations so vivid, so all-embracing, so readily explanatory that all kinds of tenuously related notions gravitate towards it. The conception of the usurer is one example of this; another is the subject of 'degree, priority, and place'. We can also see from the pamphlets how strong an influence the oral tradition maintained on written English, especially in the light of the fact that a large part of the pamphleteers' public may well have been made up of first generation readers. The act of reading in itself must have been a novelty for many of these people, the printed pamphlet with its pages that one could turn back and forth and read over and over again as unfamiliar and upsetting an object as a microfilm reader can at first be for someone accustomed only to books. How understandable then that despite the clamour for 'new' and 'strange' and 'marvellous' accounts of prodigies, for matter 'never before imprinted', for 'novelties' and 'new-fangledness', what the public most wanted was the traditional, the familiar, the reassuring.

But it is not to be denied that we can also see how changes taking place within Elizabethan life and thought at large, the general outline of which is doubtless much clearer to us than it was to those living at the time, are reflected within the pamphlets. The whole movement away from fixed standards of authority, from analogical structures as a basis for the conception both of the universe and of man's place within society, from the style of writing and thinking expressed in the formal periods of Ciceronian prose, is one that the pamphleteers feared and often tried to reject but nonetheless could not escape.

G. R. Owst in his pioneering book, *Preaching in Medieval England*, justified his study of minor and neglected material, the manuscript sermons of the Middle Ages, on three main grounds: that their wealth of 'illustrative social detail' provides an important source of information on matters of medieval social history; that the study of them may help to dissipate the errors of historians; and that they throw new light on contemporary literature. These claims may all be made for the pamphlets. The first is obvious. They contain a wealth of vivid and detailed observation of contemporary life, of a London underworld of taverns, brothels, and bowling alleys, of country boys at risk in the big city, of wide-scale and organized petty crime, of extravagant and fast-changing fashions, of a rising class of middlemen and profiteers, and of an all-pervasive and disquieting sense of social upheaval. The third claim, too, is readily validated. Prose deliberately designed for the humbler members of the reading public can tell us things about the contemporary use of language which are outside the range of aristocratic literature. The colloquial rhythms and the reproduction, in news reports especially, of plain everyday speech, help us to imagine how people actually spoke and also to appreciate the close relation between the written and the spoken word. And if we can trace in popular prose the infiltration of the styles and tendencies of aristocratic literature we can appreciate differences of emphasis between the two, as for instance when throughout the period in the pamphlets Ramus is resisted and Aristotle acclaimed,[35] and Ciceronian rhetoric persists till the 1620s and beyond. The interest in and use of rhetorical terms and devices in the pamphlets furnishes evidence that the linguistic vitality of the age permeated all social levels. The manner in which news pamphlets often treat sensational stories, providing dialogue, soliloquies, and psychological motivation for the characters, throws an interesting light on the drama itself and on the relationship conceived between dramatic convention and real life.

The second of Owst's claims, that the study of secondary literature can help to dissipate the errors of historians, is one that I would also make for the pamphlets, if more diffidently. What seems of importance here is to recognize tone, topics, and ideas as conventional; if we know that a certain subject appears traditionally in a certain sort of writing, and that it is invariably presented in a particular way, we may be spared from making wrong assumptions on the basis of its appearance in the work of an individual author. If we did not know, for instance that Alexander Niccholes' *A Discourse of Marriage and Wiving* derived its cynical attitude from a long tradition of anti-feminist satire and its structure from a medieval parody of a religious poem on the sorrows of the Virgin Mary, we might think Niccholes both more misogynistic as a man and more original as a writer than he deserves. If we had not Middleton's *Father Hubburds Tales*, the pamphlets of Dekker, and Lodge's *An Alarum against Vsurers* to compare with Greene's *Groats-Worth of witte* and his *Repentance*, we might stand in danger of relating the prodigal son theme too exclusively to Greene's own circumstances. If we knew nothing of the oral tradition and of its influence on the style and structure of popular prose we might be inclined to dismiss almost all of this writing as hastily conceived and carelessly executed.

If it is helpful to relate the pamphlets to a modern counterpart, the nearest thing is journalism. In function, if not necessarily in style or intention, we may regard the milieu of Nashe and his fellows as the forerunner of Fleet Street, this writing as the Elizabethan predecessor of the features, editorials, serials, personal columns, human interest stories and news reports of our newspapers and magazines and the pamphleteers' professional lives as those of freelance journalists at a disadvantage in a buyer's market. At the same time we must not forget that some of the pamphleteers are writers not to be confused with hacks and newsmerchants, who would be seen as guardians of taste, standards and morality, as well as arbiters of literary style. The Elizabethan pamphlet has no exact modern equivalent. 'Pamphlet' itself is an unsatisfactory term, but usefully vague. It defines a category of writing largely by negatives, yet it brings into relation writers and work that were closely interconnected but had no well-defined function in the literary organization of their day. It is a stop-gap, a makeshift form, 'that accommodating but shapeless holdall', as Nashe's biographer, George Hibbard, calls it, used by most from necessity rather than, as far as we can tell, from choice. Saintsbury, praising Dekker's prose, regrets that it was 'wasted on the ephemeral and barren fashion of composition, which, as a hack writer, he probably had no choice but to adopt'.[36] Nashe's talents, too, were inhibited by the lack of a suitable outlet. Nonetheless the productions of these writers, abundant in the face of many difficulties and a distinct lack of either prestige or profit, are of real interest in showing how writers combined tradition and their own resources, channelling their literary abilities into such directions as lay open to them, at the same time creating and supplying a taste for reading in people to whom the printed word had never been directed before.

1
Rogue and Prison Literature

The life of rogues and vagabonds as a subject for satirical literature had grown increasingly popular both on the continent and in England since the end of the Middle Ages. The cony-catching pamphlets of Robert Greene, the best-known exponent of the rogue genre in Elizabethan times, have often been praised for their realistic manner of reporting, and described as accurate reflections of the low life of the late sixteenth century, but it is important to realize that there was a considerable tradition of rogue writing behind Greene's works and that he drew very fully upon it. In fact, the blend of observed detail and conventional moralizing, of colloquial dialogue and traditional anecdote, which characterizes Greene's writing in this mode, is a feature of most rogue literature at least as far back as Robert Copland's *The Hye Way to the Spyttel Hous* (c. 1535), and conversely, a tendency in English rogue writing away from the personified abstractions of medieval literature and towards what is seen as Renaissance realistic description has been marked since the anonymous *Cocke Lorelles Bote* (c. 1510).

Initially, the life of rogues and vagabonds, both urban and rural, seems to have formed a small subdivision of the kind of medieval satire that surveys the misdeeds and vices of the world by means of a catalogue or list of fools or folly. Sebastian Brant's poem *Narrenschiff* (1494), in the English version of Alexander Barclay, *The Shyp of folys* (1509), is one of the most popular and influential examples of this, though by no means the earliest; the poem has only one chapter dealing with beggars, but its method of proceeding by listing types of fool, each described in a self-contained section, is used as the basis for much later English rogue writing, and it is a direct influence on the most important early work of rogue literature, Copland's *The Hye Way to the Spyttel Hous*. This poem consists of a dialogue between the author and the porter of an almshouse about those kinds of beggars who are allowed lodging and those who are turned aside. It is really a general warning, in the manner of *The Shyp of folys*, against the kind of folly that leads to beggary and not a description of contemporary rogue life, but the interest for my purposes is in the account of the applicants for charity whom the porter rejects,

> As losels, mighty beggars and vagabonds,
> And truants that walk over the lands

as well as counterfeit soldiers, false scholars, clerics and physicians, and confidence tricksters with fake crutches and make-believe diseases, and the many kinds of sturdy rogues who chose to win a living by dishonest use of their wits rather than by working.

Three prose pamphlets of the mid-century follow in Copland's wake: *A manifest detection of the most vyle and detestable use of Diceplay* (1532), attributed to the otherwise unknown Gilbert Walker, *The Fraternitye of Vacabondes* (1561) by John Awdeley, and *A Caueat or Warening, for Commen Cursetors vulgarely called Vagabones* (1566) by Thomas Harman. Between them they contain almost all the features of rogue literature that later writers, Greene and Dekker particularly, made standard. As the change in medium from verse to prose suggests, the primary function of these pamphlets was to inform rather than to entertain, and they are presented as factual accounts of the deceptions currently practised by rogues and vagabonds. But it does not do to take them entirely at face value; undoubtedly they are factual, truthful, realistic—to different degrees—but none of them is without an element of literary artifice, and the desire to tell the truth is modified by pressures conscious and unconscious, to entertain, to moralize, to conform to traditional ways of telling a tale.

A manifest detection, one of Greene's primary sources, concerns itself with a particular kind of urban rogue, the card-sharper, whose main victim is the inexperienced young gentleman up from the country. It is in the form of a dialogue between one such novice, R., 'a raw courtier, as one that came from school not many months afore, and was now become servant to my lord chancellor of England' (*The Elizabethan Underworld*, ed. A.V. Judges, London, 1930, p. 29), new to London life, who has unknowingly fallen into the hands of a gang of card-sharpers, and the experienced M., the main speaker, who gives him a full account of the methods of such people, how they cheat with dice and cards, pick pockets, and use whores to attract their victims, together with specimen speeches of the various types of cheaters at work on their victims, and one or two anecdotes. M. sees the proliferation of such cheating gamesters as a sign of the times; they are not only craftier and more successful than in earlier days but they have the gall to insinuate themselves into the company of the highest in the land. This sense of the cony-catcher as a symbol of universal corruption throughout the commonwealth is shared by Harman and by Greene. So too is the view of the thieves' world as a kind of anti-society, with its own rules and organization, its own secret language; M. describes not only the various 'laws' of cheating, sacking (prostitution), figging (purse-cutting), the high law (robbery), the barnard's law (a complicated group swindle), and the cant terminology, but also an intelligence network by means of which rogues are informed of each other's successes, a division of London into various 'beats' or private territories, and a common fund of money, administered by a 'treasurer' to be used to save members of the fraternity from the penalty of the law. Doubtless there is some element of invention in all this, but it is impossible to define; and an act of parliament against cony-catchers of 1566 (8 Elizabeth, c.4) which describes them as 'a certayne kynde of evill disposed persons commonly called Cutpurses or Pyckpurses . . . [who] doo confeder togethers making among themselves as it were a Brotherhed or Fraternitie of an Arte or Mysterie' helps to confirm some of these details.

The Fraternitye of Vacabondes is a more fragmentary work in three separate parts, first of all, the 'fraternity' itself, a series of short descriptions of country rogues like the abraham man, the ruffler, the palliard, the prigman, and so on, then 'the company of cozeners and shifters', three longer descriptions of urban cony-catchers, and finally 'the XXV Orders of Knaves Confirmed for ever by Cock Lorel', a list of misbehaving servants. The last section owes everything to the moralizing literary tradition of *The Shyp of folys* and nothing to observation of or interest in the detail of contemporary life; but the rogues and vagabonds, who are treated, interestingly, with almost no censure, are so close in the account of their mode of life to similar figures in the works of Harman and Greene that it is tempting to see them as drawn from reality. Indeed, F.R. Aydelotte, in *Elizabethan Rogues and Vagabonds,* takes Awdeley at face value, accepting both his claim that his information has been supplied by a reformed vagabond in return for official protection, and the view that the first two sections constitute 'a trustworthy picture of the terrible social conditions of the early part of Elizabeth's reign' (p. 118). But the reformed vagabond is plainly a device of the kind that Greene and his followers often used to lend verisimilitude to a fiction or semi-fiction, and while Awdeley's descriptions no doubt reflect certain aspects of low life in the 1550s and 1560s, the story-telling element in the longer sections is very strong, and the view of social conditions by no means 'terrible'.

Harman's *A Caueat . . . for Commen Cursetors* is a different kind of work, and much more significant as a source for later writers, especially Greene and Dekker. It is enlivened throughout by the personality of the author, a wordy inquisitive magistrate, full of the upright citizen's disapproval of idle layabouts, thoroughly convinced that the rogues he describes constitute a powerful threat to the well-being of the countryside and of law-abiding citizens, yet nonetheless able to absorb himself in the fascination of relating their exploits. His contribution to what was to become a fund of conventions is threefold: the determination to warn his readers against an ever-increasing menace, the emphasis on his personal knowledge of what he describes, and the concern with an appropriate style. The warning he gave was both a social and a moral one; on the one hand he felt that the presence and practices of sturdy rogues and vagabonds made country life unattractive and deprived the deserving sick and poor of relief and comfort rightly theirs, and on the other he regarded their power and increasing numbers as symbolic of the state of the whole country. If they are justly punished, he wrote,

> Then shall not sinne and wickednes so much abound among us; then wil gods wrath be much ye more pacified towards us; Then shall we not tast of so many and sondry plagues, as now dayely raigneth ouer us. And then shall this Famous Empyre, be in more welth & better flourish, to the inestymable ioye & comfort of the Quenes most excelent maiestye (sig. A3).

The social awareness was peculiarly his own, but the moral feelings were shared by later writers, especially Dekker. On several occasions, however, both are subordinated to Harman's interests as a storyteller, and there are anecdotes, like the story of the two rogues who rob a parson despite his impenetrably locked and bolted house, or that of the woman who, with the aid of an itinerant prostitute, is enabled to catch her husband in the act of adultery, which have the style and feeling of fabliaux. The tale of the parson ends simply: 'Why then quoth this parson, the deuyll goe with it, and their an end.' But whatever its relation to earlier writing, Harman's work genuinely originates in his personal first-hand knowledge. His characters and anecdotes are presented in terms of eye-witness reporting or reliable hearsay—'such haue I seene at my house', 'I was credebly informed', 'of all that euer I saw of this kynde, one naminge him self Stradlynge, is the craftiest and most dyssemblyngest knaue', 'Apon Alhollenday in the morning last . . . there came earely in the morninge a Counterfet Cranke under my lodgynge at the whyte Fryares'. He obtains revelations from a doxy who comes to his gate by offering her food and money, and promising anonymity; he exposes the craft of a dummerer, a beggar who pretends dumbness, by having him strung up by the wrists to a beam until he calls for mercy. He uses friends, acquaintances, and servants to get information, and he trades on his own reputation as a magistrate in order to prevent the circulation amongst underworld traders of a copper cauldron stolen from his own backyard. These details bring a sense of reality to his work that no later writer was to achieve. All Harman's successors tried to put their work over as fact; Greene in particular went to some lengths, and the documentary aspect became a convention of the genre, although, despite the passing of years, the rogue life described by conycatching writers retained much the same basis of information as Harman supplied in the 1560s.

While Harman was not by intention a writer or stylist, he was not without literary awareness. In his Epistle to the reader he belittles his style: 'Eloquence haue I none, I neuer was acquaynted with the muses, I neuer tasted of Helycon.' Later writers took up this protestation; Greene defended the plain style as necessary to the subject,[1] while others felt or claimed to feel that their style required some apology. Harman was genuinely interested in language; his style was by no means as plain as he pretended, and he indulged frequently in alliteration and word-play:

> This amerous man be holdinge with ardante eyes, thys glimmeringe glauncer, was presentlye pyteouslye persed to the hart, and lewdlye longed to bee clothed under her lyverye and, bestowinge a fewe fonde wordes with her, understode strayte, that she woulde bee easlye perswade to lykinge lechery, and as a man mazed, mused howe to attayne to his purpose, for he hadde no money (sigs. C2^v–C3).

And the pamphlet is often enlivened by his understated humour:

> He . . . offeres . . . [the whistle] to this manerly marian that yf she would mete him on the backesyde of the towne and curteously kys him with out constraynt, she shoulde bee mystres thereof and it weare much better (sig. C3).

More unusual and significant is his discussion, in the Epistle to the reader of the second edition, of the etymology of his terms:

I thought it necessary now at this seconde Impression to acquaynt ye with a great faulte as some takethe it, but none as I meane it, callinge these Vagabonds cursetors in the intytelynge of my booke as runneres or rangers aboute the countrey, deriued of this Laten word, (CURRO) neither do I wryght it Cooresetores with a double oo or Cowresetors, with a w, which hath an other signification, is there no deversite between a gardein and a garden, mayteynaunce & maintenance, streytes and stretes, those that haue understanding knowe there is a great dyfference, who is so ignorant by these dayes as knoweth not the meaning of a vagabone and yf an ydell leuterar should be so called of eny man, would not he thik it bothe odyous and reprochefull? (sig. B1)

He was interested also in the language that the vagabonds themselves used, and the glossary of 'pedlars' French' and the specimen dialogue in canting terms between an uprightman and a rogue with which the pamphlet concludes were features taken up in later rogue writing, and formed the basis of much dramatic dialogue in plays concerned with cony-catchers.[2]

Aydelotte cites convincing documentary evidence to support some of Harman's findings: of Harman's list of three hundred upright men, rogues, and palliards living at his time, at least twenty may be found in official records.[3] But it is impossible here to go into detail about the relationship of Elizabethan rogue literature to the facts of life at the time. The reader who knows something of Elizabethan habits of mind will have learnt to be wary of making too simple an equation between what is stated and what was true, and so to take with a pinch of salt any claim that this material gives an authentic account of first-hand observation of contemporary life. There is no doubt that beggars and vagrants who chose a wandering life in preference to one of immobility in a small rural community were evident in large numbers in the sixteenth century and constituted a grave social problem to contemporary chroniclers and economic theorists. The increasing amount of legislation after 1530 directed at controlling them, often very severe, indicates the importance of the problem in the eyes of governments interested in suppressing any manifestations of anarchy and disorder within the commonwealth. Contemporary estimates of the numbers of unlicensed beggars and masterless men at large are often improbably high, perhaps as a reflection of current hysteria on the subject,[4] but there is objective documentation to support a number of the details about rogue life given in the earlier pamphlets. The existence of cheating tricks and cony-catching devices as first described in *A manifest detection* are also vouched for. Acts of parliament, local records, orders for the poor, descriptions of beggars arrested in searches, and so on provide evidence of child beggary, of fraternities of beggars and cutpurses, of counterfeit licences, of manufactories for false dice, of feigned diseases, and false wounds. The 'Acte for Punyshment of Rogues, Vagabondes and Sturdy Beggars' (39 Elizabeth, c.4, 1597) asserts that:

> All persons calling themsleves [sic] Schollers going about begging, all Seafaring-men pretending losses of their Shippes or Goodes on the Sea going about the Country begging, all idle persons ... using any subtile Crafte or unlawfull Games and Playes, or fayning themselves to have knowledge in Phisiognomye Palmestrye or other like crafty scyence ... all Juglers Tynkers Peddlers and Petty Chapmen wandring abroade ... and all such persons not being Fellons wandering and pretending themselves to be Egipcyans, or wandering in the Habbite Forme or Attyre of counterfayte Egipcyans; shalbe taken adjudged and deemed Rogues Vagabondes and Sturdy Beggers, and shall susteyne such Payne and Punyshment as by this Acte is in that behalfe appointed. (Quoted from Tawney and Power, eds., *Tudor Economic Documents*, 3 vols., London, 1924, III, 355.)

A letter from William Fleetwood, Recorder of London, to Lord Burghley, written on 7 July 1585, describes a school for pickpockets in Billingsgate and notes the use there of various cant terms:

> He that could take owt a cownter without any noyse, was allowed to be *a publique Foyster:* and he that could take a peece of sylver owt of the purse without the noyse of any of the bells, he was adjudged *a judiciall Nypper*. Nota that a Foister is a Pick-pockett, and a Nypper is termed a Pickepurse, or a Cutpurse ... Note that ... *lyft* is to robbe a shoppe or a gentilmans chamber, *shave* is to fylche a clooke, a sword, a sylver sponne or suche like ... Nota, that *mylken ken* is to commyt a roborie or burglarie in the night in a dwelling house (Tawney and Power, II, 338–39).

F. R. Aydelotte may well be right in his view that the statutes of 1572 and 1575 against vagabondage (14 Elizabeth, c.5 and 18 Elizabeth, c.3), in providing stricter punishment for sturdy beggars, establishing houses of correction in every county, and organizing the idle to labour began to bring to an end the old vagabond way of life. It is very clear that after Greene rogue writers had little more factual material and information to add, and so it seems that they contented themselves with wholesale plagiarism, or else utilized the established conventions as a basis for creating new forms and styles.

Greene's cony-catching pamphlets form the heart of the genre. They are among the best-known of all Elizabethan pamphlets as Greene, with his 'iolly long red peake, like the spire of a steeple'

(Nashe, *Works*, I, 287) and his early death after a 'fatall banquet of Rhenish wine and pickled hearing' (Nashe, *Works*, I, 287-8) is one of the most vivid figures of the period. There is much uncertainty about the facts of Greene's life, in particular about the extent of his personal knowledge of the rogues and cozeners with whom he claimed close acquaintance, but no doubt that he was a notorious character in literary London for at least his last four years, and the major source for the contemporary image of the bohemian pamphleteer. Greene's literary relationships provide much of our information about him as a man. To lovers of Shakespeare, he has a small dark corner in fame because his attack on 'that upstart crow, beautified with our feathers' testifies to the significance of Shakespeare's reputation in 1592. In *Foure Letters and certeine Sonnets*, published in December 1592, Gabriel Harvey, spoiling to have his revenge for some malicious remarks in Greene's recently published *A Quip for an Upstart Courtier*, heaped insult upon insult on the newly dead writer for nearly a page:

> Who in London hath not heard of his dissolute, and licentious living; his fonde disguisinge of a Master of Arte with ruffianly haire, unseemely apparell, and more unseemelye company: his vaineglorious and Thrasonicall brauinge: his piperly Extemporizing, and Tarletonizing: his apishe counterfeiting of euery ridiculous, and absurd toy . . . hys villainous cogging, and foisting; his monstrous swearinge, and horrible forswearing; his impious profaning of sacred Textes: his other scandalous, and blasphemous rauinge . . . his infamous resorting to the Banckeside, Shorditch, Southwarke, and other filthy hauntes: his obscure lurkinge in basest corners: his pawning of his sword, cloake, and what not, when money came short; his impudent pamphletting, phantasticall interluding, and desperate libelling, when other coosening shifts failed?
> (*Foure Letters and certeine Sonnets*, ed. G. B. Harrison, Bodley Head Quartos, 1922, pp. 19-20.)

But all this, very much the substance of the modern view of Greene, was, as Harvey admitted, based entirely on hearsay: 'I was altogether vnacquainted with the man, & neuer once saluted him by name' (*Foure Letters*, p. 19). Nashe, who did know Greene personally, does not refute these charges directly in his answer to Harvey; although he wanted to defend Greene, he preferred to ridicule Harvey and turn his accusations aside with flippant rejoinders rather than attempt the perhaps impossible task of exonerating the dead man. 'Greene inherited more virtues than vices . . . his onely care was to have a spel in his purse to coniure up a good cuppe of wine with at all times' (*Works*, I, 287). Greene's biographers generally accept Harvey's implications about Greene's manner of life and his assertion that Greene died in poverty and squalor, and it seems certain that Greene did know the lives and habits of London's petty criminals more intimately than any of the many other pamphleteers who found saleable material in them. It is not so much his frequent insistence on presenting himself in the role of reformed profligate, as he does, for instance, in *Greenes Mourning Garment, Greenes Never too late, Greenes farewell to Folly, Greenes Groats-Worth of witte,* and *The Repentance of Robert Greene,* or even the references in the cony-catching pamphlets to his personal acquaintance with individual rogues that lead us to see him in this way, but the general air of real interest and observation that pervades these works.

In the last year of Greene's life appeared, amongst other writings, six cony-catching pamphlets: *A Notable Discouery of Coosnage* and *The Second part of Conny-catching* (entered together in the Stationers' Register 13 December 1591), *The Thirde and last Part of Conny-catching* (entered 7 February 1592), *The Defence of Conny-Catching* by 'Cuthbert Cunny-catcher' (entered 21 April 1592), *A Disputation, Betweene a Hee Conny-catcher and a Shee Conny-catcher* (not entered), and *The Blacke Bookes Messenger* (entered 21 August 1592). They achieved immediate popularity.[5] Although *The Defence* is often grouped with Greene's pamphlets its authorship is not established but much about it points to Greene as the author.[6] These six pamphlets form two groups: first, *A Notable Discouery of Coosnage, The Second part of Conny-catching,* and *The Thirde and last Part of Conny-catching,* which consist basically of descriptions and anecdotal illustrations of the workings of various 'laws' of the criminal underworld that Greene claimed to have discovered, and second, *The Defence of Conny-Catching, A Disputation,* and *The Blacke Bookes Messenger,* each different and more experimental in form. In style, and in tone and attitudes, they are all basically alike. Greene has often been praised, sometimes exaggeratedly, for the plain style of his cony-catching pamphlets, which is seen as a development away from the Euphuism of his romances. In *The Second part* he draws attention to his plain style and to the decorum he is observing in using it:

> A certaine decorum is to bee kept in euerie thing, and not to applie a high stile in a base beside the facultie is so odious, and the men so seruile and slauish-minded, that I should dishonor that high misterie of eloquence, and derogate from the dignitie of our English toonge, eyther to employ any figure or bestow one choyse English word upon such disdained rakehels as those Conny-catchers (p. 7).

But Greene did not entirely avoid figures and choice words in treating his base subjects, and the reader does not have to search hard to find the kind of alliteration and balanced periods, classical tags and quotations, learned comparisons, and proverbial phrases that are typical of his earlier prose. Conventionally emotional subjects especially seem to call forth his instinct for elaboration:

> So gentlemen, my younger yeeres had uncertaine thoughts, but now my ripe daies cals on to repentant deedes, and I sorrow as much to see others wilful, as I delighted once to be wanton (*A Notable Discouery*, p. 2).
>
> The Crocodile hath not more teares, Proteus, more shape, Janus more faces, the Hieria, more sundry tunes to entrap the passengers, than our English Curtizans, to bee plaine, our English whores: to set on fire the hearts of lasciuious and gazing strangers (*A Disputation*, p. 5).

But the stories and anecdotes are generally more economical and direct in their language; Greene provides plenty of lively and colloquial dialogue, and gives his tales the air of factual report with details of names and places, of clothing and of gestures. The whores in their 'rich garded gowns, queint periwigs, rufs of the largest size, quarter and halfe deep, gloried richly with blew starch, their cheekes died with surfuling water' (*A Notable Discouery*, p. 44), the merry gentleman who 'holding his gowne open with his armes on either side as verie manie doe, gaue sight of a faire purple veluet purse' (*The Thirde and last Part*, p. 22), the card-sharper dressed like a gentleman who wears boots to conceal his want of stockings—such characters bring Elizabethan London vividly to the mind's eye.

Greene's moral tone, while never in itself consistent, maintains the same variations in all his cony-catching pamphlets. The objects of his censure do not vary. The dying confession of Ned Browne, cutpurse and narrator of Greene's last cony-catching pamphlet, *The Blacke Bookes Messenger*, carries the same stresses as *A Notable Discouery*—on the deceptions of whores, the idle wasteful lives of rogues who prefer crime to honest labour, and the undermining of the whole commonwealth that comes about through their behaviour. Greene wants to warn against the enemies of society in general, and more specifically to advise the innocent and the honest on the preservation of their property while they are in London. But he does not maintain a high moral tone throughout. Sometimes he presents himself as the purveyor to the general public of inside information on the methods of the criminal fraternity; the Elizabethan reading public was plainly interested in the sheer mechanics of cozenage, and Greene's description of the barnard's law, the prigging law, the vincent's law, and the rest of it were designed to exploit this interest to the full. Sometimes he takes the stance not just of the guardian of honest citizens' purses but also of the upholder of the health and well-being of the whole state; but often these roles are cast aside to reveal Greene the storyteller and lover of wit who delights in a good joke or a clever trick even if perpetrated at the expense of the simple citizen. His characters are sometimes made to share this taste; a cheated lawyer admires the skill of the cutpurse who robbed him: 'In the middest of his griefe, hee remembred him that said, who am I? Wherewith he brake foorth into a great laughter' (*The Thirde and last Part*, p. 25). A story in which a young pickpocket gets away with robbing an old one is concluded without moral comment: 'Onely this makes me smile, that one false knave can beguile another' (*The Thirde and last Part*, p. 39).

Many of the anecdotes are told simply for what they are, merry jests; the exploits of thieves are enjoyed for their originality, and the qualities of the perfect foist, or cutpurse, 'properties that a good surgeon should have', are described with the enthusiasm of Mosca in *Volpone* dilating on the profession of parasite. In 1591 Greene wrote in the dedication to his *Farewell to Folly* that it was to be the last of his 'superficiall labours' and thereafter took as a motto for his title pages 'Nascimur pro patria', but it is clear that his didacticism, though more than merely a gambit, is not the shaping inspiration behind any of the cony-catching pamphlets, with the possible exception of *The Defence of Conny-Catching*, if it is his. Greene was never a master of structure, and often the moralizing element in his pamphlets takes the form of passages of advice or indictment included at the expense of the unity of the rest. In *A Disputation*, Laurence the thief and Nan the prostitute, who have been vying with each other as to whose trade makes the most money and does most harm, are obliged to step out of their characters in order to indict the evils they embody; Nan herself is made to speak one of Greene's strongest condemnations of prostitution:

> Search the Gayles, there you shall heare complaintes of whoores, looke into the Spittles and Hospitalles, there you shall see men diseased of the Frenche Marbles ... bee an Auditor or eare witnesse at the death of any theefe, and his last Testament is, Take heed of a Whoore: I dare scarce speake of Bridewell because my shoulders tremble at the name of it, I have so often deserued it (*A Disputation*, p. 38).

In the same pamphlet, the story of the courtesan who is converted by her client's pointing out to her that even in the darkest room God can see all she does is simply told and moving. It makes a fitting climax to a pamphlet whose main theme is the power for destruction of woman as whore. Yet Greene cannot leave well alone; he appends a short and pointless 'merry Tale taken not far from Fetter Lane, of a new found Conny-catcher, that was Conny-catcht himselfe' which has no relation to the rest and changes the whole tone of the pamphlet. In *The Blacke Bookes Messenger*, the ending is equally discordant; Ned Browne, who has enthusiastically recounted merry jests and pleasant tales of criminal exploits for the main body of the pamphlet, finally undergoes a lightning repentance and leaps to his death from a window, shouting moral counsel as he goes.

The main line of development within Greene's cony-catching pamphlets is towards fiction. This was, of course, no new departure for Greene, but rather a regression, since he had claimed in the preface to *A Notable Discouery* to be turning his back on the wanton follies of his misspent youth in order to write something of practical value for the benefit of his countrymen. The emphasis in *A Notable Discouery* is on fact and information. The author has been many times a witness to the cozenage practised by wily city crooks on both 'men of good calling' and 'poor ignorant country farmers', and has personal knowledge of their methods; it is his duty to expose them, even at the risk of his safety: 'Yet Gentlemen am I sore threatned by the hacksters of that filthie facultie, that if I sette their practises in print, they will cut off that hand that writes the Pamphlet but how I feare their brauadoes, you shall perceive by my plaine painting out of them' (p. 14).

His attack is specifically directed against two kinds of villainy: that of cony-catchers who band together to lure the innocent into taverns and then cheat them at cards or dice, and that of cross-biters who use prostitutes to pick the pockets of their victims or else entrap them in compromising situations where they may be blackmailed. Information is always spiced with entertainment. Greene reveals his rogues by means of anecdotes and dramatically realised scenes with vivid dialogue. Names of people and places give a sense of authenticity, and Greene, like a good journalist, is often on the scene in person to conduct interviews: 'Coming downe Turnmil street the other day, I met one whom I suspected a conycatcher, I drew him on to the tavern, and after a cup of wine or two, I talkt with him of the maner of his life' (p. 35). He aims to create a mystique around the activities he describes, and to convince the reader that he is being initiated into a special world, a fraternity of criminals with their own jargon, meeting-places, and way of life. *The Second part of Conny-catching*, although apparently first published at the same time as *A Notable Discouery*, is written as if it were a sequel; Greene answers those who have criticized the low style of his first pamphlet, and boasts of the widespread effects his discoveries have had:

> The Professors of this law, beeing somewhat dasht, and their trade greatly impouerished, by the late editions of their secret villanies, seeke not a new meanes of life, but a new method how to fetch in their Conies, and to play their pranckes . . . But the country men hauing had partly a caueat for their cosenage, feare their fauorable speeches & their curteous salutations, as deadly as the Greekes did the whistle of *Poliphemus* (pp. 23–24).

He builds upon the self-created reputation for fearless exposure of valuable secrets of the underworld by describing several new criminal 'laws' and providing more up-to-date information; the tone is intimate and confidential:

> I remember their Hall was once about Bishopsgate, neere unto Fishers folly, but because it was a noted place, they have remooued it to Kent-street, and as far as I can learne, it is kept at one *Laurence Pickerings* house, one that hath bene, if he be not still, a notable Foist. A man of good calling he is, and well allied, brother in law to *Bul* the hangman (p. 36).

At the same time a high proportion of the pamphlet consists of anecdotes, most of them ostensibly illustrating one or other of the 'laws'. Greene several times makes claims for the authenticity of his stories, in terms of personal acquaintance with either the rogue or the victim, but the jestbook origins of many of them are betrayed by the neatness of the plotting, the way in which the outcome is made to depend upon some ironic twist of fortune, or the punchline provided by a play on words. Some of them are very amusing in the manner of a fabliau, like the last one in the pamphlet which tells of how an old gentleman gets a witty revenge on the tinker who has picked the locks of many of his tenants. The gentleman invites the tinker to his home and wins his confidence by innocent curiosity about the tricks of his trade, meanwhile plying him steadily with strong beer; eventually he rewards the tinker richly for agreeing to take a letter to the jailor of Lancaster. The tinker pockets the money and hurries on his way, unaware that the letter is of course his own *mittimus*. In general, *The Second part* seems less planned and more haphazard than its predecessor; the anecdotes all concern cony-catching in some form, but they are not related to the law which they are supposedly included to illustrate. The fact that a plan for the pamphlets is set out in the prefatory letter and not carried out has caused critics to think that the work was somehow mixed up in the printing and the sections set out of order. The haste with which these works were launched on the market makes this very likely.

In *The Thirde and last Part of Conny-catching* the transition to fiction is complete; the pamphlet consists entirely of tales supposedly compiled from notes supplied to Greene by an elderly justice of the peace. The devices for authenticity are fewer; his main claim for the stories is their value in warning potential victims rather than their truth, and on occasion even this claim is hardly asserted with conviction. In the first story, of a cony-catcher feigning acquaintance with a maidservant up from the country so as to rob her rich employers, the loving detail and implicit admiration for criminal ingenuity overshadow any moral intention. The naive girl, convinced that the persuasive young thief is really a hitherto unknown relative, 'seemed proud that her kinsman was so neat a youth'. The thief labels a cheese that he means to present to the family as a gift from the country with elaborate carelessness 'that it could not bee discerned, but that some unskilful writer in the Country had done it.' The mistress of the household, having invited the impostor to supper, gets out all her best linen and plate on display 'to have the better report made of their credite amongst their servants friends in the Countrey'. The girl sees her kinsman off early to bed 'with a low courtesy', anxious not to offend him with 'long talk', after which he promptly makes off with all the valuables of the household to the headquarters of his accomplice. 'Imagine these villaines, there in their iollitie, the one reporting point by point his cunning deceipt, and the other (fitting his humour) extolling the deede with no mean commendations' (*The Thirde Part*, p. 20). In comparison with the denunciations of rogues as despoilers of the commonwealth that Greene used to whip up excitement in the prefaces to *A Notable Discouery* and *The Second part* the final comment here is markedly lacking in censure: 'How [this] may forewarne others, I leaue to your own opinions that see what extraordinarie devises are now adayes, to beguile the simple and honest liberall minded' (*The Thirde Part*, p. 21).

The second three cony-catching pamphlets maintain the trend towards fiction, but they are more experimental in form. Each utilizes at least one persona other than that of the author-narrator, and in *A Disputation*, the most inventive and lively of the three, Greene takes pains to distinguish between the several narrative styles. The idea behind *The Defence of Conny-Catching* is a good one, although the pamphlet itself is repetitive and without vitality; Cuthbert Cunny-catcher, its supposed author, is a master of cheating at cards and dice who has found his livelihood eroded because his potential victims have been forewarned by reading Greene's pamphlets. In order both to have his revenge on Greene and to show how trivial are the misdemeanours of cony-catchers in comparison with the cheating and deception practised on a grand scale by all the major professions, Cuthbert proposes to open Greene's eyes to the crimes perpetrated by the mighty ones of the commonwealth against the humble and innocent:

> You decypher poore Conny-catchers, that perhaps with a tricke at cardes, winne fortie shillings from a churle that can spare it, and neuer talke of those Caterpillers that vndoo the poore, ruine whole Lordships, infect the common-wealth, and delight in nothing but in wrongfull extorting and purloyning of pelfe, when such as be the greatest Conny-catchers of all, as by your leaue, maister R.G., I will manifest (*The Defence of Conny-Catching*, p. 13).

But the ambitious plan is not realized; the pamphlet consists of a series of denunciations of and tales about the dishonest practices of various stock figures, such as the usurer, the miller, the lawyer, the fake traveller, the pawnbroker and the tailor. Some of the malpractices are very small beer indeed, and the stories, many of them adapted from earlier sources and all highly conventional, have nothing at all to do with wickedness in high places. It is likely that the important language of the prefatory matter is designed only to attract the reader, and that the author did not care, or expect his reader to care, that his claims were not borne out.

A Disputation, Betweene a Hee Conny-catcher and a Shee Conny-catcher is a more satisfying piece of work, especially inventive in its exploitation of a new point of view which does much to transform the now familiar material. The concern of the earlier pamphlets with disclosing information and revealing valuable secrets is gone; Greene's manner is straightforwardly didactic: 'Heere shall parents learne, how hurtfull it is to cocker vp their youth in their follies, and haue a deepe insight how to bridle their daughters, if they see them any waies grow wantons' (*A Disputation*, p. 7). The two parts of the pamphlet are linked by the theme of woman as criminal; in the first part, the dialogue between Laurence and Nan, Nan proves with the aid of several cony-catching tales that not only are women as skilled as men in all the various kinds of cozenage that Greene has described earlier but also that their abilities as prostitutes give them a power to corrupt and destroy that men can never achieve: 'You men theeues touch the bodie and wealth, but we ruine the soule, and indanger that which is more pretious then the worldes treasure, you make worke onely for the gallowes, we both for the gallowes and the diuel' (p. 40). The tales of cozenage are familiar enough. The novelty lies in presenting them as part of a contest in villainy between the man and the woman in which it is the woman's criminal abilities that are highlighted. The second part consists of the life story of a reformed courtesan, recounted by the girl herself, a conventional exemplum with several moral warnings, against doting parents, wanton girls, and feminine inconstancy, enforced emphatically. The style, unlike that of the dialogue, often reverts to that of Greene's Euphuistic romances.

When the girl is grown up and has become a professional courtesan, her career gives opportunity both for moralizing and for racy anecdotes, and Greene makes her manner of narration vary accordingly; in the scene of her conversion, a story from Erasmus's *Colloquia*, when her young client insists on having his dealings with her in the darkest room possible, the style initially is simple, and the dialogue direct:

> How now sir quoth I, is not this darke inough, he sitting him downe on the bed side, fetcht a deep sigh, & said indifferent, so, so, but there is a glimpse of light in the tyles, some bodie may by fortune see us, in faith no quoth I, none but God, God saies hee, why can God see us here? (pp. 76–77).

But when the client delivers his lengthy conversion speech, calling on the whore to look on her 'miserable trade' as living off 'the vomit of sin', Greene deserts the realistic mode for a more conventional style of moral exhortation. The problem of finding an appropriate narrative manner for the self-conscious or reformed criminal is one that he seems largely to sidestep in *A Disputation*, although there is an obvious difficulty when Nan and Laurence are made at one moment to boast of their criminal techniques, and at the next to condemn themselves for viciousness. In *The Blacke Bookes Messenger*, a short and clearly hasty production, Greene is hopelessly torn between making his narrator, Ned Browne, an unrepentant reprobate, and having him reformed so as to moralize on his past follies. Ned begins boldly enough:

> If you thinke (Gentlemen) to heare a repentant man speake, or to tel a large tale of his penitent sorrowes, ye are deceiued: for as I haue euer liued lewdly, so I meane to end my life as resolutely, and not by a cowardly confession to attempt the hope of a pardon (p. 5).

But a few sentences later he assumes exactly the proverbial, moralizing style of the repentant courtesan in *A Disputation:*

> As one selfe same ground brings foorth flowers and thistles; so of a sound stocke prooued an vntoward Syen; and of a vertuous father, a most vicious sonne (p. 5).

The main part of the pamphlet is devoted to Ned's exploits as a cheat and cutpurse, somewhat monotonously interspersed with assertions of his unbelievable wickedness—'Gentlemen, this is but a ieast to a number of villanies that I haue acted', 'It were too tedious to holde you with tales of the wonders I haue acted, seeing almost they bee numberlesse'—until at the very end, after a dull and dirty 'merry Ieast how Ned Brownes wife was crossebitten in her owne Arte', Greene plumps for a moral conclusion and has Ned make a hasty repentance before committing suicide. Stories of prodigals, usually but not always reformed, seem to have fascinated Greene; he had used them in *Greenes Mourning Garment* and *Greenes Never too late,* and was to follow Ned Browne with two accounts of his own career of vice in his last two pamphlets. In an obvious way, *A Disputation* and *The Blacke Bookes Messenger* are concerned with Greene himself, in that they both contain much publicity for his current work and for the *Black Book* that never appeared. Perhaps the preoccupation with the individual criminal career and with the moral life of the criminal, in contrast to the disinterested description of criminal techniques and successes in the earlier cony-catching pamphlets, also reflects upon the author's personal feelings during the last months of his life.

Very soon after Greene's death, writers began in different ways to capitalize on his popularity and reputation. Gabriel Harvey, whose family had been mocked by Greene in *A Quip for an Upstart Courtier,* first published in the summer of 1592, responded at once with the well-known vituperation against him in the second of the *Foure Letters.* Several pamphlets were published using Greene's name in their titles, such as *Greenes Newes both from Heauen and Hell,* probably by Barnaby Rich, in 1593, *Greenes Funeralls* (1594), John Dickenson's *Greene in Conceipt* (1598), and *Greenes Ghost Haunting Conie-Catchers* (1602). More cony-catching pamphlets were written; dull work, with few exceptions, and largely plagiarized from Harman or Greene.[7]

A more interesting and original pamphlet—at least insofar as no specific sources for it have been identified—is *The Discouerie of the Knightes of the Poste* (1597) by E.S. In the form of conversations taking place over several days between several travellers journeying from London to Plymouth the author exposes the practices of 'knights of the post' or 'bailers', petty criminals who lived by taking money to stand bail for known felons or to perjure themselves in court. The knight of the post was a low-life figure who obviously captured the Elizabethan imagination, and appeared in several pamphlets, particularly, after the success of Nashe's *Pierce Penilesse,* as a messenger between earthlings and the devil; *The Discouerie* is significant in that it gives more detail about the methods of such people than any other work, and more especially because it seems to allude to individual knights of the post who would have been well known to the readers. Minutely detailed and authentic sounding descriptions, such as the following, apparently intended to make clear identifications without providing names, make Greene's cony-catching pamphlets seem contrived and literary by comparison:

> There is a most braue fellow but very newly crept into this crewe, and his name is N. well knowne, one that lookes very high, and at euery word casteth his eye aboue Powles steeple, as if he would quarrel with the Moone . . . In his attire, he is neat and fine, and in his speech stately, with a long piccadeuant after the French cut, and of a scornefull countenance . . . Also at the same time as I wel remember P. the golden fethered bird was with him, very braue, with a faire cloake of somewhat a gray colour on his backe (sig. C1^v).

But the author of this little work is also a conscious story-teller, and he takes great care with details of the journey, with names of good inns in Basingstoke or Andover, with descriptions of characters met en route like the garrulous hostess whose style of badinage is interestingly similar to Mistress Quickly's, or the footpost from London who wears a flannel waistcoat and a Spanish hat, and with the day-to-day minutiae of travel, meals, hangovers, running out of money for the reckoning, and so on. Whether or not the accounts of the criminals and the lists of their hideouts are true, the pamphlet as a whole seems to convey an authentic sense of Elizabethan inn life, and of a certain kind of London gossip.

A more worthy heir of Greene was Thomas Dekker, who was a young man of about twenty, just embarking, like Shakespeare with whom he was then associated, on a career in the theatre when Greene died. Dekker did not at once take up the trade of pamphleteer in Greene's wake; his first interest was the theatre, and by the end of the century he had written enough for Francis Meres in *Palladis Tamia* to number him with Shakespeare as among the best for tragedy. Henslowe's diary shows that between 1598 and 1600 he had a hand in thirty-two plays for the Admiral's Company. He had plays performed at court, and together with Jonson, surely an uneasy partnership, he was chosen to prepare pagents for *The Magnificent Entertainment* to celebrate the would-be triumphal entry of the newly-crowned James I into the City of London. Despite this, his first pamphlet, *The Wonderfull Yeare*, written in 1603 when plague closed the theatres, was published anonymously. It was popular enough to go through three early editions, and Dekker lost no time in consolidating his reputation in his new medium while continuing active in the old one; in the years from 1604 to 1607 he wrote eight more pamphlets, experimenting all the time in subjects and styles.

Then in 1608, for no obvious reason, he turned his attention to the rogue tradition and produced *The Bel-man of London*. It is a curious pamphlet, much more literary and meditative than any of Greene's rogue writing, and the rogue material is so placed within a context of conventional melancholia about the transitoriness of life, alternating praise and dispraise of the country and of the city, and complaint about the decay of familiar institutions, that it is completely transformed in its effect. The preliminary address by the Bellman, a man with a bell who walked the streets acting by day as a town crier and by night as a watchman ringing the hours 'to all those that either by office are sworne to punish, or in their owne loue to vertue, wish to haue the disorders of a State amended', suggests a certain confusion of purpose. The Bellman forcefully urges his readers, as did Greene, to band together against certain enemies of the commonwealth, 'those Monsters', 'these Sauages', 'the wilde beastes', and boasts of his intention to 'deuote my life to the safetie of my country in defending her from these Serpents'; but he never specifies the nature of these enemies or of their crimes, and he concludes with a kind of face-saving withdrawal from the intention to cause particular offence:

> None can be offended with it, but such as are guilty to themselues, that they are such as are enrold in this Muster booke, for whose anger, or whose stab, I care not. At no mans bosome doe I particularly strike, but onely at the bodie of *Vice* in *Generall* (*Non-Dramatic Works*, III, 67).

The table of contents, listing 'A discouerie of all the idle Vagabonds in England' and 'certein secret Villanies, which borrow to themselues the name of Lawes' is redolent of both Greene and Harman, but the pamphlet opens in a mode quite foreign to either of them, with a meditation on time and change. This develops into a conventional pastoral eulogy in the high style, elaborately written and ornamented to the best of Dekker's ability with rhetorical schemes and tropes. A narrator emerges, with a simpler though by no means colloquial style, who draws the reader into an Eden-like grove within a wood; at this point the reader is pleasurably surprised to discover that the whole of the introductory section has been contrived for ironic effect, when it turns out that the earthly paradise is in fact the site of a thieves' kitchen, where a feast is being prepared. But this is no vagabonds' lair such as Harman might have discovered in the Kent countryside; it is a decidedly more literary and imaginatively conceived location:

> Some sate turning of spits, and the place being al smoaky, made mee thinke on hell, for the ioynts of meate lay as if they had beene broyling in the infernall fire; the turne-spits (who were poore tattered greasie fellowes) looking like so many hee diuels. Some were basting and seemed like feindes powring scalding oyle vpon the damned: others were myncing of pye-meate, and shewed like hangmen cutting vp of quarters, whilst another whose eies glowed with the heate of the fire, stood poaking in at the mouth of an Ouen, torturing soules as it were in the furnace of Lucifer (*Non-Dramatic Works*, III, 78–79).

The narrator spies on the proceedings and describes the rogues' convention, at which a novice is initiated into the brotherhood in the terms of a romantic fantasy about carefree vagabonds, colourfully patched and weatherbeaten, who roam at liberty, fearless of society and its constraints. So far, all is Dekker's invention, loosely based on the work of Awdeley and Harman, but owing nothing to them in spirit. The head of the fraternity makes a rousing speech to the assembly, beginning

> My noble hearts, my old weather-beaten fellowes, and braue English Spirits, I am to giue you that which all the land knowes you iustly deserue (a Roaguish commendation)

and ending

> Let vs my braue *Tawny-faces*, not giue vp our patched cloakes, nor change our coppies, but as we came beggars out of our mothers bellies, so resolue and set vp your staues vpon this, to returne like beggars into the bowels of the earth (*Non-Dramatic Works*, III, 89–90).

The rogues go off to sleep, the narrator questions the old beldam in charge of the kitchen, and she tells him all she knows of them. This part of the pamphlet consists entirely of material from Harman, much abridged and partially rewritten, with all the anecdotes left out. Only the account of the Abraham-man is significantly different, including the detail that 'he calls himselfe by the name of *Poore Tom*, and comming neere any body, cryes out, *Poore Tom* is a cold', which perhaps Dekker found in *King Lear*. Even the details of the rogues' meeting places, apparently so authentic-sounding, are taken straight from Harman. A short passage of narrative, in which the authorial persona, now disillusioned with country-life, makes his way to London and meets the Bellman, the symbol of society's efforts to protect itself against the criminal outsider, allows Dekker to make a transition to the material of his other sources, which is, by what is now a convention, introduced as new: 'I learnt much by the Bell-mans intelligence but more afterwards by my owne obseruation and experience: what merchandize I stored my selfe with by both the *Voiages* here doe I vnlade' (*Non-Dramatic Works*, III, 116).

The rest of the pamphlet is concerned with city rogues, and is compiled from *A manifest detection, Mihil Mumchance,* Greene's first three cony-catching pamphlets, and *Greenes Ghost Haunting Conie-Catchers*. Dekker does not straightforwardly steal from the earlier pamphlets, but rewrites much of his source-material, condensing it considerably, and by omitting the anecdotes and illustrations, and using only what can be presented as fact and information he makes *The Bel-man* more emphatically and single-mindedly moralistic than any of Greene's pamphlets. It is a major difference between them that in his prose—some of the plays are exceptions—Dekker neither treats the underworld as a subject for amusement and entertainment nor allows himself to be seduced by the fascination of roguery. His standpoint is consistently moral. He concludes with a ponderous rhetorical diatribe against the powerful menace of the criminal underworld:

> Who would imagine that in a Kingdom so fertile in all sorts of wholesome discipline, there should grow vp such ranck and such pestilent beds of hemlock: that in the very hart of a state so rarely gouerned & dieted by good lawes, there should breede such loathsome and such vlcerous impostumes? That in a City so politick, so ciuill, and so seuere, such vgly, base, and bold impieties dare shew their faces? What an Army of insufferable *Abuses*, detestable *Vices*, most damnable *Villanies*, abominable *Pollutions* . . . and *Hel-hound-like-perpetrated* flagitious enormities haue beene here minstred together? . . . What Artillery haue they to batter downe Order, Law, custome, plaine dealing, and all the goode guards and defences of Gouernement? (*Non-Dramatic Works*, III, 167–68).

Such writing is difficult for the modern reader to take seriously; it is readily dismissed as merely inflated and sensationalistic. And indeed there are a number of insoluble problems confronting anyone who tries to estimate the contemporary impact and significance of such a work as this. For instance, how was the rogue tradition in general and the work of Harman and Greene in particular regarded at this time? Were they largely forgotten, remembered but moribund, or still fresh and topical? Harman's work was more than forty years old by now, and Greene's more than ten; on the one hand, they were deliberately ephemeral works, essentially newsworthy and relevant to current events at the time of publication, and on the other, this was a period when there were, by our standards, few new books available, and when change in all walks of life took place more slowly. The question here is not one of plagiarism and its status; in the years immediately following Greene's death, when there can be no doubt that the life and works of this notorious writer were still fresh in the mind of the reading public, writers were able to bring out cony-catching pamphlets plagiarized almost entirely from Greene and still to call them new. What is important is how Dekker saw the rogue material for which he devised such an elaborate context. Did he mean to create a new, totally literary and fictional form out of material that had once been of social and practical relevance? And if he was working in this way, how much irony should be seen in *The Bel-man of London* in view of elements of contemporary life such as the unrest of the rural poor in the North in 1607, that he might have expected his readers to bear in mind? No amount of historical or literary evidence can provide certain answers to these questions. But they are nonetheless worth asking.

Whatever the answers, Dekker's public clearly liked *The Bel-man*, since it went through four editions in the year of its publication, and was followed a few months later by a sequel, *Lanthorne and Candle-light. Or, The Bell-mans second Nights Walke*. Despite the fact that the first edition was published anonymously, this is a more polished and self-confident production than its predecessor, set out with a certain amount of conventional literary apparatus, such as three complimentary sonnets, separate chapter headings, and marginalia, often in Latin, to direct the reader's attention to parts of the text, and it was to prove the most popular of Dekker's pamphlets, with a second edition in 1609, an enlarged edition under the title *O per se O* in 1612, another called *Villanies Discouered* in 1616, another in 1620, another as *English Villanies* in 1632, and two further in 1638 and 1648. Although it makes some use of the conventions of cony-catching pamphlets, beginning with a table of contents listing new 'laws', 'Of Gul-groping', 'Of Ferreting', 'Of Hawking', and followed by a chapter 'Of Canting', its real interest is more diverse, and it is probably the wide range of subject-matter and of tone and style that help to account for the pamphlet's popularity. The theme of roguery unifies the work, and cony-catching terminology provides a fund of metaphor to be applied to many kinds of dishonest endeavour, but after his opening chapter on thieves' cant, Dekker moves largely away from the subject-matter of Greene and his fellows.

As in *The Bel-man* he gives his pamphlet a narrative framework, of a kind that had become popular since Nashe's *Pierce Penilesse*, with the familiar satirical device of a devil sent up from hell to investigate the state of sin on earth. A knight of the post brings to hell a letter from the Devil's ambassadors on earth, urging that the Bellman's activities in suppressing cony-catchers be stopped because they are too successful: 'A Foyst nor a Nip shall not walke into a Fayre or a Play-house, but euerie cracke will cry looke to your purses: nor a poore common Rogue come to a mans doore, but he shall be examined if he can *cant*? (*Non-Dramatic Works*, III, 212).

A messenger is selected to visit those city locations where vice might be expected to flourish—taverns, theatres, ordinaries, alehouses, and prisons—and thus Dekker creates both a setting for social satire and an opportunity for the ironic description of vice; the devil sees so much villainy that he cannot contain himself for delight: 'His spleene leap'd against his ribbes with laughter, and in the height of that ioy resolued to write the villanies of the World in *Folio*' (*Non-Dramatic Works*, III, 285). In the end he meets the Bellman, fails to recognize him, and by mistake reveals to him all that he has observed.

On his travels he sees sights familiar to the connoisseur of cony-catching, such as the cheating of gentlemen in ordinaries by organized trickery, which Dekker calls 'Gul-groping', although in fact it is only a sophisticated version of the old barnard's law, and the methods of 'rancke-riders' who defraud innkeepers of their horses and wheedle loans out of country gentlemen and farmers under the pretence of being well-born men of substance. The cony-catching terminology is extended also to less familiar abuses, such as those of 'fawlconers', who extort money from would-be patrons of literature by botching up pamphlets from 'certaine small paringes of witt' enticingly bound with 'forepenny silke ribbon at least, like little streamers on the top of a Marchpane Castle, hanging dangling by at the foure corners', printing a number of copies of the same dedicatory epistle, each addressed to a different knight or gentleman by name, and hawking the pamphlet round as if it had been specially produced for each separate individual. The detail of this chapter, with its account of the preliminary research carried out by the Falconer into the likely dedicatees living in a particular area, the collusion between the printers and the Falconers, and the travelling pedlars who buy up old books and insert new epistles into them, printed with the aid of an alphabet of portable type, suggests both personal knowledge and special interest on Dekker's part. His own livelihood was threatened by such practices.

The chapter on 'Moone men', or gipsies, is interesting as a treatment of a kind of rogue neglected by Greene and Awdeley, and only briefly mentioned by Harman. In the horrified fascination with which he describes 'these Egiptian lice', so cruelly persecuted by Elizabethan law,[8] Dekker typifies the attitude of the Elizabethan bourgeois to the social outsider. The gipsies' exotic appearance and association with forbidden arts of magic such as palmistry and fortune-telling made them in his eyes almost more to be feared than the conventional country rogues, especially since to him they seemed to be daily gathering strength:

> For if the vgly body of this Monster be suffred to grow & fatten it selfe with mischiefs and disorder, it will haue a neck so Sinewy & so brawny, that the arme of the law will haue much ado to strike off the Head, sithence euery day the mēbers of it increase, & it gathers new ioints & new forces by *Priggers, Anglers, Cheators, Morts,* Yeomens Daughters . . . and other Seruants both men & maides that haue been pilferers, with al the rest of that Damned Regiment (*Non-Dramatic Works,* III, 264).

Greene and Harman also used military metaphors to convey their sense of the strength and organized menace of the rogues, but they did not make the constant association that Dekker does between the criminal and the demonic underworld. What is peculiar to Dekker in *The Bel-man* and *Lanthorne and Candle-light* is the intensity of his conviction that the moral health of the whole commonwealth is being threatened by the growth of the criminal fraternity and the way he encapsulates it in his nightmare vision of London as a kind of hell of proliferating crime:

> In euerie Corner did he finde Serpents ingendering: vnder euerie roofe, some impyetie or other lay breeding.
>
> Not farre frō *These,* came crawling out of their bushes a company of graue & wealthy *Lechers* in the shapes of *Glowe-wormes* who with gold, Iyngling in their pockets, made such a shew in the night, that the dores of Common *Brothelryes* flew open to receiue them . . . Then came forth certaine infamous earthly minded Creatures in the shapes of *Snailes* . . . A number of other monsters, like *These,* were seene (as the sunne went downe) to venture from their

dennes, only to ingender with *Darknesse* (*Non-Dramatic Works*, III, 285, 296–97).

This sort of writing seems remote in tone and feeling from Greene, but in fact it represents a development of a side of rogue literature always latent in the subject, which Greene chose not to emphasize. Greene was interested in cony-catching for its potentialities in combining instruction with entertainment; moralizing was generally a secondary consideration, brought to the fore in prefaces and conclusions. Dekker traded on the achievements of Greene and his predecessors, but made something entirely his own out of them.

His success was the inspiration of another rogue pamphlet, *Martin Mark-all, Beadle of Bridewell*, whose author, identified by the initials, S.R., was quick to exploit openings provided by *The Bel-man*. The only extant edition of *Martin Mark-all* was published in 1610.[9] Like Dekker's pamphlets, it combines rogue materials and conventions with other kinds of social satire to construct a work of wider and more varied appeal. The author begins with an exposé of Dekker's plagiarism from Harman, interesting in that it is the only pamphlet condemnation of this offence, and also because it imputes to the sole charge of Dekker a crime of which every writer after Harman might with equal justice be accused. He himself is not entirely innocent of the same offence.[10] Like Dekker he uses underworld allegory as a framework for his material. The rogues of the land hold a meeting to try the Bellman for his attacks on their profession: a jury convicts him of slander, and censures him, as Cuthbert Conny-catcher did Greene, for wasting his time on petty crimes when greater ones go unassailed. Corporal Fize sends a letter to the devil, 'Don Purloyningo, chief Gouernour of the Region of Theuingen', asking for protection, since rogues are now so persecuted and exposed. The devil promises them a territory of their own, in the country of Thevingen, an account of which is given in the manner of Spenserian allegory. The description of the rich and embattled city, Gazophilacium, 'enuironed about with a wall of siluer beaten out with the hammer', whose grasping inhabitants live in constant fear of being robbed by their neighbours, the lawless population of Thevingen, 'naturally given and inclined to idleness and lazy lives, insomuch that it cometh to pass, that being hungry they will steal from one another, and often cut one another's throats', is a cynical variation on Dekker's view of the honest members of the commonwealth preyed on by the criminal underworld; the author finds those who hug their wealth to themselves as worthy of derision as those who try to snatch it away.

The author then moves into another mode, with a section correcting and updating Dekker's chapter on canting: 'I haue thought good not only to show his errour in some places in setting downe olde wordes . . . for wordes that are used in these dayes . . . But haue enlarged his Dictionary (or Master Harmans) with such wordes as I thinke hee neuer heard of' (sig. El^v). The enlargement in fact consists of only about a dozen terms, but these are of interest in being almost the only additions made to the original fund of words and phrases supplied by Harman and drawn upon by every subsequent writer who described thieves and beggars. Finally comes the history of rogues, as promised on the title-page, part fact, part fiction, part tradition. It is less interesting in itself than for what it implies about the ways rogue literature had developed, and for the suggestion that the author felt a need to emphasize that a subject which lent itself so readily to invention and to fantasy still had respectable roots in fact.

A final contribution to the Bellman/Martin Mark-all feud was the anonymous pamphlet, *O per se O,* almost certainly by Dekker,[11] published in 1612. The first part of this is merely a reprint of *Lanthorne and Candle-light,* but the second, promises new material gleaned at first hand:

> For my better painting forth these Monsters, I once tooke one of them into my seruice . . . So what intelligence I got from him, or any other trained up in the same Rudiments of Roaguery, I will briefely, plainely, and truely set downe, as I had it from my Diuellish schoolemaister, whom I call by the name of O per se O (sigs. L2–L3).

Here Dekker entirely foregoes the use of any allegorical or satirical framework, and concentrates instead on providing factual descriptions of country rogues and details of their tricks and devices, with an apparently straight-faced insistence on the authenticity of his material. Unusually for him, the style of writing makes its impression, not by the use of rhetorical figures or puns and witticisms, but through simply related factual detail, where the bizarre and often horrifying quality of the rogues' way of life is the more forcefully conveyed for not being insisted on:

> Some of these abrams haue the letters E. and R. upon their armes: some haue Crosses, and some other marke, all of them carrying a blew colour: some weare an iron ring, &c. which markes are printed vpon their flesh, and by tying their arme harde with two stringes three or foure inches asunder, and then with a sharp Awle pricking or raizing the skinne, to such a figure or print as they best fancy,

they rubbe that place with burnt paper, pisse, and Gunpowder which being hard rubd in, and suffered to dry, stickes in the flesh a long time after (sig. M2^v.)

The description of the way that counterfeit soldiers produce their sores owes little to its original in Harman:

Take unslaked lime and Sope, with the rust of olde yron: these mingled together, and spread thicke on two pieces of leather which are clap upon the arme, one against the other: two small pieces of wood (fitted to the purpose) holding the leathers downe, all which are bound hard to the arme with a Garter: which in a few howers fretting the skin with blisters, and being taken off, the flesh will appeare all raw, then a linnen cloath being applyed to the raw blistered flesh, it stickes so fast, that upon plucking it off, it bleedes: which bloud (or else some other) is rubd all ouer the arme, by which meanes (after it is well dryed on) the arme appeares blacke, and the soare raw and reddish, but white about the edges like an old wound: which if they desire to heale, a browne paper with butter and waxe being applyed, they are cured (sig.M4).

Needless to say, the pamphlet is not without its pieces of unacknowedged plagiarism and its literary flights of fancy, like the rogues' version of the ten commandments, but it is significant amongst Dekker's work for the unstrained vividness of its best sections, and for the conviction with which it shows that the rogue life of Harman's time, even if dying out in actuality, still exerted a strong hold over the popular imagination.

In such pamphlets as *The Bel-man of London, Lanthorne and Candlelight, Martin Mark-all* and *O per se O,* the cony-catching material forms only an element, small though not insignificant, of a larger whole, and this reflects a general trend in that the interest originally aroused by rogue literature has by this time shifted from information and anecdote to moralizing and social satire. But there are two other kinds of pamphlet, the criminal biography and the prison pamphlet, both popular in the early seventeenth century, in which cony-catching plays a large part.

Two of the most interesting rogue biographies are *The Life and Death of Gamaliel Ratsey* and *Ratseis Ghost. Or the Second Part of his madde Prankes and Robberies,* which both appeared in May 1605, not much more than a month after Ratsey was executed for crimes committed during his notorious two-year career as a highwayman. He was famed for carrying out his robberies in a particularly hideous mask.[12] Although the second pamphlet purports to be a sequel to the first, each was the work of a different writer, put out by a different publisher, and each forms an independent unit with its own beginning and conclusion. Both, like much popular biography of the time, are written in the manner of jestbooks as a series of unconnected anecdotes. They are similar in style and tone to Greene's *The Blacke Bookes Messenger*, although Ratsey, as a highwayman, has a superior status in the criminal hierarchy. The authors have mixed a few true stories of Ratsey's life with apocryphal folk-hero tales and accounts of cony-catching tricks from Greene and his followers.[13] One of the few incidents from real life is the story from *Ratseis Ghost* about Ratsey's encounter with the players which has won Ratsey his modern notoriety amongst Shakespeare scholars, because it contains allusions to *Hamlet*. The author of *The Life and Death* claims as usual that his account is both authentic and of moral value, if not straight from the horse's mouth then at least set down as told by Ratsey to his friends: 'After the time of his imprisonment, with desire it might be published, as well to testify unto the world his repentance, as to giue cawtion to his country-men to eschew his follie, and preuent his fall' (sig. A2^v). That this is no more than a catchpenny opening gambit is evident from the entirely different approach adopted by the author of *Ratseis Ghost* who uses essentially similar material but introduces it as a kind of dream-vision, using an opening gambit borrowed from Chettle's *Kind-Harts Dreame*.

The Ratsey pamphlets resemble Greene's work both in the nature of the hero's activities and in the authorial attitude taken towards them. Ratsey is a stylish villain and carries out his crimes with wit, bravado, and an understanding of human weakness. He cozens a servingman of a horse by 'borrowing it' on the pretence that he is a gentleman abandoned by his servant who must have a horse to keep up appearances, and with his accomplices he steals three post-horses from an inn by posing as a gentleman who needs to ride to London to repay gambling debts. He escapes from prison because he is daring enough to cross 'a very dangerous great water . . . for he knew none of them durst follow', and he robs nine men at once, single-handed. Some of his exploits reveal a sense of irony. He robs a scholar, and then makes him preach a sermon of repentance: 'For, sayes he, I haue been a long male factor, and it may so preuaile with me, that it may worke me to some good deed' (*The Life and Death*, sig. C2). He is outwitted by a man he intended to rob, but bears him no malice: 'If I could see the man himselfe, quoth Ratsey, I would giue him a gallon of wine; there is all the ill I owe him, for in my life I neuer had such a prancke passt upon me' (*Ratseis Ghost*, sig. B4^v).

In a story borrowed from *The Second part of Conny-catching*, he cheats a pick-lock, and has him sent to jail. But unlike the cony-catchers, Ratsey has several of the sympathetic traits of the folk-hero, such as kindness to the poor, and courtesy to women. He lends a poor farmer money to pay a creditor, and then robs the creditor; to an impoverished old couple he had meant to rob, he instead gives forty shillings, and to the daughter of a miserly parson with barely enough money to buy a new dress he gives three angels for a petticoat as well. The highwayman is a gentleman among cony-catchers, and often appears as a rather heroic figure. Even Dekker in *The Bel-man* shows a grudging admiration for him when he says that 'the *High Law* stands both vpon *Wit* and *Manhood*'.

It is not until the end of the second pamphlet that any note of moral condemnation is heard, and not loudly even here. The author seems to be preparing for Ratsey's death with a flourish of moralizing:

> But as the heauens are doomers of mens deedes, and God holds a ballance in his fist, to reward with fauour and to reuenge with Justice . . . for as folly perswaded Ratsey to leade a sinfull life, soe Justice at length brought him to a sorrowfull end, and as his faults were fond, so his successe was foule (*Ratseis Ghost*, sig. F2^v).

Ratsey makes a short penitent speech protesting that there is no hell to be compared to a guilty mind, and ascends the scaffold. But his last words are bold and jaunty, and the author declares finally that he 'shewed an end of courage euen to the resolution of his death, confession made he none'. The amoral picaresque qualities of the Ratsey pamphlets, and of others such as *The Life and Pranks of Long Meg of Westminster* and *The Life and Death of Griffin Flood Informer* relate them to the fiction of Nashe and Deloney, but in their blend of fact and fiction, of admiration for successful criminal trickery with a sense that the wicked are, or at any rate ought to be, always found out, they stand in a direct line from Greene.

Prison pamphlets are linked with rogue writing in terms both of form and of feeling, but with significant differences. It is the prison officials, ostensibly the agents of law and order, who are the cony-catchers and exploiters of the simple, and the condemned prisoners their helpless victims. The stories usually spring from the personal experience of the author: Dekker, who wrote much and eloquently on the subject of London's prisons, which he called 'Thirteene strong houses of sorrowe,' spent seven years in the King's Bench for debt; William Fennor, author of *The Compters Common-wealth* was in the Wood Street Counter; Luke Hutton, author of *The Blacke Dogge of*

Newgate, spent some time in the notoriously ill-run Newgate for felony, and Geoffrey Mynshul wrote *Certaine Characters and Essays* while in jail. As with cony-catching pamphlets, life must be presented in terms of art, and personal experience is constantly modified and elaborated by means of fictional conventions, but here that experience is so strongly felt as to justify the claims of moral and reformatory intention. In fact, the prison pamphlets are part both of a literary tradition and of a practical campaign for the reform of prison conditions; they represent a closer correspondence to contemporary life than did the cony-catching pamphlets. The most significant result of the campaign, which had been under way since before the beginning of the seventeenth century, was achieved in 1618, when the King revived the *Commissio pro Revelatione Debitorum* to seek relief for helpless debtors. But it was only an interim measure and did not eradicate the evils of the situation; agitation for reform continued strong in the next decade.

The subject of prison and the sufferings of prisoners did not evolve its own form in the way that cony-catching did; jestbooks, the seven deadly sins, the paradoxical encomium, and especially the Character, a newly popular form, all provided convenient structures and devices, but each prison pamphlet is essentially a separate and individual work. Forms such as the paradoxical encomium or the Character are often used to create self-contained units within a larger framework, so that the subject of prison may represent only one of several topics dealt with in a single work. But in the sense that they too were exposing enormities and revealing the secrets of an enclosed world unfamiliar to the general public, the prison writers felt themselves akin to the cony-catching pamphleteers, and sometimes harked back to them. In *The Blacke Dogge of Newgate* by Luke Hutton, published about 1596, two years before Hutton was hanged for highway robbery, one of the narrators, a well-informed Newgate prisoner called Zawny, who is initiating the author into the ways of the jail, which he calls 'the superlative degree of cony-catching', recalls his predecessor: 'Maister Greene, God be with thee! for if thou hadst been aliue, knowing what I know, thou wouldst as well haue made worke as matter' (sig. E2^v).

The revelations in *The Compters Common-wealth* by William Fennor explicitly claim to surpass those of Greene and his successors, including Hutton, and even Dekker, 'the true heir of Apollo'. The author presents himself as a novice to the prison world who cannot conceive of greater vices still to be discovered; his informant, a seasoned prisoner, knows better: 'These indeede . . . haue done . . . most exquisitely, both for their owne reputation and their countreyes good, but I haue that lockt vp in the closet of my brest, that, when it is opened and made apparent to you will amaze you' (p. 16). For once, this is no conventional hyperbole; Fennor's pamphlet gives one of the fullest and most detailed accounts of prison life that we have.

Going to prison was a sufficiently common occurrence in Elizabethan times for the pamphleteers to be able to draw on a large fund of cynical and familiar notions about jail and jailors as a source of bitter humour. In a piece of characteristic exuberance Nashe praises the counter as an unrivalled source of worldly education:

> Heare what I say; a Gentleman is neuer thoroughly entred into credit till he hath been there; & that Poet or nouice, be hee what he will, ought to suspect his wit, and remaine halfe in a doubt that it is not authenticall, till it had beene seene and allowd in vnthrifts consistory.
> ... I protest I should neuer haue writ passion well, or beene a peece of a Poet, if I had not arriu'd in those quarters.
>   Trace the gallantest youthes and brauest reuellers about Towne in all the by-paths of their expence, & you shall vnfallibly finde, that once in their life they haue visited that melancholy habitation.
> ... I vow if I had a sonne, I would sooner send him to one of the Counters to learne lawe, than to the Innes of Court or Chancery (*Strange Newes*, in *Works*, I, 310).

Nashe's claim to first-hand experience of prison life is probably an idle boast, but many playwrights and pamphleteers of his time had seen the inside of one of London's eighteen jails. Imprisonment was not regarded as a punishment, and only a few of those imprisoned had been found guilty on criminal charges. Death was the penalty for common felons; for lesser offences there was whipping or the stocks, or some kind of physical mutilation. Galley-service was a new alternative to incarceration in the overcrowded jails. In general, prisoners were people awaiting trial, or those kept in safe custody for an unspecified length of time, either because they were regarded as politically or socially too dangerous to be allowed their freedom, or because they had committed some civil offence, in particular by getting into debt, and might evade the execution of the law if they were at large. The law made no provision for the insolvent debtor who had fallen into his creditor's power, either to work off his debt or to achieve solvency in some other way; he simply went into one of the debtors' prisons, Ludgate, the Wood Street Counter, or the Poultry Counter, the Fleet, the Marshalsea, or the King's Bench, and stayed there until he died. Nothing was freely provided for the prisoner except shelter; almost anything, from special accommodation and plentiful food and wine to permission for leave of absence, could be obtained by payment, and there is much evidence that life in jail could be comfortable and convenient for those with money. But the poor debtor had to rely for food, warmth, clothing, and bedding on the charity of the outside world; and when such charity was not available, as for instance in plague time, the warden of the prison had no responsibility to keep the prisoners alive.

It is no wonder, then, that the pamphleteers stress above all the chaos and horror of prison life, and the helpless misery of the prisoner. Going to prison is like making a voyage over 'tempestuous seas, in which ten thousand are euery day tossed, if not ouerwhelmed', (Dekker, *Villanies Discouered*, sig. I3ᵛ), to an 'infernal island', while prison itself is 'a mans graue, wherein he walkes aliue', (Dekker, *Iests to Make you Merie*, in *Non-Dramatic Works*, III, 340), a pest-house, a dunghill, a purgatory, a hell. Nashe's idea of prison as a bizarre source of education is also one that occurred to many writers. Fennor, for instance, calls the debtors' prisons 'these City universities', and the character of a prison in *The Overburian Collection* concludes: 'It is an university of poore Schoolers in which three Artes are chiefly studyed. To pray, to curse, and to write letters' (ed. W. J. Paylor, Oxford, 1936, p. 84).

The jailor is a tiger, a wolf, a cur, a scavenger battening on the corruption of the age, a cruel surgeon bleeding his patient to death. His treatment of the prisoners is worse than bestial:

> If a man should trauell to the Wildernesse or some vast desert, and bee deuoured by some Beare, or Boare, or such-like sauage Creature, it were but their kinde to doe so being prickt and stung with hunger; But for one man like a Canniball to feed vpon the other, what more monstrous and worse then crueltie is this, which euery day is seene in this place (Fennor, *The Compters Common-wealth*, p. 59).

The prisoner is a chained animal, a hunted victim, a drowning man whose struggles everyone pities but whom no one will save. His creditor is a torturer and a 'bloodhound of the law'. The serjeant who arrests him at the creditor's instigation is 'the excrement that proceeds from the body of the common-wealth'. In the emotive presentation of their subject the prison pamphlets are all very similar; the same melodramatic images recur repeatedly. But there are other aspects to the presentation of prison life; the pamphlets were part of a movement for practical reform in prison conditions, and as such they needed to supply facts and details as well as appealing to the sympathy of their readers. They were also the successors to the cony-catching pamphlets; and therefore they utilized anecdotes of jailors' villainy, of serjeants' craftiness, of witty prisoners' clever devices, to provide entertainment and a moral viewpoint.

The earliest pamphlet devoted entirely to the subject of prison life, Luke Hutton's *The Blacke Dogge of Newgate*, is unusually close to the cony-catching pamphlets in form and manner, and strongly influenced by Greene. Hutton was a highwayman, and perhaps also the son of Matthew Hutton, Archbishop of York, but he makes no use of his own career of crime and downfall in this pamphlet; he may, in fact, have written about them already in the *Repentance* that was published in 1595 or 1596 but no longer exists. Instead, *The Blacke Dogge*, a two-part pamphlet in verse and prose, is concerned with the abuses of prison life. In the verse section the narrator dreams of being thrown by a Cerberus-like prison serjeant into the lowest ward of Newgate, where he listens to the despairing complaints of prisoners who have no hope of release and to the moans of the sick and starving, where he sees the condemned, their necks bound with halters, taken off in carts to execution, and where he himself lies down to sleep with forty others on the filthy floor of the cell. By comparison, the tone of the prose section, a dialogue 'pithy, pleasant, and profitable for all the readers' is brisk and factual. The author insists that his intention is to bring about reformation, and not to arouse emotion:

> I wil name no man, for if they should be named, their friends would be angry: and more than that, I rather wish their amendment, then their publike infamie (sig. D2^v).

His emphasis on maintaining a moral stance despite the threats of violence from those he exposes recalls similar protests by Greene:

> I will not regarde the mallice of the threatning Cunnycatcher; who hath sworne, if I publish this Booke, they will do one what mischiefe they can (sig. A3).

Although Hutton's attitude is in general more moral and condemnatory than in the rogue pamphlets, since he had himself been a victim of some of the malpractices of prison officials, the manner in which he reveals their trickery is essentially similar to Greene's method; general descriptions of cheating devices are followed by illustrative anecdotes and specimen speeches: 'Now first will I begin with their petty practises in theyr lewd actions. Say there is a man or two robd by the highway not farre from London. . . These and such like speaches he useth' (sigs. D3–D3ᵛ). The pamphlet consists of a dialogue between two speakers, the author, and Zawny, a Newgate prisoner, who compete in telling stories of dishonest serjeants, how they extort money from the victims of pickpockets by the pretence that they will help to find the robbers, how they threaten innocent citizens with arrest on trumped-up charges unless bribes are paid, how they force payment from known thieves by threat of exposure. As in *The Discouerie of the Knightes of the Poste,* identities are hinted at,[14] but the descriptions of the villains and their activities are very general. The relation of a 'wonderfull piece of villainy', of pranks and witty practices, is ultimately of more concern to the author than any real exposure of a social evil. Despite the fact that the pamphlet was probably written while Hutton was imprisoned for crimes committed as a highwayman, it conveys no sense of personal suffering, or even of grievance; nor does it attack the failings of a system which allowed the serjeants to abuse their powers. Under the influence of Greene, Hutton saw that he could make a cony-catching pamphlet out of prison life, and he sought to do no more.

Of the other pamphlets entirely devoted to the subject of prison, William Fennor's *The Compters Common-wealth* is the best and the most ambitious. Fennor was one of those odd Jacobean characters whose career seems curious to us but also typical of the minor literary men of the time. He was once a soldier, had connections with the stage, and earned a living as a poet and entertainer as well as a pamphleteer. The number of his publications to have survived is not large enough to suggest that writing was his main source of income, although some of his work may well be lost. In 1614 he notoriously failed to turn up at a contest of wits against John Taylor the Water Poet, due to be held in the Hope Theatre on the Bankside, and thereafter the two men indulged in a minor pamphlet war. In 1616 he was imprisoned for debt in the Wood Street Counter, and wrote *The Compters Commonwealth* during his term there.

It starts out as a first-person account of Fennor's own experiences in prison, beginning with his arrest, but it turns into something larger. For once, the description given in the preface is accurate:

The first three chapters shew how distresse and oppression ioin'd hands to wound my weake and unprouided estate, by which single example, all other may discerne the true vsage they shall receive from the kinde Keepers if their meanes once faile or their friends forsake them. The foure chapters following, lay open the foure armes or currents, with their seuerall natures, that bring supply to this body or maine Ocean, which in the last three chapters is liuely anatomized. The cruelty of Keepers and the misery of prisoners (sig. A4^v).

In order to introduce the more general material of prison life, and also to allow for a more elevated style of narration, Fennor uses the familiar device of the knowledgeable informant, a gentleman prisoner whom he meets at a drinking party in the jail. This prisoner promises amazing revelations, not specifically about prison, but about the vices of the time. Fennor seems to have felt that social satire and moral exhortation were more likely to allure the readers than a factual account of life inside a jail. To make it clear that these will be no ordinary discoveries, Fennor has his prisoner explicitly claim that he will overgo the best-known works of criminal exposé, here named as 'a book called *Greenes Ghost haunts Cony-catchers;* another called *Legerdemaine,* and *The Black Dog of Newgate,* but the most wittiest, elegantest and eloquentest peece, (Master Dekkers the true heire of Apollo composed) called *The Bellman of London*' (p. 16).

What follows is a well-ordered account, much of it written in a more lively and colloquial style than the prisoner's exordium would suggest, of the ways in which careless young gentlemen and heirs are trapped into debtors' prisons by the villainy of city tradesmen and brokers and the craft of decayed gallants, and the nature of the abuses they suffer once inside. The theme of the prodigal heir, newly up from the country, who 'scarce having scented the City air, all this while thinks himself in a heaven upon earth' (Judges, p. 450) and readily falls a prey to moneylenders because of his love of gallant living, or else out of sheer foolish generosity signs a bond on behalf of some confidence trickster which eventually lands him in jail, is familiar from Greene's pamphlets, and the anecdotes of cheating serjeants and constables owe much to the cony-catching tradition. But Fennor has a lively way with a story, and is capable of considerable variation of emotional tone. In one tale, a debtor evades his creditors with great success, until they hit on the idea of having a serjeant disguise himself as a porter to gain entrance to the man's lodging; the conclusion of this is successfully muted:

> As he was opening of [a letter brought by the 'porter'], what doth my Porter doe, but pulls his mace out of his pocket (The Gentleman not dreaming of such a breakfast) and laide on his shoulders, and

arrested him, telling him that he was not what he seemed to be (a Porter) but what hee was a Sergeant, . . . therefore make yourselfe ready, and along. So hee seeing how hee was betraide and arrested went quietly along with him to the Compter, and died in execution (p. 43).

In another story, two serjeants who 'being well oyled in the hand with *aurum potabile,* were as hot vpon the exploite as an Italian on a wench of fifteene' (p. 44) dress up as a counsellor and a scrivener so as to gain access to their victim, and force him to pay up. The victims for their part are not without wiles. One poor debtor, having spent several years in the Hole, as the lowest ward of a prison was named, persuades a keeper to accompany him out into the city on promise of payment to be obtained from friends, lures the keeper into a barber's shop for a 'shaving', and then, while the keeper has his eyes shut against the soapsuds, makes his escape. Fennor's use of detail brings the tale to life. The keeper, realizing that his charge has made off, 'ran into the streetes with the Barbers cloaths about his shoulders, with his choppes all white with the froth and sudds that hung about them, so that he looked like a Boar that foamed at mouth, or a well-travelling horse' (p. 76). But there is also plenty of conscious effort to arouse emotion and win sympathy. The practices of the jailor and other prison officials in extorting money from their helpless charges are related in detail.

> What extreame extortion is it when a Gentleman is brought in by the watch for some misdemeanour committed, and staies but while the next morning, that must pay at least an Angel before he be discharged, hee must pay twelvepence for turning the key at the masterside dore, two shillings to the Chamberlaine, twelvepence for his garnish for wine, tenpence for his dinner, whether he stay or no, and when he comes to be discharged at the Booke it will cost at least three shillings and sixpence more, besides sixpence for the Book-keeper's paines, and sixpence for the Porter (p. 66).

The keepers, it seems, had no scruples, even in purloining legacies left for the relief of the poorest prisoners in the Hole for their own use, and they did not hesitate to maltreat those who could not pay their fees. The narrator's informant tells briefly of one poor serving-man arrested for debt at the beginning of August 1616, who 'took a strong conceit', i.e. contracted some infection from ill-treatment, and died nineteen days later.

Fennor supplements the emotive qualities of his factual details with the use of various literary devices. A flow of sea imagery is maintained throughout the pamphlet,[15] developed from the idea in the subtitle of prison as 'a voyage made to an infernal island'; the counter is 'a turbulent sea' nourished by four currents, by which its victims are driven, and Fennor makes out the analogy between prison and the ocean point by point:

> As the sea is oftentimes disturbed with stormes, gusts, and tempests, so is the Compter with continuall stormes of grief; gusts of sorrow, and tempests of tribulation... The Sea, as *Philosophers* hold is rul'd by the Moone... So is the Compter maintained by the Law and the foure-Tearmes, and, according to their nature and property, it is full and empty. The sea hath many fearefull monsters in it; so hath the Compter an abundance of Sergeants (pp. 53–54).

He is fond of set-pieces like this, and includes also 'the character of a prison', which consists of a series of metaphorical definitions striving after aphoristic wit, a punning paradox in praise of serjeants, and, in order to heighten the tone of his last chapter, first of all a comparison between the Hole and Jerusalem when sacked, and finally an ironic description of the Hole as 'a little Citty in a Commonwealth' with its organization of a Master Steward and twelve senior prisoners to keep order in the wards.

But some of his best effects occur more spontaneously. None of Fennor's other extant pamphlets shows the skill in colloquial descriptive writing of this one; this description of a prison warder gets its vividness from the easy use of imagery from everyday life:

> Hee was a tall rawboned thing, and might very well at Midsummertime haue serued instead of a May-pole, had he been in a contry town, for all the hob-nail wearers in the parish to dance about; his face was much like a withered warden, and wrinckled all over like an *Apple-Iohn* of a yeere old, he was chapfalne, and lookt like the picture of *Famine*, the haire that grew vpon his mussell was so blacke that I thought he had a couple of blacke puddings round about his chaps (p. 13).

Although Dekker is the best-known of all prison pamphleteers, he did not devote any work entirely to the subject. His longest sections on prison and prisoners come in *Iests to make you merie* (1607), which he wrote in collaboration with George Wilkins,[16] and the fourth and seventh editions of *Lanthorne and Candle-light*, respectively entitled *Villanies Discouered by Lanthorne and Candle-light*, published in 1616, and *English Villanies Seven Several Times prest to Death*, published in 1632, perhaps posthumously.[17] When he first came to write about prison in his prose, in *The Seuen Deadly Sinnes of London* (1606), he had already a little personal experience of it because of a short stay in the Poultry Counter in 1598 from which Henslowe released him by lending the forty shillings he owed, but his earlier prison writings, with the exception of *Iests* do not reflect it. *The Seuen Deadly Sines* opens with a very literary description of the allegorical figure Politic Bankruptism, who leads a triumphal procession of seven contemporary sins into the city of London: the *Foure Birds of Noahs Arke* (1609) contains a moving, but totally impersonal prayer for a prisoner, and *A Strange Horse-Race* (1613) ends with a description of a 'Bankrouts Banquet', another allegorical attack on the politic bankrupt. He wrote *A Strange Horse-Race*, it appears, in some haste, with the explicit hope, expressed with unusual directness in the address to the readers, of financial gain: 'The Title of this booke is like a Jesters face, set (howsoeuer he drawes it) to beget mirth: but his ends are hid to himselfe, and those are to get money' (*Non-Dramatic Works*, III, 312). The dedication to his play *If it Be not Good*, published the previous year, also suggests that at this time Dekker was in grave need. Plainly he did not get as much money as he required, for in 1613 he went into the King's Bench prison for debt,[18] and did not emerge until January 1620. From prison he wrote six new chapters for the fourth edition of *Lanthorne and Candle-light*, and these show interesting differences from the earlier prison writings, undoubtedly the results of the suffering he was then enduring. It is probable that he also wrote the six prison Characters that make their first appearance in the ninth edition of *The Overburian Collection*[19] in 1616. Shortly before his release he wrote the strange visionary poem with a prose commentary, *Dekker his Dreame*, published in 1620, which alludes to his life in prison—'a long Sleepe, which for almost seven yeares together, seized al my sences, drowning them in a deepe Lethe of forgetfulness' (*Non-Dramatic Works*, III, 11)—plainly his source of inspiration, but never deals directly with it. His financial troubles were never over,[20] but he managed to stay out of jail; the subject of prison stayed at the back of his mind, and his last publication was yet another edition of *Lanthorne and Candle-light* with three new prison chapters.[21]

Throughout Dekker's long career of prison writing, certain subjects continued to interest him. The figure of the politic bankrupt, the man who lives at ease in the debtors' prison having first taken care to obtain money or goods on credit and then defaulted on his creditors, appears in almost all of his prison work. He distinguishes sharply between this kind of debtor, 'a ten-groates-in-the-pound Banck-rupt, a voluntary Villayn, a devouring Locust, a destroying *Catterpiller*, a golden theefe' (*English Villanies*, sig. I4) and the 'honest Bank-rupt, undone by suretiship, Casualities, or losses at Sea'. The politic bankrupt defies the law and gets away with it; in *The Seuen Deadly Sinnes* he is seen hiding himself in the security of the prison until his creditors cancel his bonds, and then boldly re-emerging to flout all those he has cheated:

> The victory being thus gotten by basenes & trechery, back comes he marching with spred colours againe to the City; aduances in the open streete as he did before; sels the goods of his neighbor before his face without blushing: he iets vp and downe in silks wouen out of other mens stockes, feeds deliciously vpo other mes purses, rides on his ten pound Geldings, in other mens saddles, & is now a new man made out of wax, thats to say, out of those bonds whose seales he most dishonestly hath canceld (*Non-Dramatic Works*, II, 23–24).

In *English Villanies* Dekker sees him as another of those caterpillars that devour the commonwealth:

> How are these wholesome lawes (and the good Princes that made them) abused, by these corroding cankers that eate into the hearts of ten thousand mens estates, to the undooing of families, cozening of whole Parishes and dishonouring of a Noble Kingdome. Such a Banckrupt, is a Devill in a Vault, and so he may stand, cares not whom he blowes up (sig. I4^v).

The helpless debtor and the stony-hearted creditor are the other two figures that haunt Dekker's imagination. The wailing and lamentations of the prisoners, 'Ululations, Deplorations, Groanes, Cries, Sighes, and Complainings' (sig. I3), are the only music of his jails. He does not, like Fennor, stress the sufferings of the prisoners through the extortion of jailors, and he gives few realistic details of prison life; instead, he emphasizes two things, the spiritual misery of losing one's liberty and facing the prospect of indefinite confinement, and the fact that the incarceration of the head of a household almost always brought about the ruin of his family and dependants. Implicitly, he assumes that the typical prisoner is a man of some status in the community. Thus the prisoner in *Iests* soliloquizes:

> Better had it beene for thee to haue beene the sonne of a common Begger, for if then thou hadst beene smitten by the Lawe, the houres of thy punishment would quickly haue runne out: But these are like Shelues of Sande growing in Riuers, neuer to be taken away: so long hast thou worne the fetters of miserable thraldome, that thou canst scarce remember that there is such a thing as libertie (*Non-Dramatic Works*, II, 340).

He conjectures that London's prisons hold at least a thousand debtors: 'What a losse is this to the King? What dishonour to the Countrey? What scandall to Christianity? What Derision to Policy?' (sig. 13ᵛ). Worst of all, the creditor is wronging God, and sacrificing his own eternal soul by acting like a murderer, especially like those who crucified Christ; the passage from *English Villanies* last quoted continues:

> But remember thou (whatsoever thou art) that art a Creditor, and hast inclosed thy heart between walls of Flint and Marbles remember that a Prisoner is Gods Image, yet mans Slave, and a Scriveners Bond-man. He is Christs Pawn, Redeemed from one Hell, and cast in to another.

The religious emphasis is always present in Dekker's prison writing, but it is noticeable that in the writing during and after his long jail term a new tone of stoicism starts to appear; in *Jests* Dekker's attitude is one of hopeless pity towards the lamenting prisoner, or of impotent bitterness towards the serjeants and prison officials, but in *Villanies Discouered* and *English Villanies* he has positive advice to give the prisoner on how to bear himself in jail. The chapter 'Of prisoners' in *Villanies Discouered* begins:

> Hope to escape this wreck, albeit thou swimmest sitting on a mast. The ocean hath both a shore and a bottom. Cities on fire burn out, of themselves. No misery is endless. It behoveth a prisoner to say as Caesar did to the pilot when he was afraid—'Thou carriest,' quoth he, 'Caesar' (*Thomas Dekker*, ed. E. D. Pendry, The Stratford-upon-Avon Library 4, London, 1967, p. 258).

The prisoner is urged never to give up hope, but for the sake of his wife and dependants to find any way of getting out; if this proves impossible, then he should take to himself the comforts of Christian consolation:

> Why is the name of a prison loathsome to thee? Is it because thou art cooped up under lock and key? Or is it because thou feelest wants? Hadst thou the air free as the fowls of it have, yet thy soul must be a prisoner to thy body and thy body commonly be a subject and slave to base and vicious passions.
> ... A bird in the cage sings as sweetly as that in the field; and thou, being in prison, mayst so physic thy sick fortunes that thy mind never took hold of more noble liberty (Pendry, p. 258).

The advice is a mixture of stoic platitude and common sense learnt from experience. The prisoner should take care in the choice of friends—'be sociable to all, acquainted with few'—and especially in selecting a room mate, who should be chosen 'as swans do their mates.' He should not rely for help on former friends. Dekker writes in his later prison pamphlets as a man long past the initial violent reactions of indignation or despair; he has come to terms with the life that has been forced upon him. He is even able to take an objective attitude towards the jailors, and to see them as hard and pitiless only in response to the demands of their job. In *Iests*, as in most prison writing, they were devils and tormentors; in *Villanies Discouered* they are sour and obdurate, but they are also men who in their own way suffer:

> The prisoner cries out he lies upon an ill bed. But upon what bed sleeps his keeper? I think he sleeps upon none—I think he cannot sleep, for his pillow is not stuffed with feathers but with fears. Every prisoner sinks under the weight of his own debts, but his keeper feels the burden of all (Pendry, p. 271).

While Dekker was in the King's Bench, there was agitation from many quarters for reform of the laws relating to debtors and bankrupts, and in 1618 James I revived the commission set up by Elizabeth to bring about a settlement between debtors and creditors in the King's Bench and the Fleet, the *Commissio pro Revelatione Debitorum*. In the years between 1618 and 1625 the pressure for reform continued, and there were numerous petitions to the King and to parliament for a bill to be passed for the relief of poor debtors. The writing of the prison chapters in *Villanies Discouered* and *English Villanies* may well be seen as part of this reformatory movement.

The style of *The Seuen Deadly Sinnes* and of Dekker's part of *Iests* is distinctly more formal and self-conscious than in his later writing; and there is an extravagance of fancy that perhaps owes something to the influence of Nashe; this description of an old prisoner from *Iests* shows Dekker at the height of his style:

> In his face were the *Ruines* of youth, in his garments, of *Time:* in both, the *Triumphs* of pouerty. His Armes were seuen times folded together, like a withered garland of willow, worne carelessly by a forsaken Louer: Sometimes did he vnwinde them, but then did his handes claspe each other so harde, that betweene them they embraced many witnesses: for now his eyes stood like floating Islands compassed rownde with waters: his cheekes like Bankes to Riuers, eaten hollow by cruell torments (*Non-Dramatic Works*, II, 338).

The later writing strives less after its emotional effects, and, to our taste at least, often achieves more; its syntax is less complex, its sentences shorter, its language plainer. The following from the chapter 'Of visitants' in *Villanies Discouered* is vivid and moving, and at the same time almost aphoristic:

> A small end of a cord saves a man from drowning; and a finger of a friend to a prisoner is a full hand. They that cheer up a prisoner but with their sight are Robin Redbreasts that bring straws in their bills to cover a dead man in extremity. Such acquaintances grow like strawberries in a barren country; you shall hardly in a day gather a handful (Pendry, p. 269).

But it is only fair to say that Dekker is not often as successful as this.

In general what stays the same in Dekker's prose is more evident and significant than what changes. Almost all of his prison writing is set out roughly in the form of Characters; in the main he does not construct narratives, or, with the exception of the bankrupts' banquet in *A Strange Horse-Race*, create dramatic settings, and he does not use the anecdotal techniques practised by Greene and the cony-catching writers. Nor does he claim to reveal tricks and devices or to expose new enormities. The prison chapters of *Villanies Discouered* are very modestly presented: 'I make not an orchard but a private walk or rather a small garden-plot set with pot-herbs for the kitchen. This which I write is not a book but a mere rhapsody of mine own disturbed cogitations' (Pendry, p. 257). Dekker never loses his religious awareness, nor his fervency; and the sense of moral purpose in his prison writing is more convincing and deeply felt than in any of his condemnations of rogues and vagabonds.

It remains to say something brief of the treatment of prison and prisoners in Character books of the period. The first genuinely Theophrastan Characters in English appeared in Joseph Hall's *Characters of Vertues and Vices* (1608), and the first prison Character in John Stephens's *Satyrical Essayes Characters and Others* (1615). Thereafter it became usual to include one or two prison Characters in any Character book, and among others *The Overburian Collection*, in its ninth edition of 1616, John Earle in *Micro-Cosmographie* (1628), R.M. in *Micrologia* (1629), Richard Brathwait in *The Whimzies* (1631), Wye Saltonstall in *Picturae Loquentes* (1631), and Donald Lupton in *London and the Countrey Carbonadoed* (1632) all did so, while Geoffrey Mynshul, for a time Dekker's fellow-prisoner, devoted the whole of *Certaine Characters and Essayes of Prison and Prisoners* (1618) to the subject.

Most of these works treat prison only as a conventional subject for the epigrammatic style of moral and social description of types of people and places associated with the Theophrastan Character and its later developments; the aim of their authors is to display a talent for writing in a concise, witty, and morally penetrating manner, and not to describe personal experience or to expose abuses and enormities. Two Character works stand somewhat apart from these generalizations, the prison Characters in *The Overburian Collection,* and Mynshul's *Certaine Characters and Essayes of Prison and Prisoners;* these show something of the Character-writers' approach to the subject of prison, and also relate, for different reasons, more closely to the prison literature I have discussed than the other Character books.

The Overburian Characters first appeared in 1614 appended to the second impression of Sir Thomas Overbury's poem *A Wife*. This composite work proved extraordinarily popular, and new Characters by various unnamed authors were added to each subsequent impression until the total reached eighty-three in 1622. In the ninth impression six Characters dealing with prison life appeared, now thought to be the work of Thomas Dekker.[22] Four of these, *A Prison, A Prisoner, A Creditour,* and *A Jaylour* duplicate subjects treated in chapters XI, XII, XIII and XVI of *Villanies Discouered,* which was published in the same year. The Character of a prison was in itself a novelty, since this was the first time that the Character of an institution, rather than of a human type or quality, had been included in a collection. Dekker's description of a prison in the last part of *Iests* is a kind of early study for it, and sufficiently similar to support the theory that he wrote the Overburian prison Characters. Its influence seems to have been felt immediately, for Fennor in *The Compters Common-wealth,* which came out the year after the Overburian prison Characters, inserted a Character of a prison, with a conspicuous flourish, into his personal reminiscences of prison life. Although the subject-matter of *Villanies Discouered* is similar, the Overburian prison Characters are quite different in effect. They are more tersely and impersonally written; the author's aim is to define the moral nature and significance of each topic, and not, as in *Villanies Discouered* to draw on or describe his own experience of prison life in order to arouse the reader's sympathy. Where, in *Villanies Discouered,* in the chapters 'Of a prison' and 'Of prisoners', Dekker lists and anatomizes the different classes and kinds of prisoner to be found—the sick, the old, the young, the wealthy, the poor—and addresses each in turn, offering a different sort of consolation for his condition, in the Overburian *A Prison* the author summarizes the nature of the single and only consolation in one sentence:

'One thing notwithstanding is heere prayse-worthy, for men in this persecution cannot chuse but proove good christians in that they are a kinde of Martyres, and suffer' (*The Overburian Characters*, p. 82). The tones of pity and of stoic advice in *Villanies Discouered* turn into a kind of bitter wit in *The Overburian Collection;* the prisoner 'lives betwene two Tropiques (Cancer & Capricorne) and by that meanes is in Double danger (of crabbed creditours) for his purse, and hornes for his heade if his wives heeles be light' (*The Overburian Characters*, p. 86).

The imagery and some of the moral attitudes in both works are similar; in both, metaphors from the sea are used to describe going to jail, prison officials are seen as animals or as diabolic creatures, the prison is a wilderness or hell, the creditor is a rapacious torturer with a heart of stone. But the feeling behind the Overburian Characters is either disgust at human degradation, as in *A Sarjeant*, 'the spawne of a decayed shop keeper', or sour acceptance of it. The description of the prisoner's helplessness from *A Prisoner* plays wittily on the two meanings of 'execution', as either death by capital punishment or seizure of the person of a debtor:

> The Barber Surgeons may (if they will) beg him for an Anatomy after he hath suffered execution; an excellent lectuarie may be made upon his body: he is a kinde of dead carcas, creditors, lawyers and Jailours, devoure it, creditors picke out his eyes with his owne teares, Lawyers flea him of his owne skinne and lap him in partchment, and Jaylours are the *Promethean* vultures that gnaw his very heart (*The Overburian Characters*, p. 85).

But his writing impresses more with its eloquence and its punning than with the intensity of its pity, and there is none of the warmth and humane concern of Dekker's other prison writing. Benjamin Boyce's awareness in the Characters of 'Dekker's pity for the prisoner and his burning hatred of creditors and jail-keepers'[23] takes into account only the other Characters in the collection, and not Dekker's prison writing generally.

It is also in the context of Dekker and of *Villanies Discouered* that Geoffrey Mynshul's *Certaine Characters and Essayes of Prison and Prisoners*, which I have cited in its second and enlarged edition, *Essayes and Characters of a Prison and Prisoners*, must first be seen. Mynshul wrote, or rather compiled, this work while he was in the King's Bench, and claimed that he never intended to have it published, but did so in the hope that 'some obdurate creditors may reade it, & by reading mollifie their strong hearts' (sig. A4) and that young gallants might be warned against running into debts. He put his name only to the second edition. Perhaps his reluctance, if it is anything other than a literary convention, was due to the fact that at least half of the pamphlet was plagiarized, mostly from *Villanies Discouered*, which was of course the work of Mynshul's fellow-prisoner, Dekker.[24] Mynshul made no attempt to rewrite his borrowings in the impersonal style of true Character-writing, and as well as using Dekker's work he also took some details from Fennor's *The Compters Common-wealth*, especially for his section 'of entertainment in prison', so that the tone of the whole is less homogeneous and more subjective than in the prison Characters of *The Overburian Collection*. He alternates essays and so-called Characters, devoting one of each to each subject, and the first two-thirds of the pamphlet follows exactly the sequence of topics in *Villanies Discouered;* only the last four chapters, 'Of the Miserable Life in Prison', 'A Locker up at Nights', 'A Noble understanding Prisoner', and 'Observations of a Prison', which were added in the second edition, do not derive directly from other literature.[25] Despite the fact that this is ostensibly a Character book, the Character is in reality only one of many forms that Mynshul tries out. There are passages of stoical moralizing and exhortation to cruel creditors and sinful politic bankrupts in the manner, and often the words, of Dekker, factual details of jailors' extortion, cony-catching anecdotes about keepers' trickery, and would-be gnomic witticisms:

13. It is full Sea when three men are forced to lye thrusting in one bed.
14. A snorting bed fellow, is that great Organ pipe, whose base sound sets all the Quire a roaring (p. 45).

Between his borrowed passages Mynshul inserts sentences insisting on his personal knowledge of his subject: 'So if I should haue studied all the dayes of my life, and that my yeares should be doubled, I should neuer haue imagined either to haue inuented, or to haue been an eye-witnesse of such vnnaturalnesse as is here exemplary' (p. 13). The artless colloquialism of some of the passages that appear to be Mynshul's own conveys the sense of a plain man's response to prison life. He cannot, like Dekker, see his jailors as men of tormented conscience; instead they are the scum of society, 'as Cabbage-carriers, Decoyes, Bum-bayliffes, disgraced Purseuants, Botchers, Chandlers, and a rabble of such stinkardly companions, with whom no man of any reasonable fashion, but would scorne to conuerse' (pp. 30-31). He often tries for literary flourishes, but is more interesting when he abandons them. His bald conclusion gives an authentic feeling of words having failed: 'What els ye shall heare both touching the place, the Persons, and their hangers on, hang me if the tryall make you not say report hath beene too sparing' (p. 48).

Mynshul's little pamphlet is far from being a high point of prison literature but it makes a not unfitting conclusion for this subject. In the hands of professional writers, prison and the sufferings of prisoners could easily become no more than piquant topics for the exercise of wit. Mynshul's barren and derivate effort was the work of someone without literary gifts who wanted to express something of the sordid and horrifying, yet all too common, experience he was undergoing, and by its very lack of sophistication it succeeds.

2
News Pamphlets

'It is an itch in our nature to delight in newness and varietie, be the subject never so grievous', wrote Sir Richard Hawkins in the preface to his pamphlet *Observations of Sir R. Hawkins in his voiâge into the South Sea 1593* (1622) and he is typical of his times in his attitude towards news. Prince Hal in *I Henry IV* talks of 'smiling pickthanks and base newsmongers', and Nashe, being rude about Richard Harvey's *Astrological Discourse* called it 'viler than newsmungrie'. Nonetheless, in the latter half of Elizabeth's reign interest in news of many kinds was on the increase, and news writing for its own sake had become a recognized kind by the early 1620s when the first regular newsbook to be printed in England appeared.[1] Elizabethan news pamphlets represent at least as wide a range of journalistic attitudes and styles as that between, say, the *Financial Times* and the *News of the World*. They were written to cater for a readership extremely diverse in its expectations and in the extent of its literary sophistication. Official news publications, put out by some agency of the church or the state, were intended to present orthodox and approved views and to prevent or correct any tendencies to heterodox thinking on significant current events; as such they were designed to appeal to that class of readers whose attitudes were worth official consideration. An anonymous pamphlet, *A Declaration of the Demeanor and Cariage of Sir Walter Raleigh,* published after Raleigh's execution in 1618 by the King's printer, to show, as the title-page says, 'the true motiues and inducements which occasioned his Maiestie to proceed in doing iustice vpon him', is typical of news put out to establish an official line. It begins

> Although Kings be not bound to giue Account of their Actions to any but God alone; yet such are his Maiesties proceedings, as hee hath alwayes been willing to bring them before Sunne and Moone, and carefull to satisfie all his good people with his Intentions and courses . . .

It is long and carefully printed, and implies the existence of a good number of literate, informed, and politically aware readers. The other end of the scale might be represented by a little pamphlet printed two years earlier called *Miraculous Newes, From the Cittie of Holdt, in the Lord-ship of Munster (in Germany) the twentieth of September last past* (1616), supposedly a translation from an original published in Cologne, which begins with an intriguing woodcut on the title-page showing three skeletons rising from their graves, and goes on to describe how three 'most ghostly and fearefull dead Bodyes' appeared to the people of Holdt to warn them against their wicked ways. In a short appendix called 'The Bookes Apologie' the author owns that this sort of phenomenon is rarely taken seriously: 'Euery one almost is ready to make a tush at it, before hee vnderstand either the probabilitie or the credible testimony, or the authority by which it is published' (sig. C2). But it is unlikely that his readers set great store by credible testimony or authority; it is to a taste for sensationalism tempered with moralizing that this pamphlet and many like it appealed.

My concern is with moralistic pamphlets and so with the kind of news generally classified as 'popular' rather than official or political. In the sixteenth and early seventeenth century the subjects of such news were, as they are now, mainly of sensational interest: murders and other crimes, cases of witchcraft; prodigious events such as the appearance of portents, the birth of monstrous children, or freak weather conditions; and the plague. One area of great interest to modern readers of popular news is missing: accounts of the everyday lives of famous or notorious personalities. It is not that Elizabethan news lacked detail, as the accounts of witchcraft trials show, but that the cult of personality—that peculiar interest in the most private aspects of the lives of the great which is sanctioned in the general public—was given no scope to develop. Domestic news, other than the popular kind, remained a forbidden commodity until the abolition of the Star Chamber in 1641, censorship was strict, and the lives of the great had to be treated with extreme circumspection; the death of the Earl of Essex could not be lamented in print in Elizabeth's life-time, the involvement of the Earl and Countess of Somerset in the notorious Overbury murder was never mentioned in any of the many popular news pamphlets on the crime, and no news report was written to account for the mysterious death of the young Ferdinando Stanley, Earl of Derby, according to Stow's *Annales*,[2] from witchcraft.

The writers of popular news, the majority of them anonymous, express a variety of attitudes towards their work. Many claimed to be writing to satisfy a demand, sometimes overcoming personal reluctance to publish in order to please the public. Henry Goodcole, for instance, stated in his preface to *The wonderfull discouerie of Elizabeth Sawyer a Witch, late of Edmonton* (1621): 'The Publication of this subject whereof now I write, hath bin by importunitie extorted from me, who should haue beene content to haue concealed it, knowing the diuersitie of opinions concerning things of this nature' (sig. A3). Some news appeared very promptly[3] in response to a desire for topical sensation; Goodcole prepared his account of Elizabeth Sawyer to correct the impression given by 'most base and false Ballets, which were sung at the time of our returning from the Witches execution.' The story of the latest murder might well be in print before the execution of its perpetrator, and many books of news were entered in the Stationers' Register within two or three days of the occurrence of the event. But a different sort of demand was behind much publication, as for instance of compilations of anecdotes like Munday's *A View of Sundry Examples Reporting Many Strange Murders* (1580), Churchyard's *The Wonders of the Ayre. The Trembling of the Earth, and the Warnings of the World before Iudgement Day* (1602) and Richard Johnson's *A Lanternelight for Loyall Subiects. Or, A terrour for Traytours* (1603). News readers enjoyed not only the latest crimes and scandals; they also liked reports presented in the form of warnings and direful examples, and seemed not to mind if they described events long past. Biographies and confessions were often prefaced with the sort of claim that Henry Arthington attaches to his repudiation of the fanatical preacher William Hackett, executed in 1591 for proclaiming himself to be the Messiah:

> I haue added my indeuor (the Lorde bearing witnesse, with a single heart) to set downe the storie of my fearefull fall, that all others (if possible) might by my example be warned betimes to forsee and preuent the practises of Satan (*The Seduction of Arthington by Hackett especiallie, with some tokens of his vnfained repentance and Submission*, 1592, sigs. A2–A2ᵛ).

It is not uncommon to find an account of a crime concluded with a separate short section headed perhaps 'Observations gathered out of the former discourse', where the author lists various moral lessons and warnings to be gleaned from the story. Lives were moralized in the interests of religious or political propaganda, especially those describing the trials, confessions and executions of religious heretics, traitors and would-be regicides. If the malefactor did not repent or recant, then the degree of his villainy or the horror of his death was given extra stress. In the case of William Parry, a Jesuit accused of conspiring against Queen Elizabeth, who 'most maliciously and impudently' continued to insist on his innocence up to the point of execution, the author makes much of the Queen's mercy and humanity in pardoning Parry for a minor felony committed earlier in his life;[4] Nicholas Anthoine, a former Catholic who became a Jewish convert because of 'finding several difficulties in the New [Testament] which seemed to him unanswerable', was punished by God with fits of madness before he was burnt for heresy.[5] Even the most virtuous and uneventful lives could be used in the cause of propaganda; both Katherine Brettergh and Katherine Stubbes, pious young women who died in their early twenties, are depicted disputing on their death-beds with Satan who tried to tempt them to heresy.

It is clear that sixteenth and seventeenth century news reporting was in some ways very different from our own. The influence of moral attitudes is a major reason for this; it was generally felt that every event could be seen and shown to illustrate some facet of God's relationship to man, especially his providential control of human affairs and his careful and constant warning of the inevitable consequences of sinful living, and so the reporting of news was often done in such a way as to emphasize these things. Also important was the belief that the individual life or the single sensational event could always be seen as typical exemplifications of some truth, and that it was in the general rather than the particular aspect that their importance lay. Hence, Elizabethan news placed relatively little stress on precise factual detail: the names, places, dates, and figures which are so essential to modern reporting were often very summarily treated. Arthur Golding, in *A discourse vpon the Earthquake that hapned throughe This Realme of England* (1580), while far from underestimating the cosmic significance of the tremor, affords almost no description of what actually happened: 'it overthrew fewe or none that I have yet hearde of, saving certaine stones, chimneys, walles, and Pinacles, of highe buildings' (sig. C4ᵛ). The anonymous pamphlet, *Sundrye strange and inhumaine Murthers, lately committed* (1591), recounts three cases; in two of these no names are given, and in the third, of a girl and two suitors, the men are identified as 'Mr. Padge' and 'George Strangwich' and the girl left anonymous. No details of time, date, or locality are given. From the several pamphlets extant which describe the phenomenally windy winter of 1612-13 it is very hard to discover the nature and extent of the damage done. The author of *The Windie Yeare* (1612) looks only for anecdotes to illustrate his thesis that 'These tempests, as they haue been ill windes to blow many upon the rockes of ruine, and poverty, so haue they blowne some to profit' (sig. B3), and hence gives no figures of loss at all. In other pamphlets the figures are either quite obviously the result of guess-work, or else too huge to be plausible. In *The Wonders of This Windie Winter* (1613) the author writes that 'The seas have bereaued 7000 and od people of their lives and that neere the sea side there are knowne to be fourteene hundred sea-faring mens widdowes'. From *The Last terrible Tempestious windes and weather* (1613) we learn that 'many hundreds of acres of pasture and erable land was . . . turned into a maine Ocean (sig. A3), and that deaths from the wind in London alone numbered 'one hundred and odde thousands'.

Undeniably some news did appear promptly,[6] and names, facts and figures were accurately reported, but these things were not taken for granted, as they are now. There were indeed signs that factual news was coming to be valued for its own sake, for instance, the increasing use of words like 'report', 'news' and 'true' in the titles of works, even of those with little claim to any of them.[7] But, at least until 1620, the titles stress wonder as much as truth. The tendency towards informing is constantly counteracted by that towards amazing, warning, and teaching by example. Alongside 'true' and 'just' stand 'wonderful', 'rare', 'dreadful' and 'unnatural'. In *A true Relation of the Travels of M. Bush* (1607) the author, perhaps Anthony Nixon, describes the vessel built by Bush for his journeys, a ship which could travel by land, sea, or (with stiff cables acting as runners) air, in such a way as to bring out both the wonder and the truth of his account, with the emphasis on the former: 'such as have been in the South Sea, and at the Cape of *Bona Speranza*, could neuer report of such a performance as this gentlemans, which for rareness, hath the wonder and approbation of all men, and for trueth the confirmation of many thousand eye-witnesses' (sig. B2). An account of diabolic possession is the more saleable for being 'true' as well as 'most dreadful', and for the confirmation of named witnesses, but in most news writing it does not essentially matter that the author writes from hearsay, nor in *True and Wonderfull. A discourse relating a Strange and Monstrous Serpent (or Dragon)* (1614), that more than three-quarters of the pamphlet is designed to arouse the reader's amazement, while the truth is dealt very summarily with, in a page or two at the end:

> The serpent (or dragon as some call it) is reputed to be nine feet, or rather more, in length . . . The scales along his backe seeme to be blackish, and so much as is discovered under his bellie appeareth to be red; for I speake of no nearer description than of a reasonable ocular distance (in *The Harleian Miscellany*, III, 111).

News was of typical rather than individual significance, as the frequent citation of historical precedents well illustrates. Arthur Golding, writing on the earthquake of 1580, concentrates not on the tremor itself, which lasted but a minute, and did little damage, but on its resemblances to other monstrous events, an earthquake in Naples in 1566, a famine in the time of Queen Mary, and various prodigious births. Thomas Twyne treats the same subject in *A shorte and pithie Discourse, concerning the engendring, tokens, and effects of all Earthquakes in Generall* (1580), where his title makes explicit his view of the earthquake, not as a singular event in itself, but as one example from a significant number. He begins his pamphlet:

> Before we enter any further into the bare bewraying of the matter, it is expedient that I discouer unto you the cause, and substance of euerie Earthquake, which I must be fayne to borrowe from the Prophane wryters ... And therefore following *Aristotle* as cheefe in this behalfe: we must understand, that the efficient causes of an Earthquake are three (sig. A1).

And before he finally gets round to describing the event, which is done in two pages, he gives first in thirty-seven unnumbered paragraphs, an elaborate account of the causes, kinds, and incidence of earthquakes in general. Shaaber given an explanation for his habit which is only part of the truth; he calls it 'an imitation of the style of the standard historical works of the day, the nearest precedent familiar to the literary soldiers, lawyers, scholars and gentlemen amateurs who wrote the news of wars, state ceremonies, and political developments' (p. 213). Undoubtedly the need for a formal model has something to do with it, but there is also the point that news writers associated their works with historical writing because they believed them to share the same function. News was not only interesting, but useful, and useful in the same way as chronicles and lists of exemplary lives, like the *Mirror for Magistrates* (1559), Foxe's *Acts and Monuments* (1563), Beard's *The Theatre of Gods Judgements* (1597) and Reynolds's *The Triumphs of Gods Revenge Against the Crying, And Execrable Sinne of Murther* (1621), from which stories cited as precedents in these pamphlets are often taken. The distinctions between individual events, between contemporary fact and centuries-old legend, are less important than the fact that they can all be used to inculcate the same morality.

Popular news pamphlets take three main forms: biographies (including confessions), compilations, and reports. Biography as a word had not yet come into the English language;[8] the Elizabethans used instead the term 'lives'. The concept itself was not clearly defined, and no distinction was made between biography as a form of history, as Bacon saw it, and biography as the life of a significant or curious individual. Although the motivation behind the writing of many biographies and confessions is clearly the desire to provide sensation or novelty, the authors always insist on the didactic value of their accounts. The lives of the good, of public benefactors, great travellers, protestant martyrs, chaste wives, are exemplary, those of the wicked, of thieves, murderers, traitors, prodigals, sorcerers, stand as solemn warnings. Even in the most sensational, freakish, or bizarre lives, like those of Faustus, or Stubbe Peeter, the Dutch mass-murderer, or Henry Welby, who lived for forty-four years in total solitude, the authors are concerned to discover what is typical or representative, to trace a familiar pattern shaping the course of the oddest career.

Some of the most interesting popular biographies are confessions by repentant criminals; no doubt the lives of the unrepentant might have been more interesting, but no one wrote them. The numerous Catholic recantations are usually dull and stereotyped, but criminal confessions, though circumscribed by the need to present the world with a penitent face, can be very lively and full of personal detail. *The Life, Apprehension, Arraignement, and Execution of Charles Courtney* (1612) is a vivid first-person account of a career as thief and jailbreaker. Courtney presents himself in the Robin Hood tradition as one who took only from 'such Curmugions, who care not who starues themselues to bee Corne-fed'; his crime was to rob a rich usurer called Gardner, and he describes in an accomplished narrative how he eased himself into Gardner's confidence by pretending to be pious and thrifty, and how he organized the burglary while the old man was out at a tavern. The fluent unstructured prose vividly communicates the excitement of the discovery:

> Maister Gardner with his wife come home to their house, find their doore shut, there was no hurt in that, bids his wife light a candle, there was no hurt in that, but missing his key, was forced to breake the doore open: coming up into his chamber, espying the feathers scattered all about one roome, and money about another ... my old friend began to wonder at that: and beeing suddainly affrighted flees to his Counting-house, where, when he saw what ransacke was made, what a pittiful heat was my olde Grandsire in, let euery one iudge (p. 9).

It is when Courtney fails to break out of Dunstable prison that he becomes aware of God's intervention in his affairs, and his pamphlet ends with a typical statement of penitence which follows leadenly after the relish of the first part:

[In jail] I spent my time onely in praier, being still frequented with divers good & godly men, who laboured zealously for the good of my soule, and who I hope can testifie to the world, that I died a true penitent & servant of God, God for his mercie grant vnto al other offenders the like contrition, and true feeling of his benefits, and vnto me life everlasting, Amen (p. 18).

The repentant, whether or not destined for execution, present their changes of heart as direct examples of God's work, and emphasize their criminality to the fullest extent. Francis Cartwright, who murdered two men, survived a shipwreck, escaped from Turkish capture, and narrowly avoided falling on his own sword, describes the beginning of this life of misadventure in the archetypal manner, by disobeying his parents: 'Vpon this foundation of my disobedience, the Deuill began to build a Mansion for himselfe to inhabite, and so grew my soule a Cage of uncleane Birds, wherein many foule sinnes were bred' (*The Life, Confession, and Heartie Repentance of Francis Cartwright, Gentleman*, 1621, sig. A3ᵛ).

Greene in his confessional pamphlet *The Repentance of Robert Greene Maister of Artes* (1592) makes his change of heart more striking by stressing the dual theme of 'the graceless endeuours' of his youth, accusing himself of atheism, drunkenness, gluttony, and blasphemy, and the constant providence of God, manifested particularly in the efforts of his friends to bring about his repentance. He quotes the frivolous answers he made to them:

Tush, what better is he that dies in his bed than he that endes his life at Tyburne, all owe God a death (p. 11).

Hell (quoth I) what talke you of hell to me? I know that if I once come there, I shal haue the company of better men than my selfe (p. 11).

But, as he relates, 'the mightie hand of God' struck him down with an illness which, in combination with his reading of Father Robert Parsons's 'booke of *Resolution*', induced terrible thoughts of damnation and brought him into the depths of self-loathing. The language of his agony recalls not only the book of Job, but also the topical repentance of Dr Faustus, another sinner claimed by hell at the end of his life, published in its English version a few months earlier:

O cursed and vnstable life! O blinde and carelesse wretch that so hast abused thy body, sence and soule! O foolish pleasure, into what a weary labyrinth hast thou brought me, blinding mine eyes in the clearest day: Ah weake heart! O troubled soule, where is become

> thy knowledge to comfort thee: O pitifull wearinesse! (*The Historie of the damnable life, and deserued death of Doctor Iohn Faustus*, 1592, p. 76).

The tracing of God's influence during the whole course of a lifetime which Greene's *Repentance* shows is a common feature of repentance pamphlets. Sir Gervase Elwes, Lieutenant of the Tower of London, in a speech supposedly made immediately before his execution for his part in the Overbury affair, describes how events in his life have anticipated his fate, especially an incident at gambling in his youth:

> Vpon a time, being much displeased at my losse, I said, (not in a careles manner) would I might be hanged, but seriously, and advisedlie (between God & myself) clapping my hands vpon my breast, I spake thus, If euer I play againe, then let me be hangd. Now gentlemen here you may behold the justice of God, paying me my wish and imprecation home (sigs. B3^v–B4).

Francis Cartwright, who was luckier than Elwes, constantly emphasizes God's efforts to preserve him; on one occasion, 'my Sword suddenly fell out with the point up, nor could I stop my selfe: but violently with all my weight I fell upon it; yet the Lord turned the harme from mee, and betwixt my arme and bodie it slided' (sig. C2^v). Charles Courtney, in the last part of his work, ascribes the failure of his frequent efforts to escape from prison to 'the will of our just God, that giues preuention to euill, for the prosperitie of honest and good men (which I now heartily pray for)' (p. 12). It seems also to have been conventional for the penitent to show how he has profited from his experience, by giving suitable advice to the reader; Arthington concludes with a warning to beware of Satan's temptations, and Greene, both in his *Groats-worth of witte, bought with a million of Repentance* (1592) and in his *Repentance*, gives a series of specific injunctions against drinking, blaspheming, and harlots.

The demands of this moralistic attitude serve not only to emphasize aspects of these lives that lack particularity to a modern reader but also to diminish the significance of areas where our curiosity is aroused. *The Phoenix of these late times: Or the life of Mr. Henry Welby Esq.* (1637) by Thomas Heywood[9] is about a man who retired completely from human society at the age of forty, and lived for his remaining forty-four years in total solitude. But rather than examine the motives for this strange way of living the author devotes himself to unoriginal definitions of Welby's virtues and laboured wit:

What should I say? hee dyed living, that hee might live dying: his life was a perpetuall death, that his death might bring him to an eternall life; who accounted himselfe no better than a Glow-worme here on Earth, that hee might hereafter shine a most glorious saint in heaven (sig. A2).

Clearly the details are less important than Welby's value as an exemplar of virtue; the same aspect is stressed by the more elementary didacticism of other writers. The author of *A true Discourse. Declaring the damnable life and death of one Stubbe Peeter* (1590), describing the life of a lycanthropist and sex-murderer who was also convicted of incest and sorcery, strove to find generally applicable truth from a singularly inimitable case-history, and began his work:

> Those whome the Lord dooth leaue to followe the Imagination of their own hartes dispising his proffered grace, in the end through hardnes of hart and contempt of his fatherly mercy, they enter the right path to perdicion. . . as in this present historie in perfect sorte may be seene (p. 1).

Undeniably there are pamphlets which simply exploit the bizarre or sensational possibilities of their subject, but these are rare. John Taylor's *The Great Eater of Kent* (1630?) an account of Nicholas Wood of the celebrated appetite who was said to have eaten a whole sheep raw at a sitting, is one such, but even so it gives little factual detail and consists entirely of witticisms and hearsay. Taylor, a great provider of impromptu entertainments, invited Wood to the Bankside to put on an eating display, promising a wheelbarrow full of tripes as an inducement, but Wood refused.

The use of newsworthy events mainly for their value as moral examples derives from the same mental outlook as that which produced collections of moralized lives such as *The Mirror for Magistrates.* This attitude of mind is seen also in that odd journalistic form, apparently popular in this period, the news-compilation. Some compilations are made up of three or four news pieces describing various celebrated events of the relatively recent past, published together as a sort of bargain offer to attract sales, a newspaper in miniature, but more of them consist of a number of shorter pieces or anecdotes arranged in a roughly chronological order to illustrate some uncontroversial theme such as the imminence of judgement day. Anthony Munday's *A View of Sundry Examples* (1580) and Thomas Churchyard's *The Wonders of the Ayre* (1602) both take this line, and in doing so leave undeveloped potentially interesting narratives. Many compilations are political, like

Richard Johnson's *A Lanterne-light for Loyall Subiects*, which acclaims the doctrine of divine right and illustrates the inevitable downfall of all regicides, and those anti-Catholic histories in the tradition of Foxe like Edmund Rudierde's *The Thunderbolt of Gods Wrath* (1618). Others are domestic like *A Divine Tragedie Lately Acted, Or, A Collection of sundrie memorable examples of God's judgments* (1641) by the puritan preacher Henry Burton, which illustrates God's anger against Sabbath-breakers. Two features of popular news-writing particularly stand out in these compilations: one is that attitude towards pamphleteering and its raw material which treats the sources and published texts as all part of a single common fund on which any writer may draw without question of another having exclusive rights, and the other is the influence of the chronicle histories on popular reporting.

The notion of utilizing a common fund of material is reflected in compilations in several ways. A writer may compose his pamphlet largely with material from someone else, as Richard Johnson does in *A Lanterne-light* with extensive and unacknowledged passages from Whetstone's *The Censure of a loyall Subiect* (1587); or, he may deliberately set out to make up a pamphlet from anecdotes collected from numerous sources, like Munday in *A View of Sundry Examples* or the anonymous *A World of Wonders* (1595); finally, he may simply republish, as nearly as possible verbatim, two or three earlier news items, without adding anything of his own, as in the collection entitled *A Miracle, of Miracles, As fearefull as euer was seene or heard of in the memorie of Man* (1614). Johnson's *A Lanterne-light* is essentially a simplified and generalized version of Whetstone's *The Censure*, a comment in dialogue form on the recent execution of Anthony Babington and his thirteen fellow rebels. Johnson takes many passages direct from Whetstone,[10] making only the changes necessitated by the passing of time, but by rearranging them, omitting the dialogue framework, and shifting the emphasis from a single event to a multitude of similar examples, he turns a news pamphlet into an illustrated discourse 'describing many fayre examples of Traytours foule ends'. Munday's *A View* is also a reworking of old material but done in such a way as to involve almost no additional writing or commentary; the author has simply collected, and where necessary rewritten, accounts—sometimes, apparently, even his own accounts[11]—of recent crimes and portentous events from various sources, inserting Biblical quotations and emotive asides. The compiler of *A World of Wonders*, perhaps the printer John Trundle or one of his hacks, put his book together in the same way, although his material ranges more widely, from the legendary times of King Arthur and the ancient Britons to the story of a corpse dug up whole and intact in 1594. His comments are briefer than Munday's, like this one which is appended to the story of Walter Gray, Archbishop of York in 1234, who hoarded corn during a famine and was punished for it by finding his granary made 'The beds of wormes and of toades and horrible serpents': 'Beholde this true example and repent thou covetous rich man and doe good while time is offered thee, and God will blesse thee the better' (sig. D3). The conclusion of this pamphlet clearly shows that the compiler did not see the necessity of recounting a contemporary event with the detail that he gave to history or legend:

> It shall be needlesse to report unto you the most hainous murther committed uppon the Chaundler neer broken Wharff in London the matter being so fresh in memorie, the malefactor still hanging as a notable example to our eyes, a greif to the godly a terrour to the wicked and reprobate; which God graunt for our Lord Jesus sake. Amen (sig. F4).

A third method of re-using old material, by simply republishing it, is also demonstrated by John Trundle, one of the most active news publishers of the early seventeenth century, in *A Miracle, of Miracles, As fearefull as euer was seene or heard of in the memorie of Man*, containing three separate accounts which had all been published before. The first, 'strange newes out of Sommersetshire', is a reprint of a pamphlet entitled *A true and most Dreadfull discourse of a woman possessed with the Devill*, which Trundle, by subtle omissions, presents as contemporary, although the events took place in 1584. The second story, though dated 'the first of October last past, 1613' is probably even older, and recounts events of 1580.[12] The third which has a separate title-page, tells of floods in Lincolnshire in 1613; it had already been published in the same year by Trundle as a separate account. The fact that old stories could be retold and republished in this way clearly shows that news was of interest as much for its moral and didactic value as for its contemporaneity.

The influence of chronicle histories on these compilations comes out both in their form and in the assumptions on which they are based. Some of them are abridged versions, with additional contemporary items, of the great prototypes; Foxe's *Acts and Monuments* gave rise to a tradition of anti-Catholic compilations, while the *Mirror for Magistrates* by Baldwin and his successors directly inspired collections of domestic tragedies like Beard's *The Theatre of Gods Judgements*, and Reynolds's *The Triumphs of Gods Revenge*. Henry Burton's pamphlet, *A*

Divine Tragedie Lately Acted, Or, A Collection of Sundrie memorable examples of Gods judgements is a good example of the influence of the chronicle way of thinking and writing. Although the pamphlet is a piece of Puritan propaganda and part of the revived Sabbatarian controversy,[13] Burton in his letter to the Reader places himself in a tradition of writing which links the Protestant biographies of Foxe with the domestic anecdotes of Reynolds and Beard through the common theme of God's judgements. Burton's own contribution to the subject is to consist of 'many memorable presidents of Gods avenging justice upon Sabbath-breakers'. There follow fifty-six numbered examples, varying in length from a sentence to a paragraph, of judgements executed on Sabbath-breakers incited to licentious acts by Charles I's so-called *Declaration for Sports and Pastimes after Evening Prayer on the Lords Day* (1633). They are economically written, but not without vigour:

> In Yorkshire at a Wake, in the Parish of Otley at Baildon, on the Lords Day, two of them sitting at drink, late in the night, fell out and being parted, the one a little after finding his fellow, sitting by the fire with his back towards him, comes behinde him, and with a hatchet chines him down the back, so as his bowels fell out; the murtherer flying immediately, and being hotly pursued, lept into a river, and so drowned himself. O fearfull fruits of carnall liberty! (p. 7).

Sources and dates are sometimes given, sometimes not; total accuracy is less important than overall credibility:

> If it shall so fall out, that one or two, or so, should prove otherwise, either for the substance, or circumstance; let not the Reader blame me, who have used my best diligence to enquire out the certain truth of them all, and I am sure the most of the examples are confirmed by witnesses without all exception, and none of them is to me of any suspected credit (p. 2).

Burton emphasizes the fact that all his examples postdate the King's Declaration, as if to render unassailable conclusions reached by evidence and observation. He implies that he is making social criticism on the basis of his stories, whereas in fact the reverse is true, and his stories are all selected or slanted to verify the commonplaces of popular thought, especially that with which he concludes:

> Inferiour persons exalt themselves in high contempt against their Superiors, as the common vulgar against the Magistrate and Minister, servants against their masters, Children against their parents,

and wanton wives against their husbands, which hath caused such outcries and complaints of masters, for their servants unbridled and uncontrouled outrage on the Lords day (p. 29).

Compilations in general share these attitudes to events; hence legend, history and contemporary news are treated together, in a single work, on a single level of validity. In *A World of Wonders* there are stories of a woman who falsely accuses a minister of stealing her ring, making such an outcry in public that he gives her ten groats to be rid of her; of a woman who grew a horn because she had committed adultery; of a man who was hanged for stealing a chicken to give a harlot; of a flesh-eating fish shaped like a man; of a whale discovered on the Isle of Thanet twenty-two yards long. And, as they are presented, all these are true, and are assumed to testify with equal authority to the fact that Doomsday is at hand.

On the third and largest category of news-writing, straightforward reports, the effect of the didactic treatment of news is considerably modified by a newly emerging interest in facts for their own sake, and by a number of functions other than warning or instruction given by the authors. Reports were sometimes written to convey information to answer a specific request, as Alexander Gurth makes clear in the dedicatory letter of his *Most true and More Admirable news, Expressing the Miraculous Preservation of a Young Maiden of the towne of Glabbich in the Dukedome of Gulische* (1597) 'to his especiall freind, Master Ed Hare': 'Sir (as you have desired) I have done all my endeavour to satisfie you with the truth of such noteworthy things, as in these parts happen; beeing recompenced by you with like for like from London, our naturall and beloved Citie' (sig. A3). Many reports claimed to correct false information or furnish a definitive account of a well-known case, and writers were keen to stress their authority as eye-witnesses or acquaintances of those involved; Gilbert Dugdale in the dedication to *A True Discourse Of The practises of Elizabeth Caldwell* (1604) asserts:

> True it is that diuers reports passed vp and downe the streets of London as touching this act of murder, but how scandelously, as fiue murdred, three murdred, by the meanes of six persons, which your Worships know is false, only three murdered one; marry the intent was to him that now lives. Therefore being an eare-witness to this false alarum, it made me more diligent in the setting foorth the truth (sig. A3^v).

Pamphlets on witchcraft, to the Elizabethans one of the gravest and most serious subjects for reporting, stand out as a group for their stress on fact and authenticity. Lists of witnesses and minute details of evidence are given, interrogations and confessions presented verbatim; some authors emphasize the part they themselves have played in questioning suspects and taking notes at the trial. But witchcraft was a subject to be treated with especial delicacy because of the dangerously controversial religious issues involved. The series of pamphlets concerned with the exorcist John Darrell at the turn of the century, written by state officials or ministers of the church, combine news, propaganda, and special pleading. Darrell, who had no episcopal licence for exorcism, had been involved in three famous sixteenth-century cases of witchcraft, those of Thomas Darling, the boy of Burton, bewitched by Alice Gooderidge, of the seven members of the Starkey household in Lancashire, and of William Sommers and his sister in Nottingham.[14] In 1599, Samuel Harsnett, secretary to the Bishop of London and a member of the ecclesiastical commissioners who had investigated Darrell's exorcisms, published *A Discovery of the fraudulent practises of Iohn Darrel Bacheler of Artes* to expose Darrell as a fake; Darrell replied with *A Detection of that Sinnful, Shamful, Lying, and Ridiculous Discours of Samuel Harshnet* (1600) the next year, and was supported in print by at least three other pamphlets. The case was brought to a hasty and probably official conclusion by the publication of Harsnett's *A Declaration of Egregious Popishe Impostures* (1603).[15] Other accounts of witchcraft cases came with official backing: *The Wonderfull discouerie of witches in the Countie of Lancashire* (1612) contains a statement by one of the judges, Sir Edward Bromley, that he had personally overseen the report which had been written by the clerk at the sessions. Henry Goodcole, Chaplain to the prisoners at Newgate, made use of his official position to provide the public with information. His covertly sympathetic narrative, *The wonderfull discouerie of Elizabeth Sawyer a Witch*, was written to offset the false impression given in ballads sung at the witch's execution.

In another pamphlet, *Heavens Speedie Hue and Cry sent after Lust and Murther* (1635), Goodcole uses the story of Thomas Sherwood, a London cony-catcher, and Elizabeth Evans, a country girl turned prostitute and Sherwood's accomplice in two murders, to give needful advice on city life to 'vulgar Ignorants'. He provides two separate sections of information, entitled 'A briefe observation for all persons, both in Citty and Countrey, to know lewd tempting persons lurking in the streets and High-wayes, by these tokens following' and 'An intimation of such places in, and about the City of London, that Harlots watch their opportunities to surprise men'. At the end of the pamphlet he gives directions on where the bodies of the two criminals, now executed, are to be seen. A case of infanticide in Ewell in Surrey is used by John Taylor the Water Poet to draw attention to the fact that the town 'hath neither Preacher nor Pastor' because the living is in the gift of a layman and the stipend available for a Reader is a mere £11 a year, (John Taylor, *The Vnnaturall Father: Or, The Cruell Murther committed by one Iohn Rowse of the Towne of Ewell,* 1621). During the period from 1600 onwards there is a movement away from the chronicle-didactic style of reporting in pamphlets like Arthur Golding's *A discourse vpon the Earthquake that hapned throughe this Realme of England* (1580) and Francis Shakelton's *A blazing Starre or burnying Beacon . . . to call all sinners to earnest & speedie repentance* (1580) towards fact, useful information, and even, later on, advertisement. The author of *A certaine Relation of the Hog-faced Gentlewoman called Mistris Tannakin Skinker* (1640), after describing the unfortunate lady and comparing her case with various historical examples, reminds his readers that she can be seen 'at Blackfriars or Covent-Garden'.

Although some reports may remind us more of sermons than of news stories, many of them use literary techniques common to the popular journalism of all periods, which will not be unfamiliar to anyone who has ever picked up the *News of the World* or the *Daily Express*. There is a strong attempt to win interest by presenting the story in as sensational a manner as possible, and by stressing its unique and newsworthy qualities. The writers make free with superlatives. 'The most strange and cruell Murther that euer I read of', 'a murther so detestable that were it not it desires record for example sake, Humanitie could wish it rather utterly forgot', 'a fellow not to be fellowed, and one that scarce hath an equall, for matchlesse misery, and unnaturall Murther', 'Of all other that euer liued, none was comparable unto this helhound'—such feeling phrases abound in the pamphlets. Title-pages and prefaces, like modern fly-sheets, advertise what is to come in terms of horror, wonder, and uniqueness. The anonymous author of *A True report of the horrible Murther, which was committed in the house of Sir Ierome Bowes* (1607) is careful to distinguish this from similar cases, although in fact it is a very straightforward account of robbery with violence:

> I haue sometime heard, and oft times read of murthers, as hainous in the fact, as this was, that I am to write of: but of none did I euer heare or reade, more audacious in the attempt, than was this, or more odious to God and man (sig. A4ᵛ).

In *True and Wonderfull. A discourse relating a Strange and Monstrous Serpent (or Dragon)* (1614) the author promises mind-expanding revelations: 'Believe it, or reede it not, or reade it (doubting) for I believe ere thou hast read this little all, thou wilt not doubt of one, but believe there are many serpents in England' *(Harleian Miscellany,* III, 228). But although he personally viewed the serpent he could supply little in the way of convincing factual detail because he dared not go too near it.

Other writers create interest and excitement by their descriptive style. Philip Stubbes in *Two wunderful and rare Examples of the Vndeferred and present approaching iudgement of the Lord our God* (1581) makes his account of a blasphemer's death hideously vivid with a multitude of adverbs:

> [He] dyd most hardlie, in the verie anguishe of death, starte vp in his bedde, and sware by Gods blood, this Bell dooth towle for me. Whereuppon immediatlie, the blood aboundauntly, from all the iountes of his body, as it were in streames, did issue out, most fearfullie, as well, from mouth, nose, wrestes, knees, heeles, toes, with all other ioynts not one left free: whereupon he most myserablie yeelded up the ghost (sig. A3).

The author of *A True Relation of the most Inhumane and bloody Murther, of Master Iames Minister and Preacher of the word of God at Rockland in Norfolke* (1609), who had obviously studied the arts of rhetoric and meant to show it, uses a kind of pathetic fallacy to arouse the reader's horror and anticipation immediately before the occurrence of the murder:

> The offended winde put on his roughest wings and beate against the doores as if it ment to rush in and discouer, or blow downe the house and couer the bodie of the murtherer. The heavens threatned vengeance in thunder, if he desisted not, the melancholy night though naturally prone to outrages, could not but blush for shame (sig. B).

These writers deal very directly with their readers, deliberately stimulating response like a speaker to a live audience. They describe their own reactions to arouse the reader's:

> How shall I be able to express this strange crueltie without distilling tears from mine eyes (apt to put me in remembraunce, of such a wickedness) whensoeuer I doe but take my penne in hand or how can it be, that any one in reading this tragicall subiect, should not consider and weigh my hardines and courage? *(The Life and Death of Lewis Gaufredy,* 1612, sig. D2^v).

They constantly urge the reader to feelings of outrage: 'Now whose heart is so stonie, that reading this bloody letter will not burst foorth into teares?' (Philip Stubbes, *The Intended Treason of Doctor Parrie*, 1584, sig. A3^v). The author of *A True Relation* invites the reader to put himself into the position of the murderer at the time of the crime: 'Wel, into his chamber he enters, where alasse, what hand, if but humane would not have trembled? What hart, if not flint but would have melted at the very thoughte of the attempt?' (sig. A4^v).

In *The Bloody Downfall of Adultery, Murder, Ambition* (1615), a comment on the Overbury case which avoids the dangers of discussing so controversial an affair by never referring to any of those involved by name, the author invokes each of the major participants in turn, and involves his readers in a communal threnody for the fall of princes:

> All you that haue your hearts pierced with sad considerations, take this for a remembrance of greefe, that is: that when a woman of noble Parentage, placed on the mountaine of smiling chance, hauing the dignity of Greatnesse shining on her forehead, should humble her selfe to base conditions... Oh was not this woman created for a deep sorrow to her Aliance, a great greefe vnto her country, and a foule staine vnto her owne reputation? (sig. Cl^v).

In this oblique way, safe allusion is made to the complicity of Lady Frances Howard in witchcraft and murder.

While the lives of the well-born had to be treated carefully, popular writers could exercise their imaginations to the fullest on the misdeeds of the humble. They are rarely at a loss to give some sort of psychological account for the behaviour of the criminals, although there is much recourse to conventional explanations such as provocation by the devil, wrongful ambition to improve one's social status or the prick of a guilty conscience. The most inexplicable actions could be ascribed to fits of madness, inflicted as a divine punishment. The writers frequently describe the inner feelings of their characters, or provide them with some sort of expository monologue. The author of *Two most vnnaturall and bloodie Murthers* (1605), who had a stronger sense of the dramatic than most of his fellows, gives his protagonist, Walter Calverley, a vivid style of soliloquy; after a duel with a man who has defended Mrs Calverley's honour, Calverley is described: 'looking upon his wounds, and seeing them bleed, [he] said to himselfe strumpet, thou art the cause that I bleede now, but I will be the cause that thou shalt bleede heereafter' (p. 9).[16] This sort of imaginative treatment of news items is not uncommon; and although it seems to suggest a different conception of the relationship between fact and fiction from that of contemporary journalism, it has a modern counterpart, not in written news, but in the reconstruction of criminal acts in the form of films and plays.

A mode of thought popular in Elizabethan times that is foreign to us is the tendency to find evidence of the outrage of nature at the crimes of men. In Renaissance drama supernatural portents symbolized God's anger at human misdeeds; real life, even contemporary life, it seems, imitated art. The bleeding of the corpse in the presence of a murderer is reported in *Sundrye strange and inhumaine Murthers, lately committed* (1591), where it identifies the hired killer who has made away with three unwanted children, and in *The Most horrible and tragicall murther of. . . John Lord Bourgh* (1591), thus exposing Arnold Cosby, the servant who treacherously stabbed his master. Murders are followed by supernatural events. In *Sundrye Strange and inhumaine Murthers*, after the killing of Mr Padge by his wife, a strange portent appears: 'Vpon the same night three nights after, there was seen an ugly thing formed like a Beare, whose eyes were as it had been fier, bearing about him a linnen cloth representing the instrument wherewith the said M. Padge was murdered' (sig. B4ᵛ).

If the murderer tries to escape on horseback, his horse invariably stumbles and falls. In two accounts of the celebrated case of George and Annis Dell, who murdered a two-year-old boy and cut out the tongue of his sister, the little girl, after being dumb for four years, regains her power of speech when she hears the crowing of the cock 'that bird that put *Peter* in minde of his great sinne in denying our Sauiour and his Maister' (*The Most Cruell and Bloody Murther*, 1606, sig. C1). There is a similar improbable neatness in the way that many crimes meet appropriate punishments. Examples of curses and blaspheming ironically fulfilled are legion: a wastrell husband, urged to remember his pregnant wife's condition, 'unadvisedly made answere: she may beare the Deuill of hell', and was presented with an infant covered in black hair and adorned with horns and claws. Anne Avery, unable to pay her bill at a tow-merchants, 'desired of God that she might sincke where she stood if she did not pay for it',[17] and at once disappeared into the earth. Traitors meet their ends by treachery, corn-hoarders have their secret supplies devoured by worms, and 'one Marlin [Marlowe], a Cambridge schooler, who was a Poet, and a filthy Playmaker' dies of wounds inflicted by his own dagger. As always, observers interpreted mysterious events according to what they expected or felt proper should happen; this is so in Thomas Cooper's *The Cry and Reuenge of Blood* (1620), where a farmer's desire to have his pond dragged, revealing, unbeknown to him, two murdered bodies and so bringing to light a long-concealed crime, is imputed to the will of God working through him:

> The *Farmer* cannot rest till the *Pond* be clensed. *Why?* His own *profit* was against it, because it would be great charge and no benefit to him, that had but a short time to enjoy it. And therefore his *Wife* and *Friends* are also against it, as consulting no *Further* then with flesh and blood. But *God* was *for it*, and therefore he must be *for God*, or else he shall not be for himselfe, nothing will go downe with him, till this be done (sig. F4^v).

The Cry and Reuenge of Blood, far from being a journalistic account of a murder, is in fact a rhetorical and moralistic study of crime and the revelation of God's purposes with particular reference to a topical example, composed in eight chapters with all the paraphernalia of a table of contents, marginal notes, citations from authority, and numbered points. Cooper dedicated his pamphlet to the judge who tried the case, Sir Henry Montague, stating openly that he had long sought for a opportunity to win the knight's favour, and so he perhaps felt it necessary to inflate his subject in this way to create a better impression.

Writers like Cooper did not regard themselves as journalists or reporters; they were historians, chroniclers, interpreters of the world of events, and as such they used all manner of devices to elevate their work to a status higher than a mere factual account. Some drew attention to the plainness of their style while others seized the opportunity to display their command of rhetoric. The author of *The Most horrible and tragicall murther of . . . John Lord Bourgh*, a servant of the dead man who had perhaps no other chance to get into print, begins his account with an amazing flourish:

> Not to painte it out with vainglorious termes of a large Exordium in a matter where throbbinge sorrowe breaketh of superfluous circumstances, and overwerying plaints abreuiate the libertie of speach, nor to use the choice inuention of a pleasinge discourse where nothing but heavy misfortunes minister cause of melancholike and pensive contemplations: But to explain a tragicall trueth, and set foorth the lamentable order, of a premeditated murther, I will brieflie prosecute my owne greefe (sig. A2).

In some instances, stylistic displays such as this are confined to the prefatory or moralistic matter, while the events themselves are described quite separately in a plain and factual way; in *Looke up and see*

Wonders (1628) the author moralizes gracefully for twelve of his nineteen pages: 'Though Death knockes at our very Doores, nay; albeit wee see him sit at our Bed-side, yet the hope of Life, playes her idle, vayne, and wanton Musicke under our Windowes' (p. 2). Then he turns abruptly to his account of a shower of meteors in Berkshire: 'The weather was warme, and without any great shewe of distemperature . . .'

Accounts of crimes of passion are often written with an almost novelistic interest in story-telling and characterization. Even the simplest reports are shaped into a story by their anonymous authors. At the outset, a narrative tone is established, and the reader put at his ease: 'In South Tavistocke, an ancient place in Devonshire, distant from Plimouth somme ten miles, dwelt a worshipful gentleman, called Maister Fites' (*The Bloudy booke*, 1605, sig. A3).

'At Perin, a Towne in Cornwall, liu'd a man of honest life and ample possessions.' So begins *Newes from Perin in Cornwall: of A most Bloody and un-Exampled Murther* (1618), a grim family saga that deals with a fatal homecoming.[18] The man's youngest son leaves home in search of adventure, and spends many years at sea, first as a pirate, and then as a Turkish galley slave. Eventually he returns to Cornwall, and goes back late at night to his family home. After so long an absence no one recognizes him, and, like many a returned wanderer, he proves his identity by displaying to his sister 'a great red Moale'. The author does not linger over the reunion scene. 'So leave we them', he counsels, 'and speake a worde or two of the good olde man their Father'. The father meanwhile has married again; the second wife, learning that her step-daughter has offered lodging for the night to a sailor, is prompted by a devil-sent impulse and decides to kill him for his money, not, of course, knowing who he is. The old man demurs; but 'When he refold [*sic.* refused?] by urging the unlawfulnesse of it, she burst out into bitter extreames and cursings, calling him faint-hearted coward' (sig. C), and Lady Macbeth-like 'she thrust the knife in his hand, and stood hastning of him on at the dore'. The murder takes place hastily in the dark, and although the returned son recognizes his father he has no opportunity to make himself known. At this point the author urges his readers for a sympathetic response: 'To see what a pitteous groane and ruthfull looke the dying sonne cast upon the murtherous father, I leaue to their consideration, that either know the loue of a father to a sonne, or a sonne to a father' (sig. C). In the morning the sister reveals the stranger's identity; father and step-mother kill themselves in remorse. It is a stark story and an inartistic narrative, but even so there are many touches which betray the writer's sense of himself as the teller of a tale.

Altogether more ambitious is *Two most vnnaturall and bloodie Murthers*, whose literary possibilities were at once recognized by two dramatists who used the first murder story as a basis for the plays *A Yorkshire Tragedy* (1605) and *The Miseries of Enforced Marriage* (1607). The story is of a Yorkshireman,[19] Walter Calverley, an unstable and quick-tempered prodigal, who in a fit of murderous rage wounds his wife and stabs two of his children to death from motives which the pamphlet writer implies are guilt and a strong sense of inferiority. The narrative is intensely contrived and metaphorical; this is no mere domestic drama to be allotted, as fitting, the low or middle style, but a high tragedy of passion. Mrs Calverley's grief at her husband's infidelity is described: 'Shee brought her selfe to a consumption; who so plaide the insulting tyrant over her unblemished beautie, that the ciuill contention dwelt in [her] face of white and redde, was turned to a death-like paleness' (p. 3). All sense of facts being reported is quite lost; the writer sees himself as a story-teller who must keep his reader's attention: 'Shee . . . laid her downe upon her bed, where in her carefull slumbers we will leaue her, and attend the conference betweene Maister Caverly and this Gentleman' (p. 11). Calverley himself is given strongly characterized moods and speeches like a dramatic protagonist; urged by his wife to spend less freely he replies abusively: 'Base strumpet (whom thogh I maried I neuer loued) shall my pleasure be confined by your wil? if you and your bastards be in want, either beg, or retire to your friends, my humor shal haue the auntient scope' (p. 5). Later, Calverley's eldest child comes to ask for him, and the writer, obviously having to hand no factual reasons to account for Calverley's actions, calls his own imagination into play and gives him the motivation of a dramatic villain:

> And as the sea, beeing hurled into hideous billowes, by the fury of the winde, hideth both heauen and earth from the eye of man: so he being overwhelmed by the violence of his passion, all naturall loue was forgot in his remembrance, caught his childe up by the necke, and striking at him with his dagger, the childe lent him such a looke, would haue driuen a hand seuen yeares prentice unto murther to an ague (p. 13).

The extent to which the writer has translated his subject into the realm of imagination appears again in the account of Calverley's behaviour after the killings; having hurled the children's nurse to her death from the top of a high staircase he leaves his maimed household and takes to horse: 'Not earnest to escape, but thirstie after more blood: for hauing an infant of halfe a yeare old at nurse some twelue mile off, he prickt by his preposterous fate, had a desire to roote out all his own generation' (p. 16).

Few reports manipulate and heighten their material to this degree; speech and dialogue are common, and no distinction is made between what is recorded, remembered, or invented, but the tone is usually more colloquial than in *Two most vnnaturall and bloodie Murthers,* and the effect intended is realistic rather than dramatic. Yet however simple and appropriate the language and phrasing it is almost impossible not to be aware of at least the possibility of literary contrivance on the author's part. For instance in *A pitilesse Mother. That most vnnaturally at one time, murthered two of her owne Children* (1616) where Margaret Vincent, tempted by the devil, decides to do away with her family because she cannot convert them to Roman Catholicism, the dialogue after the murders between the grief-stricken husband and the desperate wife sounds at a first impression entirely credible:

> O Margret, Margret, how often haue I perswaded thee from this damned Opinion, this damned Opinion, that hath vndone vs all. Whereuppon with a gastly looke and fearefull eye shee replyed thus, O Jaruis, this had never beene done, if thou hadst beene ruld, and by mee conuerted (sig. A4ᵛ).

So too the quarrel in Kyd's *The trueth of the most wicked & secret murthering of Iohn Brewen* (1592) between the adulterous Mrs Brewen and her lover John Parker after she had poisoned her husband; here, Parker refuses to marry his pregnant mistress:

> If I were so minded (quoth he) I would be twice aduised how I did wed with such a strumpet as thy selfe ... whereunto shee answered shee had neuer been strumpet but for him, and wo worth thee (quoth she) that euer I knowe thee, it is thou and no man else that can triumph in my spoyle (sig. A4ᵛ).

But in both accounts the author is reporting a scene that he cannot possibly have witnessed personally, and where it is highly unlikely that either of the participants would have reported their speech to him verbatim, so that to some extent at least what we are convinced by is his power of imaginative reconstruction.

Nonetheless, it still seems true to say that simple reports of this type, in their choice of detail and lively colloquial writing, can provide us with a greater and more intimate sense of the life and popular speech of the times than any other writing. Witchcraft pamphlets, which contain a higher proportion of eye-witness reporting than most Elizabethan journalism, are a particularly rich source; the subject was of such universal appeal that it needed no further sensationalizing, and it is the very starkness of these accounts that makes them so compelling to a modern reader. The grim confessions of old women who believed they had trafficked with familiar spirits in the shape of dogs, cats, mice, or toads with names like Hob, Dick, or Willet in order to maim children or livestock, the avid searches for proof of diabolic intercourse signified by bodily marks and deformities, the evidence of frightened or malicious neighbours, the long account of exorcisms of those possessed by demons, are all essentially similar in outline, and both tedious and harrowing to read. But every so often there is some bare detail, some trick or chance of phrasing, that brings vividly to life this bizarre side of the Elizabethan consciousness. In *The Apprehension and Confession of three notorious Witches. Arreigned and by Justice condemned and executed at Chelmesforde* (1598) the author describes in a long sentence, loosely constructed but finely built to a climax, how the devil appeared to Joan Prentice:

> Imprimis, this said examinate saith and confesseth, that about six years last past, between the feasts of All Saints and the birth of our Lord God, the Devil appeared unto her in the almshouse aforesaid about ten of the clock in the night time, being in the shape and proportion of a dunnish coloured ferret, having fiery eyes; and the said examinate being alone in her chamber, and sitting upon a low stool preparing herself to bedward, the ferret standing with his hinder legs upon the ground and his forelegs settled upon her lap, and settling his fiery eyes upon her eyes, spake and pronounced unto her these words following, namely; 'Joan Prentice, give me thy soul.' (In *Witchcraft*, ed. B. Rosen, The Stratford-upon-Avon Library, London, 1969, p. 186).

In *The Triall of Maist. Dorrell, Or, A Collection of Defences* (1599) a spirit called Giles is sent to afflict Joan Jorden, a kitchen-maid; again it is the description of physical activity and the plain yet precise vocabulary that evoke the scene:

> he came down the chimney in the likenes of a cat. . . first scraping on the wals, then knocking, after that shufling in the rushes; and then (as his vsual maner was) he clapped the maide on the cheekes about halfe a skore times as to awake her; and (as oft times else he did) he kissed her 3 or 4 times and slauered on her (p. 93).

It often happens that the unintentionally apt choice of detail and grimly honest writing reveal to a later age terrible cruelty and suffering of which the recorder was quite unaware. In John Denison's account, *The most Wonderfull and true storie, of a certaine Witch, named Alse Gooderige of Stapenhill* (1597), the witch is brought to the bedside of the child who has accused her to be given one of the standard tests for guilt:

> Some of the standers by, persuaded the Boye to scratch her; which he did upon the face, and the backe of the hands, so that the blood came out apace: and she stroked the back of her hand upon the child, saying, take blood enough child, God helpe thee (sig. Bl^v).

In Goodcole's *The wonderfull discouerie of Elizabeth Sawyer* the old woman's innocent answer to the question whether she ever touched the devil when he appeared to her as a dog is intensely poignant: 'Yes, I did stroake him on the backe, and then he would becke unto me, and wagge his tayle as being therewith contented (sig. D). Undeniably the power of language such as this is as often the result of good fortune as of conscious literary sensibility; but it is nonetheless valuable to us in conveying, through simple, uninterpreted observation, more truth than the writers knew.

An offshoot of news reporting worth a little separate attention is the group of pamphlets dealing with the plague of London which erupted in major epidemics in 1603 and 1625, and minor ones in 1592/3 and 1630. This is only one subject chosen from several available—recusant confessions, witchcraft trials, and travel pamphlets, for instance—which would in various ways repay a consideration of their different aspects. But it was a particularly good subject for pamphleteering and it produced some of the most lively writing; it gave opportunities for both sensational description and for moralizing, it lent itself to sermon, textbook, and anecdote, it allowed for the treatment of certain social topics which had not much stirred the surface of popular awareness so far, and it provided a focus for a wealth of Elizabethan commonplaces on life, transience, and death.

Between 1580 and 1640 there were few years in which no single Londoner died of the plague, and during the epidemics of 1603 and 1625 it took off more than 70,000 people, at least a sixth of London's population, at the rate of nearly 3000 a week in high summer. Although the plague had been endemic in England since the Black Death, the Elizabethans had no truly effective measures against it; they wore amulets and fumigated their houses with herbs and raw

News Pamphlets

onions, they smoked tobacco and ate garlic and what they thought was the powdered horn of unicorns, they appointed officers to shut up infected houses and mark their doors with crosses, clean the streets, and remove the dunghills, they closed their theatres and, if they could, they escaped from their city, but they knew no sure way to prevent or cure the disease. Those who woke one day to find swellings in their armpits and red or black plague tokens on their bodies knew that they could well be dead within a week. Pest carts rumbled through the streets by day, and by night fearful citizens crept out of their houses with corpses on their backs to bury them by stealth, so that their doors should not be sealed with the fatal red cross. Stricken servants and apprentices were taken out of the city to the fields and hedgerows and there abandoned to die. Some of the sick went mad with terror and ran raving from house to house openly displaying their sores. Poor prisoners who relied on public alms died of starvation. The city stank.

Compared with subjects like witchcraft or cony-catching, the literature of the plague is not large, and much of it is purely medical. But Dekker, forced by the closure of the theatres in 1603 to abandon his established profession of playwright and turn for the time being to pamphleteering, luckily for us found it a good theme for his first prose piece, *The Wonderfull Yeare* (1603), and returned to it five times more, in *Newes from Graues-end* (1604), a verse pamphlet, *The Meeting of Gallants at an Ordinarie* (1604), *A Rod for Run-awayes* (1625), *London Looke Backe* (1630), and *The Blacke Rod: and the White Rod* (1630)[20] Although, like all literary plague pamphlets, they were written either during an epidemic or its aftermath, none of these is a news report as such. Dekker does not set out to bring his readers facts and information about the state of the disease, nor does he describe what he personally experienced in plague-stricken London. The only pamphlet which gives figures for plague deaths, *The Blacke Rod*, compares totals for 1603 and 1625 with those of the current year in a spirit of warning; in *A Rod for Run-awayes* Dekker rejects factual information in favour of 'sad Relations' because they are both 'true . . . and fuller of horror': 'Shall I tell you how many thousands haue beene borne on mens shoulders in the compasse of fiue or six weekes? Bills sent vp and downe both Towne and Countrie, haue giuen you already too fearefull informations' (*Plague Pamphlets*, p. 158). The plague orders and weekly bills of mortality were publicly displayed; the pamphleteers had other things to do than repeat their grim news. Dekker prefaces *The Wonderfull Yeare* by stating that the stories which conclude his pamphlet, 'a certaine mingled Troope of strange Discourses, fashioned into Tales' are the product of 'flying Report' and so may not be entirely true, but to him and his readers this is obviously immaterial. On the other hand, he says, to list the names of those thrust out to die 'in fields, in ditches, in common Cages, and Vnder stalls... would weary a second *Fabian*'.

The Wonderfull Yeare is justly one of the most often reprinted of Elizabethan pamphlets. In a long preliminary section of stylish and witty writing Dekker establishes his subject in the context of the extraordinary sequence of events of the year 1603: the brilliant spring-time brought to an untimely end by the death of the Queen, the universal lamentation followed by rejoicing at the accession of the King, and 'in the Appenine heigth of this immoderate ioy and securitie' the outbreak of the plague. The writing is exuberant, the tone fanciful; Dekker delights to show off his talents as a prose stylist, and is in no hurry to get to the point. He composes a neat cadenza on the subject of Elizabeth's death:

> Shee came in with the fall of the leafe, and went away in the Spring: her life (which was dedicated to Virginitie,) both beginning & closing vp a miraculous Mayden circle: for she was borne vpon a Lady Eue, and died upon a Lady Eue (*Plague Pamphlets*, p. 17).

and follows it with a paradoxical meditation on change:

> Upon Thurseday it was treason to cry God saue King Iames King of England, and upon Friday hye treason not to cry so. In the morning no voice heard but murmures and lamentation, at noone nothing but shoutes of gladnes & triumph (*Plague Pamphlets*, p. 21).

Here Dekker is not a chronicler or reporter but a performer in language; he is practising styles, and he wants his readers to appreciate his skill in each one before he moves on to the next.

'A stiffe and freezing horror sucks vp the riuers of my bloud: my haire stands on end with the panting of my braines: mine eye-balls are readie to start out, being beaten with the billowes of my teares' (*Plague Pamphlets*, p. 25). So, at last, he introduces the plague itself, remembering Nashe's technique of arousing feeling in *Christs Teares over Ierusalem* by describing the body in violent and distorted images, and he takes a ghoulish pleasure in filling several pages with predictable horrors: there are enough handwringing widows, distracted mothers, heaps of dead men's bones, groans of raving sick men, hungry graves gaping, and worms breeding out of putrifying carcasses to satisfy the largest appetite for sensation. But Dekker's repertoire is not yet exhausted, and he devotes the remaining half of his pamphlet to a variety of jestbook-like tales, bringing 'a kind of sad delight': 'Some of them yeelding Comicall and ridiculous stuffe, others lamentable: a third kind vpholding rather admiration, then laughter or pittie' (*Plague Pamphlets*, p. 38). They are linked by the theme of the reversal of expectation: a man orders a coffin for a sick friend, and then shares it with him; a traveller goes to the Low Countries to escape the plague, and when it follows him returns to England, where he dies; an unfaithful wife, imagining herself to be dying, confesses her misdemeanours and subsequently recovers. These stories are wonderfully enlivened by Dekker's rich graveyard humour, his relish for macabre irony, and they display to the full his versatility in narrative.

The sad little tale of the young bride sickening of the plague at the very altar where she is about to be married allows Dekker to indulge his taste for paradox: 'She was a wife, yet continued a mayd: he was a husband and a widower, yet neuer knew his wife: she was his owne, yet he had her not: she had him, yet neuer enioyed him' (*Plague Pamphlets*, p. 46). In the contrasting account of the adulterous wife who makes an ill-timed confession of her sins, Dekker's colloquial, punning description of the sorrowful cuckold recalls the concrete language and vigorous wit of *Nashes Lenten Stuffe:*

> Such Thicke teares, standing in both the gutters of his eyes, to see his beloued lye in such a pickle, that in their salt water, all his utterance was drownde: which she perceiving, wept as fast as he: But by the warme counsel which sat about the bed, the shewer ceast: she wiping her cheekes with the corner of one of the sheetes, and hee, his sullyed face, with his Lethren Apron (*Plague Pamphlets*, p. 47).

As a narrator Dekker is ribald and irreverent, constantly pausing for a decorative detail, a pun, or a mocking aside. Midnight in one of his stories is the time when 'not a Mouse dare stirre, because Cattes goe a Catterwalling', a drunkard reeling out of an alehouse thinks that 'the ground vnder him danced the Canaries', a fat innkeeper has legs 'that were thicke & short like two piles driuen vnder *London-bridge*'. A country household is turned upside down in its efforts to escape from a visiting Londoner:

> Mine Host and Hostesse ran ouer one another into the backside, the maydes into the Orchard, quiuering and quaking, and readie to hang themselves on the innocent Plomtrees (for hanging to them would not be so sore a death as the Plague, & to dye maydes too! Oh horible!) (*Plague Pamphlets*, p. 42).

Dekker did not tell stories like this in all his plague pamphlets; but in *A Rod for Run-awayes* he felt it necessary to defend the practice on the ground that a lightening of tone was both emotionally desirable and a good moral tactic:

> In the middest of my former compassionate complaynings (ouer the misery of these times) let me a little quicken my owne and your spirits, with telling you, how the rurall *Coridons* doe now begin to vse our Run-awayes; neyther doe I this out of an idle or vndecent merriment ... but onely to lay open what foolery, infidelity, inhumanity, nay villany, irreligion, and distrust in God ... dwell in the bosomes of the vnmannerly Oasts (*Plague Pamphlets,* pp. 152–53).

Not everyone approved of his jocularity, and Benjamin Spenser in *Lachrymae Londinenses* (1626) attacked the use of 'scarce credible or feigned matters of wonderment' in 'spuriall Pamphlets' which 'dare venture to vent their Quacksaluing Conceipts, to moove mirth, in time of a mightie Mortalitie' (quoted in *Plague Pamphlets,* pp. 245–6). *The Meeting of Gallants,* which consists of a dialogue between Signors Shuttlecocke, Ginglespurre, Stramazoon, and Kickshaw at an ordinary, and several tales told by their 'honest-larded' Host, was, if anything, more jocular than *The Wonderfull Yeare,* but Dekker's last two plague pamphlets were as solemn and exhortatory as anyone could wish, urging his fellow sufferers to accept the plague as God-given and turn their eyes toward heaven: 'Remember why Those Tokens are sent: To make all the hast thou canst to set forward, for away thou must: Hug them therefore, and thy Louer; Kisse, and bid them welcome, thanke that sweet Token-sender for his guift' (*Plague Pamphlets,* p. 216).

A Rod for Run-awayes contains several stories against the inhumane and stupid behaviour of country people towards Londoners, but they are short and bitter, and do not show the gusto of those in *The Wonderfull Yeare*. There is a characteristically sour tale of a young girl of Kent who goes to town to stay with her sister but on account of her 'very good apparell' is driven out by the townspeople with bills and halberds because they think she comes from London; homeless, she retreats to the open fields and there sickens and dies. No one comes near her for several days until an old woman, bolder than the rest, ventures out of the town, strips her body of clothing and money, and then buries it. The old woman is then banished from the county for fear of infection.

The plague revealed Dekker's gifts not only for narrative but also for the prose of meditation. The subject of death inspired his powers of rhythmical writing and his eloquence in metaphor. In this famous passage from *London Looke Backe* the diction and syntax are simple, even prosaic, and Dekker subdues his usual tendency to self-conscious punning and paradox, although he chooses his phrases with a lively sense of their resonance:

> To dye is held fearefull: and the Graue hath many formidable shapes.
> A prisoner being drag'd to a Iayle, out of which he can neuer be deliuered, may truely call his chamber, his Liuing Graue, where his owne sorrowes and the cruelty of creditors, bury him.
> They, who with fearefull labour, maintaine life by digging vnderground, goe daily to their Graue; So doe all Traytors that lay traynes to Blow vp their K. and Countrey: So doe all those whose blacke consciences prick them on to digge Pitts for others, into which they fall themselves.
> But to open a graue as it is indeede, the graue is our last Inne, and a poore wooden Coffin our fairest Lodging Roome. No: the Graue is not our Inne, (where we may lie to Night and be gon to Morrow) but it is our standing House, it is a perpetuity, our Inheritance for euer: A peece of ground (with a litle garden in it,) fiue or sixe foot long, full of flowres and herbes, purchas'd for vs, and our posterity, at the deerest Income in the world, the losse of *Life*.
> The World is our common Inne, in which wee haue no certaine abyding: It stands in the Road-way for all passengers: And whither we be vpon speed, or goe slowly on foot, sure we are that all our Iourneyes are to the land of death, and that's the Graue (*Plague Pamphlets,* p. 182).

In some pamphlets the plague is treated in a more factual way, from a social viewpoint; here, Dekker's theme from *A Rod for Runawayes* predominates, the relationship of Londoners to country people in plague time. Dekker based many of his best anecdotes on their mutual hostility; a tinker is allowed to strip and rob a city corpse while country people stand aside because they won't touch a Londoner's body; a band of thieves escapes trial because a judge is afraid to confront Londoners; a sleeping drunkard, believed to be a plague-corpse, is set on fire by country men afraid to bury him. But he used the subject only as a basis for stories, whereas other writers such as Henry Petowe in *The Countrie Ague* (1625), B.V. in *The run-awyaes Answer, To a Booke called, A Rodde for Runne-awayes* (1625), and Benjamin Spenser in *Vox Civitatis, or Londons Complaint against her Children in the Countrey* (1625) and *Vox Ruris, Reverberating Vox Civitatis* (1636) treat it more extensively. None of them is objective; they do entertain mixed feelings about the ethics of deserting plague-stricken London, but they always depict the countrymen with whom the deserters take refuge as stupid, covetous, and ungracious, 'rustique irrational Beasts', 'hob-nailed Boores, inhumane Blocks', 'Grunting Girigashites, Hog-rubbing Gadarens', eager to cheat and defraud the citizens. That the countrymen might have a very real cause for their fear and hatred is rarely taken into account. Their fear is continually satirized in bitter anecdotes which mock at their stupidity, and revile their inhumanity. In one story a countryman refuses to eat a spotted cod because he thinks it has the plague and elsewhere countrymen are unwilling to help a Londoner give fitting burial to his dead children, or prevent a city man's corpse from being devoured by animals. The mutual resentment between country and town is particularly evident in descriptions of the normally accepted bearing of the countryman towards the Londoner:

> That *Name* (of *Londoner*) which had wont to draw out a whole *Towne* to stare vpon him, and a Church-yeard full of People (after Seruice) to gape vpon his fine Cloathes, spruce Silke-Stockins, and neate steeletoo-fied Beard: That *Name*, to be Called by which, all the Land . . . sends her Sonnes . . . That Name is now so ill, that he is halfe hanged in the Countrey that has it (*The run-awyaes Answer*, sig. C1^v).

The country, it was thought, owed a great debt of gratitude to London; John Taylor in *The Fearefull Sommer: or London's Calamitie* (1625) chides the 'country canibals' for their behaviour towards the men responsible 'for repairing their Churches, Bridges and high-wayes, for their wrackes by sea, for their losses by fire . . . for many Free-Scholes, Alme-houses & other works of piety and charity'. In this context there is not the smallest hint of pastoral idealization; townspeople doing country tasks are demeaning themselves: 'Many Citizens that haue been brauer Fellowes than Whisslers on Simon and Iudes Day, are fayne . . . to turne Hay-makers, Cock Barley, and sweat with Pitching the Cart with Corne' (*The run-awyaes Answer*, sig. C2).

The fate of the poor in plague time is a subsidiary theme and the feeling against them very similar to that against countrymen. Sometimes the two are equated; Spenser, personifying the countryside, writes:

> I must confesse, ignorance and arrogance are the badges of many with mee, and the ruine of many Schooles which are founded to instruct me better. Some will not have their children taught though it cost them nothing; others will not have them corrected to gaine the Muses dowry . . . I speake not this out of a discontented, but a

pitiful spirit . . . to shew how hard a yoake poverty is to morall men, not onely making men slavish, but even void of good manners and also necessarie knowledge (*Vox Ruris,* p. 24).

In the pamphlet to which this is a complement—*Vox Civitatis*— London berates the rich for leaving the city poor to perish, and while Spenser is ostensibly making the point that the plague attacks the rich as well as the poor, his feelings implicitly contradict his reasoning and he manages to imply that the poor are largely to blame:

> I know *they are,* for the most part, *ill livers, intemperate of tongue, and appetite, grosse feeders;* all this may cōspire to their ruine, *and such as disorderly thrust themselues into danger,* specially by preparing their bodies for other diseases as well as the *Plague* (*Vox Civitatis,* p. 21).

The city poor, of course, were the greatest sufferers from the disease, because of their cramped insanitary dwellings, infested with plague-carrying rats and fleas, and their lower physical stamina. Most plague pamphleteers took no account of the fact that they were at the mercy of their conditions, partly because they did not know of the connection between the nature of these conditions and the incidence of the disease, but also because it was common to link poverty with idleness and irresponsibility. Thomas Brewer in *A Dialogue betwixt a Cittizen, and a poore Countrey-man and his Wife* (1636) shares with Dekker a rare humane concern for the helpless poor; he berates the 'braue, rich people' who flee the stricken city in their coaches: 'How little doe they regard the poore, which they leaue behinde them?' (sig. C1). And in his dialogue, set in the country between a citizen who has escaped from London and the suspicious countryman whom he asks for food and shelter, the countryman and his wife, after some prevarication and warning anecdotes about friends who have caught the plague through helping Londoners, actually invite the citizen into their house. But the ambivalence of Benjamin Spenser is a much more usual attitude; that the rich should have provided for the poor is grudgingly recognized, but nevertheless there is the sense that the poor have done nothing to deserve it.

In the treatment of the runaways who desert the city some very primitive religious and moralistic attitudes emerge. The ethics of escape were much debated. Despite the fact that most medical books advocated flight as the first measure to be taken in the avoidance of plague[21] and quoted Hippocrates' rule, 'Fuge longe, cito, tardo', those who did escape were often harshly attacked. Dekker, for instance, claimed that they were neglecting their duties:

How shall the lame, and blinde, and halfe-starued be fed? they had wont to come to your Gates: Alas! they are barred against them . . . Where shall the wretched prisoners haue their baskets filled euery night and morning with your broken meat? These must pine and perish. (*A Rod for Run-awayes, Plague Pamphlets*, p. 148).

In getting out of the city they were making things much worse for those who were forced to stay behind. In fact, this must have been true;[22] but given here, it almost seems like a rationalization of the real reason for condemning the runaways—that they were trying to escape the judgement of God: 'Why should any man, (nay, how dare any man) presume to escape this Rod of Pestilence, when at his back, before him, round about him, houses are shut vp, Coarses borne forth, and Coffins brought in?' (*A Rod for Run-awayes, Plague Pamphlets*, p. 152). This was a feeling endorsed both by medical writers and sermonists; W. T. in *A Casting Up of accounts of certain Errors* (1603) expresses a fatalism typical of the time: 'our physitians searching into the natures of diseases, finde a supernatural cause in the secret will of God hidden from us in this pestilence, which they cannot finde, and then the cause being not found, how should it be prevented?' (sig. B2).[23] The Reverend John Sanford of Oxford in his sermon *Gods Arrowe of the Pestilence* (1604) concludes with awful certainty: 'it is he alone that can salue & cure the wound that it maketh, & therefore vaine is it for us to seeke for helpe from any other.' It was felt that, in any case, only those whom God had specially appointed would die, however infectious the disease might be, and in some strange way, the plague could even be looked on as a blessing: 'There bee men that dare eate spiders: Monkeyes swallow them, and by them get sweet breaths: why then should not many Limbes of our Estates bee made the sounder by this Infectious fracture?' (*The run-awyaes Answer*, sig. B3).

Much is implied here about the significance of London in the whole life of the nation and the extent to which the newly-grown nationalism of the Elizabethans centred on their capital. The city is frequently personified as a mother weeping over her children; so in Henry Petowe's *The Countrie Ague* she regrets the desertion of her citizens: 'I haue beene (most deere and more intirely beloued Children) so much burthen'd, pressed down and ouerladen with Lamentations, complaints, Miseries and Calamities for your long absence. . . that I am almost dead with languishing (p. 1). To many it seemed as if London '*Empress* of *Citties*, faire *Troynouant*' 'tender & delicate, the Mistress of felicity, the Imperial chamber of this Kingdome' had been specially chosen by God for the venting of his wrath. The city, once the largest in Europe, excelling, as Lyly had said, all the cities in the world, had grown too great in its pride, and God had sent the plague to temper the excess of worldly joy. 'So I now poore, distressed, reiected, diseased London, once the Phoenix, now the Owle, once the Paragon of beautie, now a Patterne of deformitie... know not which way to turne me first (Spenser, *Vox Civitatis*, sig. A3). It is Dekker who most movingly evokes the dereliction of his beloved city, where, it was said, grass had begun to grow in Cheapside:

> How many goodly streets, full of beautifull and costly houses, haue now few people or none at all (sometimes) walking in the one, and not so much as any liuing rationall creature abiding in the other? Infection hath shut vp, from the beginning of Iune, to the middle of Iuly, almost (or rather altogether) foure thousand doores (*A Rod for Run-awayes, Plague Pamphlets*, p. 147).

With such desolation at the very heart of the nation it is not surprising that men began to think of the end of the world; those whose pessimism was a degree less were certain that England had in some way aroused God's wrath, and that the only remedy must come from a change in its people's relationship with God.

The question of responsibility for the plague brought all writers together; they were agreed that men had brought the plague on themselves through their sinfulness. Thomas Brewer in *Lord have Mercy vpon Vs* (1636) describes the sins of the country at length and concludes:

> For these, and their spotted companions, did the Pestilence, that Tyrant, in the yeare of that never to be forgotten number, 1625, Arrest, and Imprison (in that Goale in which they must rot that enter) so many, many thousands of people: sparing neither the silver head of the old man, nor the golden hopes of the young man; the strength of the Male, nor the beauty of the Female (p. 16).

The plague is an arrow, striking down God's enemies, and it is a physical counterpart to the sickness in man's soul. Though practical measures against it—medicines, hygiene, flight—are advocated, the only true cure, for which physicians and preachers use both the same term, is repentance. 'Art thou sick!', writes Dekker. 'Thy best and onely Doctor dwells above.' Further, it was urged that if men did not repent, there would be worse to come. London had been greatly favoured by God; comparable cities, like Jerusalem and Sodom, with comparable sins, were utterly destroyed. Nashe, in *Christs Teares over Ierusalem*, written during the epidemic of 1592/3, complained that no one took the plague seriously enough, and urged London to take warning from Jerusalem: 'God hath striken vs, but we haue not sorrowed, of hys heauiest correction we make a iest. Wee are not mooued with that which he hath sent to amaze vs (*Works*, II, 157). George Wilkins in *Three Miseries of Barbary* (c. 1606–7)[24] compared London with Barbary, which suffered not only plague but also famine and war, concluding severely:

> You see howe the Great Father of Nations, keepes us under his wing, he is loth to chide, more loath to strike us, let us not therefore. . . prouoke him too often. . . least he take up his triple Mace. . . as he hath already and stretch out his Arme to smite those of Barbarie (sig. D4).

Plague writing contains many expressions of the common Elizabethan sense of the transitoriness of the world. Dekker's view of life as a brief stay at an inn is the most memorable. In a more despairing spirit, Dekker was brought to affirm the positive values of death, and to rejoice in the tokens of the plague:

> Hath Infection blowne vpon thee with her Contagious, noysome and stinking breath! Hath the Pestilence. . . Printed her nayles within they Flesh. . . Fall on thy knees, Call for mercy. . . shake off the world, looke vp at Heauen, Thither is thy Iourney, prepare for no voyage else! Art thou all-spotted over! They are GODS rich Ermines; to Inrobe thee like a King, and to set a Crowne of Glory on they Head (*The Blacke Rod, Plague Pamphlets*, p. 215).

Between 1580 and 1640 attitudes to the plague changed very little. The fatalism, the tendency to treat physical measures as second best beside hoping and praying, are as typical of the pamphlets of 1630 as of those of 1603. The city authorities were taking more steps to alleviate the suffering and to prevent the spread of the disease;[25] but the imaginative significance of the plague remained unchanged.

3
Social Satire

Many moralistic pamphlets of this period are not confined to a single or specific subject; their authors strike us as journalists who had no newspaper to write for, writers with nothing to write about. They condemned their own itch to get into print, but they could not suppress it. What C. S. Lewis has to say of Nashe applies also to his contemporaries, if one assumes no value judgement in the word 'literature':

> Paradoxically, though Nashe's pamphlets are commercial literature, they come very close to being, in another way, 'pure' literature: literature which is, as nearly as possible, without a subject. In a certain sense of the verb 'say', if asked what Nashe 'says', we should have to reply, Nothing (C. S. Lewis, *English Literature in the Sixteenth Century*, p. 416).

What Nashe and his fellows were doing, ostensibly, was describing from a satirical or moralistic point of view the vices and follies of contemporary society; but they did not write in such a way as to make a strong protest against some enormity, although there are exceptions to this, or so as to plead for reform, but rather because they liked writing and they wanted to interest and delight their readers with the variety of devices they could use to display their material. The material was for the most part familiar enough: attacks on various social and professional groups such as usurers, lawyers, atheists, and so on, and vices and abuses like blasphemy, drinking, or the use of cosmetics. Some of the topics had formed the basis of popular preaching and complaint for a couple of centuries, while others emerge from the preoccupations of a new era: the politic bankrupt, the lecherous actor, the unemployed soldier, the tobacco-taker are not conspicuous before the 1580s.

The title-pages of these miscellanies, in their effort to suggest novelty, inclusiveness, and moral warning, convey something of their flavour: *A meruailous combat of contrarieties. Malignantlie striuing in the members of mans bodie, allegoricallie representing vnto vs the enuied state of our florishing commonwealth: wherin dialogue-wise by the way, are touched the ex-treame vices of this present time*, by William Averell, or *The Curtaine-Drawer Of the World: OR, The Chamberlaine of that great Inne of Iniquity. Where Vice in a rich embroidred Gowne of Veluet, rides a horse-back like a Iudge, AND Vertue in a thrid-bare Cloake full of patches, goes a foot like a Drudge. Where he that hath most mony may be best merry, and he that hath none at all, wants a friend, he shal daily haue cause to remember to grieue for* by William Parkes, or Nashe's *The Anatomie of Absurditie: Contayning a breefe confutation of the slender imputed prayses to feminine perfection, with a short description of the seuerall practises of youth, and the sundry follies of our licentious times.* Many title-pages make reference to the forms or formal devices employed in the pamphlets; it was clearly an added attraction to consider the advantages of marriage or of the single life as discussed in a dialogue, or to read of the vices of actors in an allegory. It tends to be the forms and devices rather than the subjects or attitudes that distinguish pamphlets of this kind from each other. Such devices—and many pamphlets make use of more than one—include the dream vision; the visitor from the underworld who comes up to London and describes in satirical fashion what he sees; the satiric persona such as Piers Penniless, Cock Watt, ghost of Nashe or Greene, even the devil himself, as narrator or mouthpiece; the mock almanac and the burlesque prophecy; the allegorical narrative; the warning exemplum; the historical comparison as suggested in titles such as *Englands Sicknes, Comparatively Conferred with Israels, Londons Warning by Ierusalem,* or *Londons Warning, by Laodiceas Luke-warmenesse;* the procession of the Seven Deadly Sins; satire by Estates; the formal defence or attack, conducted according to the principles of rhetoric; and the dialogue.

In a later chapter, I shall deal with typical pamphlet subject matter and the conventions by which it is presented. Here I want to make an introductory foray into the large mass of miscellaneous and uncategorizable works of popular satire, mainly by examining some of its forms and formal devices. This is not to say that moralistic or satirical pamphlets could not be written at all without the supportive framework of an allegory or a dialogue or the structural basis of the Seven Deadly Sins, but that they were uncommon. Two examples are the anonymous *A Health to the Gentlemanly Profession of Seruingmen* (1598) and John Taylor's *The World runnes on Wheeles: or Oddes betwixt Carts and Coaches* (1623). In each the author has a distinct idea to express, which is unusual, and, even more surprising, he does so in a straightforward way. In *A Health* the author laments the decline in status of the servingman or chief servant, which he sees as directly related to the decay of the aristocracy and the noble tradition of hospitality. In *The World runnes on Wheeles* Taylor makes a case for the idea of the new four-wheeled coach in opposition to the old two-wheeled cart as a symbol of a decadent modern society. The coach is symptomatic of the new wealth and luxury that causes social divisiveness; coach travel encourages proud manners and effeminacy in men, it makes the streets noisy and dangerous, and it can even be held responsible for the decay of housekeeping:

> The witchcraft of the Coach quickly mounted the price of all things (except poore mens labour) and withall transformed, in some places, 10, 20, 30, 40, 50, 60, or 100 proper seruingmen into two or three Animals (videlicet) a Butterfly Page, a trotting foot-man, a stiffe-drinking Coachman, a Cooke, a Clarke, a Steward, and a Butler (*All the Workes*, p. 243).

Such pamphlets may appeal to us now because they appear concise and pointed, with all parts relevant and directed to an obvious end. That we expect such qualities of good journalistic prose now goes without saying; but in Elizabethan pamphleteering they were the exception, and there is not much contemporary evidence for Spenser's idea that many readers preferred 'good discipline delivered plainly'.

Spenser puts forward this idea in the letter to Raleigh that prefaces *The Faerie Queene*, and then goes on to explain why he has chosen, in despite of it, to write an allegorical poem; he gives one reason for his choice and implies another. He states that allegory is more 'delightfull and pleasing to commune sense' than plain precepts, and he implies that there was considerable convenience for him in allegory's oblique method. On both counts allegory appealed strongly to the pamphleteers. 'Tart meates go easily downe, being strewd with sugar', wrote Dekker to account for the variety of allegorical devices he used in *A Strange Horse-Race*. Many pamphleteers referred to the advantages of sheltering their satire behind the cloudy devices of allegory, even when they had no need of its protection. There could be disadvantages in being too open about the objects of one's satire, as Nashe found to his cost more than once, but for the most part the pamphleteers really used allegory for the sake of variety and narrative interest rather than as a cover for satirical attacks, despite claims to the opposite effect. Averell in *A meruailous combat of contrarieties* promises to strike at certain groups from whom opposition might be expected, 'our proud Pares', 'our wanton wiues and mincing minions', 'our gluttonous Sanctrae', 'our couchant papists', and therefore 'if we touch these men, it must be figurate but not aperte, closelie and cunninglie, not openly or plainely' (sig. *3ᵛ). But in fact the attacks are so traditional and unspecific that Averell could have had no particular individuals in mind, and no real cause for timidity.

The taste for allegorical narrative had been strong in the Middle Ages and the mode remained popular for its simple combination of entertainment and instruction. Any kind of subject could be treated in terms of an allegorical fiction, from attacks on usury or acting to the search for wisdom. But the forms were traditional ones: the journey or search, the debate, the contest or trial, the procession, and the feast. Journeys might be made to imaginary places like the Palace of Worldly Felicity in Jean de Carthenay's *The Voyage of the Wandring Knight*, the Fort of Folly in *Laugh and lie downe: Or, The Worldes Folly*,[1] the shrine of learning in John Day's *Peregrinatio Scholastica*, or through London itself in William Rowley's *A Search for Money*, where a band of adventurers explores the city and finally descends to hell in quest of the elusive Monsieur Money. The butt of the satire may be general or particular. In *Moriomachia* by Robert Anton, an amazing amalgam, and perhaps a parody, of Spenser and Cervantes, a bull is transformed into a knight errant and sent to 'the coasts of Morotopia' to be educated; his adventures give scope for picaresque battles between knights and giants, tournaments and magic armour, as well as satire on neglectful landlords, usurers, brokers, drunken millers, and city low-life. Other pamphleteers used allegory as a means of attacking a specific abuse; Gerard de Malynes in *Saint George for England, Allegorically described* (1601) contrived to show the fair island Niobla (Albion) tyrannized by the Dragon Usury, although he found some difficulty in embodying all of the usurer's social and economic characteristics in the form of a dragon. Richard Brathwait in *The Smoaking Age* (1640) more inventively described the genealogy and birth of Tobacco, only son of Nepenthes, a rich native of Bermuda, and his wife Usquebaughin, and predicted the child's glorious future:

> Thou shalt be hissed out of the schoole of Hypocrates, Aesculapius, and Galen. Not a Quack-saluer Doctor upon the Universe, but shall reade Lectures on thee, as if it were upon an Anatomy. The mercinary Pedler shall counterfeat thee: and drying some Walnut leaues shall forsweare himselfe for thee (pp. 146–47).

In *A Mirrour of Monsters* (1588) by William Rankins, the allegory is devoted to a vitriolic attack on the stage, the last, in fact, of the secular attacks.[2] The narrator sails to Teralbon, a country ruled by 'a most vertuous and godlie princesse, whose fame spreddeth to infidels, whose noble vertues are wondered at amongst the Heathen, whose peaceable gouernement Pagans doo adore' (sig. B1ᵛ). The only blemish on the face of this paradise is the presence of actors, men 'such as liue by others losse, laughes, at others languishing, florish by others fading, sing at others sorrow, consuming caterpillers cleaning to forward branches, canckers that cauterize Roseall youth' (sig. B2). The narrator gets into the actors' headquarters, 'The Laborinth, where lodged these monstrous Minotaures', where he attends a wedding between their patrons, Fastus and Luxuria, performed in the Chapel Adulterinum, identified in the margin with the Theater and the Curtain. The couple are honoured by Lust and Curiosity, and married by Confusion. Masquers from hell, Idleness, Flattery, Ingratitude, Dissention, Blasphemy, and Impudence, entertain them. They feast in the Hall of Misery, and the narrative peters out into moral exhortation against the sin of theatre-going. As an allegory, it is ingenious rather than morally penetrating; Rankins can make only the most obvious points through his narrative. The figures have the static significance of emblems, and must be translated back into abstract qualities before he can frame from them any attack on the stage. These authors rarely take any pains to bring their narratives to an appropriate conclusion; it is typical that the hero of *Peregrinatio Scholastica*, Philosophos, is forgotten long before he reaches Latria's shrine.

Trials and contests demand less in the way of narrative development and more easily allow for the contrasting of vices and virtues, so that they are often more consistently worked out. In such very different allegories as Averell's *A meruailous combat of contrarieties*, Greene's *A Quip for an Upstart Courtier* (1592), Richard Bernard's *The Isle of Man* (1627) and Dekker's *Worke for Armorours* (1609) and *A Strange Horse-Race* (1613), opposed forces, both within the commonwealth and within the individual psyche, are displayed in action. *Worke for Armorours*, one of Dekker's best pamphlets, depicts the enmity between rich and poor, the Two Nations as he calls them, through a battle. Although Dekker uses stock figures on either side—in Poverty's army are poor scholars, younger sons, old servingmen, and returned soldiers, with Wealth are foreigners, farmers, landlords, and engrossers—two features prevent the pamphlet from becoming dull and conventional. First, there is Dekker's realistic awareness of the moral issues involved in that Poverty's army includes not only the deserving poor but also bankrupts, pimps, and bawds, and second, the strongly-felt bitterness that enlivens the traditional attacks. The allegory is set in plague-time London; the narrator, unable to visit the theatre, is reading at his window when he hears a riotous commotion outside, a renewed outbreak of the long-standing enmity between Poverty and Wealth. The London setting is a significant context for the allegory which follows, in this city where 'poore starued wretches' are led like bears 'to the whipping posts in London (when they had more need to be releeued with foode)'. The perennial conflict is given a directly contemporary application. It is likely that the pamphlet was written partly in response to the general sense of economic and commercial crisis towards the end of this decade, and perhaps in particular to the recently concluded Dutch/Spanish peace.[3] Money is an Empress, the aggressor in the conflict. She wants 'to roote the name, not onely of that infortunate and deiected Princesse from the earth, but euen to banish all her people to wander into desarts, & to perish' (*Non-Dramatic Works*, IV, 108). She guards her kingdom with hard-hearted constables who prevent the poor from coming within two miles of the city gates lest they try to steal the golden keys. Dekker's attitude towards poverty is ambivalent. He evokes sympathy for the poor with his description of soldiers from the Low Countries come to fight against Money

> Because for her sake, and vpon her golden promises they had ventured their liues, spent their blood, lost legges and armes, had beene pinched with cold, parched with heate, fed upon cabbage, vpon rootes, & vpon Christmas day (in stead of minched pyes) had not better cheere then prouant (mouldy Holland cheese, and course browne bread) (*Non-Dramatic Works*, IV, 117).

He identifies himself with the cause of the poor: 'Beggery, and Miserie, are so well knowne to us, I shall not neede to draw their faces' (*Non-Dramatic Works*, IV, 116). He makes Poverty founder of hospitals and friend of poets yet he gives her as Councillors not only Discontent and Despair, but also Sloth and Repining, and he describes Bankrupts fighting in her cause although they are morally distinguished from the rest by being put in charge of the mines 'As beeing the onely rare fellowes for damnable and speedy blowing up of men in any assault'. Money has as advisers, Covetousness, Providence, Parsimony, Deceit, Violence, and Usury, and Dekker's moral sympathies are made obvious in his enumeration of her allies within the city—mercers, silk-merchants, goldsmiths, and old misers. Money issues commands to her subjects, the 'Money-mongers', especially farmers, landlords and engrossers to perseuere in those sanctioned abuses that keep the poor oppressed:

> Let the times be deere, though the grounds be fruitfull, and the Markets kept empty though your barnes (like Cormorants bellies) breake their butten-holes (*Non-Dramatic Works*, IV, 146).
>
> Hire ware-houses, Vaults vnder ground, and cellers in the City, and in them imprison all necessary prouision for the belly, till the long nailes of famine breake open the dores (*Non-Dramatic Works*, IV, 148–49).

There is no doubt direct contemporary relevance in the details of how Money's commands are carried out:

> Corne skipt from foure to ten shillings a bushell, from ten to twelue shillings, stones of beefe began to be pretious, . . . Mutten grew to be deere, two crownes a buttocke of peefe, and halfe a crowne a wholesome breast of mutton (*Non-Dramatic Works*, IV, 150).

The battle itself never takes place. The troops of Poverty besiege the City, and during the siege both sides become so enfeebled that they finally agree to a perpetual truce. Poverty's men are to be ever ready to fight for Money, and Money to help Poverty, and a Utopian law is enacted whereby Fortune is to be cured of her blindness, so that 'she maight see those vpon whom shee bestowes her blessings.' But when the siege is raised there is only one conclusion possible, a return to the status quo:

> shop-keepers fell to their old *What doe you lacke:* the rich men feast one another (as they were wont) and the poore were kept poore still in pollicy, because they should doe no more hurt (*Non-Dramatic Works*, IV, 165–66).

In Greene's *A Quip for an Upstart Courtier* a consistent allegory is again used as a means of social criticism. Neither Greene's material nor his social and economic comments were original,[4] but the pamphlet clearly had something which drew readers, since it went through six editions in six months. The first edition contained a short but highly wounding attack on the Harvey family,[4] which was immediately suppressed; this, along with the pamphlet's timely appearance during a period of economic depression and the notoriety of its dying author, no doubt contributed to its popularity. The striking form of the allegory, a dream debate between two claimants, Clothbreeches and Velvetbreeches, as to which has the greater right to residence in the commonwealth, and the choice of a jury of citizens to try the case, Greene took directly from Francis Thynne's *Debate between Pride and Lowliness* (c. 1570)[5], but as with all of his borrowings, he added enough to mark the work as his own.

The two figures are contrasted without subtlety. Clothbreeches wears clothes 'such as in Diebus illis our great Grandfathers wore', while Velvetbreeches is dressed in the Italian style; Clothbreeches's associations with the past relate him to that golden age of acquiescence in the ideal of fixed social hierarchies: 'Then the farmer was content his sonne should hold the plough, and liue as he had done before: Beggars then feared to aspire, and the higher sortes scorned to enuie' (sig. Cl^v). Velvetbreeches's foreignness and novelty epitomize the menace of Italy: 'Thou camest not alone but accompanied with multitude of abhominable vices, hanging on thy bumbast nothing but infectious abuses, and vaineglory, selfeloue, sodomie and strange poisonings, wherewith thou had infected this glorious Iland' (sig. B2). The two debate as to which has the better right to be regarded as an Englishman and a jury is chosen to arbitrate from a selection of representatives of different trades. By this means Greene shifts his focus from the conflict of values between the old ways and the new, the English ideals and the Italian, to satire by Estates, as candidates for jury service appear one by one and are accepted or turned down by the two claimants. The novelty of the treatment results from Greene's ability to use the point of view of both antagonists in his critical attitudes to the various trades and professions. The broker, for instance, is rejected by Velvetbreeches for his 'monstrous exacting upon Gentlemen' and by Clothbreeches as a thief. The serjeant is rejected by Velvetbreeches as 'the vserers executioner, to bring such Gentlemen to Limbo, as he hath ouerthrowne with his base brocage and bad commodities', and by Clothbreeches for his cruelty and covetousness. The Knight is challenged by Velvetbreeches—'Why this Knight is a mortall enimy of pride and so to me'—but praised by Clothbreeches. Clothbreeches challenges the bricklayer for building great houses with too many chimneys, but is corrected by the narrator, who says that the apparent superfluity of chimneys is due to the niggardliness of great lords: 'For would they vse ancient hospitality as their forefathers did, and value as lightly of pride, as their great grand fathers, then should you see euery chimny in the house smoke, and prooue that the pore artificer had done his part' (sig. E2^v). Once the jury of twelve is complete, they pronounce the judgement that Clothbreeches's claim is 'by many hundred yeeres more entient', and the narrator is woken from his dream by the triumphant shout of Clothbreeches's supporters.

Two of the most popular allegorical pamphlets were without social or economic satire: *The Voyage of the Wandring Knight* (1580–81), a translation from the French of Jean de Carthenay (or Cartigny) by William Goodyear, a London merchant, and *The Isle of Man: Or, The Legall Proceeding in Man-shire against Sinne* (1627) by Richard Bernard, another very popular allegory, which went into six editions in the year of its publication. Between the Euphuistic style and elements of medieval romance in De Carthenay's story of the Wandering Knight's forlorn search for happiness on earth, his deception by Dame Folly, and his seduction by Voluptuousness in the Palace of Worldly Felicity, his stay in the School of Repentance and his vision of the City of Heaven, and Bernard's simple colloquial prose lies the distance that separates Spenser from Bunyan, on whom Bernard was a direct influence. Bernard's seriousness and his lack of interest in chivalry and romance mark a distinctively seventeenth-century puritan sensibility.

The Isle of Man concerns the pursuit, capture, and trial of the criminal Sin. Bernard uses his allegory as a homiletic technique; his whole structure is based on the exposition of the text, 'Let us search and try our ways' (Lamentations, 3.40); the process of searching, which involves descriptions of the searchers, Godly Jealousy assisted by Lovegood and Hate-ill, the place they search, which is called Souls Town, the friends of the criminal, and the place of his capture, the inn kept by Mistress Heart who lives incestuously with her father Old Man, is at least as long as the trial. The interest of the pamphlet comes, not as in Dekker's from strength of feeling, but from the inventiveness with which the allegory is extended. There is an originality in the choice and application of detail, coupled with a neatness of description that perhaps derives from the newly popular Character writing, which at many points entirely removes the tedious sense of inevitability so common in allegory. The description of Sin's kindred shows Bernard's strong sense of moral discrimination; the family includes not only Ignorance and Error, but also subtler types like Sir Sampler 'who produceth for patternes great mens and learned mens examples, as if they could not do amisse; but whatsoeuer they doe or say, it must be good and lawfull' (p. 33); and Sir Silly, 'one made all of good meaning, who will qualifie the fact by thinking no harme, or intending well'(p. 34). The centres both of the symbol patterns and the intellectual conception coincide in the description of the inn of Mistress Heart where Sin is finally run to earth. The metaphor of a lodging house with its innkeeper and attendants is both ingeniously and accurately extended to suggest the complex of relationships between the sins which stem from the original corruption of the human heart. The five senses are the doors of the house, and the eleven passions the daughters of its lady; her servingman is Will, who has three assistants, the Hands, the Feet, and the Tongue; the dishes served for the guests include the Lusts of the Flesh, the Lust of the Eyes, and the Pride of Life, eaten with the Salt of Opportunity and the Bread of the Fitness of Every Sin's Proper Object. But it is only the first part of the allegory which is sustained with this skill; the second part, the trial of Sin, grows narrowly sectarian, and ends flatly with Papistry being sentenced to Perdition.

Allegory was not the only mode of narrative available to the pamphleteers for moralizing. They were very fond of stories on all occasions, both those of a sentence or two in length and those which took up a whole pamphlet. The stories can be roughly divided into two groups, warning exempla, either in the form of cautionary tales or of didactic accounts of virtue triumphant, or else satirical narratives. In the warning pamphlets, the stories exist only for their value as examples; they are hardly stories at all, rather fragments of narrative, and they function like the exempla in a sermon, as a focus for the moralizing in concrete illustrations. In Averell's *A Dyall for dainty Darlings* (1584) the author moralizes long and enthusiastically on the folly of feminine vanity, with much recourse to exhortation, apostrophe, citations from authority, and Euphuism:

> Draw neere you wanton worms, that leaue your lofty heades, upon the dainty pyllowes of pride, you that haue periwigs to curl your heaire, colours to paint your face, art to square your shoulders, bolsters to fashion your wast, inuentions to chaunge nature, and deuises to alter kinde, consider what Cyprian sayth: *De habitu virginis, quod natum est, ex Deo est, quod mutatum est, ex demone* (sig. B3).

The account which follows this address of the woman who pampers her body to excess and rots away while she is still alive is done with in a couple of sentences; it is an extended and literalized metaphor rather than a narrative. In the other two stories that compose the pamphlet the proportion of story to moralizing is higher, but even so Averell is clearly interested in fiction only for its power to instruct.

In *An Alarum against Vsurers* by Thomas Lodge, published in the same year as *A Dyall*, the author again uses devices of fiction to illustrate a didactic point and to render his warnings more effective, without actually telling a story. His subject is the exposure of the practices of London usurers and moneylenders, and he enlivens it by giving a narrative account, with many apostrophes and passionate speeches, of how a typical wealthy young gentleman falls into their hands. His method is very similar to that used in the cony-catching pamphlets; he provides a general account of the tricks of brokers, some examples of their persuasive speech, and the outline of a representative history of a broker's exploitation of a gentleman. To arouse emotion, he introduces the gentleman's father and gives him a long and very rhetorical speech of lamentation; the son is then brought to life to answer the father with a speech of dissimulation, and the inevitable sequel of his enslavement to Mistress Minx the courtesan, Master Scrape-penny the broker, and the usurer himself, is rapidly unfolded. It sounds like a story but in fact the narrative is very generalized and Lodge makes no attempt to bring his imaginary instance to life with characterization or realistic detail; he constantly turns aside to address his readers, and the speeches of the characters are only extensions of his own voice.

Lodge's pamphlet has been thought by some critics to be partly autobiographical, which is not impossible from the facts of his life, although there is little enough in the style of the piece to suggest it. The little bits of didactic narrative are really devices for raising the emotional temperature of the pamphlet. The imaginary instance is used in a very similar way in John Deacon's pamphlet, *Tobacco Tortuered, Or, The Filthie Fume of Tobacco Refined* (1616), a vehement exhortation in dialogue form against another contemporary abuse, which has never been thought to have any bearing on the life of its author. In order to illustrate the idea that tobacco is to be avoided because, amongst other reasons, it makes men waste the money that is due to their families, Deacon presents a highly charged scene of family conflict:

> Imagine thou beheldest here such a fume-suckers wife most fearefully fuming forth very fountaines of bloud, howling for anguish of heart, weeping, wailing, and wringing her hands together, with grisly lookes, with wide staring eies, with minde amazed, with thoughts perplexed, with body shiuering and quaking in euery ioynt: wouldest thou not wonder greatly at this her so sodaine change? (p. 72).

The wife breaks out into lamentations:

> Am not (I alas) thine onely wife; thy best beloued wife; yea and the onely wife of thy youth? Out, out (alas) why art thou then so carelesse of this my present estate? Why dost thou so vainely preferre a vanishing filthie fume before my permanent Vertues? before my amourous imbrauings; yea before my firme setled faith & constant lone? (p. 72).

In the margin Deacon notes the usefulness of this device: 'The same or the like complaint may also be taken up against adulterous husbands' (p. 72). Then the eldest child is made to implore his father:

> Dad, hearke Dad in thine eare. Am not I thy best boy, am I not, Dad? And doest thou not loue me thy best boy, Dad? . . . And wilt thou now let me—thy white-headed boy runne barefoote and barelegged without hose or shooes? Why harke Dad, hath the fire of *Tobacco* filched thy purse? (p. 74).

The other speaker in the dialogue, who has been called upon to picture to himself this likely situation, finds it all too much to bear, and brings the scene to an abrupt end: 'Forbeare (I beseech you) all such your further patheticall *Prosopopoeias*' (p. 76). This technique has served its turn and Deacon proceeds in a factual tone to the next reason for abolishing tobacco.

A completely different use of narrative techniques is made in the pamphlets of Greene, who is of course both the great exponent of warning literature and a skilful story-teller. Admittedly, it was the same story that he told over and over again, and no doubt because it was Greene's own life that provided him with his favourite cautionary tale, the story and the moralizing work as a powerful combination. *Greenes Mourning Garment* (1590), *Greenes Neuer too late* (1590), *Greenes Groats-Worth of witte* (1592), and *The Repentance of Robert Greene* (1592) are all versions of the tale of spendthrift youth, dissolute living and betrayal by courtesans, followed, too late, by repentance. The motif of the prodigal son had appeared in Greene's first pamphlet, the Italianate romance *Mamillia* (1583), and recurred frequently throughout all of his prose. To begin with, his interest was in fiction, following the popular modes established by Sidney and Lyly, but in the last two years of his life he used the story increasingly as a means to point a moral, and each version grew nearer in form and details to autobiography.

In *Greenes Mourning Garment*, the first of his pamphlets to bear the motto 'Sero sed serio' and to talk in its dedication of repentance and reformation, the prodigal is Philador, the younger son of a wealthy rabbi in Callipolis, who, after various adventures in Arcadian countryside, is taken into the house of three beautiful and witty courtesans until his money runs out and they send him packing. He makes his way sadly home and is received with rejoicing by his old father. In *Greenes Neuer too late. Or, A Powder of Experience* a palmer tells the story of Francesco, a scholar, who runs away with, and marries, Isabel, against her father's wishes; after five happy years together Francesco goes on business to Troynovant, and there is seduced by the courtesan Infida. This is no such novelettish instant infatuation as Philador's, but a genuine encounter with human weakness. Francesco's belief that he is proof against Infida's beauty is mere self-deception; and his strong protestations of love for Isabel are immediately followed by capitulation to Infida. 'None like Isabel', he tells himself firmly, after reading over one of her loving letters: 'But when he went fourth of his Chamber, and spied but his Mistresse looking out of her windowe, all this gear chaungde, and the case was altered: she calde, and in hee must, and there in a ieast scofft at his wives letters.' (sig. H2^v). Like Philador Francesco runs out of money and finds his mistress's love grown cold; like Robert Greene, he then joins a company of actors and writes a successful comedy. At last comes the reconciliation that Greene in his own life never achieved when Francesco returns home penitent, to be completely forgiven by his uncomplaining wife. In the posthumous *Greenes Groats-Worth of witte*, said on its title-page to be published at Greene's dying request and entered in the Stationers' Register shortly after his death by William Wright, the prodigal is called Roberto, a scholar and the elder son of a mean old usurer called Gorinius, who bequeathes all his money to the younger son, leaving Roberto but a single groat. Roberto plots with a prostitute, Lamilia, to defraud his brother and share the fortune with her, but in the event she takes all the money and betrays him. At this same moment of desertion Roberto, like Francesco, falls in with a company of players and becomes successful, 'famozed for an Arch-plaimaking poet'; but this time success goes along with depravity, and Roberto's name becomes a byword for lewdness, perjury, and cozenage. Greene bodies out Roberto's viciousness much more fully than Philador's or Francesco's; the account of his downfall is both Greene's self-flagellation and self-advertisement. At the moment when Roberto is at his lowest, when 'his immeasurable drinking had made him the perfect Image of dropsie, and the loathsome scourge of Lust tyrannized in his bones' (p. 38), he discovers his one remaining groat and Greene, with perfect timing, breaks his cover: 'Heere (Gentlemen) break I off *Robertoes* speach; whose life in most parts agreeing with mine, found one selfe punishment as I haue doone' (p. 39). The fiction thrown aside, Greene completes his pamphlets with general moral precepts to young gentlemen, and with the well-known advice to his fellow-playwrights to beware of actors. Finally, the printer includes 'a letter written to his wife, founde with this booke after his death'.

The world had not heard the last of Greene and his misspent life, for the following month a different publisher, Cuthbert Burbie, put out Greene's final work, *The Repentance of Robert Greene*,[6] at last a first person account. It is shorter and more fragmentary than the other pamphlets, perhaps because Burbie was putting together such bits and pieces as he could find of Greene's unpublished papers, and contains alternative versions of all the major elements of *Greenes Groats-Worth*, the breast-beating life story and repentance, the moral precepts, even the death-bed letter to his wife. Burbie, who had a different sense of an ending from Wright, gives a few conventional sentences on the penitent poet's last hours and concludes with a properly humble prayer. Greene's life many have been a common paradigm of dissolution in his day, but his literary use of it was unique.

His follower Dekker produced one pamphlet only in the form of a cautionary narrative, *Penny-Wise Pound-Foolish Or, a Bristow Diamond, set in two Rings, and both Crack'd. Profitable for Married men, pleasant for young men, and a rare example for all good Women* (1631). The story, a traditional one, bears certain resemblances both to *Greenes Mourning Garment* and to *Greenes Groats-Worth*, although what is known of the sources does not suggest any direct relationship.[7] Again it concerns a wandering husband who is lured away by courtesans, here on more than one occasion, and a faithful and forgiving wife; and the penny of the title, like Greene's groat, represents the wit that cannot be purchased by the prodigal's gold but is only to be found in the true virtues of fidelity and repentance. But the narrative itself is more sophisticated than anything of Greene's, and its morality more complex. The story falls into two similar parts, and in each Ferdinand, the prodigal, a young merchant, betrays his wife Annabell with a courtesan who rejects him once she has gone through his money, and is rescued and rehabilitated by the wife. The two parts are connected by the figure of Theobald, a sailor on the voyage Ferdinand makes to Turkey, who gives Ferdinand the moral counsel that will save him and is paid for it with the penny that Annabell originally gave Ferdinand to buy a penny worth of wit. At the end of the story, when the once-prosperous Ferdinand is reduced with his wife to a life of mean scraping as a shopkeeper, Theobald reappears, now a merchant and rich on profits all stemming from the penny, and sets Ferdinand up in business again. In two particular respects this tale of prodigality redeemed differs from Greene's accounts: first, in the unabashed admiration for the prudential citizen virtues of thrift and sound business dealing, and second, in the stress on the positive moral strength of the wife who understands her incorrigibly feckless husband and learns how to make the best of him. In both instances Dekker's moral emphases are those of the seventeenth century; in Greene's decade money-making was not respectable, nor wives strong and intelligent as well as faithful.

Money is also an important subject in several satirical narratives, which take as their theme its lack or misuse. In Middleton's *The Blacke Booke* Lucifer comes up to London from hell to reward Piers Penniless for his supplication, and meets several of the city's inhabitants who complain to him of their poverty, especially the pimp, Lieutenant Frig-beard, who protests that 'What with this long Vacation, and the fidging of Gallants to Norfolke and up and downe Countries, Pierce was neuer so Pennilesse, as poore Lieutenant Frig-beard' (sig. C4^v). In Rowley's *A Search for Money* (1609) a group of travellers scour all quarters of the city in quest for 'the wandering knight, Monsieur Money', and fail to find him in tailor's shops, taverns, or brothels, amongst usurers, merchants, or students. In the end they discover that money is imprisoned in hell in order to provide dowries for the devil's huge family, and will never be released. In neither of these pamphlets is there anything that could be called a story, although each has a clear and sustained narrative line; the fiction is tailored to the subject—the satirical portraiture of contemporary London life— and although the character-studies are often sharply detailed and very funny they exist in isolation, each for its own sake.

But in Middleton's other prose pamphlet, *Father Hubburds Tales* (1604), the first of the three sections is a story, an unusually complete and consistently sustained account of social change seen through the eyes of an old ploughman. The main events are familiar ones: a foolish country heir on inheriting his father's estates goes up to London and ruins himself and his dependants in his efforts to become a gallant. It is the use of the old retainer's point of view that gives the story both humour and pathos. In his eyes the young heir's fashionable headgear of white feathers looks like a shuttlecock and the scabbard for his sword is embossed in pearl 'as thick . . . as the white Meazells upon hogs flesh'; he watches the facial contortions of the youth smoking a pipe and is reminded of a sowgelder blowing his horn. To the countryman the youth's behaviour is absurd and undignified; and the thoughtless waste and irresponsibility of this new landlord as he signs away his estates and his tenants' well-being become very poignant as observed by the ploughman who cannot read but knows too well the power of the written word: 'Now was our young Maister with one pen-full of Inck doing a farre greater exployt then all his forefathers: for what they were a purchasing all their life time he was now passing away in the fourth part of a minute' (sigs. C3ᵛ–C4).

Few satirical pamphleteers show this sort of skill in integrating their social criticism so completely with their fiction; Averell's method in *A Dyall* whereby the narrative is constantly interrupted for an outburst of moralizing, is much more common. Only in Dekker's *The Guls Horne-booke* (1609), a parody of the Renaissance courtesy-book, is the criticism similarly implicit and contained by the consistency of the narrator's tone. After the first chapter, headed 'The old world and the new weighed together: the tailors of those times and these compared; the apparel and diet of our first fathers', which makes obvious Dekker's detestation for 'The corrupt humours of this ages phantastickness', the insidiously bland and soothing quality of the voice that guides the foolish aspirant to modishness is always maintained, so that the absurdity of the gallant's life is presented as if it were perfectly reasonable, and his boorishness as the height of good manners. The gallant is urged to lie in bed as long as possible in the morning, both on account of the example of Endimion 'who slept threescore and fifteene yeare, and was not a haire the worse for it' and for more practical considerations: morning sleeps 'make us thrifty, both in sparing victuals (for breakfasts thereby are saud from the hell-mouth of the belly) and in preseruing apparell: for while wee warme us in our beds, our clothes are not worne' (*Non-Dramatic Works*, II, 218). He is advised to grow his hair long after the manner of the Greeks and the people of the Golden Age: 'It is in peace an ornament; in war a strong helmet—it blunts the edge of a sword and deads the leaden thump of a bullet' (*Non-Dramatic Works*, II, 229). He should display himself in St Pauls Walk, though not 'above three or four turns' so as not to become 'cheap and ordinary'; during services there he should appear in the open choir and 'draw forth a perfumed embrodered purse (the glorious sight of which will entice many Country-men from their deuotion, to wondering) and quoyt siluer into the Boyes handes, that it may be heard aboue the first lesson' (*Non-Dramatic Works*, II, 233). At the playhouse he should sit on the stage so as to make the acquaintance of the boy actors, laugh aloud in the most tragic scenes, and take every opportunity to rail against the author. This satire on affectation is unfailingly light in its tone, but nonetheless it penetrates beyond the conventional butts and the fashionable forms of its day to the heart of human frivolity and pretence.

It is not consistency that characterizes the pamphleteers' use of narrative and fictional devices. In general they preferred, rather than sustained fictions, to use devices which could be taken up and abandoned piecemeal, or else those which required little contrivance to maintain. Hence the popularity of the dialogue, a very unobtrusive literary form, and the use of prosopopoeia, a rhetorical figure by which an imaginary person or personified abstraction (like London and Westminster in Dekker's *The Dead Tearme,* Time in Brathwait's *The Smoaking Age,* or the distraught wife and child in *Tobacco Tortuered*) is made to speak. Hence also the convenience of two other formal devices which link the new prose of the late sixteenth century very strongly with traditional medieval complaint and satire. They are the procession of the Seven Deadly Sins and satire by Estates. As formal expressions of impersonal and inherited religious attitudes they were on the decline; Protestantism claimed that all sins were deadly, and in Elizabethan times the medieval division of society into three Estates, nobility, clergy, and commoners, did not reflect the social complexity of urban life. But so useful were they as devices for structuring all-purpose social condemnation and so ingrained in popular thought that vestiges of them appear everywhere. Few pamphlets were based entirely on the Sins. *Wits Miserie, and the Worlds Madnesse* (1596), the best pamphlet by Thomas Lodge, is one that is. In it he sets out to describe the Sins as 'Deuils incarnate in clokes of the new fashion', and the traditional seven, each with its many offshoots, appear as vivid and penetratingly satirical portraits of contemporary types. Boasting and Contempt are two of the many descendants of the first sin, Pride. Boasting

> draweth his mouth continually awry in disdaine, and what day sooner you meet him, he hath a sundrie apparel . . . In the stationers shop he sits dailie, jibing and flearing ouer euery pamphlet with Ironicall ieasts; yet heare him but talke ten lines, and you may score up twentie absurdities: I am not as this man is, is his common protestation, yet a more aranter Diuel is there not betwixt S. Dauis and London (pp. 9–11).

Contempt

> neuer speaks but he first wags his head twise or thrise like a wanton mare ouer her bit. To his seruant hee chops the fragments of Lattin in euerie feast of his phrase, My deminitiue and defectiue slaue (quoth hee) giue mee the couerture of my corpes to ensconse my person from frigiditie; (and al this while he cals but for his cloak) (p. 23).

Lodge keeps consistently to his structure, but so varied and inventive is his range of sins, and so wittily detailed his presentation of them, that the pamphlet seems to give us a rich panorama of sixteenth-century London life. Under Pride he also invokes the upstart whose 'studie is for ostentation, not vertues sake', under Avarice the coughing usurer in his fur-edged coat, the glib-tongued broker, the traveller with his tall stories—'he will tell you of monsters that haue faces in their breasts, and men that couer their bodies with their feet' (p. 35)—and the bawd, with her smooth invitation to the merchant's aspiring young wife: 'I know you are fair & yong, fresh, & full as a pullet, & this is not to be lost & laid up niggardly; proue, proue the pleasures of loue' (p. 39). Lodge had learnt much, as he acknowledged, from Greene and Nashe, and the bare framework of the Sins provided all the structure he needed for his blend of anecdote, observation, and moral comment.

Dekker in *The Seuen Deadly Sinnes of London* (1606) also based his pamphlet on the traditional structure, but produced a modernized version of the original seven; his new sins are Politic Bankruptism, Lying, Candlelight, Apishness, Shaving, and Cruelty. He describes a pageant of personified vices, individually entering London in a stately procession, joyously received by supporters like a foreign potentate. The very structure of the pamphlet gives it a biting contemporary relevance. Dekker's London readers must surely have drawn a parallel between the curious pageantry of Dekker's sins and the real pageantry of August 1606 celebrating the state visit of the King of Denmark.[8] The Induction admonishes London for its sinfulness and makes covert reference to the Gunpowder Plot of 1605: 'Once againe hath [God] gone about (and but gone about) to call thee to the dreadfull Barre of his Iudgement' (*Non-Dramatic Works*, II, 13). The Sins themselves are conceived and described so as to be directly appropriate to the moral and spiritual condition of the city. Each is received at one of the city's seven gates and welcomed; Politic Bankruptism is greeted at Ludgate, the site of a debtors' prison, by the keepers and inmates of the jail, Candlelight enters at Aldersgate 'for though the streete be faire and spatious, yet [there are] few lightes in mistie euenings' and Cruelty at Aldgate 'beeing drawne that way by the smell of bloud about the Barres'. Dekker presents his sins in terms both of moral emblem and of contemporary social observation. Cruelty, the last and most emotionally treated, is a strikingly Spenserian personification, riding in a chariot of flint:

> The Spokes of the Wheeles, are the Shin-bones of wretches that haue bin eaten by misery out of prison. A couple of vnruly, fierce, and vntamed Tygers (cald *Murder* and *Rashnes*) draw the Chariot.

Ignorance holds the reynes of the one, and *Obduration* of the other: *Selfe-will* is the Coach-man. In the vpper end of the *Coach*, sits *Cruelty* alone, vpon a bench made of dead mens sculls (*Non-Dramatic Works*, II, 80).

But it is also seen as a vice peculiarly characteristic of London; despite the fame of London's charity to widows and orphans, to the leper and the lunatic, the city harbours many forms of cruelty, from the pitilessness of creditors towards their debtors who die in jail, the hard hearts of masters who turn out old servants to beg in the street or abandon plague-victims to die in a ditch, to the vividly evoked misery of forced marriages:

> He into whose bosome three score winters haue thrust their frozen fingars, if hee be rich (though his breath bee rancker than a Muckhill, his bodye more drye than *Mummi*, and his minde more lame than *Ignorance* it selfe) shall haue offered vnto him (but it is offered as a sacrifice) the tender boosome of a Virgin, vpon whose forehead was neuer written sixteene yeares (*Non-Dramatic Works*, II, 70).

In many pamphlets, individual Sins in a form recognizably derived from the processional treatment are incorporated into other satirical modes. In Nashe's *Pierce Penilesse*, an important work which had great influence on the moralistic pamphlet as a genre and on Lodge and Dekker particularly, the second section, Piers's supplication to the devil for money and patronage, consists of a lively attack on the Sins in their current forms. The various social types are sketched in with a spontaneity and a malicious precision of satirical detail very characteristic of Nashe, as for example in the forms of Pride. Pride is first exemplified in the upstart:

> All malcontent sits the greasie son of a Clothier, & complaines (like a decaied Earle) of the ruine of ancient houses: whereas the Weauers loomes first framed the web of his honor ... *Al Italionato* is his talke, & his spade peake is as sharpe as if he had beene a Pioner before the walls of Roan (*Works*, I, 168–69).

It appears, too, in 'Mistress Minx, a Marchants wife, that wil eate no Cherries, forsooth, but when they are at twenty shillings a pound' (notice the economical mockery of that 'forsooth'), and in aging ladies who 'weare nosegayes of yeolow haire on their furies foreheads, when age hath written, Hoe God, be here, on their bald burnt parchment pates'. Nashe shared with his disciple Dekker a mobility of formulation that enabled him to move easily between the Sins as social types and as allegorical emblems; Greediness who guards the inner rooms of hell in a cap befurred with catskins, breeches bombasted with statutes and forfeitures, and shoes toed with sixpenny nails so as to dig up all the dunghills for gold, recalls the tableau effects of Spenser and of Dekker in *The Seuen Deadly Sinnes*. But the Supplication does not merely consist of an array of vices; Nashe packed into it several merry tales, attacks on poetasters and puritans, on antiquaries, which evidently caused offence, and on Richard Harvey, and vigorous defences of poetry and the theatre. He made the form serve his own purposes, and amid the conventional, if vivid and witty, moral commonplaces, there is some independent and strongly-felt writing:

> Our Players are not as the players beyond sea, a sort of squirting baudie Comedians, that haue whores and common Curtizens to playe womens parts, and forebeare no immodest speech, or vnchast action that may procure laughter, but our Sceane is more statelye furnisht than euer it was in the time of *Roscius*, our representations honourable, and full of gallant resolution (*Works*, I, 215).

What is particularly interesting is the way that *Pierce Penilesse* begins as something quite different and becomes so to speak magnetically attracted to the pattern of the Sins. At the beginning Piers complains, like a neglected postgraduate, of his poverty and the unrewarded status of the serious writer:

> Hauing spent many yeeres in studying how to liue, and liu'd a long time without mony: hauing tired my youth with follie, and surfetted my minde with vanitie, I began at length to looke backe to repentaunce, & addresse my endeuors to prosperitie: But all in vaine ... I my selfe (in prime of my best wit) laid open to pouertie (*Works*, I, 157).

He hears that 'a certaine blinde Retayler called the Deuell' lends money to parasites and fools, and writes out a supplication to him which he gives the Knight of the Post to deliver. The Supplication begins as if it is leading up to a meeting between Piers and the guardians of the Devil's gold; Piers describes two of them in detail, Greediness and his wife Niggardize, who hoards her nose-droppings and 'would not aduenture to spit without halfe a dozen porringers at her elbow'. Hell, their habitation, is a vast stately house with a small bare kitchen where even the spiders can find nothing to eat. But instead of bringing the characters to life and having Piers encounter them Nashe abandons the scheme entirely; having described Greed he is drawn on to Pride, from Pride to Envy, and so on until he has covered all seven. When the Supplication has been read, the Knight of the Post remarks on Piers's digressive style:

> A Supplication calst thou this? (quoth the Knight of the post) it is the maddest Supplication that euer I saw; me thinks thou hast handled all the seuen deadly sinnes in it, and spared none that exceedes his limits in any of them. It is well done to practise thy witte, but (I believe) our Lord will cun thee little thanks for it (*Works*, I, 217).

The Sins provided a ready-made and reliable formula for many a pamphleteer who wanted to castigate contemporary vice in a comfortably traditional manner. They appear, invariably led by pride, in allegorical narratives, in processions and masques, at the wedding of Fastus and Luxuria in Rankins's *A Mirrour of Monsters*, pitted against virtues in Dekker's *A Strange Horse-Race*, inhabiting the palace of Sin in *Peregrinatio Scholastica*, and embodied in foreign archetypes such as the proud Spaniard or the lecherous Italian. In laments for London, like George Whetstone's *A Mirour for the Magestrates of Cyties* (1584) and Nashe's *Christs Teares over Ierusalem* (1593) the specific vices of the capital are seen in the general terms of Pride, Gluttony, and the rest. In the railing pamphlets that seem to grow more prevalent in the reign of James they are an invariable ingredient, although no longer in the traditional processional order. They sometimes appear rearranged, with new interrelationships, and ingenious subdivisions. For instance, Nashe in *Christs Teares* makes Ambition a son of Pride, and Avarice, normally a Sin in its own right, a branch of Ambition; Vainglory is Pride's second son, and Atheism, Discontent and Contention the others, while Disdain, Gorgeous Attire, and Delicacy are Pride's daughters; surprisingly, Gluttony, Lust, and Sloth are offshoots of Delicacy. Sometimes one or two of the Sins will appear in a compendium of vestigial forms for social satire, almost as if by chance. Barnaby Rich, in *Faultes faults, And nothing else but Faultes* (1606) asserts that he will avoid 'this pleasant imperfection of *Pompe, Pride, Adulterie, Gluttonie, Drunkennesse*, and such other' because he knows himself not to be innocent of them, but very soon he is writing in a traditional way of the fruits of Drunkenness, of the 'hatefull, pernicious, detestable wretch Couetousnesse' and Pride 'the ouerthrow of many flourishing Citties'. In William Parkes's *The Curtaine-Drawer Of the World* (1612) a hectic and savage vision of life in terms of man's blind commitment to sin, all human activity is seen as dominated either by Pride 'the Minion and wel beloued sinne of women' 'the badge and ensigne both of Court, Citie, and Country', or by Lust 'the marrow-eater of the world, the canker of health, the azure complectioner of the eyes, the azure infeebler of the backe, the consumption of the braine' (p. 8). The anonymous *This Worlds Folly* (1615), a hell-fire sermon of a pamphlet, begins with Pride and procedes to Blasphemy, a sin often elevated to the rank of the Seven, and Lechery, all of which are associated with the depravity of theatres and of poets; but the author's real subject is the imminence of Judgement Day and the citation of the Sins is merely a prelude to it.

Satire of Estates, another medieval form, is similarly treated. Originally, it arose as the literature of feudalism, an expression of the division of society into strictly classified occupational groups and of the hierarchical theory behind the division. Unlike the Seven Deadly Sins the literature of Estates was recognized as a distinct form in its own right, with four particular characteristics: an enumeration of the Estates, aiming at total inclusiveness, a lament over the shortcomings of the Estates, an expression of belief in their divine ordination, and an attempt to find remedies for their defections. Although in Elizabethan times the medieval groups or divisions had broken down, and many more classes of people and criteria by which to categorize them were recognized, the well-defined political and religious beliefs in which the genre had originated were still strongly maintained, at least by such conservative and traditional social theoreticians as the pamphleteers. Such notions as the importance to the commonwealth of every class, the mutual dependency of the classes and the obligation resting on each to fulfil its duty towards the others, the necessity for every man to be content with his degree, and the superiority of olden times when men kept to their naturally appointed places, are basic to popular Elizabethan satire. In some pamphlets it is the Estates philosophy which is most significant, in others, though fewer, the Estates form. William A'verell's *A meruailous combat of contrarieties,* a pamphlet partly in dialogue form, uses the Estates device of the analogy between the structure of the commonwealth and the members of the human body, as in *Coriolanus,* to justify differences in rank and to show the mutual dependence of all parts, but only as a preliminary to a work of anti-Catholic propaganda. The Belly accuses the Back of Pride and Envy, and the Back replies in kind:

> You forget your owne delicacie, that consume more at one banquet in a day, then I doe uppon apparrell in a yeare (sig. B1).

The Belly defends itself by pointing out its necessary physiological functions:

> I drawe from the entrailes and bowelles certaine filthie vapours, of which matter are ingendered wormes (sig.C2ᵛ).

The other members are persuaded:

> As we see that in a politique state diuerse men haue diuerse duties . . . so in a naturall bodie each member hath his seuerall dutie (sig. C3ᵛ).

Averell then completely redirects his satire by introducing the Tongue, and making it represent the papists, who undermine the security of the state with lies, and the second part of the pamphlet turns into an orthodox exhortation of religious unity in the state.

Estates satire provided the pamphleteers with literary devices and with a social philosophy sanctioned by tradition, but rarely with an entire literary form. They abandoned the hierarchic distinctions and the old divisions in favour of a survey of mainly middle-class professions, although it was still strongly felt that many of the ills of the commonwealth could be ascribed to the nobility or the commons not performing their traditional functions. The emphasis on the pride of upstarts is one aspect of this; its obverse is the stress on the decay of hospitality. So William Parkes in *The Curtaine-Drawer* censures the country gentleman for not fulfilling the role ascribed to the first Estate:

> And whilst he should maintaine with his hospitality, from the gates of his charity, the daily resort of the impotent and the needy, he shuts his doores, and allows his chimnies no smoke, keeps his Christmas Hall in a Citizens chamber, turns his men into boyes, and sometimes into women, regards not his place of calling, the honour of his house, the end of his beeing (p. 38).

Barnaby Rich, an intensely conservative writer, frequently expressed the view that many of the sins of the age were due to the pride of the lower classes who tried to ape the nobility:

> The pride of this age is growne to that height, that wee canne hardly knowe a Prince from a pesant, by the view of his apparell, and who is able by the outward show, to discerne betweene *Nobilitie* and *Seruilitie*, to know a Lord from a Lowt, a Lady from a Landresse, or to distinguish betweene a man of worthinesse and base

> Groome, that is not worth the clothes that belonges to his backe (*The Honestie of This Age*, p. 47).

Estates satire underlies Rich's thinking more obviously than in many writers. He deals out blame for the state of decadence very much in terms of the failure of the Estates to do their duty. Courtiers and princes he sees as susceptible to bribes and flattery, and guilty of self-seeking and covetousness. The court can both make and mar. Knights no longer carry out their former roles: '*Knights* in former ages haue been assistant vnto *Princes,* and were the staies of the Common-wealth; but now, they liue by begging from the *Prince,* and are a burthen to the common-wealth' (*My Ladies Looking Glasse*, p. 66). Churchmen are guilty of hypocrisy and dissembling; and often they 'set the holy scriptures at a iarre, that will many times make the glose to ouerthrow the text' (*Roome for a Gentleman*, p. 14^v). But Rich, like most pamphleteers, used only certain elements from Estates litera-ture. He did not aim at an all-inclusive survey of professions, and while he readily pointed out defects, he did not supply remedies.

An exception is one of the pamphlets of Nicholas Breton, a belle-lettrist rather than a pamphleteer, who tried his hand at all the fash-ionable forms of verse and prose. Breton takes a very feudal viewpoint in his *A Dialogue full of pithe and pleasure* (1603). The three speakers, Antonio, Meandro, and Dinarco, consider the social hierar-chy in strict order from King and counsellors, through professional and working classes, to labourers and beggars. Antonio, who presents the extreme view of man's indignity, considers only the worst charac-teristics of each class, omitting the clergy.

> If [he is] a King, he may be a tyrant, and that is odious: or a sheepe, and that is erronious. If a Counsellor, he may be proud, and that may breed enuy: he may be couetous, and that may corrupt con-science (sig. B4).

Meandro, in the manner of a scholastic debate, gives the opposing view in the same terms:

> If a King in his tiranny ouer the wicked, he may be a friend to the vertuous: in his clemency to the repentant, he may reclaime the malignant. If a Counsellour, his auarice may teach the prodigall thriftinesse: and if haughtie, if may breed feare in the enuious (sigs. C3–C3^v).

Dinarco, in a more strictly traditional manner, shows how the Estates fail in their duties to each other:

What dishonour it is to a King, to be ungratious to his subject? What dishonour in a subject, to be disloyall to his Prince? What Indignitie it is to the Counsellour, to be either faithlesse to his King or carelesse of his commaund? (sig. D4).

The summary of his argument for the indignity of man finds all faults stemming from man's inability to rest content with his appointed Estate, and he concludes with the wish for each class to find again the contentment of its proper state of mind:

O then let the Prince be gratious: the Courtier vertuous; the souldier mercifull: the Lawier conscionable: the Merchant charitable: the Farmer no Snudge: the Labourer painfull: and the Begger thankfull (sig. E2).

In the first decade of the seventeenth century these medieval forms began to be superseded by a new mode, the Theophrastan Character. Benjamin Boyce, in *The Theophrastan Character in England to 1642*, shows how many literary cross-currents including the Sins, Estates satire, certain kinds of Elizabethan psychological writing like the influential *Batman uppon Bartholome* (1582), courtesy and conduct books, and florilegia, combined to produce the genre which began with Joseph Hall's *Characters of Vertues and Vices* in 1608, the Overburian Characters, and Earle's *Micro-Cosmographie*, and flourished until the days of Addison and the *Spectator*. The seventeenth-century Character has much in it of moral and social characterization according to the traditions of the Sins and of satire by Estates, as can be seen in such examples as Thomas Tuke's 'Pictur of a Pictur, Or, the Character of a Painted Woman' which forms part of his *A Treatise Against Painting and Tincturing of Men and Women* (1616) and owes much to descriptions of Lechery, and Richard Young's *The Drunkard's Character* (1638) which is very like a sermon against the evils of drink; but in this genre the portraits are separate rather than interconnected, and not arranged in any sort of social or moral hierarchy. Boyce has surveyed the Character so thoroughly that there is no need to do more here than briefly indicate how it is used in popular pamphlets, especially since the relation of the Character to the literature of the Elizabethan criminal underworld has already been mentioned.

Nashe, Lodge, and Rich all included Character-writing of a kind in their pamphlets, although it was not in the consciously and deliberately formed manner of Hall or Earle. Some of Nashe's witty sketches in *Pierce Penilesse* and Lodge's in *Wits Miserie* show the interest of the Theophrastan Character writer in the balance of typical qualities and vivid, recognizably individual details, but their moral and social types, the spendthrift heir or the merchant's wife in Nashe, Lying, depicted as a boastful traveller, or Fornication, a perfumed gallant, in Lodge, have their origin in some branch of the Sins. In *Catharos. Diogenes in his Singularitie* (1591), a dialogue between three citizens of Athens, Lodge presents an array of professional types such as magistrates, divines and lawyers, merchants and usurers, so as to correct the vices of the city 'that finding the imperfection of euerie member, we may the better establish and bring in frame the whole city' (sig. Cl^v). But he was following the manner of his source, *The Dialoges of Creatures Moralysed*,[9] an anonymous collection of fables printed in 1480, and describing the moral characters of his types in terms of animal images and beasts fables. Rich, in *Faultes faults* (1606) and *My Ladies Looking Glasse* (1616) includes many wittily detailed portraits, full both of moral intelligence and precise observation, like Captain Swag, the red-faced counterfeit soldier, who 'will atchieue greater victories, but sitting at a dinner or a supper, than euer did Alexander', the Ninihammer, a foolish gallant, with his feather and his lovelocks, and the Amorist, who puts on mourning for the death of his mistress's monkey.

The anonymous *The Man In the Moone, Telling Strange Fortunes, or the English Fortune-teller* (1609) illustrates in its form a transitional stage between Sins and Estates writing, and the Character. It opens with a vestige of narrative, a traveller finding himself at nightfall lost in an enchanted world and taking refuge in a mysterious house. The house is inhabited by an old fortune-teller called Fido and his assistants Mockso and Opinion; a series of visitors call, and each is described in turn. Mockso gives a physical description, Fido a moral assessment, and Opinion 'somewhat criticall and taunting' a Character. Mockso and Fido moralize in the manner of the earlier writing on their guests, who include a drunkard, a glutton, a prodigal, and a parasite, but Opinion's views are usually expressed tersely and objectively. The writing is colloquial and accurate, and sometimes even funny; some of the portraits are as detached as a Character should be, like that of the Glutton:

> he is none of your great talkers, but will do prettie well at a dinner: if silence be a vertue, he is a vertuous Gentleman, for at meate he cannot entend to talke for eating, and betweene meales, hee sleepeth soundly: to be briefe with him, he is a pestilence to Pastries, which sweepeth many of them sheere away, a consumption to capons, chickins, and other poultry, a sepulchre to seafish, and

others in ponds, moates, and Riuers, a sharp sheep-biter, and a marueilous Mutten-monger, a gorbelly Glutton (sig. E2^v).

But in those descriptions which are more akin to the old Sins tradition than the new Theophrastan style the tone can change suddenly from sardonic humour to straight-faced moralizing. The last sentence of Opinion's verdict on the drunkard contrasts with his lighter-toned conclusion on the glutton:

> To be briefe with him, hee is his Masters hindrance, if he be a seruant: his seruants torment, if he be a Master: his wifes crosse, if he be an husband: his childrens beggaring, if he be a father: his owne ruine, whatsoeuer he is, a detested drunkard (sig. B3^v).

Anthony Nixon imitated the hybrid method of *The Man In the Moone* and plagiarized from some of its description in *A Straunge Foot-Post, with A Packet full of Strange Petitions* (1613), which also consists of a series of type portraits presented with an exhaustive amount of commentary from several points of view. There is first a physical/moral description of the Harlot or whoever it may be, then a moral 'Character' given by Opinion, here personified as a monster with Hydra heads and Argus eyes, then a first-person petition to fortune; the petitioner is followed by an attendant, the Harlot, for instance, by a Bawd, who gives yet another description of him and is himself assessed by Opinion. Nixon was a dull and uninventive writer who compiled his pamphlets from the work of others rather than composing them himself; he was obviously attracted by the Character as a device for social criticism, but he had nothing of his own to contribute to it.

The pull towards overt moralizing was always very strong, and the pamphleteers did not try to resist it. They rarely achieved or even aspired to the consistent detachment that Boyce sees as characteristic of the true Theophrastan Character, nor did they try to interrelate their separate Characters or fit them into narratives. It is on the stage, in the plays of Ben Jonson or Middleton, that the boastful soldier, the fop, the city wife, the would-be poet and their like live and move, not in Renaissance prose fiction. To the pamphleteers, the Character-portrait was a device for varying the form of their satire, a traditionally sanctioned structure for inveighing against the ills of society.

It is in their structures and devices that the pamphlets show their greatest variety. One of the most fruitful sources for devices to mingle pleasure and profit was the realm of the supernatural. That 'undiscovered country, from whose bourn no traveller returns' was in itself intrinsically fascinating to the Elizabethans and perhaps had for them something of the imaginative compulsion that the world of science-fiction has for us. Undoubtedly it was a good way of locating any sort of satirical matter at several removes from reality; as Chettle says in *Kind-Harts Dreame* (1592), safeguarding himself against the spite of 'enuious misconsterers' by framing his satire in a dream vision: 'Neither can they what euer they be, deale hardly with Kind-hart, for he onely deliuers his dreame; with euery Apparition simply as it was vttered (ed. G. B. Harrison, Bodley Head Quartos, p. 10). And it could be used to preface or frame almost any subject. A writer could refurbish his familiar material by setting it out in the form of a dream or vision, a communication from a ghost, an account of the visit to earth by an underworld inhabitant or of a visit to hell by someone who had returned to tell the tale; the Devil might be supposed to send forth prophecies, to disguise himself or his emissaries and visit London, to make a will. Most of these devices had a considerable literary ancestry. The visit to the underworld, for instance, was pioneered by the Greek Sophist Lucian, whose *Dialogues of the Dead* furnished some source material for the pamphleteers, in particular for Dekker in *Newes from Hell*. The dream vision was one of the most popular devices, and one with an even longer literary tradition. The idea of the dream as a vehicle of divine revelation occurs both in classical writing and in the Bible. In the Old Testament the dreams of Daniel, Ezekiel, Isaiah, and Zechariah are prophetic. In classical times, probably largely because of the conception of the oracle manifesting the divine will through a human agent, the dream came to be accepted as a literary convention for presenting material concerned with other worlds. In medieval times the fictional dream as a device for showing higher truth became mingled with the real dreams through which saints and mystics experienced their visions of God. The emphasis on other worlds combined readily with a critical attitude towards this one, and so the dreamer became a convenient device to introduce satire or complaint. And it was also in the medieval period that allegorical elements were introduced into the dream vision, and dreams came to involve personifications as often as real people.[10]

Since the dream vision was a highly conventional form, pamphlets constructed as dreams open in very similar ways. The dream takes place at night, in the countryside, or sometimes in a precisely located spot in or near London; Chettle's Kind-Hart, for instance, in an opening copied verbatim in *Ratseis Ghost* (1606), falls asleep while 'sitting alone not long since, not far from *Finsburie*, in a Taphouse of Antiquity' (sig. B2). The narrator of *Tarltons Newes out of Purgatorie* (1590) 'stept by dame Anne of Cleeres well, & went by the backside of Hogsdon' (p. 2) before he fell asleep and began to dream. In *All to Westminster* (1641) the narrator is also sleepless, and goes on a long walk through the country and city before reaching Westminster Hall where he has a dream about Charon's boat being shipwrecked. The setting of the dream often corresponds in some way to its contents. In *Tarltons Newes* the narrator, deterred from visiting the playhouse by a large and rowdy audience, goes off into the country, and dreams of an actor; Lupton's Eumenides, in *A Dreame of the Devill and Dives* (1615) has been carousing late in a tavern with depraved companions when he has a vision of hell. In *A Dreame: or Newes from Hell* (1641) the narrator, an 'honest yeoman', comes up to London from the country to submit to parliament a petition against enclosures, dines in a tavern called Hell, and dreams of the real Hell, and of Pluto's servants, the oppressors of the poor. But John Dickenson's narrator in *Greene in Conceipt* (1598) is surprised to have a vision of the ghost of Greene after he has been reading Lucian's *Timon* because of Greene's reputation as a sceptic. Dickenson conveniently ignores *Greenes Vision* (1592), one of those pamphlets published after Greene's death, which describes how Greene, in a fit of remorse for his lewd life and 'laciuious Pamphleting' has a dream in which Chaucer and Gower appear to him. Chaucer urges Greene not to worry because 'thou hast doone Scholler-like, in setting foorth thy pamphlets', but Gower advises repentance, and more attention to divinity. Greene prepares to follow Gower.

The dreams often show clearly visualized apparitions. Some stay and tell stories, like Tarlton who sits down 'crossing one leg ouer another', or inveigh against abuses like Nashe, 'a poore olde swarty fellow, with stareing haire, Neglected beard, Ashy gastly looke, with a black Cloath Cloak upon his back' (J. Taylor, *Crop-Eare Curried, Or, Tom Nash His Ghost*, 1644, sig. A2). Others, like the five figures who appear to Kind-hart, depart after some brief badinage, leaving their manuscripts to the author to read. In the dreams of more obviously solemn intention, like Lupton's *A Dreame of the Devill and Dives* or Dekker's *Dekker his Dreame* (1620) the narrator's vision is of a whole scene, peopled by characters who are real or allegorical, living or dead, historical or contemporary. Except where the narrator is himself involved in the action of his vision, the dream form itself is not an integral part of the pamphlet; it serves as a convenient opening, which absolves the author of the necessity of explaining how he came by his material, and it gives an effect of distancing from reality. It also provides a neat ending. The ghosts vanish, the narrator awakes, wiser for what he has seen, picks up his pen and starts to write. This kind of ending was so handy and economical that writers sometimes used it in pamphlets that were not initially presented as dream visions at all. *A Knights Coniuring* (1607), the second edition of Dekker's *Newes from Hell*, does not begin as a dream, but it ends with the narrator waking up: 'They made such a mad noyse, that all this Coniuring which is past (beeing but a dreame) I suddenlie started up, and am now awake' (sig. Ll^v). Anthony Nixon's *The Scourge of Corruption* (1615), a satire in dialogue form, similarly alludes to this device in its conclusion. The four speakers depart, leaving alone the narrator who has all along been a silent witness; he picks up his pen to record what he has heard, begging the reader 'Pardon me if it answere not your expectation, being it was done in hast, and but the indigested remnant of a dreame' (sig. F2^v).

The idea of putting out a pamphlet as a communication from a ghost or underworld inhabitant was also a convenient one. The communication could take the form of describing the other world, commenting on the state of things on earth, warning of disasters to come, or making a prophecy, and the form lent itself readily to political or religious satire, as in *Greenes Newes both from Heauen and Hell* (1593), the pamphlets of Thomas Scott, the two accounts of Nashe's ghost, and many crude satires of the 1640s. In *Greenes Newes* the scene is carefully set; the narrator is out walking one evening in a disreputable locality 'betweene Pancredge Church & Pye-Corner, beeing somewhat late in the euening, about an hour after the setting of the Sunne' (sig. A2) when he meets Greene's ghost, which is of unusual appearance, being 'wrapt up in a sheete, his face onely discouered.' The meeting is described like a dream vision, except that the narrator is awake: it is night, the action is carefully located, the ghost appears suddenly; he makes a short speech, presses his manuscript upon the narrator, and vanishes. The 'manuscript' contains some crude anti-Catholic satire and some ribald anecdotes about priests and young women, as well as reminiscences of Greene, rejected both by heaven and hell, and left 'a walking spyrite, restlesse and remediless to wander through the world.'

In many pamphlets the preliminaries are less detailed, although the supernatural narrator often introduces himself briefly. In the anonymous *Tom Nash his Ghost* Nashe announces himself boldly: 'I am a Ghost and Ghosts doe feare no Lawes.' Cock Watt, in *Iests to make you merie* (1606) by Dekker and George Wilkins, describes himself as a spirit of doom which appears only between sunset and sunrise: 'Know that to those to whome for that moment I am visible, the horror of thunder, mixt with the flashes of affrighting lightning . . . begets not a more Earthquake in the bosomes of the wretched, then doth my light increase in my beholder' (*Non-Dramatic Works*, II, 302). Robin Goodfellow in *Tell-Trothes New-Yeares Gift* (1593) gives some details of his spirit nature, for instance that he 'crossed the riuer *Stix* in *Carons* boat without his leaue', but will not describe hell: 'To tell what I there say, were no newes: because it hath beene tolde by so many, whereof some of them haue not reported amisse' (ed. Furnivall, New Shakespeare Society, p. 4).

Nashe performed his own variation on the device of the underworld visit or visitant with his invention of the character of Piers Penniless, which was taken up by many of his successors who made their own adaptations of it. Piers, whose name puns on a current pronunciation of 'purse,' is a poor scholar who can find no way of employing his talents so as to make himself a living, and so decides to write a supplication to the devil for money. He was both a dramatization of Nashe himself and a topical figure whose plight was all too familiar to the literary men of the time. Nashe built up a character for him and used him as a mouthpiece for his attacks on Gabriel Harvey in *Strange Newes, Of the intercepting certaine Letters* (1592). In several of the sequels to *Pierce Penilesse* Piers appears as the representative of the unrewarded scholar. In Middleton's *The Blacke Booke* Lucifer comes to earth to look for him, and finds him in poverty, asleep 'vppon a Pillow stuft with Horsemeat, the Sheetes smudged so durtily, as if they had ben stolne by night out of Saint Pulchers Church-yard when the Sexton had left a Graue open' (sig. Dl^v), and promises him a happier future when 'his palme shall bee pawnde with Pence'; in Dekker's *Newes from Hell* the Knight of the Post comes up to earth, receives Piers's letter, and, having travelled through Europe and decided that Italy contains all the varieties of sin to be found in the world, returns to hell, collects the Devil's answer, and finally delivers it to Piers in Elysium. In the anonymous *The Returne of the Knight of the Poste from Hell*[11] the narrator out walking in London chances on the Knight who gives him the Devil's answer to Piers, a desolate account of the decline in cultural values, which concludes by asserting that Piers and his fellows will never receive any just reward, not even praise.

The liveliest of these sequels is *The Blacke Booke*, which uses the theme of the Devil's search for Piers as a framework for vigorous social satire. The Devil is the narrator; he comes up to earth, disguises himself as a London constable, and heads for the notorious district of Picthatch. There he amuses himself by scaring the inhabitants of a brothel:

> Two or three vaulted out of their beddes at once, one swearing stockes and stoones, he could not finde his stockins, other that they could not hit upon their false bodies, when to speake troath and shame my selfe, they were then as close to their flesh as they could, and neuer put them off since they were twelue yeare old. (sig. B3^v).

The Devil and the brothel-keeper argue as to whether brothel-keeping is a profitable practice, and in the ensuing discussion of vice and money the author manages to satirize usurers, lawyers, upstarts, and gallants with their 'prodigall glistrings and spangled damnations'. Piers is discovered in a dirty room in a brothel, even in his sleep railing at the injustice of the world, and the Devil decides to relieve his poverty. So he summons together all the greatest villains of the city, notably moneylenders, thieves, cutpurses, and pandars, and makes his will, leaving to Piers as his final legatee the title of the profits from all the brothels of London, and free access to the girls.

Dekker's *Newes from Hell* pays a more solemn tribute to Nashe. This pamphlet also uses Piers, the Devil, and the Knight of the Post, to satirize the vices of France, Spain, and Italy, as well as those of London. In the second edition, *A Knights Coniuring,* Dekker adds material, no doubt inspired by *The Returne of the Knight of the Poste from Hell*, on Nashe's favourite theme of the decay of the arts, which is skilfully inserted into the existing narrative structure. The temple of the Muses is falling into disrepair, and 'many that seemd to hate *Barbarisme* and *Ignorance*' decide to raise a general subsidy to put it in order. But their efforts are thwarted by the refusal of large numbers of people to contribute. Gentlemen 'swore by their bloud, & by the tombs of their ancestors, they would not lay out a peny'; many noblemen agree. Soldiers claim the exemption of their peace-time impoverishment, and lawyers 'knew there was no Statute in anie Kings time, could compell them to disburse'. The gods are fearful that knowledge will vanish from the earth, and so they send down Apollo, in the shape of Nashe, who 'full of the *Diuine Furie,* taking a deepe bowle of the *Helliconian* liquor in his hands, did in a brauery write a Supplication in the behalfe of God for his enlargement' (sigs. B4–B4^v). At the end of the pamphlet the Knight of the Post travels to Elysium to deliver the Devil's reply to Piers; there he finds a special place set aside for poets: 'When these happy Spirits sit asunder, their bodies are like so many Starres, and when they ioyne togither in seuerall troopes, they show like so many heauenly constellations' (sig. K4ᵛ). In this celestial group sit Chaucer 'reuerend for prioritie', Spenser, 'learned Watson, industrious Kyd, ingenious Atchlow', and recent arrivals including Marlowe, Greene, Peele, and of course Nashe.

Dekker obviously found the underworld congenial as a satiric device, for he used it once again in *Lanthorne and Candle-light* (1609), as a framework for cony-catching material. *Pierce Penilesse* and *The Blacke Booke* both contributed to the punning account of the law term in hell where Rhadamanthus tries courtiers for riotous living and citizens for city-sins, and Satan, the Lord of the Fiery Lakes, chooses a devil to go to earth and sabotage the efforts of the Bellman of London to expose crime. But the Stygian traveller is only an eyewitness, and Dekker tends to forget his existence once the action has moved up to London and its low life.

A common and traditional form for the underworld figure to take is that of a ghost or apparition who sends messages of warning and advice to those on earth. The messages may consist of political or religious satire as well as straightforward complaint. Thomas Scott uses well-known historical figures in his anti-Catholic pamphlets; in *Robert Earle of Essex his Ghost* (1624) the Earl writes to King James with practical warnings 'that the Spanish Kings reuengefull humour was insatiable . . . that all Treaties with Spaine . . . were both vnsafe and dangerous' (p. 10). In *Sir Walter Rawleighs Ghost, Or Englands Forewarner* (1626) the ghost of Raleigh appears to Count Gondomar, the Spanish ambassador, and upbraids him for the crimes of Spain against England: 'Behold, I thy Tormentor will never be absent from thine elbow, and whatsoeuer thou shalt contrive or plot for the hurt of Great Britaine, I with the help of the holy Angels will returne upon thine owne bosome' (p. 40).

Chettle's *Kind-Harts Dreame*, which came out in the same year as *Pierce Penilesse* about three months after Greene's death, was the product of a period when the popular pamphleteers were less politically involved. Five apparitions, accompanied by the Knight of the Post, appear to the sleeping Kind-Hart and inveigh against contemporary subjects of controversy: Anthony Now-now, a street fiddler and balad-singer, against ballad-singers, Dr Burcot against quack doctors, Greene against his detractors, Tarlton against those who would ban plays, and William Cuckoo against jugglers both literal and metaphorical. In some ways Chettle makes an original use of his form. He employs the device of a double narrator—Kind-Hart is presenting the complaints of a third party—for juxtaposing points of view. For instance, after Anthony Now-now's diatribe against lewd ballad singers, Kind-Hart rids himself, and by implication Chettle, of any responsibility for these views: 'When I had read this rabble, wherein I found little reason, I laide it by' (ed. G. B. Harrison, Bodley Head Quartos, sig. C4). In addition, the choice of well-known and only recently dead spokesmen allows for references to be made to identifiable contemporary figures. Anthony Now-now addresses himself to 'Mopo and Pickering, Arch-overseers of Ballad singers', meaning Bancroft and Whitgift, and refers to the two sons of Old Barnes the plumber at Bishops Stafford, who, 'the one in a sweaking treble, the other in an ale-blowen base carrowle out such adultrous ribaudry, as chast eares abhorre to heare'. The section given to Greene's ghost is of special interest. Greene addresses himself to Piers Penniless; he speaks of the malicious attacks recently made on his memory by Gabriel Harvey, of the mysterious 'Blacke Booke' which never saw the light of day, and of his desire for Nashe to be revenged on Harvey:

> Awake (secure boy) reuenge thy wrongs, remember mine: thy aduersaries began the abuse, they continue it: if thou suffer it let thy life be short in silence and obscuritie, and thy death hastie, hated, and miserable.
>
> All this had I intended to write, but now I wil not giue way to wrath, but returne it unto the earth from whence I tooke it: for with happie soules it hath no harbour.
>
> Robert Greene
(sig. E2).

In a neat and appropriate way, Chettle remembers his dead friend, clarifies his own position in a prominent literary controversy, compliments a living friend, and makes a strong appeal to public interest in very topical events.

Variations on the underworld devices are many; but the pamphlets are bound together by the common fund of notions about the devil and hell on which they all draw. The Devil, for instance, is almost always presented as a comic, never a terrifying figure. His disguises, such as 'the habits of a knight *Errant*, a swearing knight, or a knight of the Poste', or as an ingrosser, an intelligencer, a constable, or a usurer, are devices of social satire. The nickname that Nashe and Dekker use for him, Signior Cornuto, suggests the image of the demon with a tail and three-pronged fork that sometimes appears in woodcuts at the front of pamphlets.

If the devil has children or attendants they are usually personified sins. In Dekker's *A Strange Horse-Race* he begets Hypocrisy, Ingratitude, Schism, Atheism, Paganism, and Apostasy. In *Greenes Newes* he has as servants Ambition, Pride, Ignorance and Obstinacy. In *The Blacke Booke* he summons his relations to hear his will made, including 'all my Striplings of Perdition, my Nephewes of Damnation: my kindred and alliance of Villany and Sharking (sig. E). In *Pierce Penilesse* and *The Returne of the Knight of the Poste* Greediness, Famine, and Desolation are servants of hell. Emblematic scenes or tableaux are sometimes devised to show the activities in hell. *Greenes Newes* describes the triumphant arrival of a cardinal: 'Then was there brought foorth a most stately Chayre, which was prepared of purpose, in which Chayre *Ambition* and *Pryde* having placed the *Cardinall*, old *Ignorance* and young *Obstinacy* . . . taking it upon theyr shoulders . . . they returned to Hell' (sig. G4). In *A Strange Horse-Race* there is a masque performed by catchpoles and a banquet of bankrupts, who dine off bonds, bills obligatory, statutes, and executions.

The inhabitants of hell include personified sins, classical and biblical figures, and all the common butts of Elizabethan satire, especially those such as apothecaries, tailors, barbers, and doctors whose life on earth is seen as dedicated to the preservation of the body. On the whole, historical figures, apart from the Pope and his entourage, are not described in hell until the pamphlets of the 1640s, although they often come out of hell to visit the upper world. The pamphleteers made nothing of Lucian's form of the dialogue of the dead in which historical figures of different periods were brought together in hell for the purpose of satirical conversation. Perhaps it was the product of the kind of sceptical and enquiring mentality they did not possess.[12] The classical figures are either types of the eternally damned, such as Ixion and Sisyphus, always pictured in everlasting torment, or occasionally active beings like Charon and Mercury who derive their characters from Lucian and play an important part in the running of hell. In Dickenson's *Greene in Conceipt* Greene has to ask leave of Mercury to visit the upper world, and must return to his quarters when 'the power of Mercuries caduceus drawes me hence.' In Dekker's *Newes from Hell*, a very Lucianic Charon with 'a beard filthyer then a Bakers mawkin that hee sweeps his ouen, which hung full of knotted Elf-locks, and serues him for a swabber in fowle weather to clense his Hulke' (*Non-Dramatic Works*, II, 120) rows the damned to hell in his leaky boat built out of bits of coffins and fleshless shinbones. There is also a three-headed Cerberus to be pacified and a Mercury who runs messages between Elysium and the Underworld.

In *Lanthorne and Candle-light* and in *Dekker his Dreame* Rhadamanth, Aeacus, and Minos are servants of the Devil. Christian and Pagan elements usually co-exist easily, except in the work of Dekker who occasionally feels a need to allegorize his classical borrowings. Charon 'by interpretation is Ioy' in *Dekker his Dreame*, and also 'Good Councell, & Sweete Perswasion to prepare for death', characters very unfitting for the bleary old boatman of *Newes from Hell;* the rivers of hell are each given a 'morall and Mysticall' meaning with Acheron as 'the river of Bitterness' and Cocitus the Water of Repentance.

The torments of hell include the standard classical punishments of Hades, raging heat which burns and scalds but does not consume, and innumerable forms of retributive punishment. *Dekker his Dreame* is one of the few pamphlets to use the idea of extremes of temperature, which so caught the imagination of Dante. Hell-fire is the first feature of his lower world: 'About This, Diuels stood round, still blowing the fire, / some tossing soules, some whipping them with wire' (*Non-Dramatic Works*, III, 30). But infernal cold, though a more controversial idea, has Biblical precedents:

> I called to minde . . . that vpon earth I had heard many great Schollers defend, that there was no Cold in hell: But then (turning ouer the leaues of my memory) I found written there, that Iob once spake thus. They shall passe from the waters of *Snow* to too much *Heate* (*Non-Dramatic Works*, II, 46).

His verse description of the damned freezing in hell has a rugged power much stronger than anything in the humorous pamphlets:

> *Heere* I beheld (mee thought) *Soules* scar-crow-like,
> Some bound, some hang bi'th' heeles, whose heades did strike
> The *Icy-knobbed-roofe*, toss'd too and fro,
> By Gusts implacable, able down to throw
> Rampires of *Brasse;* which still beate out the *Braines*,
> And still Renewde them with Plangiferous Paines.
> (*Non-Dramatic Works*, II, 44)

In accounts of retributive punishment the pamphleteers excel in vindictive fancies. Nashe has Piers Penniless conjecture as to whether hell is truly a place where

> one ghost torments another by turnes, and he that all his life time was a great fornicator, hath all the diseases of lust continually hanging vppon him, and is constrained (the more to augment his misery) to haue congresse euery houre with hagges and old witches . . . as so

of the rest, as the vsurer to swallow moulten gold, the glutton to eate nothing but toades, and the Murtherer to bee still stabd with daggers, but neuer die (*Works*, I, 218).

By implication Nashe dismisses the idea as popular fantasy here, but in his more ambitious work *Christs Tears over Ierusalem* there is no doubt as to what lies in store for the damned:

Wherein sooner thou hast tooke extreame delight and glory, therein shalt thou be plagued with extreame & despiteous malady. For thy flaring frounzed Periwigs lowe dangled downe with more Snakes than euer it had hayres. In the moulde of thy braine shall they claspe theyr mouthes, and gnawing through euery parte of thy skull, ensnarle their teeth amongst thy braines, as an Angler ensnarleth his hooke amongst weedes (*Works,* II, 140).

Few writers could match the grotesque fertility of this conception, but instead were content to allow the idea of retribution to find its natural expression in the antithetical phrases of Euphuism:

For gaudie geane on earth, they shall haue gnashing of teeth in Hell: for vaine fame on Earth, they shall haue shame in Hell: for curtesie, and wayting, they shall haue cursednesse and wayling: for short wealth, endless want . . . for pleasant perfumes, most stinking smels: for short pleasure on earth, euerlasting paines in hell (Lupton, *A Dreame,* sig. B4).

And they were not sparing of horror in expressing the idea that hellish torments were eternal.

Boyce has it that the popularity of the underworld genre in the Renaissance was due to a combination of two motifs, 'a literary motif—the vision of the lower world—and an ethical or philosophical motif—the idea of the democracy of death'.[13] But in fact despite the basis of moralizing on which most of these pamphlets are set, the ethical motif that Boyce mentions is not very prominent. Death the Leveller may rule in Lucian's hell, but not in that of the pamphleteers. Their major emphasis is on the fact that the damned are getting the punishment they deserve, not that they are people from all ranks of society at last made equal in death. It is a more limited concept, born partly from feelings that those who have become more than usually prosperous on earth should afterwards have to pay for it, and partly perhaps from the guilt felt by those whose prosperity was growing in the face of a traditional sense of the worthlessness of earthly goods. Only Dekker makes anything of those themes that enrich and universalize Lucian's *Dialogues,* on both occasions in passages of consciously Lucianic material, concerned with Charon and with the crossing of Acheron rather than with hell itself. In *Newes from Hell* he translates the idea of Death the Leveller into English terms in describing Charon's barge:

> It is for al the world, like *Graues-end Barge:* and the passengers priuiledged alike, for ther's no regard of age, of sex, of beauty, of riches, of valor, of learning, of greatness, or of birth . . . *Will Summers* giues not *Richard* the Third cushions, the Duke of *Guize* and the Duke of *Shoreditch* haue not the bredth of a bench between them. *Iane Shore* and a Goldsmiths wife are no better one then another (*Non-Dramatic Works,* II, 117–18).

In a passage of *Dekker his Dreame* clearly separated from the Bible-inspired body of the work by its Lucianic tone, he describes Charon taking from his passengers all they have owned on earth:

> As *Death* hath no respect of persons, for the beggers dish & the kings standing cup of gold, are to him of one weight; so he spoyleth all men of all that they possesse, *Princes* of their *Crownes* . . . *Age* of *Experience, Youth* of *Comeliness.* And as they enter into the *Lists* of the world, weake and vnfurnished; So must they go forth, *Beaten, Vanquished,* and *Disarmed* (*Non-Dramatic Works,* III, 34).

But the theme is not an intrinsic part of this sort of conception of hell, only a borrowed idea; nor is there much development of the notion that those who suffer on earth will be rewarded after death; Lupton's emphasis in *A Dreame* is typical in being on the sufferings of Dives in hell; Dekker's Elysium for poets and malcontents is hardly what Christ envisaged in his sermon on the mount. Although these pamphlets borrow indiscriminately from the Bible, from folklore, and from pagan legend, more often treating their material satirically or comically than seriously, the spirit of religious scepticism associated with Lucian and with later dialogues of the dead is absent. The values are those common to Elizabethan popular satire.

Most of these devices of form have the effect of emphasizing the pleasure rather than the profit to be gained from the pamphlets. One mode of writing that they did often use which does the opposite, their most overtly didactic method, is the formal defence or attack on a specific subject or point of view, mounted with the aid of the forms and terminology of rhetoric. This form is used in a less fragmentary way and seems to bear a less arbitrary relationship to content than, say, the underworld devices or the dialogue, but nevertheless it is, like the others, a chosen rather than a necessary structure, and the kind of material it is used to present is essentially the same, although more clearly defined. The subjects discussed in this way are various, but all of them lend themselves to polemical treatment: the merits and demerits of women, for instance, the taking of tobacco, dancing, drinking, usury, even sleeping in church. Such pamphlets draw attention to their formal organization, with headed chapters, numbered and subdivided points, the citation of authorities, marginal notes calling attention to points of style or indicating a transition to another section, and all the paraphernalia of learning. Rather than beguile, exhort, or terrify their readers out of vicious practices and anti-social behaviour these authors choose to argue, reason, and if necessary baffle with logic.

A pamphlet on drink, *Englands Bane: Or, The Description of Drunkennesse* (1617) by Thomas Young, a former student of the Inns of Court, illustrates the method at its barest. It begins dully, but ends entertainingly with many touches of real observation. It is constructed like a sermon on a text, and designed as a kind of handbook for those in need of guidance on how to admonish drunkards. Predictably the emphasis is moral and religious, not social, and Young hopes to 'Set downe all the subtle sleights, tempting baites, and craftie allurements, which Satan useth for the ouerthrow of mankinde, by this vice of drunkenness' (sig. A2^v). To achieve comprehensiveness, he divides the sin, following Plato, into six heads, filthy talk, fornication, wrath, murder, swearing, and cursing, and devotes half the pamphlet to an academic discussion of these, chiefly consisting of quotations and examples from the Bible, with one or two from classical sources, and, the better to drive the point home, a few modern anecdotes, such as the one from Foxe's *Acts and Monuments* of John Peter, 'a horrible swearer, with whom it was vsuall to say, if it be not true, *I pray God I may rot ere I dye.*To which God said, Amen, and so he rotted away indeed, and died miserably' (sigs. C3–C3^v). Next comes a short section on the fleeting pleasures of drinking, followed by several vividly written pages on the pains. Drink not only brings about physical decay but also leads on the worse vices: 'First they visit the Tauerne, then the Ordinarie, then the Theater, and end in the Stewes. From Wine to Ryot, from that to Playes, from them to Harlots, from thence to the Diuell' (sig. E3). Some of the anecdotes are recounted with enjoyment, like the little story of the drunk who

> cralled vnder all the signes from Holborne Bridge to Saint *Giles*, because in a Moone-shine night his eyes being glazed (with the mist

of Mellego Sacke) and seeing the shaddow of the Signes vpon the ground, swore they were arrant knaues for setting the signes so low, that a man could not goe vpright under them (sig. F2ᵛ).

To finish, Young draws on the rhetorical figure Division, and categorizes drunkenness in nine species, each corresponding to an animal: it is a familiar formula which Nashe among others[14] had used earlier, but Young's observations still please. The third and fourth kinds of drunkenness are particularly vivid:

> The third is sheepe drunke, who is very kinde and liberall and sayes, by God captaine I loue you. Goe thy wayes, thou thinkest not so often of mee, as I doe of thee, and in this sheepish humour giues away his Horse, his Sword, the clothes off his backe. The fourth is Sow drunke, who vomits, spewes, and wallowes in the mire, like a Swine, and seeing the Moone shine, sayes, put out the Candle lets goe to bed, lay a little more on the feete and all is well (sigs. F2ᵛ–F3).

The Pamplet hardly seems persuasive to us now, but the form it takes is such a common one that the Elizabethans must have felt it to be effective.

An Alarme to Awake Church-Sleepers (1640), another pamphlet which combines the functions of handbook and sermon, is similarly constructed. Chapter III lists some of the most common reasons for sleeping in church, ranging from personal debility—'I am old and weake, and so am to bee borne withall'—to detailed academic objections to the preacher's style—'Hee is no scholler; Hee is not read in humane writers. Hee is no Logician, Historian, Linguist. He is not acquainted with the Schoole-men. He citeth not the Testimonies of the Fathers, and Doctors of the Church' (p. 104). These are followed, for the benefit of those called upon to admonish such sinners, by suggested answers, the four for the first objection being honest rather than diplomatic:

> A.1. The older thou art, the more need hast thou to abstaine therefrom, as being nigh thine end. 2. Thou wouldest be loath, that whilst thou art thus sleeping death should seize on thee. 3. As old as thou art, thou canst watch longer about thine owne businesse, or in hearing some vaine, triviall, sinfull discourse, or in seeing a Play, or some vaine show . . . 4. *Simeon* was as old as thou art, yet when he came into the Temple, did hee not thus behave himself (pp. 96–97).

In the first chapter, 'The seuerall kindes of sleepe', the author makes use of the figure Similitude as a means both of varying his material in the approved rhetorical manner, and also of showing off his style, with a comparison between death and sleep opening with the traditional image of the beds as graves that George Herbert uses in his poem 'Mortification'. Such diversion was not uncommon in plainly-written handbook-style pamphlets. John Blaxton, in *The English Vsurer* (1634), an equally closely argued pamphlet constructed also in the logical manner, has a section entitled 'similitudes to which usurers, and usurie are resembled', some of them borrowed from Henry Smith's *The Examination of Vsury;* a usurer is like a man who pretends to rescue a drowning person but actually kicks him back into the sea, or like ivy round an oak, and usury 'is like that Persian tree, that at the same time buds, blossomes, and beares fruit'. This sort of fanciful folk-wisdom was perhaps intended to supply ammunition for argument, and certainly to constitute a source of authority.

The pamphleteers believed stoutly in the value of authority and precedents, and had little confidence in the judgement of the individual; many pamphlets proved their points simply by listing a vast number of authorities who agreed with them, along with traditional examples. Anthony Gibson in *A Womans Woorth* (1599) proves that 'the body of a woman is the heauen of humane perfections, and her soule the treasurie of celestiall and diuine vertues' by this method, contributing nothing whatsoever of his own except the selection and arrangement of the authorities. The printer of *Conclusions Vpon Dances* (1607) by John Lowin, the actor, makes it clear that none of the conclusions on this controversial subject are Lowin's own: 'The Author . . . doth not lay the foundation of his arguments upon his owne opinion, nor upon the fantasticall imaginations of some others: but upon the word of God it selfe' (sig. A4). And indeed every single point in the pamphlet is referred to the authority of the Bible. From biblical quotations it is discovered that dancing in former times could be holy, profane, or indifferent; the occasions on which holy dancing was permitted, the grounds for justifying 'indifferent' dancing, who might dance and with whom, and at what times dancing should be entirely forbidden, were all questions settled by recourse to biblical evidence.

Occasionally a writer did use his own judgement as the basis for his conclusions, although in handbooks or pamphlets offering moral guidance on troublesome issues this was rare. William Heale wrote *An Apologie for Women* (1609) to refute the views of William Gager who held that wife-beating was permissible; his structure and chapter-headings suggest the usual method of arguing from authority:

> An Introduction to the discourse following . . . That it is not lawfull for a husband to beat his wife is proued by reasons drawne from

Nature . . . The same confirmed by rules of morallitie or ciuill policie . . . The same discussed by the Ciuill and Canon Lawes . . . The same euinced by the law of God . . . The Conclusion.

But Heale's pamphlet is distinctly different in that it argues from branches of knowledge other than literary authority, as well as using a far greater variety of literary devices. He argues methodically, from point to point; there are three ways of interpreting civil law on the subject of wife-beating, three grounds on which a husband may be judged the superior marital partner, three kinds of faults wives commit, and three corresponding kinds of punishments. But all the paraphernalia of rhetorical organization with which Heale's argument is tricked out does not conceal the underlying commonsense and humanity. Never mind the fact that birds and animals furnish human beings with examples of mutual devotion and kindliness between the sexes; a man should not beat his wife, not just because of this, but because, on a basis of moral equality, if a wife's adultery wrongs her husband, then equally, his adultery wrongs her. Literature may well furnish precedents for misogyny, particularly the works of 'olde Tragedians', but the truth is that a wife is what her husband makes her; if he plays his part well, so will she play hers:

> In agreeing matches, where man and wife make up the sweet harmonie of mutual loue . . . yee may obserue a heauen of gouernment, the Husband intent on his businesse, the wife imploied in her house, the children brought up religiously, their attendants, their seruants, eueryone . . . busied in his place (p. 12).

None of these observations will seem to us especially striking, and it would be wrong to regard them as unusually progressive for their day; but what is significant and refreshing in this context is Heale's straightforward good sense which dictates to him the views to take and permits him to argue confidently from natural feeling without having to refer to the pronouncements of Plato or Moses as standards.

Heale was not alone amongst writers of pamphlets in having something serious to say and in stating it directly and personally, but he was unusual. Much commoner is the attitude taken by Barnaby Rich, author of more than two dozen pamphlets, in the preface to *The Fruites of Long Expeience* addressed to 'the kinde and curteous reader: "To avoyd Idlenesse, I haue betaken me to write, and to make my selfe sociable with the multitude, I haue mingled matters of importance, with matters of small regarde" (sig. A2). The implications of this, arbitrariness, desire for popular approval, willingness to mix the light and the serious, characterize much pamphlet satire and go a good way towards accounting for its miscellaneous flavour. The taste for literature which castigated vice in general terms and a sensational manner was widespread, and pamphleteers were prepared to try every trick in order to satisfy it.

> The *Printer* praies me most vncessantly,
> To make some *lines* to lash at *Lechery*

wrote John Davies of Hereford in the *Epigrams* that were ordered to be burnt by official edict in 1599, and we can be sure that this printer's motives were not those of the Puritans. More than anything these writers wanted to be read, and they had discovered that combining a censorious tone with novelty of form was the way to do it.

4
Conventions of Subject Matter

i

The aim of this section is to begin drawing together the pamphlets as a group by considering their typical subject matter and the attitudes and ideas which determine its treatment. The prose-pamphlet as a genre was new to the sixteenth century, and the pamphleteers rejoiced in a wide freedom of form, borrowing from established writers old and new, inventing to suit themselves, even improvising in the course of composition. By contrast, the subjects of these pamphlets and the range of their attitudes strike us as remarkably limited and conventional. Anyone even slightly familiar with medieval satire will find himself at home with them. The mode of writing was new, but the purposes it served were not; nor was the pamphlet audience one to which literary work had never been addressed before, although many pamphlet readers would probably have had fathers who were illiterate.

In the Middle Ages there existed at least one literary mode which reached a mass audience, that is, the spoken sermon, and it was the tradition of the sermon that popular moralizing pamphlets followed. Sermon themes and attitudes permeated secular written literature, in particular popular poetry, and formed that element in the literature of attacking abuses that John Peter in *Complaint and Satire in Early English Literature*[1] called 'complaint' in distinction to the other mainstream of didactic literature, satire. Peter distinguished complaint from satire in five particulars—its conceptual nature as opposed to the dealing of satire with the 'concrete particularity' of real life, its impersonality, a range restricted by adherence to a rigid moral system, a corrective aim, and a tendency to generalize. Peter in fact asserts that during the period when the popular pamphlet was on the upsurge complaint as a mode was rapidly disappearing and being replaced by satire. He suggests that the complainant as a figure was no longer in touch with the mood of the times, and that moralists themselves recognized that the style and attitudes of complaint had become, by the last decade of the sixteenth century, passé (p. 111). But in moralistic prose such developments are much slower to take place than in, say, the work of satirists such as Donne, Hall, and Marston, who wrote for a generally more educated public.

While the pamphlets often merge the methods of complaint and satire, the subjects most commonly singled out for attack in them are essentially similar to what Peter saw as the major themes of medieval complaint. He divided the themes into four categories: attacks on professions, attacks on non-professional malefactors, attacks on abuses, and finally the fundamental ideas about life in which the whole attitude of complaint had its basis. The professional group most subject to attack in medieval literature was, according to Peter, the clergy, followed by the law, the city as represented by usurers and merchants, the medical profession, and lastly beggars and prostitutes. The pamphlets concerned themselves far less with religious abuses, which by this time had largely been hived off into a literature of controversy of their own. But perhaps because of the current spate of popular writing on crime and prisons, or at any rate because of the same impulse that gave rise to it, both major and minor representatives of the law, lawyers, attorneys, and solicitors, as well as constables, serjeants, and jailors, come in for much attention. The view of the law that is implied suggests that the Elizabethans found a good deal wrong with those aspects of legal administration which impinged upon their daily lives.

The ignorance and inefficiency of constables were topics for amusement, but the jailor's failings were more serious. 'For cruelty they exceede *Nero*', claimed Geoffrey Mynshul,[2] and in *The Overburian Characters* the jailor 'is a creature mistaken in the making, for he should be a Tyger. But the shape being thought too terrible, it is couered and he weares the vizor of a man: yet retaynes the qualities of his former fiercenes, currishnes; and ravening' (ed. W. J. Paylor, p. 91). William Fennor also used animal images to describe the serjeants who arrested him, calling them 'a brace of bandogs', 'ravens' and 'cormorants'. The serjeant was commonly seen as hard and pitiless. 'For mony he wil betray his own father', wrote Mynshul, and he was also prepared to connive at the crafty escape of a well-heeled suspect, as Hutton and others illustrate. Feelings ran high against several aspects of the legal system, especially against debtors' law, but they were vented, at least in the pamphlets, not against the most influential administrators, judges and Justices of the Peace, and not, as in medieval sermons, against injustice in a large and abstract sense, but against the enforcers of the law and against lawyers. Nashe allowed that the best lawyers were men to be held 'in high admiration, as well for theyr singular gifts of art and nature, as theyr vntaynted consciences wyth corruption', *(Works,* III, 215), but he shared the general view that such men formed a minority. The typical lawyer was venal and covetous, outwardly respectable, inwardly deceitful, pretentious and hypocritical, 'compounded of nothing but vociferation and clamour' *(Works,* III, 214). Greene in *A Quip for an Upstart Courtier* called lawyers 'extorting Ambodexters that wring the poore'. Rich wrote tartly, 'They make their plea according to the pennie, not according to the trueth', and he included in his condemnation 'Clarkes and vnder officers, that are cryed ovt vpon by poore sutors, for their extorting & taking of vnreasonable fees' *(Roome for a Gentleman,* p. 23). The highwayman Ratsey, who sometimes, though not always, robbed the rich to pay the poor, saw his robbery of a lawyer as a kind of rough justice: 'You picke euery poor mannes pocket with your trickes and quillets, like Vultures praying uppon your Ayents purses' *(Ratseis Ghost,* sig. 4ᵛ).

The proliferation of lawyers as a class was seen as symptomatic of the degeneracy of the times; in the good old days 'When lowlinesse, neighbourhood, and hospitality liued in England', when virtue predominated over pride, and simplicity over fine clothing 'then the lawier was a simple man, and in the highest degree was but a bare scriuener, except Judges of the land which tooke in hand serious matters, as treasons, murthers, felonies and such capitall offices' *(A Quip,* sigs. C4ᵛ–D). But now went the cry, despite the law's delays, which the pamphleteers lamented as much as anyone in *Bleak House,* laws multiply, men grow increasingly litigious, and even a poor man will raise a law-suit 'if a Hen do but scrape in his orchard'.[3]

This traditional hatred of lawyers is here reinforced by a perception of what we can now see to have been a highly significant cultural change. In *The Irish Hubbub* Barnaby Rich wrote, attacking the lack of moral conscience in contemporary society. 'If mens words, and deeds, and thoughts, did concurre in one, we should vndoe the lawyers, neither should wee neede so many scryueners, to write obligations' (p. 29). This expression of longing for a simpler past may remind us of Jack Cade's bitterness against those who can read and write in *II Henry VI;* he wished to kill all lawyers:

> Is not this a lamentable thing, that of the skin of an innocent lamb should be made parchment? That parchment, being scribbled o'er, should undo a man? Some say the bee stings; but I say, 'tis the bee's wax, for I did but seal once to a thing, and I was never mine own man since (IV, ii, 74–79).

As Rich and Shakespeare perceived, theirs was a world where the written obligation was replacing the verbal oath, and the new currency was one where an agreement no longer took the form of spoken concurrence between two men known to each other as reliable, but rather consisted of a formal settlement arranged by a third party and enforceable by the mysterious machinery of law.

Another group also attacked for making unscrupulous use of professional expertise to exploit a helpless and dependent public was doctors. Chaucer's gold-loving physician whose 'studie was but litel on the Bible' has proved to be an enduring type. The Elizabethan physician was also avaricious, and associated with religious beliefs of doubtful orthodoxy and not infrequently with black magic.[4] He was regarded both with scepticism and with fear. On the one hand there was the image of the quaint old man with his flask of urine, his leeches for bloodletting, and his pills and suppositories, who could safely be mocked: 'Their Phlebotomies, Losinges, and Electuaries, with their Diacatholicons, Diacodions, Amulets, and Antidotes, had not so much strength to hold life and soule together, as a pot of *Pinders* Ale and a Nutmeg', wrote Dekker, in *The Wonderfull Yeare* (Plague Pamphlets, p. 36). But there was also a more mysterious figure, a combination of fortune-teller, magician, and spy like Dr Simon Forman, or Subtle in *The Alchemist* when he plays the cunning-man for Abel Drugger. The true physician was expected to be a scholar, perhaps with a degree from a continental university, and a command of Latin and Greek as well as astronomy.[5] The pamphleteers did not satirize men like this, but rather quacks and pretenders. Nashe in *The Terrors of the Night* traced the sinister career of the successful quack. He and his like begin as surgeon's apprentices, and become ambitious:

> Presently they rake some dunghil for a few durtie boxes and plaisters, and of tosted cheese and candles endes, temper vp a few oyntments and sirrups: which hauing done, farre North, or into some such rude simple countrey, they get them, and set vp (*Works*, I, 364).

They soon build up a spurious reputation amongst the ignorant by dint of 'vaunting and prating, and speaking fustian in steed of Greek', grow richer, and return to London. Their services are sought after by needy gallants, and their fame spreads up the social scale. By careful cultivation of a reputation for necromantic skills they can become the confidants of courtiers and privy to the secrets of the kingdom.[6]

Surgeons, on the other hand, were mundane figures who dealt with the less respectable ailments of the rich; in particular, they healed swashbucklers' wounds and cured venereal disease.[7] Apothecaries compounded potions and aphrodisiacs and traded on the ignorance of the poor with their fearsome mixtures. The one in Greene's *A Quip* makes 'purgation pills, and glisters' to settle the gallant's queasy stomach and prescribes 'his oyle of Tartar, his *Lac virginis*, his camphire dissolued in veriuice' to cure his pimply complexion. Chettle, in *Kind-Harts Dreame*, tells a series of anecdotes about the blunderings of quacks; in one, a physician, called upon to cure a man with one sore eye, rendered his patient totally blind and then charged him a hundred marks. In this section of his pamphlet Chettle addresses a strong admonition to 'the impudent discreditors of Phisickes Art', calling them 'blinde abusers of the blinde' and condemning their love of money, 'the marke for which ye play the makeshiftes, nay the murtherers, not of the common enimie, but your owne country-men'. William Parkes, in *The Curtaine-Drawer Of the World,* attacks the profession with greater eloquence, but this time directs his criticism not towards quacks, but towards doctors of genuine merit who abuse their gifts for venal ends:

> If he shall skant us in his skill, or slacke his indeuor, or not visite us because wee are poore, or because of our wealth shall linger out disease for expence . . . If he shall forsake a sicke body in the hospitall, to go painte a faire face in a Ladies Chamber, if he shall feare us out of our wits with strange words . . . if he shall do any of those things let him know the abuse is great, and the wrong iniurious, and that this diuine gift was not lent him to that end, and though that hee considers not these things, they shall one day be considered and laid unto his charge (pp. 41–42).

Usurers, merchants, and corn-hoarders had appeared in social satire since the days of Langland. The usurer, traditionally a figure condemned by God, had accumulated a wealth of literature to himself. His appearance and personal characteristics were standardized.[8] He was an ugly old man—'as ill a head in forme (and worse in condition) than euer held a spout of lead in his mouth at the corner of a Church'—[9] with a large worm-eaten nose, often afflicted with dropsy, rheumatism, or gout. He wore a long gown, lined with the fox fur that pamphleteers looked on as the dress of the nouveau riche: 'His gowne is throughly foxt, yet he is sober, for hee looketh as though he quenched his thirst with whay and water.'[10] He epitomized miserliness to the extent of starving himself and living in the greatest discomfort; Middleton in *The Blacke Booke* told an anecdote of a woman who scratched letters on the coals in a usurer's hearth and found them in the same place a year later. In descriptions of the Seven Deadly Sins he was named as a type of Avarice, and also of Envy, as well as being descended from Coveytise in *Piers Plowman*. His way of life was wretched, and his end damnation: 'The Vsurer shrinkes up his guts with a staruing dyet, as with knot-grasse: and puts his stomacke into his purse. He sels time to his customers, his food to his cofers, his body to languishment, his soule to Satan.'[11] He was cursed by his own children and despised by Christians. Charles Courtney, in the story of his life and crimes[12] told how he robbed a usurer without pangs of conscience. Henry Smith in *The Examination of Vsury* (1591) listed punishments for usury including excommunication and being forbidden the sacraments. Thomas Lupton in *A Dreame of the Devill and Dives* stated that 'usurers are excluded the Kingdome of Heauen whereby they are sure to be entertained in the Kingdom of hell' (sig. E5ᵛ). Gerard de Malynes, himself a prosperous merchant, urged that 'they should not be buried in a Christian buriall' (*Saint George for England*, 1601, p. 66). If the usurer was worsted in dealing, or confronted with any form of human kindness, he would hang himself.

This very completely realized figure was at the heart of a moral and ethical controversy which had centred on the subject of usury since the days of St Jerome. The pamphleteers drew on all the arguments they could muster to rationalize their desire to hold on to what remained of a vanishing society where the rich supported the poor because it was their duty. They longed to stem the growth of a profession which, in its vast contemporary expansion, seemed yet another symptom of widespread and inevitable social upheaval. One important aspect of this upheaval has been summed up by a historian of usury as 'the increasing bifurcation of human relations into distinct spheres: one, the world of friendship and free services; the other, the world of commercial intercourse and the economic calculus.'[13] Usurers sinned against God by disobeying the commandment to love one's neighbour as oneself (Smith, *The Examination of Vsury*, pp. 5–6) and against nature by causing money to engender and reproduce. Lodge in *Wits Miserie, and the Worlds Madnesse* stated the case: 'It is contrary to nature, you know, for a barren thing to yeeld fruit: How can it then be possible, that mony (being a barren thing) should engender money (?)' (p. 30). They defrauded helpless borrowers, deceived the simple, and robbed widows and orphans. Time and again the pamphleteers invoked the sanctions of traditional pieties in their denunciation: 'Where is loue, where is mercy, when lending of money is become merchandize?' (J. Blaxton, *The English Vsurer*, p. 15).

The opprobrium attached to the usurer and his profession was not an isolated phenomenon, but closely linked with a whole network of standard abuses such as the transference of English currency to foreign markets, the conversion of arable land into pasture, and the hoarding of grain, all of them connected with a perception of economic change. The usurer was often associated with the farmer, another much abused figure, for hoarding grain to sell at a high price. Both exhibited the same heartless cruelty towards the poor and needy. The devil in Middleton's *The Blacke Booke* at one point disguises himself as 'a couetous Barne-cracking Farmer', and in Dekker's *Worke for Armorours* farmers and usurers fight together in the army of Money against the forces of Poverty, and are urged by Heartlessness to hoard corn till prices rise to their highest. Significantly, the exploitation of the upper classes by the new men was another crime laid to the usurer's charge. Lodge in *An Alarum against Vsurers* linked the usurer with the broker and the whore as city sharks who combined forces to rob heirs newly come to London. The story of the simple young man of good birth who comes up to London to see the world and is defrauded of all he possesses is one of the most common cautionary tales in the pamphlets. He falls a ready victim to the conycatchers and cheats of London's underworld, but it is important that middle-class professional men, in particular lawyers and merchants are the initial agents of his downfall. A lawyer and a merchant stand at the side of the heir in Middleton's *Father Hubburds Tales* as he signs over his ancestral property to debtors, and it is the lawyer who instructs the young man in the prodigal ways of the London gallant.[14] The merchant was known for his cheating habits and tightfisted business practices, to which Richard Johnson in *Looke on me London* (1613) ascribed the enmity between gentlemen and citizens:

> Truly, truly, in my minde, this mortal enuy betweene these two worthy Estates, was first begotten by the cruell vsage of couetous merchants in former ages, by hard bargaines gotten of Gentlemen; and still nourished as reuenges taken of both parties (sig. B4).

'[They] eate our English Gentrie out of house and home', stated Lodge, who in *An Alarum against Vsurers* blamed merchants for the fact that 'the prisons are replenished with young Gentlemen'. But it was the merchant's wife rather than the merchant himself who was the more vividly evoked. Nashe's brilliant portrait of Mistress Minx epitomizes the type:

> a Marchants wife, that wil eate no Cherries, forsooth, but when they are at twenty shillings a pound, that lookes as simperingly as if she were dancing the Canaries . . . so finicall in her speach, as though she spake nothing but what shee had first sewd ouer before in her Samplers (*Works*, I, 173).

She combines all the vices of the middle-class citizen upstart within the traditional form of the 'simpering dame', Lechery, who so offended Lear. She is affected, extravagant, and vain; she tires her husband and servants with her ceaseless craving for unprocurable dainties while lying all the morning in bed; and her modest appearance and dainty manner barely cloak her lascivious desires. Rowley in *A Search for Money* tells how merchants, despite their known avarice, lose all their money through their wives' insatiable love of finery:

> They told us, that they themselues had often brought many of Mounsieur Moneys followers home to their houses with great hope (in the end) to attaine the companie of his compleate selfe, but their wiues (came he neuer so priuately) would finde him out, and then . . . straight he was transform'd into chaines, iewels, bracelets, tyres, ruffes of the fashion, which still were no longer liv'd then a wonder, nine days, then it was stale, and they must haue a new (p. 15).

While merchants and their wives were particularly at enmity with gentlefolk, and usurers with both poor and rich, landlords, in the sense both of landowners who leased land to tenants and of house owners who let out part of their property as lodgings formed a group who abused only the poor. They had fewer conventionalized features than usurers, perhaps partly because they were figures new to complaint writing in which the part they played in the transference of money between social groups and classes now procured them a place. Their habit of rack-renting[15] their tenants could be accommodated in diverse satiric contexts; in Lupton's *A Dreame of the Devill and Dives* they were blamed for living extravagantly at the expense of their tenants; in John Deacon's *Tobacco Tortuered* they were shown extorting money from their tenants in order to satisfy their craving for tobacco, and in *The Death of Usury* (1594) rack-renting was seen as a direct cause of the general increase in prices. There were country landlords and city landlords, each with their own exploitative practices. Nashe depicted country landlords in terms of foolish heirs with citified aspirations beyond what contented their fathers,

> casting that away at a cast at dice, which cost theyr daddes a yeares toyle, spending that in their Veluets, which was rakt vppe in a Russette coate: so that their reuenewes rackt, and their rents raised to the vttermost, is scarce inough to maintaine ones rufling pride, which was wont to be manie poore mens reliefe (*Works*, I, 33).

Dekker's view, in *Worke for Armorours,* of the 'young Land-lords, who haue cause to go dancing to Church after your old rotten fathers funerals' (*Non-Dramatic Works*, IV, 147) was essentially similar, and he made the common equation between landlords and farmers as 'cormorants of the countryside' who starved and abused the peasantry.[16] The more traditional figure of the oppressive gentleman farmer and landlord, who misused his position in order to tyrannize over his cottagers, encroach upon his neighbours' property, enclose the commons, and squeeze his tenants to death, was singled out for criticism by Stubbes in *The Anatomie of Abuses* and Greene in *A Quip*. City landlords had their own techniques as predators. Chettle in *Kind-Harts Dreame* asserted that their covetousness was responsible for much London crime, and also for the increasing number of brothels:

> By their auarice Religion is slandered, lewdnes is bolstered, the suburbs of the Citie are in many places no other but darke dennes for adulterers, theeues, murderers, and euery mischiefe worker: daily experience before the Magistrates confirmes this for truth (p. 46).

They ran businesses from their residences, and forced the tenants to buy all their goods from them at inflated prices; they favoured foreign lodgers over Englishmen because they would pay more; and landladies would lend impoverished tenants money in return for pawned clothing at extortionate rates of interest. The realistic depiction of these mundanely seedy practices suggests, in contrast to the accounts of country landlords, that these were abuses with which the pamphleteers may have found themselves uncomfortably familiar.

Throughout this pamphlet literature personal experience mingles with convention, social observation with moralizing tradition. Satire by trade or profession, a conventional device of medieval literature, was still common, though dying out in the seventeenth century, and the pamphleteers were as fond as medieval sermonists had been of listing the professional tricks of dishonest tradesmen, butchers, bakers, grocers, colliers, brewers, tapsters, and so on. The humbler ranks of society were as guilty of avarice and price as the nobler; several of these groups were also attacked for their social aspirations.

The baker's daughter corresponded to the merchant's wife; Clothbreeches in Greene's *A Quip* jibes at the baker 'You craue but one deare yeare to make your daughter a gentlewoman' (sig. E3), and rejects the tanner from his committee of jurymen for cheating his customers to raise the money that will push his children up the social ladder. The tailor had more individual traits than most of this group. He, too, was a type of cheating tradesman, known for giving short measures, and sometimes depicted as poor, by Rowley in *A Search for Money*, for instance, but more often he was despised because of the spurious wealth he had gained from pandering to the vanity of the rich. To writers who stood by the old values of a non-commercial, socially stable, hierarchically inflexible society he represented one form of the upstart, 'terse, spruise, neatified', as Dekker put it, symbol of a world where social distinction was defined in terms of wealth and its visible symbols; he seemed the direct agent of the deadly sin pride[17] as it manifested itself in rich clothing and superfluous living, he wore his heart on his richly embroidered sleeve, and he moved in the service of the new order to a place on the social ladder not rightfully his by birth or deserts. 'Whereas in my time he was counted but goodman Taylor,' says Greene's Clothbreeches, 'now hee is growne since veluet breeches came in, to bee called a marchant or Gentleman Marchant Taylor, geuinge armes and the holy Lambe in his creast' (*A Quip*, sig. C2). In Croshawe's *Visions, Or, Hels Kingdome* a devil at the gate of hell halts the entry of a band of a hundred tailors, with the claim that 'It is impossible if they be Taillours there should bee so few, for the least band that comes dayly of them, is not less than a thousand or twelve hundred, and we haue already so many, that we know not where to pile them' (p. 169).

At the end of the list of satirized professions comes one of the most criticized, entertainment. It was only to be expected that minstrels, ballad-singers, jugglers, conjurers, actors, and poets should on the whole get a bad press from so moralistic a group as the pamphleteers, although their own trade was by no means remote from some of those they abused. Medieval preachers had seen these popular entertainers as in some sense their rivals,[18] and had inveighed against them as sources of worldly and profitless amusement, as time wasters, and as liars. All these objections and many others were levelled against actors in Elizabethan times.[19] They were closely associated with several of the deadly sins, in particular pride, lechery, and sloth. George Whetstone, in *A Mirour for Magestrates of Cyties* (1584) suggested that the acting profession was dependent for its success in impersonation on one of the chief elements of pride: 'This badge of pryde, Brauerie in apparel, is necessarie for base persons, that publiquely in open Theaters, presente the personages of Emperoures, Kinges, Dukes, and such Heroycall Estates: For that they haue no other meane to perfourme their action' (sig. D4ᵛ). Dekker, in *Iests to make you merie* used 'proud as Player' for a proverbial phrase on analogy with 'envious as a serpent' and 'lecherous as a mountaine goate'. William Rankins, in *A Mirrour of Monsters,* an allegorical attack on the stage, described Pride and Lechery marrying in the playhouse. The author of *A Second and Third Blast of Retrait from Plaies and Theaters* (1580) claimed that not only were plays and players full of lechery but also that 'in the representation of whoredome, al the people in mind, plaie the Whores.'[20] Dekker in *The Seuen Deadly Sinnes of London* associated Sloth, his fourth sin, with the moral influence of the players: 'Tis giuen out that Sloth himselfe will come, and sit in the two-pennie galleries amongst the Gentlemen' (*Non Dramatic Works,* II, 53). Rankins, one of the players' greatest enemies, called them creatures sent by the devil, whose daily activity of impersonation was a kind of blasphemy. The author of *This Worlds Folly* considered that acting was 'barbarously diverting Nature, and defacing Gods owne image, by metamorphosing humane shape into bestiall forme' (sig. B2).

The fact that even pamphleteers who did themselves write plays, like Gosson, Rankins, Munday, Greene and Dekker, did not scruple to attack actors in their pamphlets, provides more evidence that in the eyes of the world acting as a profession was lowly, degrading, and despicable. But if the actor in general was despised, the individual talents of the great performers Alleyn and Burbage did not go unnoticed, as we know from their enormous contemporary reputation,[21] and in fact the profession had its supporters among the pamphleteers, though they were outnumbered by its detractors. Nashe, a staunch defender of the theatre, splendidly vindicated the plays from charges of time-wasting and corruption, and praised English actors, especially 'famous *Ned Allen*' above the 'squirting baudie Comedians' to be found beyond the seas (*Works,* I, 215). And Chettle was sensitive enough to realize that much of the actors' ill-repute derived from the uncouth behaviour of their audiences and the crudity of some of the plays they performed, as well as from the very exposed nature of their activities:

> Faults there are in the professors as other men, this the greatest, that diuers of them beeing publicke in euerie ones eye, and talkt of in euery vulgar mans mouth, see not how they are seene into espe-

cially for their contempt, which makes them among most men most contemptible (*Kind-Harts Dreame*, p. 44).

Although Nashe had much to say in favour of the arts of acting and poetry he was one of the most vehement in dispraise of ballads and ballad-writers.[22] He objected to their want of art and to the easy way they found popularity with an uncritical audience. Chettle, in a more moralistic vein, had his character Anthony Now-now urge the civic authorities to take action against

> a company of idle youths, [who], loathing honest labour and dispising lawfull trades, betake them to a vagrant and vicious life, in euery corner of Cities & market Townes of the Realme singing and selling of ballads and pamphletes full of ribaudrie, and all scurrilous vanity (*Kind-Harts Dreame*, p. 15).

Ballad-makers were proverbial for lying, and Will Kemp claimed that he was obliged to go into print with his *Nine daies wonder* because he was 'thereunto prest on the one side by the pittiful papers pasted on euery poast, of that which was neither so nor so' composed by the 'impudent generation of Ballad-makers'. The pamphleteers also deplored the increase in the number of poetasters and bastard poets who pestered the stationers' stalls with 'unprofitable stuffe', as Barnaby Rich called it, and the feeling against them ran high. Dekker called them 'thin-headed fellowes that liue vpon the scraps of inuention', 'Word-pirates', and 'ranck-riders of Art'. Conversely, the true poet was often looked on with affection, and his craft with admiration. The poet had his accepted stereotype, the terms of which, as Greene presents them in *A Quip*, are familiar to us now:

> An ouerworne gentleman attired in Velvet and Satin . . . a waste good and an unthrift, that he is born to make the Tauerns rich and himself a beggar . . . He is a king of his pleasure, and counts al other Boores and Pesants, that though they haue mony at command yet know not like him how to Domineere with it to any purpose as they should (sigs. F3–F3^v).

The poet's fecklessness, his poverty, his unworldly nature, were looked on in general with a tolerant eye. 'He is so oft out of his wits, as he verily imagines himself the man in the Moone', wrote Richard Brathwait.

The subject of poetry itself was a centre of moral controversy. The majority of the pamphleteers praised it for its moral qualities. Rich, for instance, admired the 'fictions of Poets' for their 'commendable resemblances' to life and their exemplary doctrine 'euermore extolling of the vertuous, and imbasing of such as do seeke their felicitie in vice' (*Faultes faults*, p. 39). Nashe, too, eulogized poetry in conventional terms—'a more hidden & diuine Kinde of Philosphy, enwrapped in blinde Fables and darke stories'—but also in *Pierce Penilesse* made the interesting claim that the practice of contemporary poets had produced a significant effect on the state of the language: 'They haue cleansed our language from barbarisme, and made the vulgar sort here in *London* (which is the fountaine whose riuers flowe round about *England*) to aspire to a richer puritie of speach, than is communicated with the Comminaltie of any Nation vnder heauen' (*Works*, I, 193). On the other hand, Stephen Gosson presented the Puritan and extreme Platonic view in *The School of Abuse*, and the author of *This Worlds Folly* extended his attack on the stage to include 'those mercenary squitter-wits miscalled Poets, whose illiterate and picke-pocket Inuentions can *Emungere plebes argento*, slily nip the bunges of the baser troopes' (sig. B3). That poetasters undeservedly flourished, labouring to please an ignorant audience 'amongst whom a strained stile is in better account than the best laboured lines' (Rich, *Faults faults*, p. 40), that poetry was an unprofitable pursuit, that poets were mad, were all truisms; and even poetry's defenders testified to the decay of the art: 'Poetry, if it were not a trick to please my Lady, would bee excluded out of Christian buriall' (Nashe, *Works*, III, 149).

The writer of pamphlets was a newer creature, and by no means so kindly regarded.[23] No writer would admit that his productions belonged to the *genus* pamphlet, and four of those best known to us in this form, Greene, Nashe, Dekker, and Rich,[24] explicitly treated the whole idea with scorn. Nashe in *The Anatomie of Absurditie* cited objections which came during the period, to be standard: that pamphleteers wrote pretentiously, presenting themselves 'as the Authors of eloquence and fountains of our finer phrases, when as they sette before vs nought but a confused masse of wordes without matter, a Chaos of sentences without any profitable sence' (*Works*, I, 10), that they relied too strongly on old and worthless romances, and that they indulged in hypocritical moralizing 'wresting places of Scripture against pride, whoredome, couetousnes, gluttonie, and drunkennesse'. There is some irony in the form of these attacks; Nashe, in this last phrase, is clearly objecting to complaint constructed in the form of set descriptions of the Seven Deadly Sins and embellished with Biblical exempla, which he used only a few years afterwards to compose *Pierce Penilesse;* Greene, whose later works traded on the legend of his own loose living, objected to the dissoluteness of pamphlets, and Dekker, never a man of few words, thought them too numerous and long. Rich, often dull, pretentious, and uninventive to the point of self-plagiarism, condemned 'our new writers of this age' along with their readers for 'these Paper monsters' with their 'dull conceits'. These attitudes, apparently so devoid of self-awareness, suggest a mixed response to the stigma of print, half apologetic, half-defiant: it is as if these writers wanted both to show a consciousness of the failings of popular writing, and at the same time to dare anyone else to find these failings in their own work.

The second category of stock subjects for criticism or abuse consists of groups identified by traits other than profession, such as women, social upstarts, foreigners, atheists, and puritans. As in medieval complaint, by far the most prominent was women. The range of attitudes towards them was vast, and took in extremes of both abuse and adulation. The basis of this literature was medieval clerical misogyny, and reactionary writers persistently referred to the old commonplaces, that women were proud, lecherous, and domineering, vain of appearance and empty of head; foolish virgins, shrewish wives, and lustful widows were still ubiquitous. But these well-established stereotypes did not go unchallenged; women writers defended their own sex, and men began to accept the blame for many female faults. That there was a boom in literature on women was in itself a subject worth mentioning. In some cases the awareness of this boom took the form of a comment by a woman or pro-feminist writer on the superabundance of anti-feminist literature. The pseudonymous author of *Iane Anger her Protection for Women* (1589), one of the earliest defences of women, combined her jibe at the literary vanity of men with a suggestion that attacks on women were the last resort of the desperate male hack:

> The desire that euery man hath to shewe his fine vaine in writing is unspeakable, and their mindes are so caried away with the manner, as no care at all is had of the matter: they run into Rethorick, as often times they overrun the boundes of their own wits ... If they had stretched their inuention so hard out at last, as it is at a stand, there remaines but one help, which is, to write of vs womē (sig. B).

But despite an increasing awareness of women as social beings and the growth of the ideal of monogamy, it was the vicious nature of women that dominated popular writing. Female faults and vices fall into several categories, those resulting from pride, or from lechery, or from the desire to emulate men, and a general group created by the traditional spirit of misogyny that had prevailed in popular literature since medieval times. This last group consists of faults rather than vices, traits such as obstinacy, contrariousness, inconstancy, spite, ill-temper, cunning, deceit, love of gossip, and inability to keep secrets. Joseph Swetnam, in the notorious *Araignment of Lewd, Idle, Froward and unconstant women* (1615), put forth a common piece of proverbial wisdom on female garrulousness: 'Diuers beasts, and fowle, by nature haue more strength in one part of the body than in another, as the Eagle in the beake, the Vnicorne in the horne, the Bull in the head . . . the Serpent in his tayle: but a womans chife strength is in her tongue' (pp. 40–41). There was a current saying that, while men have many faults, women have only two—all they say and all they do.

Most real vices were associated with pride or lechery; in particular, pride accounted for over-delicacy and the sinful desire to ape women of higher social status, while lechery led to dissimulation, the use of cosmetics, and the love of fine clothes. Over-delicacy was sometimes just a facet of feminine perversity, as in the lively description in *The Batchelars Banquet* (1603) of the gadabout wife off to a fair:

> By the way she will aske for twenty things, for milke, because she cannot away with their drink, for pears, plums, & cherries: when they come neere a towne, he must run before to choose out the best Inne: ever and anon as she rides, she will of purpose let fall her wand, her maske, her gloves, or something els for him to take up, because she will not have him idle (ed. F. P. Wilson, Oxford, 1924, p. 72).

But it could also be seen as indicative of ill-conceived aspiration towards nobility, in the merchant's wife, for instance, and in Barnaby Rich's upstart gentlewoman:

> And there is no remedy, but my Lady must be coacht, she can not go to church to serue God without a coach: shee that her selfe and her mother before her, haue travailed many a myle a foote, can not now crosse the breadth of a streete, but she must haue a coach (*The Excellency of good women*, 1613, p. 19).

The love of fine clothes, too, was regarded both as social and as personal vanity; cosmetics, on the other hand, obscured the distinction, not between high and low birth, but between honesty and prostitution. In Elizabethan popular morality virtue consisted almost as much in the appearance as in the deed: 'It is not enough to be good, but she that is good, must seeme good: she that is chast, must seeme chast' (T. Tuke, *A Treatise Against Painting*, 1616, p. 10). The author of

Hic Mulier: Or, The Man-Woman (1620) felt that city wives even exceeded whores in their love of painting: 'Nay, the very Art of Painting . . . they haue so cunningly stoln and hidden amongst their husbands hoords of treasure, that they decayed stock of Prostitution (hauing little other reuenues) are howerly in bringing their action of *Detinue*[25] against them' (sig. C).

Painting links pride with lechery. Cosmetics were seen by many as an invention of the devil to tempt women to sin, and the outcry against them was great. Gascoigne, Nashe, Stubbes, Rich, Averell, Tofte, Swetnam, Dekker and Prynne, amongst others, mentioned the subject and cited a host of imposing authorities including St Paul, St Chrysostom, Tertullian, Ambrose, Eusebius, Cyprian, and Origen in support. The dangers of cosmetics made from ingredients such as white lead, sulphur, and alum were known,[26] but rarely mentioned in the pamphlets: it was morality rather than health or hygiene that gave grounds for objection to them. First of all, painting was unnatural; it distracted the all-too-flighty feminine mind from more important considerations; it took up time that could be better spent in praying, and money that should have been used to succour the poor. Women, in any case, were excessively lustful by nature, without further incitement. 'Stay not alone in the company of a woman, trusting to thy owne chastity, except thou be more stronger than *Sampson*, more wise than *Salomon*, or more holy than *David*' (Swetnam, *The Araignment*, p. 22).

Aping of men by women was regarded as a peculiarly contemporary phenomenon, and a symbol of the turmoil of current morality. 'Since the daies of Adam women were neuer so Masculine,' exclaimed the author of *Hic Mulier*. King James himself objected to the 'insolencie of our women, and theyr wearing of brode brimed hats, pointed doublets, theyr hayre cut short or shorne, and some of them stilettos or poniards, and such other trinkets of like moment.'[27] Dekker, in *The Seuen Deadly Sinnes of London*, called modern women 'Mens shee Apes' for their absurd and slavish adherence to men's fashions.

> If men get vp French standing collers, women will haue the French standing coller too: if Dublets with little thicke skirts (so short that none are able to sit vpon them.) womens foreparts are thicke-skirted too: by surfetting vpon which kind of phantasticall Apishnesse in a short time, they fall into the disease of pride (*Non-Dramatic Works*, II, 59).

In two companion pamphlets on this subject, *Hic Mulier* and *Haec-Vir*, each illustrated with lively woodcuts showing the sexes wearing each

HIC MVLIER:
Or,
The Man-Woman:

Being a Medicine to cure the Coltish Disease o the Staggers in the *Masculine-Feminines* of our Times.

Expreſt in a briefe Declamation.

Non omnes poſſumus omnes.

Miſtris, will you be trim'd or truſs'd?

1. Title-page of *Hic Mulier: Or, The Man-Woman* (1620). This woodcut, specially designed for this pamphlet, shows two masculine women at the barber's shop, one having just had her hair cut short, the other about to do so.

HÆC-VIR:
Or
The Womanish-Man:

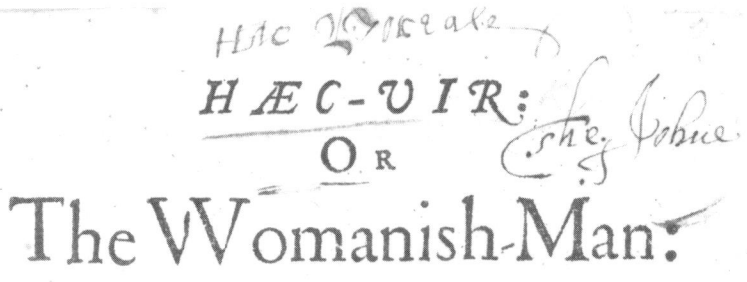

Being an Anſwere to a late Booke intituled *Hic-Mulier*.

Expreſt in a briefe Dialogue betweene *Hæc-Vir* the Womaniſh-Man, and *Hic-Mulier* the Man-Woman.

2. Title-page of *Haec-Vir: Or The Womanish-Man* (1620). This specially-designed woodcut shows a masculine woman, with short hair, mannish hat, and boots with spurs, and an effeminate man with a battledore and shuttlecock.

other's clothes, this kind of unwomanly behaviour is seen as evidence of a new desire for self-assertion. In *Hic Mulier* it is condemned as unnatural and immodest, 'an infection that emulates the plague', but in *Haec-Vir* there is an unusual and eloquent plea for liberalism towards women:

> You condemne me of Vnnaturalnesse, in forsaking my creation, and contemning custome. How doe I forsake my creation, that doe all the rights and offices due to my Creation? I was created free, born free, and liue free: what lets me then so to spinne out my time, that I may dye free?
> To alter creation, were to walke on my hands with a face erected, with a body cloathed, with a mind busied, & with a heartfull of reasonable and deuout cogitations; onely offensiue in attire, in as much as it is a Stranger to the curiositie of the present times, and an enemie to custome (sigs. B1ᵛ–B2).

This kind of attitude is rare, for the view of women as servant and vassal, as man's intellectual, emotional and spiritual inferior, was widely prevalent, but nonetheless a conception of the sex war, sometimes expressed in strikingly modern terms, was begining to emerge. The woman in *Haec-Vir* reationalizes her assumption of masculine garb as an instinctive effort to preserve the balance of the sexes: 'Now since . . . it is necessary there be a distinct and speciall difference between Man and Woman, both in their habit and behauiours: what could we poore weake women doe lesse . . . then to gather vp those garments you haue proudly cast away' (sig. C2ᵛ). In *Iane Anger her Protection for Women* the author saw the conflict in terms of animal warfare: women before men are likened to the goose before the fox. They are misinterpreted and misused by calculating adversaries: 'We being wel formed, are by them fouly deformed: of our true meaning they make mockes, rewarding our louing follies with disdainful floutes' (sig. B3). Yet men on their own are hopelessly inadequate: 'Without our care they lie in their beds as dogs in litter, & goe like lowsie Mackarell swimming in the heat of sommer' (sig. C1ᵛ). But while 'Jane Anger' claimed that women are morally superior, her real feeling was clearly that men are naturally, in every sense of the word, dominant; and, sadly for modern feminists, the woman speaker in *Haec-Vir* concludes: 'Be men in shape, men in show, men in words, men in actions . . . then will we loue and serue you; then will wee heare and obey you' (sig. C3ᵛ).

The main theme of the many pamphlets on women was twofold:

woman as related to man, and woman in society. The kind of general ideas evoked by this subject in medieval complaint, of the decay of physical beauty and the vanity of the flesh, were beginning to recede into the background. Although woman was still seen through the eyes of a male satirist as a creature enslaved by pride and lechery and degraded by a multiplicity of faults inherent in her sex, there was nonetheless a growing sense of the complexity of human relations. Some male writers saw that their own prejudices were to blame for the apparent failings of women; women had long been as men found it convenient to see them: 'Alas, poore Girles! If you appeare carelesse in your dresse, you are quickly taxed of discontent; and if neate in your dresse, you are censured of pride' (R. Braithwait, *Ar't asleepe Husband?*, 1640, p. 289). The norm of woman in society was the housewife and mother; and she was expected to conserve the marriage by modifying her behaviour and disposition to suit those of her husband. The ideal marriage relationship was often described through analogies, especially that of the mutual dependence of body and soul.[28] Dekker, in *Penny-Wise Pound-Foolish* (1631) uses a beautiful image from music to express his vision of marital harmony:

> The Bed where a Husband and Wife lyes, is that Musicke roome, where the soules of them both, play in the most excellent consort: All Discords before are here put into time, all Iarres so winded up, with the Strings of Concord, that no Harmony can be sweeter (sigs. D–D1^v).

The sense of woman's special marital function should not obscure the fact that she was coming to be regarded more often as a partner in the marriage, and as man's moral and spiritual equal in society.

The upstart was another traditional butt of complaint, and his treatment in the pamphlets also had its basis in medieval attitudes. These attitudes did not substantially alter during the Elizabethan period, despite the important changes taking place in the structure of social life and economic organization, and evidence of more widespread social mobility. The upstart aroused fear and detestation because he was the violator of a fixed social order. Although it was often conceded that nobility was, or should be, a matter of merit rather than birth, it was clear that the pamphleteers cherished a special regard for their concept of the true-born English lord who made himself worthy of his place at the top of the hierarchy by carrying out his duties to the commonwealth. Greene's adulatory Character of the Knight in *A Quip* exemplifies this belief and emphasizes the quality of humility so admired two centuries earlier in Chaucer's Knight: 'He regardeth hospitality & aimeth at honor with releeuing the poor, you may see although his landes & reuenewes be great, & he able to maintain himself in great brauery, yet he is content with home-spun cloth' (sig. E). Barnaby Rich purported to believe in nobility by desert, but his definition of the true knight in comparison with the newly created upstart makes his point by citing all the traditional qualities of knighthood:

> The one are known by their troupes of seruantes, that are attendant and waiting vpon them; the other are knowne by a poore Page or Lackey . . . The one are knowne by their hospitality and good house-keeping . . . The other are known by their frequent [sic] to other mens tables (*Roome for a Gentleman,* 1609, sig. I1ᵛ).

Social climbing was observed and condemned at all positions on the scale; merchants' wives, bakers' daughters, tanners, and tailors all practised it. Socially conscious wives vied with one another for precedence: 'One makes her plea, my husband is a Squire, and I will giue place to none but to my Lady; an other will say, my husband is a Doctor, and why should not I go with the formost?' (*Roome for a Gentleman,* sig. B3ᵛ).

The figure of the upstart had a number of recurrent characteristics: he was often the aspiring son of a father who, though wealthy, was humble and unpretentious. The son scorns the father's way of life and when he inherits, adopts a contrasting one for himself, by rack-renting or evicting his father's tenants perhaps, or by selling up his father's land and taking off to London to squander the proceeds. Alternatively he might be a citizen's son who wants to disguise his origins and become gentrified. His efforts to dress and behave modishly evoke some striking caricatures, both of the excesses of current fashions and of the awkwardness of someone trying to ape a style that is unnatural to him. At the beginning of his section on pride in *Pierce Pennilesse* Nashe details for mockery the mannerisms adopted by the bourgeois aspirant in his endeavour to cultivate an image of nobility:

> All malcontent sits the greasie son of a Cloathier, & complaines (like a decaied Earle) of the ruine of ancient houses: whereas the Weauers loomes first framed the web of his honor . . . Hee will bee humorous, forsoth, and haue a broode of fashions by himself. Sometimes (because Loue commonly weares the liuerey of Wit) hee will be an *Inamorato Poeta,* & sonnet a whole quire of paper in praise of Lady *Swin-snout,* his yeolow fac'd Mistres . . . Al *Italionato* is his

talke, & his spade peake is as sharpe as if he had been a Pioner before the walls of *Roan* (*Works*, I, 168–69).

The upstart in *Father Hubburds Tales* is more genteel in his origins as a country heir, but equally ridiculous in his city affectations, 'so metamorphosed into the shape of a French puppet, that at first we started, and thought one of the Baboones had marcht in, in mans Apparel' (sig. C2). Extravagant clothing is often the mark of the *novus homo*. Nashe writes of 'Carterly vpstarts, that out-face Towne and Country in their Veluets, when *Sir Rowland Russet-coat*, their Dad, goes sagging euery day in his round Gascoynes of whyte cotton' (*Works*, I, 160).

The pamphleteers universally deplored the breaking of class barriers and the blurring of distinctions; all kinds of satirical techniques, trades satire, Seven Deadly Sins, visits to the underworld, commentaries on English life by outsiders, allegorical narratives, were used to attack the upstart. In *Newes from Hell* Dekker includes a curious monologue spoken by the degenerate son of a wealthy upstart. The speech seems to express both the son's sense of guilt at the injustice committed by his father in order to procure wealth—'hee had ploughs to teare vp deere yeeres out of the guts of the earth i' th' country'—and his feeling that he himself has been corrupted by his inheritance:

> No man has more vndone me, than he that hath done most for me: ile stand too't, its better to be the son of a Cobler, then of a Common council man: if a coblers sonne and heyre runne out at heeles, the whoreson patch may mend himselfe, but wee whose friends leaue vs wel, are like howre glasses turn'd vp, though we be neuer so full, we neuer leaue running, till wee haue emptied our selues, to make vp the mouths of slaues, that for gaine are content to lye vnder vs, like Spaniels, fawning, and receiue what fals from our superfluity (*Non-Dramatic Works*, II, 106).

The fact that no-one was content with his allotted role in the commonweal was commonly mentioned by writers seeking to explain their dislike of comtemporary social unrest. George Whetstone, in *A Mirour for the Magestrates of Cyties*, a pamphlet intensely backward-looking in its assumptions and attitudes towards social upheaval, indulges in an elaborate conceit comparing a state disordered in the constitution of its hierarchy to an improperly clothed body. The inference that different classes and professions maintain the same sort of relationship to the state as the clothes do to the body is a medieval one:

> Where the head is crowned with a Pantofle, as the Subject of the vnconstant multitude: where the passages of the heart, which is the Organe of the Soule, are fixed with the continuall exercise of sinne, (the Figure that the Prelates sownde Doctrine, are but wordes of warnyng, and no causes of amendment: where the brest and bodie lyes naked to euery peryl, I meane, the good Maiestrates, are neither reuerenced, feared, nor obayed: where the handes are bownde to the knees, in token, that the Gentlemen are thrawle to the Marchantes:
>
> Where, on the knees is fastened a Cap and a feather, and about the legges, a Swoord and a Target buckled, in signe, that the Cittizyns desire the honour they can not gouerne, and leaue their trauayles, whiche woulde inritch the Common-wealth . . . I say: as a man thus deformed, buckled and bownd on a heape, would soone perysh, for want of sustenance: euen-so, a Common-wealth, thus confused, would soone be confownded, for lacke of good Order (sigs. C3–C3ᵛ).

Foreigners, as well as being attacked for the particular vices associated with their race, were also felt as disrupting and contaminating presences in English life. John Peter claims that in medieval literature foreigners were disliked 'mainly out of jealousy, because of their commercial success',[29] and hence that those most commonly attacked were the Lombards, the Jews, and the French. Pamphlet xenophobia ranged more widely, and attacks extended to cover all the nations of Europe, in particular the Spanish and the Italians. In general the surface of the attack was directed against conventional national traits, Spanish pride, German gluttony, the drunkenness of the Dutch and Danish, French immorality, Turkish blasphemy, and Italian machiavellianism. But the Englishman's propensity to imitate foreign models, especially dangerous at a time when it was the mark of a fashionable gentleman to travel extensively abroad, was the real source of disturbance. John Deacon, seeking in his polemic dialogue, *Tobacco Tortuered,* to account for the degeneracy of contemporary England in contrast with the golden past of Julius Caesar's day, relied heavily on the idea of native English innocence all too easily corrupted by foreign influence:

> We leaue our ancient simplicitie eftsoones in a forreine ayre: and (instead thereof) do too greedily sucke vp from forreigners, not their vertues, but vices, and monstrous corruptions, as well in religion and manners, as also, in framing the whole course of our life . . . from whence commeth it now to passe, that so many of our English-mens minds are terribly *Turkished* with *Mahometan* trumperies; thus rufully *Romanized* with superstitious relickes; thus treacherously *Italianized* with sundry antichristian toyes (pp. 6–10).

Rich more simply said

> We haue stolne away the pride and ambition of the *Spaniard*, the fraud and falshood of the *French*, the deceit and subtilty of the *Italian*, the drunkennesse and swearing of the *German:* we haue robbed the *Iew* of his vsury, the barbarous *Sicilian* of his rage and cruelty, the *Turke* and *Infidel* of his infidelity and vnbeliefe (*My Ladies Looking Glasse*, p. 10).

The English eclecticism of dress, based on a number of different foreign models, was also used in comic contexts. The Puritan William Rankins, in *The English Ape* (1588), a pamphlet largely devoted to this topic, regarded the readiness with which the English adopted foreign fashions and vices as indicative of inward corruption, and said that, instead of looking like a nation peaceably and justly governed, 'We seeme rather the men, which nature hath marked for a prodigious spectacle of her contrary operations' (p. 3). Dekker's *The Seuen Deadly Sinnes of London* replaced the old sins with contemporary ones, amongst which was Apishness, the vice of slavish imitation, exemplified by rich men's sons, prentices, tailors, haberdashers, and embroiderers. Apishness was begotten 'much about the yeere when Monsieur came in', that is, about 1580, and wore a suit resembling 'a traitors bodie that hath beene hanged, drawne, and quartered, and is set up in seuerall places' (*Non-Dramatic Works*, II, 60). English apishness represented a rejection of the good old ways of the national past: 'Other Countries fashions they see, but neuer looke backe to the attyre of their fore-fathers, or consider what shape their own Country shold giue them' (Nashe, *Works*, II, 141).

But the English were rarely compared unfavourably with other nations, and it is clear in most cases that the multitude of vices ascribed to foreigners, especially southern Europeans, were the commonplaces of a long tradition of English insularity and prejudice. For although each nation was allotted its conventional vices, they were not differentiated to a great degree; while pride was mainly associated with Spain, the French, Italians, Irish, and Jews also had their share of it, and Italian treachery was found in the French and Spanish alike. The 'southern climatic stereotype'[30] was hot-blooded, subtle, quick to anger, cheating, and deceitful, dandified, and compounded of all the vices associated with Roman Catholicism. If any one country was blamed more than another for England's degeneracy it was Italy, and Greene's Italianate character Velvetbreeches was a compound of all the viciousness and false values that have poisoned English life. The true-born Englishman, Clothbreeches, recalls his rival's origin: 'Thou camest not alone but accompanied with multitude of abhominable vices, hanging on thy bumbast nothing but infectious abuses, and vaine glory, selfeloue, sodomie, and strange poisoning, wherewith thou has infected this glorious Iland' (*A Quip*, sig. B2). The proverb, Inglese Italianato è un diabolo incarnato,[31] sums up much feeling on Anglo-Italian relations. Italy, the land of wit, culture and elegance sometimes depicted in drama and aristocratic literature, was absent from the pamphlets, and the emphasis fell on the degenerate society ridden with sexual vice and secret crime that formed the background to many Jacobean tragedies.

The Irish, England's nearest neighbours, were regarded as poor, ill-fed, and verminous, and Ireland a 'rugged country of rebels'. The policital aspects of the relationship between Ireland and England were of course hotly debated in political pamphleteering of the time, most especially in the writings of Barnaby Rich, who spent more than forty years of his life as a soldier in Ireland. It is interesting that although Rich must have acquired extensive personal knowledge of the Irish people and their ways his attitude towards them did not significantly change or develop between the publication of his first Irish pamphlet, *Allarme to England,* in 1578, and his last, *The Irish Hubbub,* in 1617; throughout his writing he continually affirms a stereotyped view of the Irish character still in most respects familiar. He emphasized the Irish vice of laziness, which Dekker in *The Dead Tearme* called 'the Irish mans disease', their rough manners and slovenly ways, and their emotional nature. Nashe noted in *Pierce Penilesse* that 'the Irishman will drawe his dagger, and bee ready to kill and slay, if one breake winde in his company' *(Works,* I, 188), and the expression 'to weep Irish' was proverbial. Rich also observed that the Irish were 'wonderfully addicted to giue credit and beleefe, not onely to the fabulous fixions of their lying Poets, but also to the Prognosticating Soothsayers and Witches' *(A New Description of Ireland,* 1610, p. 41), and criticized the excessive number of religious holidays they held. In his view the majority of their failings could be traced to their adherence to Roman Catholicism, and this was the answer with which he refuted the proposition that Irish discontent stemmed from English repression. In his dialogue *The Fruites of Long Experience* (1604), Captain Pill, who represents emotional opinion, puts the case for tolerant consideration of the Irish people:

> They complaine of too much crueltie used by our Nation . . . they say they are exacted, robbed and spoiled, & maimed no lesse by the

souldier that should defend them, then by the rankest rebell that is most readie to oppresse them (p. 40).

But he is answered by Captain Skill, the voice of what Rich calls 'temperate judgement';

> Could they now but consider, that it is their owne misdemeaners that draweth on these warres, by their owne entertaining of Jesuites, Seminaries, Fryers, and Massing Priests . . . some of them would rather blush, then complaine, and might rather looke for a due deserued punishment for their disloyaltie and contempt, then hope to be relieued in that which cannot be redressed (p. 41).

Rich was second to none in his detestation of Roman Catholicism, and the fact that Ireland provided a refuge for Catholic refugees made the country hateful to him.[32]

Of all religious groups Roman Catholics, predictably, generated the most hostility in the pamphlets. The abuses of the Catholic church had, of course, long been a subject of satire and complaint since the Middle Ages; in the pamphlets the attacks were all made from Protestant stances of varying intensity, although what the pamphleteers really wanted was not so much to satirize genuine abuses in the church as to create a vision of what C. S. Lewis, in another context, called 'the sheer bogy'.[33] In this way Christopher Ockland in *The Fountaine and Welspring of all Variance* (1589) summed up Catholicism for a gullible Protestant readership: 'Idolatry, worshipping of Images, masses, dirriges, and Heauen to be sold for mony, murdring of Saints, stewes in whole streets of Curtesans, blessings for meed, cursings for Enuy, are to be found in Rome' (sig. D2). Nearer home struck the idea of Catholics as underminers of the security of the state, depicted by Averell in *A meruailous combat of Contrarieties* as the slanderous tongue which incites the members of the body politic to rebellion one against another: 'Among all the enimies of a commonwealth, there is none more pernitious than the enuious tongue of false and lying Papists' (sig. D2^v). Papists misled the ignorant with their misinterpretations of scripture, and they were wily, treacherous, and hypocritical. Their worldliness was a common constituent of the image. Rich in *Roome for a Gentleman* compared true churchmen with Papists, asserting that while the former refuse worldly preferments in order to labour the more in their vocation, the latter take all they can get and 'hunt after temporall iurisdictions, & other proud titles of the world, to vphold and maintain their pride and ambition' (sig. E3).

Examples of God's wrath against Catholics were sometimes related in news pamphlets, such as *Two Most Strange And notable examples, shewed at Lyshborne in Kent* (1591), where two Spanish judges presiding at the trial of captured English sailors were struck dumb at the moment of passing sentence, and two French corn ships bringing provisions burnt up by lightning. The published confessions of recusants from the Catholic faith emphasized injustice within the Catholic church, the oppression of inferiors, and the abuse of the confessional. Patriotic pamphlets urged the readers to take direct action in the fight against popery: 'Where they pray for change, specially of Queenes, do thou pray for the long and happy continuance of her Highnesse raigne: where they hide rebellious stomaches, doo thou and thy children showe true and faithfull hearts' (A. Munday, *A Watch-woord to Englande*, 1584, p. 43).

Comic pamphlets drew on anecdotes about lewd priests and superstitious Catholic laymen as a reliable source of laughter. In *Greenes Newes both from Heauen and Hell* are two typical tales, one of a priest relieving a childless woman's condition with 'the holy sacrament of extreme unction', another of a priest curing a girl possessed by the devil: 'hee gaue her a glister of holie water, the which hee has no sooner put up into her bodie, but the devil immediatly forsook her' (p. 40). *Tarltons Newes* (1590) similarly tells a Boccaccio-like story of Friar Onyon who visits a beautiful woman and seduces her by pretending to be an angel.[34] Rich confirmed the stereotype of the lecherous priest from his own experience:

> A Massing Priest is such a medicine in a mans house that hath a child-bearing woman to his wife, that where they bee retained to lye lydgers, it is tenne pound to tenne pence oddes, that the good Wife, or Lady, or Gentlewoman (or whatsoere she be) will proue fertill (*The Irish Hubbub*, 1617, p. 54).

The Puritans were the only group to use the popular pamphlet to any effective extent for their own special views, and the Puritan outlook on many topics, on abuses such as drinking, dicing, and prostitution rather than on malefactors themselves, coincided with the traditional outlook of complaint to so great an extent that it is often difficult to isolate Puritan attitudes as such. Nashe, with his eye on Philip Stubbes's *Anatomie of Abuses,* lashed out at the way the Puritans bombarded the press with their second-hand denunciations of old vices:

> [They] make the Presse the dunghill whether they carry all the

muck of their mellancholike imaginations, pretending forsooth to anatomise abuses and stubbe vp sinne by the rootes, whē as there waste paper beeing wel viewed, seemes fraught with nought els saue dogge daies effects, who wresting places of Scripture against pride, whoredome, couetousnes, gluttonie, and drunkennesse, extend their inuectiues so farre against the abuse, that almost the things remaines not whereof they admitte anie lawfull vse *(Works*, I, 20).

It was the drama, the medium which Puritan opposition finally succeeded in quenching for a couple of decades, that created the stereotyped Puritan and satirized him. Individual pamphlet writers, Nashe in particular, attacked Puritan attitudes, their repressiveness, their pretentious preaching, and their intolerant zeal, but the stock figure from plays of the period of the sententious Puritan sermonizer with his sour face, his nasal voice, his cropped hair, his precise speech, his dismal moralizing, and his enthusiastic devotion is absent. Neither was the atheist, long a stock figure of complaint, evoked as a stereotype; his sin was treated as a branch of pride, and commonly used to demonstrate the futility of relying on human powers. In the face of such constant evidence of God's works as everyday events provided for the pamphleteer, disbelief in God seemed eminently unreasonable: and the literalist interpretations of the Bible so characteristic of the Puritans reinforced this view. 'No wise man living will be so foolish to think that Christ would haue made mention of hell twice in one chapter, unlesse that there had bene a hell' (T. Lupton, *A Dreame of the Devill and Dives*, sig. D6). It was the atheist's dismissal of the concept of hell, rather than his abandoning of the joys of heaven, that the moralistic writers emphasized, and in descriptions of life after death he was made to receive his due. In Croshawe's *Visions, Or, Hels Kingdome* he inhabits the infernal regions with others—apothecaries, barbers, and surgeons—who have devoted their lives to the preservation of the flesh, and with them laments his wasted days: 'O Memory! thou art to mee a cruell Divell! memory of the good I might haue done, memory of those wholesome counsels I haue despised, and the euils I haue committed. Ah! that thou dost afflict me!' (p. 187).

Many abuses were attacked without being related to the specific figure of a malefactor, and, as in medieval complaint, most of these were associated with the vanities of the flesh. Fine clothing and the use of cosmetics continued to be denounced in religious terms; the painting of the face, for instance, was blasphemous in that it obscured and implied criticism of God's image, and cosmetics precluded the users from seeking God's forgiveness: 'How shall they looke vp to

God with a face, which he doth not owne? How can they begge pardon, when their sinne cleaves vnto their faces, and when they are not able for to blush?' (T. Tuke, *A Treatise Against Painting*, p. 18). The desire to glorify one's appearance in any way was symptomatic of the deadly sin of pride; in decorating themselves women became temptresses like their mother Eve and lured men to sin. The idea of paint and rich dress to cover rotting flesh, the most potent of all conjunctions to express the perennial theme of *vanitas vanitatum*, occurs again and again. The way skulls are used in Elizabethan drama reflects this preoccupation in one form; the pamphleteers dwelt rather on the image of the physical breakdown of the flesh itself. Dekker in *The Wonderfull Yeare* evokes the horror of the plague by imagining the delicate body of the courtier 'now . . . so pampered with superfluous fare, so perfumed and bathed in odoriferous waters' as it would be in the grave 'Where his goodly eies, y^t did once shoote foorth such amorous glances, must be eaten out of his head: his locks that hang wantonly dangling, troden in durt vnder foote' *(Plague Pamphlets,* p. 29).

Nashe in a long passage in *Christs Teares over Ierusalem* rebukes proud women by reminding them of what they must come to, in similar terms but with more extravagantly unpleasant physical details: 'Your morne-like christall countenances shall be netted ouer and (Master-like) cawle-visarded with crawling venomous wormes. Your orient teeth Toades shall steale in to theyr heads for pearle; Of the ielly of your decayed eyes shall they engender them young' *(Works,* II, 139).[35] The baroque quality of Nashe's imagination entirely differentiates the tone of his writing from medieval moralizing on the vanities of the flesh, and brings to it a kind of perverse vivacity. The subject of physical decay seems to have been particularly stimulating to his sensibility. In *Pierce Penilesse* he deals with the vanity of old age and the ravages of venereal disease in prose of a grotesque vitality; his style here is terser and wittier:

> These aged mothers of iniquitie will haue their deformities newe plaistered ouer, and weare nosegyes of yeolow haire on their furies foreheads, when age hath written, Hoe God, be here, on their bald burnt parchment pates. Pish, pish, what talke you of old age or balde pates? men and women that haue gone vnder the South pole, must lay off their furde night-caps in Spight of their teeth, and become yeomen of the Vinegar bottle:[36] a close periwig hides all the sinnes of an olde whore-master; but *Cucullus non facit Monachum:* tis not their newe bonnets will keepe them from the old boan-ach *(Works,* I, 181–82).

That the sins of the flesh were visited on the flesh before and even after death was a commonplace, and warnings against pride often stressed this idea. These medieval attitudes to fine clothing were supplemented by a more contemporary awareness of the connection between changing personal appearance and changing social and moral standards. Accounts both of upstarts and of gentlemen corrupted by city ways used extravagant dress to represent false values. Even the humblest members of society were not immune from this form of pride; 'the plowman that in times past was contented in Russet, must nowadaies haue his doublet of the fashion with wide cuts', commented Lodge in *Wits Miserie*. Too much attention paid to personal appearance was seen as symptomatic of moral confusion; people respected finery without regard to what lay beneath. The author of *A Health to the Gentlemanly Profession of Seruingmen* (1598) commented sourly: 'In some places of England, let but a payr of Veluet breeches make their apparance, what personage so euer they retayne to, they shal haue more Caps, and lowe Legges, then the Lord Maior of Applebie with his whole limit, precinct, or corporation'(sig. D3ᵛ).

Clothes obscured distinctions of rank, and even of sex. Prynne in *The Vnlouelinesse, of Love-Lockes* (1628) objected to the fashion for long hair in men because it was taken up no less by gentlemen than by 'Foote-boyes, Lacquies, Coach-men, Seruingmen (yea, Rogues that ride to Tiburne, and the very froth and scumme of Men)', while Rich in *The Honestie of This Age* disliked 'this imbrodering of long lockes, this curiositie that is vsed amongst men, in freziling and curling of their hayre', because he thought it 'fitter for Mayd Marion in a Moris dance, then for him that hath either that spirit or courage, that should be in a gentleman' (p. 35). The spirit of such reflections is at once Puritan and reactionary, and the same ingredients, in different proportions, appear in most discussions of other popular habits and abuses, such as dancing, drinking, gambling, and smoking.

Dancing, an activity popular at all levels of society from the Queen to the rural labourer, had been denounced in medieval times for its association with lechery and with the unmanning influence of female company;[37] it was denounced in the same terms in the Renaissance by the influential Spanish humanist, Vives, and by the Puritans. One anonymous attack on dancing, published in 1581, was entitled *A Treatise of Daunses, wherin it is shewed, that they are as it were accessories and dependants (or Thinges annexed) to whoredome: where also is proued, that playes are ioyned with them*. In a solemn pamphlet called *Conclusions Vpon Dances* (1607) the author, perhaps the actor John Lowin, grudgingly conceded that dancing might on occasion be allowed, but subjected to so many restrictions as to nullify it entirely as a spontaneous and pleasurable pastime. Men and women might not dance together, and in any case dancing was not becoming to men; persons of different social status should not dance together, or in each other's presence 'except that superiours doe bidde or invite the inferiours to the same'; all 'profane' and 'artificial' dancing should be avoided since 'humaine mindes can not be intended nor attentive to the Art of Dancing, and to the prayse of God together'.

More interesting and various was the treatment of tobacco-taking, a new and conspicuous habit. Many pamphlets were written claiming to show the 'true use' of what some saw as a panacea, others as an invention of the devil. Full-scale attacks on tobacco, such as King James's *A Counter-blaste to Tobacco*, published anonymously but not unrecognized, were fewer in number than defences, but weightier. There were three main grounds for objections: that it harmed health, that it was socially unpleasant, and that it was morally wrong. The chief objection on grounds of health seems, at any rate in relation to the others, logical: smoking tobacco causes unnatural drying up. 'I neede not to stand long vpon this point', writes I. H. in the sardonically titled *Work for Chimny-sweepers* (1602), 'seeing that daily practise & experience teachth vs, that heat increaseth heat . . . so that in natural reason and common sence it seemeth true that the extreame & violent dri'th & heat of Tabacco, maketh it far vnfit & vnwholsome for thin & cholericke bodies' (sig. B4^v). Among the effects of unnatural dryness, which disturbed the chemical balance of the body, might be included sterility, 'rawe and undigested humours', and premature old age. Tobacco also caused melancholy, a disease to which those of too dry a nature were subject, and affected the brain. It could even bring about a general disorganization of the faculties: 'Being in any way taken into the bodie, it tortureth & disturbeth the same with violent eiections both vpward and downeward, astonisheth the spirites, stupifieth and benummeth all the members (T. Venner, *A Briefe and Accurate Treatise, Concerning The taking of the fume of Tobacco*, 1621, sig. B1^v). In addition it was poisonous: 'It hath a certaine venomous facultie joyned with the heat thereof, which makes it haue an Antipathie against Nature, as by the hateful smell thereof doth well appeare' (King James, *A Counter-blaste to Tobacco*, p. 4).

James had much to say also of the social unpleasantness of smoking, especially to non-smokers, as for instance that the wife of a smoker must either 'corrupt her sweete Breath therewith, or else resolve to live in a perpetual stinking torment' (p. 12). Tobacco-takers spit, cough, bluster, and breathe out black fumes, like the personification in the dialogue *Wine, Beere, Ale, and Tobacco* (1630). Ill-mannered upstarts were depicted annoying their neighbours at the theatre by smoking. 'There is no Gallant but hath a Pipe to burne about London', wrote Middleton disapprovingly in *Father Hubburds Tales*. The habit was seen as destructively addictive; married men were said to squander all their wages, and heirs entire fortunes on it. James upbraided smokers for allowing the habit to gain control over them: 'You are not able to ride or walk the iourney of a Iewes Sabboth, but you must haue a reckie cole brought you from the next poor house to kindle your Tobacco with' (*A Counter-blaste to Tobacco*, p. 10).

Finally, smoking was filthy; the blackness of the smoke, it seemed, must surely transfer itself to the smoker's innards. The Devil, though suspected by Nashe's Piers Penniless and Dekker in *Newes from Hell* of being himself a 'great Tobaconist' because of his black face, warns one of his legatees in Middleton's *The Blacke Booke:* 'Looke how the narrow alley of thy pipe shewes in the inside, so shall all the pipes through thy body'.

The moral objections made by the pamphleteers to smoking had more to do with emotion and fear than with logic or observation. They were also significantly similar to objections to other common satiric butts, such as new fashions, for example, or almost any one of the seven deadly sins. The first was that smoking wasted time and money. That tobacco was then an extravagance for most people might well be conceded,[38] but this reasonable point was often stretched to an amazing extent by writers who linked it quite directly with such major social and economic ills as the malpractices of landlords, farmers, and usurers, the decay of the gentry, the rebellious spirit of the people, and the general decadence of the times. Richard Brathwait, in *The Smoking Age* (1617), puts his condemnation of smoking into the mouth of a personification of Time, who treats the cult of tobacco as representative of the degeneracy of contemporary youth, with the warning: 'Your dayes, as they were imployed in smoake, shall end in smoake'. John Deacon, in *Tobacco Tortuered,* linked tobacco as an exotic import with the foreign influences that were held responsible for so many ills; he believed that for a young heir to take up smoking could only produce a series of the most disastrous of results. For smokers of lesser means the consequences were just as bad; wives had to economize on household expenses and children went hungry; landlords were forced to rack-rent tenants to keep themselves in tobacco; and men of all kinds, ruined by their insatiable craving, were reduced to beggary, crime, and finally even treason:

> They do then forthwith become professed malcontents against the well-setled peace of our publicke state: wishing and praying eft-

soones for their long expected Iubilee: and hoping earnestly after a preposterous deliuerance from all dutifull subiection towards their holie Superiours (p. 95).

One further objection to tobacco remained, to the pamphleteers, both the well-spring of and conclusion to all the rest: it was an instrument of the devil. I. H. in *Work for Chimny-sweepers* calls Monardus to witness that 'This hearbe seemed to bee first found out and inuented by the diuell, and first vsed and practised by the divels priests' (sig. F4). Brathwait, in a more light-hearted vein, calls it a 'Vassall to the Divell' and smokers' dens 'those Stygian-shops, those Cymerian hovels of darkness'. James likened the 'black stinking fume thereof' to 'the horrible Stigian smoke of the Pit that is bottomlesse'.

Casual references to tobacco in literature of the period invariably attacked it, but in fact many defences of it were written. They were based on praise for the health-giving properties of 'that divine drugge', as Nashe called it, sometimes tempered with warnings against indiscriminate usage. It was thought to be particularly beneficial to the English in its drying propensities because 'we are by nature subject, to overmuch moisture, and rhematicke matter' (Richard Marbecke, *A Defence of Tobacco*, 1602, p. 33), and good for treating diseases to which the moist-complexioned were subject, such as colds, excess of phlegm, coughs, and headaches. Claims were made for its powers as a purgative, in healing wounds, in relieving toothache, in keeping out the cold. The first reference to tobacco in English poetry, in *The Faerie Queene*, is to it as a curative herb. Belphoebe goes to the woods to find a healing plant to treat Timias's wounds:

> There, whether it diuine *Tobacco* were,
> Or Panachaea, or Polygony,
> She found, and brought it to her patient deare.
>
> (III, V, 32)

William Barclay, in *Nepenthes, Or The Vertues of Tabacco* (1614), was ecstatic in its praise: '[It] may bee vsed mortified at the fire to cure the asthma, or shortnesse of breath, dissolue obstructions, heale the olde cough, burning vlcers, wounds, migraim, Colicke, suffocation of the mother: and many other diseases, yea almost all diseases' (sig. A5^v). Even so, he urged that it be taken only on doctor's advice, although the conditions he imposed were not so stringent as those of Tobias Venner, who stipulated that it be taken not more than a pipeful at a time, not between meals, not until four or five hours after a meal, not by inhalation, not acompanied by liquor, and not immediately preceding a walk.

The social and moral aspects of smoking were less dwelt on in defences of it. The fact that it was relaxing and convivial was generally evident. The drug-like effects it produced on the brain were hardly advisable to mention, although William Barclay did allow that 'it maketh & induceth . . . the forgetting of all sorrows and miseries'. But the stereotyped conception of the smoker was as an idle gallant or upstart wastrel, whose habit had associations with time-wasting, decadence, and the fires of hell.

The pamphleteers tended to deal with what more permissive ages regard as the habits of normal social intercourse as if there were no mean between abstinence and addiction. 'If once a Custome, euer necessity', as the preacher Samuel Ward tersely put it in his sermon *Woe to Drunkards* (1622). The idea of innocent pleasure was in itself something of a paradox to them, and the danger of vicious dependence seemed always to loom large. An increasingly significant consideration was the wasting of either time or money. The conception of the virtue (as opposed to more material advantages) of giving up drinking, dancing, or smoking essentially depends on such values as thrift and sobriety. Prodigality with one's time or with one's possessions became as much a vice as moral depravity. Tobacco might well be poisonous and devil-inspired, but it involved, just as dreadfully, 'a great disspending of precious time' (Edmund Gardiner, *The Triall of Tabacco*, 1610, p. 19) and of equally precious money. That tobacco was expensive is certain; but we can be sure that not every man who smoked did so at the risk of his livelihood.[39] Richard Young condemned drinking with the sort of argument that might have worked as a deterrent, but cannot have been for many of his readers a very considerable possibility: 'The tiplers progresse is commonly from luxurie, to beggery, from beggery, to thievery, from the Taverne, to Tyburne; from the Alehouse, to the Gallowes' (R. Young, *The Drunkard's Character*, p. 65).

Behind such extravagant attacks as this on relatively harmless activities lay the new sense of the intrinsic merit of labour. The Reformation saw the growth of the idea that labour and even commercial enterprise might be identified with service of God. The temper of the age no longer found expression in the conception of the good life as that which was wholly given up to God in renunciation of the world. The man who made the best of his time on earth, both morally and economically, was as pleasing to God as the man who endured it only as a preparation for his afterlife. And it followed that almost all occupations which could not be classified as labour, even those that seem to us entirely innocuous, such as dancing and theatre-going, were at some time or another condemned, and idleness turned into the worst of offences, being both a major cause and effect of sin:

> An idle person is good for nothing but to propagate sinne, to bee a factor for the Devill: it faring with man, as with the earth of which hee was made; which if it bee not tilled, or trimmed doth not onely remaine unfruitfull, but also breeds and brings forth Bryers, Brambles, Nettles, and all manner of noysome and unprofitable things' (R. Young, *The Drunkard's Character*, p. 73).

Drinking and gaming, common pastimes for those not profitably employed, were particularly popular subjects for moralizing. Drunkenness, with gluttony, was one of the Seven Deadly Sins, and had long been the subject of censure. Drinking was perhaps the most commonly and vehemently attacked of all pastimes in this literature, and it does in fact seem to have represented a considerable social problem in many parts of England at this time.[40] Samuel Ward was not alone in seeing the English as 'a Nation ouerrun with drunkenes'. As in medieval satire and complaint, the drunkard was a figure both ridiculous and tragic, in his greasy doublet, out-of-heel hose, and tattered cloak, staggering and boasting in what Nashe called 'slauering brauery'. 'His kingdome is an Alehouse, and his Scepter a Can, which is seldome out of his hand: You queanes or knaues he crieth, no attendance vpon Gentlemen here, though he be but a Tinker' (W. M., *The Man In the Moone*, sig. B3^v).

Drink robbed men of reason, and turned them into beasts. Many attacks still proceeded through the traditional bestial stages of drunkenness, four or more, from sheep-drunk to swine-drunk,[41] citing well-known examples of downfall through drunkenness such as the overthrow of the Lapiths and the Cyclops and the drunken Alexander slaying his friend Clitus, associating the vice particularly with the Dutch, German, and English nations, and denouncing it by many of the same canons as tobacco-taking and gaming. Drink was said to be a cause of England's decline in virtue from the days of Caesar, when men were known for their 'ordinarie abstinence from wine and strong drinkes'. It brought about all manner of diseases 'as apoplexes, falling sicknesses, palsies, dropsies, consumptions, giddinesse of the head, inflammation of the blood and liuer, distemper of the braine, depriuation of the sense, and what not' (*A Looking-Glasse for Drunk-*

3. Title-page of *Philocothonista, or, The Drunkard, Opened, Dissected, and Anatomized* (1635) by Thomas Heywood. This lively woodcut illustrates the traditional stages of drunkenness by showing a party of revellers partially transformed into beasts.

ards, sig. A4). It gave rise to lechery, as the Wife of Bath well knew, and worse: 'The monstrous effects that follow it, as Incest, Parricide, Tresoun, Murther, and the like, are to frequent & familiar profes of it' (J. Day, *Peregrinatio Scholastica*, p. 60). 'Drunkennesse is modir of vices', as the medieval sermonists had it.[42] 'Was there ever any sinne committed which wine hath not beene an occasion of?' asked Richard Young in *The Drunkard's Character*.

Writers searching for social causes and effects in realistic terms suggested that there was an upsurge in the popularity of drinking because of the custom of pledging healths and the taking of tobacco, 'for Tobacco being hot and dry, must have a qualifier of cold and moist from the pot'. Drinking had spread, it was claimed, from the lower to the upper classes, being formerly 'the sinne of Tinkers, Ostlers, Beggers; &c. now of Farmers Citicens, Esquires, Knights' (*The Drunkard's Character*, p. 336). But also, like gambling, it was to be associated with 'them of the middle, and meaner rancke, as handicrafts men, workemen of all sorts, Labourers, Porters, Carmen, Water-bearers, and Watermen, Iourneymen and Apprentises' (R. Rawlidge, *A Monster Late Found Out*, pp. 17–18). The places where men gathered to drink and gamble were noted as the breeding-grounds for all manner of villainies:

> The conspiracie of *Madder* and *Barloe*, was hatched in a tabling house,[43] in the White fryers. Where is the current of newes but in tabling houses? forraine explorers and faulse subiectes, there heare much matter . . . Where is a desperate *Athiest* like unto harbraine *Someruile* so ready to be found as in a tabling house? (G. Whetstone, *A Mirour for Magestrates of Cyties*, sig. K2ᵛ).

The increase in the number of taverns and 'tabling houses' in London was strongly deplored in similar terms in two pamphlets separated by nearly fifty years, George Whetstone's *A Mirour for Magestrates of Cyties*, published in 1584, and Richard Rawlidge's *A Monster Late Found Out And Discovered. Or The scourging of Tiplers* published in 1628. Rawlidge in fact drew attention in his pamphlet to the work of his predecessor, calling him 'one amongst thousands', who took the ills of the capital to heart and denounced them. Both presented drinking and dicing as wasteful habits to be avoided in the interests of virtue and thrift. Whetstone's emphasis was on dicing, and the numbers of young gentlemen ruined by it. He especially deplored the prospering of those whom Greene and others were to call cony-catchers, and as a measure of reform suggested that dicing houses and taverns be socially segregated to prevent the lower ranks from contaminating the upper. Rawlidge, too, was concerned that 'many a young Gentleman, and prodigall Citizen' fell prey daily to the London cony-catchers, but the main stress was on the decay of the middle and lower classes through drinking. In particular he feared for the decline in family life, suffered when the head of the household went out tippling, and recommended the practice of some (unnamed) 'well gouerned Republiques' where citizens were forbidden by law to eat or drink outside their own homes unless invited into a neighbour's house. In more general terms, he saw that excessive drinking might result from the fact that Puritan preachers had outlawed alternative pastimes:

> When that the people generally were forbidden their old and antient familiar meetings and sportings, what then followed? Why, sure Ale-house hunting . . . The Preachers then did reproue dalliansey, and dancings of maides and young men together; but now they haue more cause to reproue drunkennesse and whoring, that is done privately in Alehouses (p. 13).

This interesting observation was somewhat contrary to the general trend of thought on drinking; Rawlidge, in recognizing and catering for the human need for recreation, was unusually realistic for his time. He was also one of the few pamphleteers to describe the abuses of drink from personal observation and to attempt to prescribe feasible measures for reform. Rather than fill up his pamphlet with denunciations of drinking in general terms and well-worn anecdotes of God's judgements shown in the sudden deaths of drunkards, Rawlidge insisted on the factual nature of his cautionary tales and on the practicality of his reforms. 'Some experience by my owne knowledge', 'I myself did see accidentally', 'I haue seen and doe very well know myself'—such phrases are constantly repeated. His suggested reforms were down-to-earth in the extreme: the profits to be gained from selling ale should be severely curtailed, and alehouse-keepers fined for overcharging; drunkards should be fined five shillings or made to sit in the stocks for six hours; churchwardens who failed to exact these charges should themselves be fined forty shillings for each oversight; and those who gave information against illegal practices and drunken behaviour should be paid 'some allowance towards their trouble, loss of time, and charges' (p. 25). Yet the conclusion to his pamphlet reverts entirely to emotional appeal. Medieval sermons against drinking frequently concluded with the *topos* of the drunkard's deathbed, and it seems to have been in Rawlidge's mind too, when he ended with an admonition to alehouse keepers to think of Doomsday and repent:

What a miserable, lamentable, and wretched case will you bee in, when you shall bee arraigned before the Lord our God: and so many poore men, women, and children, shall there stand to witnes against you, with their complaints, that they haue perished for want of bread, because you haue suffered and kept them night and day, swilling and drinking all they had in your houses (sig. E1^v).

The anonymous *A Looking-Glasse for Drunkards* (1627) ends similarly, exhorting drunkards to think of the Four Last Things and to envisage the torments of hell.

ii

Beneath the surface of moralizing lay a number of deeper concerns, many of them the commonplace assumptions about the human condition that formed the basis of complaint literature, but others more directly to do with contemporary social change and growth; the latter appear in the form of such themes as the decay of moral standards and of learning, the hostility between the city and country, the growth of London, the rivalry between the nobility and bourgeoisie, and the tension between the old concept of limitless hospitality extended by the landed aristocracy to the poor, whether or not deserving, and the newer ideals of thrift and self-sufficiency.

Something of the pamphleteers' feelings about the decay of moral standards had already been seen, in their constant comparisons between the present and the heroic past, their general hatred of new habits and institutions, their assertions that the English were being contaminated by their increasing contact with foreigners, and their belief that greater prosperity could only result in the flourishing of the unworthy and discontent amongst all classes. Even England's long period of freedom from war brought no satisfaction; to many, peacetime only resulted in stagnation and degeneracy, 'inordinate delicacie, ryot & ydlenes' (Rich, *Allarme to England,* sig. F1). The current debased morality gave rise to unnatural vices, and inhuman feelings, as the compiler of the collection of sensational stories known as *A World of Wonders* (1614) writes in his preface: 'Carnall and most vnnaturall murthers, detestable periuries, cankard couetousnes, incestious adulterie, hardnes of hart, peeuish extortion, exactious vsury and diuers such most horrible and abhominable practises yeerly, monthly, nay howrely are vsed and practised' (sig. A2).

The decay of learning, naturally, was a cause close to the hearts of the pamphleteers. John Day in the dedication to his allegory *Peregrinatio Scholastica* stated that it was only a few 'noble and generous sperritts' who prevented 'this land which hath been counted Hortum Musarû' from becoming a 'Stabulum Asinorum'. His narrative shows the hero Philosophos rejected by the common people of the country he visits, beguiled by Sin and Error, and deceived by the Seven Deadly Sins disguised as the Seven Liberal Sciences. This pessimism persisted throughout the period; the Puritan clamour of the *dies irae* grew louder: 'Doe wee not yet dayly feare a Chaos, and confusion in our Church, and State, and a sodaine surprisall of our Kingdome? doe not all the characters of a dying, and declining State appeare upon us?' (W. Prynne, *The Vnlouelinesse, of Love-Lockes*, sig. A4). So wrote Prynne in 1628; the immediate cause of his fears in this instance was the prevalence of long hair in men. But inoffensive habits and small causes had often disproportionate effects, and modest portents betokened great events. It was widely believed that Doomsday was near, and hence any unusual occurrence, however insignificant, might signify God's warning of it.

While this pessimism did to some extent reveal the current climate of opinion, undoubtedly much of it can be ascribed to the demands of both literary convention and popular taste. On the other hand we know this to have been an age of extraordinary material advancement for some, of adventure, discovery, and increasing national pride. These aspects of social change were not neglected, and the dichotomy between the Englishman's growing sense of himself and his country on one side, and on the other his prevailing fear that material prosperity could only betoken arrogance and its inevitable downfall was well illustrated in the pamphleteers' treatment of London. During this period London grew extensively both in size and fame. Estimates of the population and its rate of increase vary widely;[44] it has been calculated that the population nearly doubled between 1600 and 1660[45] rising from a quarter to nearly half a million at the Restoration. Visitors from abroad admired the elegance and cleanliness of the streets.[46] The pamphleteers worked in London and wrote almost exclusively for a London public. This was the literature of a single city to an extraordinary extent, and the pamphleteers sometimes wrote as if nowhere else in England existed. Richard Johnson dedicated his pamphlet *Looke on me London* (1613) to the Lord Mayor of London and to 'the young men of London, as well Gentlemen as others' claiming 'I am perswaded, that in this Dedication, I doe salute the most part of all the yong Gentlemen of England, in that they either diwell or haue been in this worthy Citty of London' (Sig. A4).

The concept of London influenced both form and subject matter in the pamphlets. The coming of visitors to London was one of the most common situations for a moralizing story; a great number of social satires took the form either of a warning to or an account of the corruption or seduction of the young and inexperienced provincial, or else of a commentary on city life by a traveller going to or coming from another country, often hell. The very topology of the city was interesting enough in itself, and by implication sufficiently familiar to the reading public, to form the main subject matter of pamphlets like Johnson's *The Pleasant Walkes of Moore-fields* (1607), Dekker's *The Deade Tearme* and Donald Lupton's *London and the Countrey Carbonadoed*. It was the London streets where cony-catchers found their victims, the London prisons were debtors declined and politic bankrupts found sanctuary, the London fashions that moralists bewailed. London's beauty was celebrated like that of a woman: 'She seems contrary to al other things, for the older she is, the newer and more beautifull' (Lupton, *London and the Countrey Carbonadoed*, p. 2). Dekker addressed the city with an almost religious veneration: 'Thy habitations stande then like a rich Embrodery about the skirts of an imperial garment' (*The Deade Tearme, Non-Dramatic Works*, IV, 20). To its citizens London was like a mother and guardian, 'Grandam almost to this Whole Kingdome, Mother of my life, Nurse of my being', as Dekker called it, especially in times of plague; and with its streets and houses deserted but for the sick and dying London epitomized beauty in decay.

The fame of the city stretched far beyond England, and to some writers it was a prototype of civic glory for all the world to admire:

> We may well vnderstand as well by the relation of Travellers, as by our owne experience, that London is not alone the Honour of our Nation, but by others reputed the Mirror of Europe, for Civill Government, and stately building, and the vnparalel'd pattern of vertue in her many graue Senators and Citizens (Rawlidge, *A Monster*, p. 2).

The Londoner's civic pride was expressed in Johnson's dialogue *The Pleasant Walkes of Moore-fields*, where a citizen amazes a country visitor with his account of the ancient glories and modern improvements of the city. The gentleman is moved to praise both the citizens' exemplary philantrophy and their architectural taste:

> All England may take example, at your London Citizens, who not onely seeke for their owne benefits, but striue to profit others, shewing themselves good common-wealths men, and as they be called the Fathers of the Citie, so be they cherishers of the poore

and succourlesse . . . to this day (I see) they continually striue to beautifie this famous Citie, for what faire summer houses with loftie towers and turrets and here builded in those fields, and in other places, the suburbs of the Citie, not so much for use and profit, as for showe and pleasure, bewraying the noblenesse of their mindes (sigs. A4^v–B).

But the plague showed not only London suffering but also London justly punished for its sins. London was like other sinful cities, such as Jerusalem and Sodom, and had earned God's wrath by its refusal to repent even after constant warnings; it was a centre where the wicked congregated, in particular rogues, vagrants, and idle beggars. Samuel Cottesford, in *A Treatise Against Traitors* (1591), warned the Lord Mayor of London and his Alderman to guard their city against the entry of ne'er-do-wells: 'Men of no busines, of no calling, idle, unprofitable, wicked and utterlye godles, thither do they fly making it their refuge . . . Thither also the companies of recusants when they cannot find harborough elsewhere, do they repaire' (**^{v}). Henry Goodcole, sometime chaplain of Newgate, in *Heavens Speedie Hue and Cry sent after Lust and Murther* (1635) advised his readers very specifically against frequenting certain locales including 'such places, in, and about the City of London, that Harlots watch their opportunities'. Dekker saw in London the originator of a new set of Seven Deadly Sins. London's sufferings in plague-time were the deserved effects of God's anger; the city personified in Henry Petowe's *The Countrie Ague* (1625), admits this: 'Had not the Lord beene angry with me for my intollerable sinnes, hee would not have suffered my poore children to runne away from me' (p. 2). Nevertheless, the pamphleteers lamented the unaccustomed stillness of the streets: Dekker noted that 'If one shop be open, sixteene in a row stand shut up together, and those that are open, were as good as to be shut; for they take no Money *(A Rod for Run-awayes, Plague Pamphlets*, p. 138); and, less prosaically, Benjamin Spenser in *Vox Civitatis* observed that 'Those great Gates, which were wont to be furnished with spangled star-like beauties, are now the lodging for poore children, or places for dung and draught' (p. 14).

When citizens returned from country refuges after the worst was over, it was with the gladness of exiles to see their mother-country after long absence. And their emotion in returning had the additional element of relief at escaping from the resentment and ill-treatment they had suffered at the hands of country people. This antagonism between Londoners and countrymen was treated in the plague pamphlets entirely from the Londoners' point of view. The natural fear and hostility felt by countrymen for the plague-tainted refugees was regarded as gross ingratitude towards superiors and benefactors. In *The run-awyaes Answer, To a Booke called, A Rodde for Runne-awayes* (1625) despondent London is consoled by being reminded of the debt which the country owes the city: 'How many of their Sonnes hast thou taken from the Plough and from their Poore and Rusticall Parents, and plac'd those Sonnes (after thou hadst Tutord them) on the *Pinacles* of *Honor?* (sig. C2^v). Dekker, John Taylor, Henry Petowe, and Benjamin Spenser filled their plague pamphlets with anecdotes insisting on the countryman's stupidity and selfishness. The Londoner was seen as a social superior worthy of respect, who only demeaned himself in visiting the countryside at all. London's increasing prosperity was achieved to some extent at the country's expense; the fact clearly did not go unresented, and something of the countryman's point of view does emerge, not in plague writing, but in other kinds of social pamphlet.

Hostilities of various kinds underlay the pamphleteers' surface themes. Discussions of discord in the social hierarchy, for instance, often implied a tension between the nobility and the bourgeoisie, and stories about the novice who comes for the first time to London were used to embody this tension. The novice, often of noble birth, was exploited not only by obvious city petty criminals such as prostitutes, thieves, and cheating card players, but also by bourgeois types, such as lawyers, merchants, and tradesmen. A good example is the young heir in the first story of Middleton's *Father Hubburds Tales*, which, since it is narrated by a ploughman, also draws on the rivalry between the values of town and country. Here it is the old country ways to which the narrator cleaves; the city prodigality into which the heir is seduced ruins not only himself but also his dependants: 'My destruction and the mine of all painefull husbandmen about me, began by the prodigall downefall of my young Landlord, whose father, grandfather, and great Grandfather for many generations had bene lords of the Towne wherein I dwelt' (sig. C1). His downfall, both moral and financial, is accomplished specifically by this adoption of the values of his *nouveau riche* city acquaintances, who quickly get him into debt. It is only after the first stage of his decline that he takes up with low-life characters, and ends his career of depravity as a pander.

Lodge's *An Alarum against Vsurers* again shows bourgeois and city types combining to win a young heir whose career follows a very similar pattern to Middleton's. The pamphlet begins with an attack on merchants, whose abuses have grown so great that 'if the thing be not narrowly lookt in to, the whole land by that meanes will grow into great inconuenience', their chief offences being the evading of statutes, the setting up of dishonest brokers, and the robbing of heirs. The heir of this story, however, is not connected with any merchant, but is taken up by a broker who introduces him to a whore. She entices him into the life of a young gallant, with all its incidental vanities and experiences; thus he inevitably falls prey to a usurer, and is finally forced to work for him at debauching other young heirs. The sorry tale ends with Lodge's wish that 'The Lord send our Gentlemen more wit, our vsurers more conscience, and vngodlinesse a fall: so Nobilitie shall not decay, but the sinner shall be reclaimed, and wickednesse confounded' (p. 20^v).

The same system of moral values is expressed in Greene's *A Quip for an Upstart Courtier* through the antithetical portraits of Clothbreeches and Velvetbreeches. Clothbreeches exemplifies the true Englishman, of noble birth but modest habits, who rejects the ways of citizens, lawyers, and foreigners; the Italianate Velvetbreeches represents the upstart aspiring courtier whose intensest hatred is reserved for the English knight and all he stands for:

> Why this knight is mortall enimy to pride and so to me, he regardesth hospitality and aimeth at honor with relieving the poore, you may see although his landes and reverences be great, and he be able to maintain himself in great brauery, yet he is content with home spun cloth, and scorneth the pride that is nowadaies used amongst young upstarts (Sig. E).

The veneration that was the commonest pamphlet attitude towards hereditary nobility was directed towards a class under threat, and the decay of the nobility along with its traditional way of life was one of the themes in which writers crystallized their fear of changing values.[47] The aristocratic ideal of the feudal landowner, living in a country house which had been the traditional home of his family for generations, acting as spiritual and financial matrix both to the community who worked for him and to any temporary residents on the territory over which he presided, still persisted. Such a concept was based on the mutual ties and obligations that bound the lord to his tenants and workers, in particular the lord's ancestral responsibilities to provide for the poor and indigent who happened to be on his territory. But many of the wealthy landowners of the period were not hereditary noblemen; they had bought their estates or won their titles in service, and they had new ideas of their social function. This change in the character of the nobility can be related to the idea of a conflict existing at this time between what has been called the functional concept of society and the freeholders' concept; the functional concept was of a society in which each of its component groups performed a special, preordained function for the good of the whole, while the so-called freeholders' concept was that society was made up of individuals who had not functions to perform in the service of the state but rights which it was the duty of the state to protect.[48] The pamphleteers viewed the change in more traditional terms as yet another symptom of the degeneracy of their age, and expressed it through their emphasis on the decay of hospitality. That the rich personally should support the poor as part of their duty to God was a traditional idea, with Biblical authority; in the sixteenth and seventeenth centuries they were ceasing to do so, partly because many of them had no tradition or ancestral sense of this sort of service, because their function as landowners had no connection with their religious duties, and partly because of the new Protestant ethic which exalted work, and along with it, self-sufficiency. In the Middle Ages, poverty had been acclaimed a virtue; a blessed state, a necessary part of God's design for human life, and the poor were entitled to relief by virtue of their condition, whether or not deserving; but in the sixteenth and seventeenth centuries poverty turned into a social failing, with avoidable, even punishable causes, such as prodigality or idleness, and hence the poor became no longer the responsibility of any group of individuals but of the state. Compulsory monthly collections for the support of the London hospitals had apparently been in existence since the 1560s, and for the parish poor since the 1570s; and though historians disagree as to the relative proportions of the poor relief[49] derived from charity and from compulsory doles, they generally accept that a new attitude towards poor relief was developing. 'Aid to the poor came to be associated with, and subordinated to, the inculcation of new attitudes to work.'[50]

The pamphleteers were divided in their attitudes to these changes; but lamentations over the degeneracy of the times frequently included a threnody for the loss of charity, though no recognition of the new role played by the state: 'In these Golden Times of yore, Charity was the rich mans Idoll: for they did emulate each other in supplying the widdowes wants, in comforting the orphans miseries, and in refreshing the trauellers wearines' *(This Worlds Folly,* sig. B4). Absentee landlords were held to neglect their duties through pride: 'A Gentleman of ancient and able reuenue, dares scarce once in seauen yeares keepe a Christmas in his Country-hall, least he should be blowne vp by the mines of this Army of *Vanity*' (Parkes, *The Curtaine-Drawer,* p. 2). Barnaby Rich distinguished between true and upstart knights according to their hospitality; the former were known for their 'good house-keeping', the latter for their miserliness, and their habit of frequenting other men's tables instead of providing their own.

That the poor were *ipso facto* entitled to support was sometimes assumed, especially in pathetic contexts, or where the topic was incidental to something else, as in Dekker's *A Rod for Run-awayes*, where those who deserted London in plague-time were charged with neglecting their dependants: 'How shall the lame, and blinde, and halfe starued be fed? They had wont to come to your Gates: Alas! they are barred against them: to your doores . . . you haue left no Key behinde you to open them: These must perish' (*Plague Pamphlets*, p. 148). Here, Dekker suggested that constables be appointed to prevent the rich from leaving their houses until they had contributed something towards poor relief. But his attitude to the poor in *Worke for Armorours*, an allegorical account written earlier of the conflict between wealth and poverty, was more ambiguous. While poverty was at one point exalted as the foundation of charity and the inspiration of poets, elsewhere the poor were held to blame for their state. Sloth, Repining, and Discontent are in the army of Poverty, but Industry is despised: 'yet stand they not so well affected to him, because he compelles them to take paines, when tis their naturall inclination (like Drones) to liue basely' (*Non-Dramatic Works*, IV, 116).

Although the situation of the poor in times of emergency such as the plague was grievous, not all writers were disposed to be sympathetic towards them. The plague was seen as a punishment fit for their idleness and 'famine and want of good workes.' Benjamin Spenser in *Vox Civitatis, or Londons Complaint* suggested that the poor were more susceptible to the plague than the rich, because they are 'ill livers, intemperate of tongue, and appetite, grosse feeders' (p. 21). London, who is personified and narrates the whole of the pamphlet, numbers the poor among her chief spiritual afflictions:

> I know also that I haue the poore with me, a rude people whom I cannot rule, whose necessity hath hardened them, and their dejection driuen them to *Commit sinne with Greedynesse*. And as Cookes frame all things to the palate, and omit things profitable; so do they (saith *Philo*) omit good, & turne all things to their present pleasure (p. 5).

In another of Spenser's pamphlets, *Vox Ruris, Reverberating Vox Civitatis*, London's poverty is partially ascribed to the fact that the citizens neglect to punish the idle: 'Notwithstanding the good orders, that Magistrates have set downe for the poores provision: yet generally neither doe (they) levie stockes to set them on worke, nay hardly haue a paire of stockes in many places to punish notorious offenders' (p. 6). S. R., in *Martin Mark-all, Beadle of Bridewell*, noticed the increase in the number of beggars and unemployed at the end of a war, but to him such people were not casualties of war but vermin of peace who 'laze in the streete, lurke in the Ale-houses, and range in the high-waies' (sig. B4). Beggars aroused no sympathy; he quoted with contempt the proverb 'if you can Cant, you will neuer worke.' Henry Arthington, in *Provision for the Poore, now in Penurie* (1597) gave several reasons why the poor 'crie hard for foode, and finde small supply.' In particular, it was because they had not confessed their sins, of which the first was 'that they haue misspent much good time in idle roging vp and downe, and woulde not work', and the second 'that in the time of abundance, they haue beene great wasters in bibbing and bellycheare' (sig. A3).

The country poor were seen as deficient not so much in desire to work as in intelligence; they rejected learning 'out of meere negative ignorance' and took for their *summum bonum* 'a pudding or a pot of good drinke'; they would not allow their children to be educated even though it cost them nothing, and they would not have them corrected 'to gaine the Muses dowry'; they had no respect for ministers of religion, and would not provide them with books. But their social superiors did not set them an example; few of the nobility were to be found who appeared other than 'puffe-paste Titilladoes, effeminated by delicacy . . . growne exorbitant by liberty' (*Vox Ruris,* p. 28).

Such mixed and inconsistent attitudes as these testify to a moral uncertainty in the pamphleteers' relationship to the world around them. Their way of lamenting the decay of hospitality implies a sense of helplessness in the face of forces too great for the individual to control or affect. The poor must be dealt with by the state and its Poor Laws. The world in which, however theoretically, poverty could be controlled by rich individuals was gone. Public services and institutions—constables, bellmen, prisons, workhouses, and hospitals—were necessary, but unpopular and openly criticized. The citizen might not rebel against the state, but there was machinery to allow him to inform against his fellows in its service. Willymat in *A Loyal Subiects Looking-Glasse* (1604) defined the subject's duty as one of passive obedience:

> Vnder this duty are conteyned especially two things, whereof the first is, that moderation which all priuate persons ought to obserue in publique affaires, namely that they may not of their owne motion

without any calling busie themselues in publike affaires, nor intermeddle in the gouerment nor reformation of them, not take vpon them rashlie any part of the Magistrates office, nor attempt any publike thing ... The second thing conteined in this fixt duty, is the casting off, or laying away all vindictiue resolutions (p. 48).

Rawlidge suggested means for tightening up on the drinking laws which included paying part of the fine for drunkenness to the man who reported the offence to the constable; payment for informers was often advocated in order that the laws of the land might be more strictly enforced. While the rich individual's role in the maintenance of social stability was decreasing in importance, the significance of his social inferiors to the state was on the rise. The pamphleteers, the first generation of writers to reach a mass audience, regretted the passing of the golden age, but did not say that increased literacy and prosperity, among other factors, had rendered the change essential.

iii

I have shown how some topics which are used as the main subject of a pamphlet very frequently, almost inevitably, give rise to moral reflections of a particular kind, as if the topic and the reflections were closely connected, not just in the minds of one or two individuals, but in the commonest habits of thought of the time. The plague, for instance, almost invariably introduces, even acts as a pretext for, a discussion of town/country hostility, and Estates satire leads on to the theme of the decay of the aristocracy. This manner of making connections illustrates several things. It testifies to the existence both of a kind of group or communal mentality among pamphleteers, and of a common fund of material, themes, and attitudes freely available for all writers to draw on, without being subject to accusations of plagiarism or lack of originality. It also demonstrates how instinctive association of ideas governs or controls literary form to a greater extent than consciously-made connections and preplanned structures. One example of such association of ideas has already been indicated in the discussion of the Seven Deadly Sins pattern in Chapter 3;[51] another can be traced in the treatment of one or two key concepts in popular thinking, such as that embodied in the term 'superfluity', a useful example to take because, although the fundamental meaning of the word has not changed, Elizabethan usage lent it a pejorative moral connotation which has now disappeared.

At this period, 'superfluity' had begun to be used absolutely, without being followed by a descriptive phrase, to signify excess, especially in diet or dress. Dekker, in *Newes from Hell,* uses the word in this way when he describes parasites as 'slaves, that for gaine are content to lye vnder vs, like Spaniels, fawning, and receive what fals from our superfluity' (*Non-Dramatic Works,* III, 106). Shakespeare coined the word 'superflux' in *King Lear* to mean the same thing but no one else seems to have taken it up. 'Superfluous' was used to mean extravagant in consumption or expenditure, and to describe a greater abundance of worldly goods than was necessary for existence in a Christian and equitable society where each man received his due. Superfluity signified excess as a moral concept especially associated with the deadly sin of pride and its manifestation in externals, particularly clothes and cosmetics. The concept was expressed by means of ideas and images, often very vivid ones, drawn from a wide area of reference. Clothes imply the animal substances of which they are made; cosmetics too are often produced from animal effluvient. They suggest the misuse of nature, extravagance, the attempt to cover up or disguise the human form, and they both accentuate and confuse social divisions, between rich and poor, between chaste and unchaste. Cosmetics traditionally mark the harlot, the woman who will sell her body for money and goods; the harlot represents the Eve in all women, who ruins man both morally and physically. Hence images of animals, of animal passions, of decay, and of sexual vice were evoked by these associations, and in combination could produce a strong emotional response to what was not a single idea but a complex referential field. Lear's great speeches on justice draw on this field:

> Behold yond simp'ring dame,
> Whose face between her forks presages snow;
> That minces virtue, and does shake the head
> To hear of pleasure's name;
> The fitchew nor the soiled[52] horse goes to't
> With a more riotous appetite.
>
> (IV, vi, 120–25)

So, too, the sexual disgust in Timon of Athens; and Webster's Bosola and Middleton's De Flores derived their loathsomeness from it. And in particular Tourneur's Vindice evoked the concept in the speech addressed to the skull of his poisoned mistress:

Does every proud and self-affecting dame
Camphor her face for this? and grieve her maker
In sinful baths of milk, when many an infant starves

For her superfluous outside—all for this?
Who now bids twenty pound a night, prepares
Music, perfumes and sweetmeats? All are hush'd;
Thou mayst lie chaste now. It were fine, methinks,
To have thee seen at revels, forgetful feasts
And unclean brothels; sure 'twould fright the sinner,
And make him a good coward, put a reveller
Out of his antic amble,
And cloy an epicure with empty dishes.
Here might a scornful and ambitious woman
Look through and through herself:—see ladies, with false forms
You deceive men, but cannot deceive worms.

(III, v, 83–98)

The pamphleteer Thomas Tuke, in *A Treatise Against Painting and Tincturing of Men and Women*, used the idea of superfluity in the same way:

> All painting or colouring of the face is not of one kind nor by one meane. The more artificiall and sumptuous is by tincture, the skinne being died and stained with artificiall colours. This it is the wealthier sort performe by the helpe of pearle. Were it not much better to bestow this cost on the poore, which are creatures and images of God, then on such idle images and workes of their owne creation? . . . A painted face is a *superfluous face:* it were well, if the world were well rid of all such superfluous creatures (p. 30).

Nashe and Dekker both chastised for superfluity those who devoted themselves to the adornment of a body that was all too soon to rot; in his section on 'Gorgeous Attires', an offshoot of pride, in *Christs Teares over Ierusalem,* Nashe berated the vanity of women:

> Theyr breasts they embuske vp on hie, and theyr round Roseate buds immodestly lay foorth, to shew at theyr handes there is fruite to be hoped. In theyr curious Anticke-wouen garments, they imitate and mocke the Wormes and Adders that must eate them (*Works*, II, 138).

Dekker in *The Wonderfull Yeare* made the same point:

> The selfe-same bodie . . . which now is so pampered with superfluous fare, so perfumed and bathed in odoriferous waters, and so gaily apparelled in varietie of fashiōs, must one daie be throwne (like stinking carion) into a rank & rotten graue (*Plague Pamphlets,* p. 29).

Earlier in his address to the skull Vindice had made a connection between the wasting of money on superfluities and the loss of ancestral rights:

> Are lordships sold to maintain ladyships
> For the poor benefit of a bewitching minute?

This was a common idea, and one that was used in a variety of contexts. It was pressed into the service of the opponents of tobacco in John Deacon's *Tobacco Tortuered*. Deacon describes addicted smokers led inevitably into 'a superfluous or riotous Waste' which brought about 'a prodigall dispending of patrimonies' and 'an vnrecouerable subuersion of that their ancient estate which they formerly received from their forefathers frugalitie' (p. 65). In Lodge's *Wits Miserie, and the Worlds Madnesse* it is wasteful spending on personal finery which is made to account for the decline of great households. In the description of a sin Lodge names Superfluous Invention, 'or as some tearme him NOVEL-MONGER of FASHIONS', one of the children of pride it is claimed that 'The chines of Beefe in great houses are scantled to buie chains of gold; and the almes that was wont to releeue the poore, is husbanded better to buy new Rebatoes' (p. 14). The monstrous extravagance of women's clothing is criticized in the same terms, though less pointedly, as in *The Revenger's Tragedy*: 'The elephant is admired for bearing a little castle on his back, but what say you to a tender, faire, young, nay a weakling of woman-kind, to weare whole Lordships and manor houses on her backe without sweating?' (p. 14).[53]

The relationship between waste, whether of money, materials, or land, and social status was an important one, but because the pamphleteers were so caught up in traditional verbal and conceptual webs, they did not move away from imposed patterns of thought to examine the ideas more closely. Such social criticism as did emerge had often little relevance to contemporary situations. I have shown, for instance, in Henry Burton's *A Divine Tragedie Lately Acted*[54], how although the writer saw evidence of social unrest around him, even on the brink of revolution in 1641 he did not relate his awareness to contemporary states of mind but instead diverted it back to the traditional idea that any change in status meant a breaking up of divine degree.

Degree itself was another of those magnetic concepts, like superfluity, around which was built up a complex of associations so vivid, so all-embracing, so universally explanatory, that all kinds of tenuously related notions were drawn towards it. Fashions and habits were deplored on the grounds that they obscured differences of degree or rank; cosmetics were said to obscure social distinctions and encourage confusion between people of different ranks, as did such fashions as men's love-locks, worn alike by lords and servants. There was great resentment at the fact that people who were once humble could now afford to look like their superiors; the author of *The Returne of the Knight of the Poste*, enumerating the factors that 'make rich Sathans Commonwealth', included pride in dress: 'Doe but cast thine eye aside, in after ages, and thou shalt see a Water-bearer as brave as a Sea-Captaine, and a Cobler as curious in his acoutermentes, as on Candlemas day at night, an Innes of Court Reueller' (sig. D4^v). Tailors themselves were some of the worst breakers of degree, since 'being the impers of Peacockes plumes [they] may best borrow some of their broken feathers' (sig. D4^v), and Greene's Clothbreeches mentions the arrogance of tailors who aspired to a coat of arms. Spurious elegance of dress was both a symptom of and an incitement to social aspiration: 'Have we not such amongst us whose attire rather shewes them to be Monarchs than meane men, Kings rather then subjects, whose mindes are neither suppressed with the loyalty of their duety, nor with the modest regarde of their meane estate' (W. Rankins, *The English Ape*, p. 8).

In the golden age, each man was content with his allocated place, but by contrast the pamphleteers saw their fellows as obsessed with clothes and titles and aping their betters. Visions of the golden age in terms of heaven or of Elysium, as in Dekker's *A Knights Coniuring*, explicitly excluded the common types of social aspirant such as lawyers and middle-class wives.

Few pamphleteers developed the degree and superfluity ideas in the direction of social reform. George Whetstone, who proposed the control of vice by means of social segregation in *A Mirour for the Magestrates of Cyties*, was an exception. His sociological method, however, was medieval in the extreme, since his proposals were derived, not from experience or analysed observation but from an analogy between sixteenth-century London and Rome in the times of Alexander Severus. It is clear from many instances that this ingrained habit of mind whereby contemporary life and society was interpreted in the light of traditional moral concepts was largely responsible for the reactionary tone of the pamphlets. There were formulae available to treat all the most popular satirical subjects, and any common moral idea automatically generated one of a number of set responses. Perhaps, with the benefit of hindsight, the popular writing of many periods appears equally standardized and incapable of development; there is certainly no doubt that at this time the magnetism of medieval ways and patterns of thought exerted a stronger hold than the desire to write from evidence or observation.

iv

The chapters preceding this one have dealt with some aspects of the relationship between the subjects of the pamphlets and the forms in which the material was embodied, showing the evolution of one new form, the cony-catching pamphlet, in its various manifestations—straightforward observation and report, informational guide-book, low-life fiction, and allegory—and the modification of some medieval forms, the Seven Deadly Sins and Estates satire to deal with any new subject-matter. The pamphleteers were generally more varied and adventurous in the use of forms than in their choice of subjects and attitudes towards them. A broad distinction could be made between those subjects which formed the staples of medieval complaint and were dealt with in traditional literary ways, and those which only came into being as the material of popular literature late in the sixteenth century and were sometimes treated without any apparent consciousness of form, or in forms evolved to suit them individually, but it would not be a specially useful one.

The diversification of familiar subject-matter by means of ingenious structural devices and frameworks is a major feature of popular moralistic writing at this time on whatever kind of topic. One common technique was the use of a visit to or a visitor from some other society or environment to comment on this one. Visitors to hell might find the activities there unexpectedly similar to those on earth; other-world travellers, whether ghosts or commuters between earth and hell like the Knight of the Post, observed doings on earth with indignation and even horror. Other writers found the use of a persona a convenient device for satire: Dekker used two such figures, Cock Watt in *Iests to make you merie* and later the Bellman of London; 'S.R.' invented Martin Markall to answer the Bellman back; William Parkes, in imitation, devised a character called the Curtain Drawer in *The Curtaine-Drawer Of the World*. Martin Markall was created simply as a device to expose the plagiarism in Dekker's rogue pamphlets, but the other three figures are more interesting. They all function mainly by night, as spies and voyeurs who lurk in the dark and watch, fascinated, while the secret sins of London are revealed. Cock Watt, an invisible spirit sent from the underworld to torment the guilty who lie in Newgate awaiting trial, appears

When the last minnit takes his farewell of the ensuing day, and that earely bird, the mornings herauld, giues his wakefull summõs to the darke clouds (vnder whose canopie theeues, baudes and strumpets doe their hatefull actiuities) to disport themselues from the desired day (*Non-Dramatic Works*, II, 204)

The Bellman spies on the doings of London's squalid suburbs; he watches a transaction between a prostitute and her client, and his tone recalls the hectically punning imagination of Tourneur's Vindice: 'What doe they? marry, they doe that, which the Constable should haue done for them both in the streetes, thats to say *commit, commit* (*Non-Dramatic Works*, III, 271). Parkes' Curtain Drawer, a figure of fluctuating significance, sometimes represents an omnipresent desire to sin—

Ther's no man liuing that the world can free
But hee's a *Drawer* in some one degree

(sig. A2^v)

—and sometimes the Devil. But he is also the instrument of God's justice, and Parkes uses him to embody the Lear-like metaphor of stripping away falsehood:

The waspe breakes through where the little flye is intangled, the poore harlot must be stript & whipt for the crime that the Courtly-wanton, and ye Citie-sinner ruffle out, and passe ouer, and glory in, and account as nothing. . . . There is a day to come, when this *Curtaine-drawer*, that now is so ready to smother, and cloake . . . will not onely withdraw his *Curtaine* and leaue them all naked & bare, panting without shelter, but stand forth himselfe to accuse them, . . . Then shall not rich robes, nor poore coverings hide any thing that hath beene done. Then shall the rich and the poore, euen from the furd gowne to the sweating frock, (without president taken from this world) in cases alike, haue reward or punishment (pp. 16–17).

The images of the fly, the poor harlot and the rich wanton, nakedness, the usurer's furred gown, and sexual disease, suggest either that Parkes was, consciously or unconsciously, influenced by the image combinations from *King Lear* or else that he was drawing on the same fund of concepts about justice and superfluity as Shakespeare.

The techniques of allegory provided many devices for satire. Travellers went on journeys to find learning or money; personified abstractions conflicted with each other in various situations. The armies of Poverty and Wealth met in battle; St George (or Queen Elizabeth) fought the dragon Usury; the criminal Sin was tracked down at the lodging house of Mistress Heart and tried by Conscience and Impartiality; Clothbreeches and Velvetbreeches were judged by a jury of Englishmen as to which had the better claim to be called English; London and Westminister compared their misfortunes in a dialogue. In some of these instances the allegorical devices were so transparent and so lacking in any structural coherence as to reveal very plainly a barren striving after novelty.

There is a point at which form appears as a substitute for content. In two of Dekker's allegorical pamphlets, *The Dead Tearme* and *A Strange Horse-Race* this is particularly apparent. Each is composed of a number of structures, and in neither case is there a single theme which connects the whole work. In *The Dead Tearme* Dekker, through the very presentation of the pamphlet, with its table of contents and marginal glosses, draws attention to the number of structures within it, as though to indicate that this variousness is one of its attractions. In the list of 'principall matters contayned in this discourse' at the front he gives not only the topics but also the styles or modes of writing that are to be used: 'a Short Encomiasticke speech' is followed by paradox, complaint, invective, description, and a concluding 'merrie iest'. The whole thing is framed as a prosopopoeia, whereby first Westminister and then London is personified and made to complain of her sorrows. Westminister addresses London as queen and her fairest neighbour, but London responds in less complimentary style, calling Westminister 'Courtly Paramour' and 'Minion now to Two mighty Nations'. Within this curious form a medley of topics is put on display, amongst others, two descriptions of the Deadly Sins in London, a list of the twenty-one rulers of England since the Conqueror, a paradox in praise of going to Law-Court, another in praise of pen and ink, an account of various notorious rebels, a complaint spoken by St Paul's steeple about its decayed condition, and finally a comic tale about Londoners getting the better of countrymen in plague time. This apparently endless string of devices is at last cut off when London remarks, not without reason, 'I see (O Westminister) thou art weary of this my tedious discourse'. *A Strange Horse-Race* is less variegated, but equally fragmentary in effect. It is rightly described in the epistle to the readers as 'a Moral labyrinth' where 'a weake thred guides you in and out'. Modern readers might well be glad if the thread had been stronger, and it seems as if Dekker's original readers did not especially like the pamphlet since it was never reprinted. The horse-race idea, in which all the usual moral subjects are rehearsed in a series of allegorical races run between virtues and vices, takes up more than half of the pamphlet; it is a rather desperate invention that does nothing to hide the emptiness of the moralizing it was devised to sustain. Then follow more allegorical devices: a masque of catchpoles, the devil's last will and testament, and finally a banquet of bankrupts. Each represents a conception in embryo only.

In these works the disparate forms appear one after the other. In other pamphlets the whole structure is like a cocoon of forms woven round some tiny theme embedded within. The outer layer is perhaps a dream vision, inside that a dialogue, and inside that an allegory with several layers of interpretation. Averell's *A meruailous combat of contrarieties,* a didactic pamphlet on dissension within the commonwealth, is such a work. It is presented in the form of a dialogue between parts of the body which accuse each other of moral failings such as pride and gluttony. The author then steps outside his dialogue to tell us first, that the parts of the body are analogous to the elements of the universe, with the breath as the air, the stomach the sea, the eyes the sun and moon, and second that they are also like the components of a commonwealth: 'The legges and feete as the lower and poorer sort, though not indued with pollicie as the head, nor stored with understanding as the heart . . . are yet furnished with greatest strength' (sig. D2). But his system of equivalents is not yet completed; for the head is also Queen Elizabeth, the senses are her bodyguards, and the tongue the Papists. Having at last reached the kernel of his matter, the author casts off his successive shells, and addresses his readers directly on their duty to the Queen in the face of the Catholic menace: 'You are called *Angli quasi Angeli,* and in deed you are as it were angels . . . The Almond tree the older it is, the more fruitfull, so the longer you haue had the word, bee you the more faithfull' (sig. E1^v). The pamphlet ends with a prayer to God and a panegyric on the Queen; the body and its parts, and the dialogue, are entirely abandoned.

Another pamphlet where forms and devices predominate over content is *Choice, Chance, and Change: or, Conceits in the Colours* (1606), probably by Nicholas Breton. It consists of a dialogue in which one speaker takes over the main body of the work to describe his travels; to begin with, the account of a shipwreck and the discovery of new countries provides an opportunity for conventional social satire. Breton tries his hand at various devices here, especially exchanges of apophthegms and proverbial wisdom between the two speakers, and lists of the 'pretty laws and pretty punishments' to be found abroad. The satirical comments are sometimes prolonged into anecdotes of a vaguely moralizing nature, like the one of an old man unsuitably married to a young girl, who dies of grief when his bride is kidnapped by her lover, which is presumably intended as a warning against such incompatible partnerships. Another anecdote begins with Sir Slapsawce, a slovenly knight, giving a wedding feast for his daughter; the knight and the wedding guests are described in considerable detail, and suddenly the reader becomes aware that he is in the middle of a long short story which is to take up the rest of the pamphlet. But the narrative line is always tenuous, and it eventually disappears entirely for some time when the narrator and wedding guests embark on a contest of wit, consisting of a series of increasingly pointless word games. Finally the narrator recites some satirical verses he has written, epigrams without any bearing on their context, on a swaggering gallant, an over-modest youth, a churlish usurer, a card-sharper, and other commonplace types. Grosart, in the introduction to his edition of the pamphlet, which he subtitled 'Glimpses of Merry England in the Olden Time', even though he found, rather surprisingly, much to admire in it, was driven by the inclusion of these verses to remark on the pamphlet's piecemeal structure, 'Evidently the Writer turned to account all odds and ends that lay to his hand, his main motif having been the working in of his epigrammatic sonnets.[55] A few pages from the end the narrative is resumed with a hasty rush of events including an interrupted wedding, the death of the bride, and the endangerment of the narrator's life: a rather extravagant way of contriving for him to be shipwrecked home.

In pamphlets such as these the intention to treat a subject or present a point of view is secondary if not completely absent; the writer is choosing and shaping his material rather to conform to such practical requirements as a certain length and a degree of novelty. These he achieved not by organizing his content in a unified and coherent manner, but through distributing it among a proliferation of unconnected forms and devices, so as to achieve surprise and variety, if nothing else.

The pamphleteers were bees rather then spiders in their methods of composition, and often in their choice of subject-matter as well; the practice of putting a work together out of fragments from other writings was so respectable that it extended easily to the choice of forms. Richard Young borrowed anecdotes and epigrams from all the well-known sources, as well as forms and devices from sermons and rhetorical manuals, to compile his vast treatise, *The Drunkard's Character* (1638). It was something of a tribute to his knowledge of the sources of commonplaces that he could preface his five-hundred page work by writing 'my selfe will acknowledge, that to this Nosegay of strange Flowers, I have put little of mine owne, but the Thread to bind them' (sig. A3). George Hibbard regretted that the pamphlet genre could not provide Thomas Nashe with the discipline of a tight formal structure to control his ebullient genius.[56] Dekker and Rich among others might have benefited from a recognized pamphlet structure. But on the other hand it was the freedom and patchwork quality of the genre that gave it its character. The limitations of more formal journalism might well have excluded much of the pamphlet's extraordinary variety.

No sudden changes in tone or subject-matter took place over the period. The new regime of James I was characterized by a decline in the old patriotism. The kind of intense nationalistic feeling expressed by Whetstone and Averell in their elaborate metaphors of the commonwealth as a body, so similar in attitude to Gaunt's speech in *Richard II,* belonged very definitely to pre-1600 pamphlets; but a new feeling, the desire to glorify London, perhaps given an impetus by the plague of 1603, which coincided with the change of ruler, threatened to render the city desolate, and make the citizens more conscious of the beauty and value of their capital, steadily increased in seventeenth-century writing. Puritan influence grew more pervasive, and at the same time attitudes to women grew more liberal; the change of feeling here was in accordance with a tendency to rely less on authority and more on observation. Thrift, labour, and self-sufficiency became ideals, but neither the accumulation of money nor the attainment of worldly success, though admired by implication, became in themselves respectable aims. Getting on in the world was in the main treated negatively by vivid description of and warnings against what to avoid, although in the handbook literature of the early seventeenth century, the word 'profit' began to be used with other than moral implications, as for instance in William Scott's *An Essay of Drapery: Or, The Compleate Citizen. Trading Justly. Pleasingly. Profitably,* published in 1635.

A contemporary work, *The Art of Thriving, Or, The Plaine pathway to Preferment* by Thomas Powell, published first as *Tom of all Trades* in 1631 and put out with a new title four years later, was unusual in its undisguised emphasis on getting on in the world. Powell prefaces his work with a jocular secularity: 'All men are or would be rich; even the sluggard wisheth though he hath not: 'Tis easie indeed to covet the top of wit or preferment but to get up the hill *hic labor, hoc opus:* there is a business indeed!' (sig. A3ᵛ). The pamphlet takes the form of a dialogue between the author and a friend in need of advice on careers for his children. The author summarizes the professions in a cynical manner, urging his friend to make use of influence and bribery wherever he can. The tone varies between the guidebook factual style—'For his Education. The Free-Schooles generally afford the best breeding in good letters' (p. 15)—and the crudely humorous—'For attaining of such a Benefice (in the Church), let him enquire where the Mattern are read with Spectacles, or where the good old man is lifted up into the Pulpit, or the like, and make a way for Succession accordingly' (p. 34). Powell could not prevent himself from time to time from falling into the pattern of Estates satire, to which his own plan was so similar, especially with such a traditionally satirized figure as the courtier; but there was no doubt that he genuinely meant to write a manual on getting on in life, and his insistence in the prefatory remarks to the reader that he has not merely 'prefixt a specious title to make the sale more oylie' makes it clear that a handbook on 'thriving' would have been popular.

In a limited way Scott's *An Essay of Drapery,* which has been called 'the first substantial piece of writing in English that exalts business as a career',[57] was just such a work, addressed particularly to the tradesman who wanted to prosper in his business. It is an ingenious blend of the moral and the expedient, on the one hand paying tribute to the claims of ethics and morality with such irreproachable propositions as the Miltonic-sounding 'Hee cannot bee a Good Draper which is not first a good man' (p. 3), and on the other allowing the subtle strategies and requirements of business life their due. It was not simply that fair trading need not preclude using the techniques of salesmanship; as Scott presents his case, the tradesman has a duty not only to be honest to his customers but also to himself. He should not, of course, deceive or lie to his customers, but he should recognize the fact that some customers positively appreciate sales talk; they 'grow dull and displeased, if they bee not often whetted by a Flatterer; downe-right honest speeches discontent them' (p. 20). Therefore 'this rule must bee observed: as wee may not lie, so we need not speake all the truth' (p. 34). Equally, a shop may be too light as much as too dark for honest dealing: 'Therefore it is, or should bee so ordered, that least commodities bee sold too deare, shops shall not be too Darke: and lest they be sold too cheap, they shall not bee too light' (pp. 41–42). A dealer must remember that 'God is *totus oculus,* all eye', and act accordingly, but at the same time he should not forget that he is in business to succeed. Scott is careful to make the point that the successful businessman is a benefactor to his employees and a force for good in the community; if he trades wisely—and this means that he can sell more dearly to foreign buyers and keep his prices up—he sustains 'many thousands which live by making, dying, dressing, selling . . . and the like' (p. 49) and he is in a position to give generously to charity. But, later, Scott does not conceal the fact that the greatest incentives to success are material benefits and power: 'Let him labour and consider it is for wealth, the moneyed man is the mighty man: Honour, Liberty, and Royalty attend on riches . . . they onely despise Riches, which despaire of them' (p. 113).

Despite the fact that Scott's modern editor thinks his work defective because he 'leaned so heavily on religious and ethical sources in his thinking about business' and says regretfully that 'his piety is immoderate',[58] the undisguised worldliness of this advice is for its time amazing. According to the dedication to an uncle, Scott was a young man when he wrote his essay; while a more experienced businessman might have dealt better with the practical realities of business life, it is unlikely he would have been so forthright about the businessman's motivation.

The account of popular morality given in the pamphlets was generally probably in the rear rather than in advance of actual beliefs and conditions; fashions were recorded by the pamphleteers, but this mass medium had not the power of its modern equivalents to stimulate and initiate trends. The cony-catching pamphlets of the 1590s were something of an exception in that they deliberately set out to record a current trend and a popular jargon, and won their popularity partly because they were so up-to-the-minute. Greene claimed to be in danger of his life from the cony-catchers for revealing their secrets: this was probably only a publicity stunt, but Greene could never have used it without some possibility of its truth. But the rogue pamphlets of Dekker and Rowlands continued to use Greene's anecdotes and Greene's jargon, ten, even twenty years, after Greene was dead, and this made them no less popular. Dekker's *Lanthorne and Candle-light* went through at least eight editions, more than any of Greene's cony-catching pamphlets. But in a world with only the sermon and the popular press as its mass media change takes place more slowly, and trends and fashions have fewer channels through which to be disseminated. Moreover, these subjects do not change because in essence they are the eternal foundations of popular gossip: the wickedness of other people, unrewarded merit and undeserved reward, the habits and vices of the rich, the decay of the times, the loosening of moral standards, the degeneracy of the young in comparison with their fathers—all these are still the themes through which the popular imagination expresses its interest in the world around.

5
Conventions of Style and Presentation

i

Whereas a general survey of the subjects and attitudes typical of Elizabethan pamphlets reveals them to be conservative, backward-looking and wary of any kind of innovation, a consideration of their style and manner of presentation does not support this impression. Stylistically, they were the product of a unique combination of influences, some of them traditional, others in line with the most contemporary currents of thought, brought together to create a new mode of writing which has a vitality and appeal that an acquaintance with their subject-matter only would never lead one to suspect.

The influence of new kinds of social thought was not yet much in evidence in the moralistic attitudes of the pamphlets, but there were other kinds of new thinking which gradually emerge in their style. It is, of course, absurd to hope to define all the stylistic qualities of any class or genre of literature so as to account for the way in which it is written, although this is what those who embark on such a task would really like to achieve; accordingly, I shall restrict myself to a brief examination of the most obvious influences on pamphlet style in the period, and then some discussion of the major structural and presentational devices, with a closing glance at the changes taking place in the nature of stylistic conventions at this time.

Perhaps the best place to begin is with the theories of rhetoric, the influence of which pervaded writing of every kind except the very lowest. 'The duty and office of Rhetoric', said Bacon, 'is to apply Reason and Imagination for the better moving of the will'. The kind of rhetoric Bacon had in mind here was the systematic description of the art of using language expressively according to lists of figures of speech and thought, as defined originally by Cicero in his *De Inventione* and in the pseudo-Ciceronian *Ad Herennium* and more recently by Renaissance rhetoricians such as Henry Peacham in *The Garden of Eloquence Conteyning the Figures of Grammer and Rhetorick* (1577) and George Puttenham's *The Arte of Englishe Poesie* (1589). Bacon, of course, was eager to distinguish between the techniques of using language for its persuasive force, for the power of images to move the affections, and the cultivation of eloquence for its own sake. The first vanity in learning came about when 'men began to hunt more after words than matter'. In general practice, such a distinction was not always made.

Mastering the art of rhetoric was an important aspect of education from the earliest level. Every grammar school child learnt enough about it to provide him with the figures to adorn his compositions and for the university student logic and rhetoric were basic studies. Any man capable of reading a pamphlet or of listening appreciatively to it being read, was in those days a man who knew something of rhetoric, the art of persuasion. And while he could not perhaps have identified by name the schemes and tropes, with which literature of any kind was ornamented, although if he had been educated at a grammar school he would have been familiar with at least a hundred of them, he accepted their presence and the value that they placed on wit and artifice as essential. He also accepted the underlying premise of traditional rhetoric, that the difficulty of writing was not so much in deciding what to say as in choosing how to say it. To use the term 'rhetoric' may imply spoken rather than written discourse; to men of the Renaissance the two were not so sharply distinguished, and one noun covered both. If the aim of all discourse was to teach, as men of the Renaissance accepted it was, then rhetoric was the means by which the author made his ideas pleasing and persuasive. The orator's power over his audience was accepted and respected; Henry Peacham in his introduction to *The Garden of Eloquence* which consists entirely of definitions of rhetorical figures, confirms the usefulness of his book: 'What he [the orator] commendeth is beloued, what he dispraiseth is abhorred, what he perswadeth is obeid, & what he disswadeth is auoided' (sig. AB4ᵛ).

The origins of Elizabethan rhetoric were moral as well as stylistic; rhetoric had considerable bearing on the content of the pamphlets as well as on their arrangement, in that one of the chief means of expansion and amplification, and also one of the sources of invention in its rhetorical sense of 'the discovery of valid or seemingly valid arguments to render one's cause plausible'[1] was the commonplace, a kind of mental storehouse or pigeonhole of information in the form of proverbs and sententious sayings on subjects to be used in speeches or arguments, which had always been closely associated with the contrast between vice and virtue. Sources of commonplaces such as Aesop's *Fables*, the *Colloquia* and the *Apophthegms* of Erasmus, and Elizabethan commonplace books like *Politeuphuia*, Francis Meres' *Palladis Tamia* and *Wits Theater of the little World* contain headings, grouped by subject, and under each a list of authoritative pronouncements on the subjects in the form of short anecdotes, fables, proverbs or aphorisms. For instance in *Wits Theater of the little World* there are several pages of sayings on the subject of women. The vicious and the virtuous appear side by side. The section begins:

> Although *Pandora* had wisedome from *Pallas*, eloquence from *Mercurie*, beautie from Venus, personage from Iuno, and from euery other God some gift, (where vpon shee is so called) yet in the nature of a woman, shee brought the whole world to confusion.
>
> Although Eve transgressed before the man, yet is the originall of sinning, ascribed to Adam, because the succession is accounted in men, and not in wemen.
>
> Thucydides was of opinion, that those wemen were most honest, of whose commendation and disprayse there is least speech vsed. (pp. 101–2).

The emphasis is very distinctly on moral judgements, and the description of each woman is so slanted as to make her an example of either virtue or of vice. J. M. Lechner considers that

> the long tedious hours spent by the students in memorising, paraphrasing, and expanding axioms of virtue would so colour their way of thinking that everything and everybody tended to be viewed through one or other set of glasses as clothed in the whiteness of virtue or the blackness of vice.[2]

The pamphleteers show the effects of such learning in several ways. One of them is in a particular use of imagery to describe some object in terms of extreme good or extreme evil, where a number of images are grouped together, either directly taken from the appropriate heading in a commonplace book or else in an arrangement based on this model. Greene frequently used such a method of description; the harlot, one of his stock figures, is evoked by means of certain image clusters, where the dominant idea of the fatal power of her charms is emphasized repeatedly:

The Crocodile hath not more teares, Proteus more shape, Ianus more faces, the Hieria, more sundry tunes to entrap the passengers then our English Curtizans *(A Disputation,* p. 5).

Beware of whores, for they be the Syrens that draw men on to destruction, their sweet words are inchantments, their eyes allure, and their beauties bewitch: O take heede of their perswasions, for they be Crocodiles, that when they weepe, destroy *(The Blacke Bookes Messenger,* p. 31).

Oh take heede of Harlots (I wish you the vnbridled youth of England) for they are the Basiliskes that kill with their eyes, they are the Syrens that allure with their sweete lookes; and they leade their fauorers unto their destruction, as a sheep is lead vnto the slaughter *(The Repentance of Robert Greene,* p. 21).

They cleaue like caterpillars to the tree, and consume the fruit where they fall, they be Vultures that praie on men aliue, and like the Serpent sting the bosom wherein they are nourished *(A Disputation,* p. 71).

Cony-catchers and beggars are defined by images of the same kind, suggesting waste and destruction in traditional terms of caterpillars and basilisks:

What is a loyterer or Drone, nothing but a sucker of honie, a spoyler of corne, a destroyer of fruit, a waster of mony, a spoyler of victuall, a sucker of blood, a breaker of good orders, a seeker of brawls, a queller of life, a Baseliske of a comon-wealth . . . (S. R., *Martin Mark-All, Beadle of Bridewell,* sig. B3^v).

The idea of a hidden evil is similarly amplified by images from animal and plant life; in Greene's *The Myrrour of Modestie* (sig. A2^v) the lustful elders hide a wolf's nature in sheep's clothing, and a kite's heart in doves' feathers. In Averell's *A Dyall for dainty Darlings* the wise man is he who knows that 'the sweetest Cedar in smell, is bitter in sent, that the fayrest fruite in touch, is not the best in taste, that the goodliest Oke in sight, is not most sound and safe, nor the ritchest state, on vertue chiefest stayed (sig. E2).

The influence of the proverbial manner of moralizing extended from the work of the best-known pamphleteers to that of the little-known. It shows in such things as *The Recantation of Thomas Clarke* (1594), a recusant confession, put out as the work of Clarke himself, a little later than most of the pamphlets which used this technique extensively. While the author insists that his writing was without conscious artifice—'I am to admonish thee not to looke for any expresse methode of my speeches . . . for I never meant to publish it eyther in print or writing' (sig. A8)—he nonetheless inserts Latin quotations, and uses an elaborate series of commonplace images, mixing simile and metaphor, to describe the false doctrine he has renounced:

> [It] will seeme in the mouth as pleasant as hony, but in the throate it will bee more bitter then wormwood and gall. It is like a canker which creepeth secretly . . . wherefore if thou wilt not be bitten with the snake, sleepe not neere the hedge: hee that toucheth pitch, must needes cary away some stayne (sigs. A7^v–A8).

A later, and more subdued example appears in *The Great Frost. Cold doings in London* (1608), an anonymous pamphlet largely written in a straightfoward descriptive style: 'I pray, sithence you crack the shell, let us see what kernel there is within it: sithence you have bestowed the sweet, let me taste the sour' (E. Arber, *An English Garner*, I, 85). This particular style of amplification, with its references to the repository of proverbial wisdom located in truisms about nature, tended to die out in the early 1590s. New subjects such as tobacco or Puritans which did not figure in the indexes of florilegia or commonplace books were still treated by means of stereotyped and conventional patterns, but they did not evolve image clusters like these.

A related method of developing a subject, by means of analogues from history and legend to reinforce moral judgement, persisted through the period, especially with such themes as the praise or dispraise of women. A typical example of a pamphlet composed by this method is *A Womans Woorth, defended against all the men in the World* by Anthony Gibson.[3] Gibson takes as his subject a proposition from Anaxagoras that 'As . . . the body of Nature is heauen, and the influence thereof her soule: euen so, the body of a woman is the heauen of humane perfections, and her soule the treasure of celestiall and diuine vertues' (sig. B1). At the beginning of his little work he lists eighty-four authorities and chooses examples from their work to illustrate each stage of his argument. Rasis Arab, Eleborus, Timaeus the Sicilian, Homer and ̓Aristotle, among others, are used to support Anaxagoras. Next, Gibson proves that women's virtue is of greater efficacy than men's in affairs of state by citing the examples of Dido, Penthesilia, the Sabine women, Volumnia, Deborah, and Judith. So he proceeds to examine other human accomplishments and virtues— eloquence, art, sobriety, liberality, humility—in each case offering a list of outstanding examples of womanhood and authoritative pronouncements on them to make his point. He concludes, predictably enough, that 'the body of a woman is a true Temple, and her soule the very image of God, or figure of his blessing' (sig. G1).

The use of commonplace books was responsible for the long lists of exempla, proverbs, fables, and aphorisms that can make moralistic pamphlets such tedious reading. Many of them were constructed entirely out of these things, works like Greene's *The Spanish Masquerado*, Breton's *The Court and the Country*, and Richard Brathwait's *Ar't asleepe Husband? A Boulster Lecture*, and many others. It was a convention in some kinds of news pamphlet on momentous events or phenomena to list all the previous examples of similar occurrences known to history or legend. In George Whetstone's *The Censure of a loyall Subiect*, a dialogue between three speakers on the Babington plot, the principle that God preserves the innocent is established by the citation of a motley collection of examples including Susanna and the Elders, the Emperor Commodus, Nero, and Elizabeth I; Adam and Eve, Cardinal Pole, and the Papists of Edward VI's reign are used, on the other hand, to prove that those who rebel against legally constituted authority always meet a bad end. Some criticism of this method of composition was offered, especially by writers on that most commonplace of all subjects, women. Christopher Newstead in *An Apology for Women: Or, Womens Defence* rejects outright the citation of authority as a means of proof:

> *Qui alium sequitur, nihil sequiture,* who makes alwayes examples his copie, shall many times erre from the rules of discretion. Should I tread in the steps of our preciseist methodists, in defining my subiect, I might seeme with Didymus to write that which each one knew, and giue a new testimonie to that old and highway Adage, to burne a Candle at Noone day (sigs. B1–B1ᵛ).

William Heale, in his *Apologie for Women*, made the point that for a hack writer short of ideas to collect a few stale examples and sentences against women was the easiest way to get something into print, and the author of *Iane Anger her Protection for Women* confirmed that literary misogyny was the standby of every would-be pamphleteer: 'If they have stretched their invention so hard out at last, as it is at a stand, there remains but one help, which is, to write of us women' (sig. B).

Then, as now, lists of commonplaces did not make exciting reading; Nashe in his preface to Greene's *Menaphon* vigorously abused those so barren of wit as to rely on 'the Latin Historiographers storehouses; similitudes, nay, whole sheetes & tractates *verbatim* from the plentie of *Plutarch* and *Plinie*' (*Works*, III, 313). In 1609 Ben Jonson was using the word 'commonplace' in its now accepted derogatory sense.[4]

Pamphlets were often constructed according to the principles of rhetorical oration with its formal parts of introduction, narration, division, proof, refutation, and conclusion. Like sermons, many such pamphlets would begin with a text or well-known quotation which was then divided into separate propositions and systematically analysed. William Willymat's *A Loyal Subiects Looking-Glasse* opens with a quotation from that 'Most Christian King, a most sincere professor, and defender of Gods eternal truth', James I, that 'next the knowledge of God, the right knowledge of subiects allegeance according to the forme of government established among them, is a thing most necessarie to be knowne' (sig. C1). It proceeds accordingly to examine the obligations of a subject to his ruler, giving first six chapters on the subject's duties, divided into obedience, fear, honour, prayer, the payment of taxes, and non-interference in the business of magistrates, then six chapters on the causes of disloyalty in subjects, which are pride, ambition, envy, lack of wisdom, discontent, and dissatisfaction with the current means of punishing malefactors. *Englands Bane: Or, The Description of Drunkennesse* by Thomas Young is constructed like a sermon. Young, following Plato, divides the consequences of drunkenness into six heads: filthy talk, fornication, wrath, murder, swearing and cursing; each is illustrated in turn with many quotations and examples from the Bible, somewhat fewer from classical sources, and one or two contemporary anecdotes. The anonymous *A Looking-Glasse for Drunkards* sets down its arguments in numbered points: accordingly, drunkenness is shown to result in five damages to the soul and four to the body; it has five causes and four methods of prevention; there are four reasons why it is wrong to entice others to drink, and four infallible means of affrighting drunkards. *An Alarme to Awake Church-Sleepers* is similarly designed as a handbook for those in need of guidance on the best way to admonish sinners, and carefully constructed according to the rhetorical principles for arranging one's material. There are chapters on 'the severall kindes of sleepe'— proper or figurative, lawful or unlawful, natural or unnatural— 'reasons disswading from Church-sleeping' of eleven kinds, reasons why people sleep during sermons, reasons why they should not do so, and finally 'the Application of the foregoing discourse for Reprehension Exhortation'.[5]

Apologies for the lack of 'method' in the pamphlets were not infrequent, and informality or disorderliness could be used as a point of attack by writers engaged in literary controversy. In the answers to Joseph Swetnam's attack on women in *The Araignment of Lewd, Idle, Froward, and unconstant women* 'Constantia Munda' disparaged 'The Vnsauory periods of your broken-winded sentences', and Rachel Speght, in *A Mouzell for Melastomus*, censured Swetnam more precisely: 'You have vsed such irregularities touching concordance, and observed so disordered a methode . . . that a very Accidence Schollar would have quite put you downe in both' (sig. Bl^v).

The theory of rhetoric at this time was by no means stable. The supremacy of scholastic rhetoric, of the Ciceronian sentence, of Aristotle's five-fold division of invention, arrangement, style, memory, and delivery, was being challenged. Ramus had taken three of these parts, invention, arrangement, and memory, and transferred them into the province of logic; rhetoric he limited only to style and delivery. The resultant confining of rhetoric to verbal techniques and to the schemata of words rather than of thought was important in the history of logic and rhetoric during the sixteenth and seventeenth centuries, but had no direct effect on the pamphlets. True, the enmity between Aristotle and Ramus was one of the subsidiary elements in Nashe's quarrel with Harvey,[6] Harvey, along with the other Cambridge Puritans, favouring Ramus while Nashe remained loyal to Aristotle, but in general the pamphleteers mentioned the debate only incidentally in passing, and then left the matter alone. Opinion generally favoured the old ways. Nashe felt that students, despite a natural inclination towards new knowledge, 'must wisely prefer renowned antiquitie before newe found toyes, one line of *Alexanders Maister,* before the large inuectiue *Scolia* of the *Parisian* Kings Professor' (*Works,* I, 43). In Earle's *Micro-Cosmographie* it was the self-conceited man who: 'prefers *Ramus* before *Aristotle,* and *Paracelsus* before *Galen,* and whosoever with most Paradox is commended or *Lipsius* his hopping stile, before either Tully or Quintilian' (sig. C9^v).

The anti-Ciceronian movement in literary prose, the turn from connection, balance, conjunction, and long sentences constructed with carefully subordinated clauses, to aphorism, brevity and disjunction, had its analogies and parallels in popular prose, but there was no sudden transition. It would be too facile to see the ornate style of such early writers as Whetstone and Averell vanishing before the low style and realism of the Greene of the cony-catching pamphlets, never to return; Greene used the low style out of a sense of literary decorum, as an alternative not as a replacement. Undeniably the pamphlets showed a trend towards plainer writing, even though the less lettered authors continued to have recourse to elaborate figures of speech, Ciceronian structures, and the devices of Euphuism in their striving for effect, as in this opening to a murder story, written up by the servant of the murdered man:

> Not to painte it out with vainglorious termes of a large Exordium in a matter where throbbinge sorrowe breaketh of superfluous cir-

cumstances, and overwerying plaints abreuiate the libertie of speach; not to use the choice inuention of a pleasing discourse, where nothing but heauy misfortunes minister cause of melancholike and pensiue contemplations: But to explaine a tragicall trueth, and set foorth the lamentable order, of a premeditated murther, I will brieflie prosecute my own greefe.[7]

But Ciceronianism was not merely a rhetorical doctrine with bearing upon no area of living other than language. M.W. Croll calls it 'the representative ... of a tendency which expressed itself in a congeries of similar dogmas in all the chief subjects of sixteenth-century learning',[8] the dogmas of philosophical and religious orthodoxy. Hence anti-Ciceronianism accompanied the kind of radical tendencies and the movement away from authority vested in a single standard of reference that many of the pamphleteers feared and rejected. Their fear was understandable if we regard this change, in the words of another writer on rhetoric and ideas in this period as 'in part a shift from the preponderant emphasis on traditional wisdom to the preponderant emphasis on new discoveries'.[9]

Just as popular pamphlets took over the forms and formal devices of literary writing, so too their style showed the influence of tendencies and movements that had their origins and chief manifestations on a higher level. Many writers made use of rhetorical terms in what might appear to us to be a self-conscious manner, although in the days when such terms were common property this might not of course be the case. Christopher Newstead excuses himself from citing many examples of female fidelity in this way: 'Should I stand to enumerate all the regular Matrons that moone within the speare of fidelitie; I might seeme by a Logical Induction, in reckoning vp all particulars, to inferre a generall' (*An Apology for Women*, p. 26). 'Jane Anger' is showing that she knows the method of logical proof when she says: 'Give me leaue like a scholler to proue our wisdome more excellent than theirs, though I neuer knew what sophistry ment. There is no wisdome but it comes by grace, this is a principle & *Contra principia non est disputandum*' (*Iane Anger her Protection for Women*, sig. C2). In a lighter mood Donald Lupton puns on some rhetorical terms when he describes the whores of Turnbull Street in his *London and the Countrey Carbonadoed:* 'They partake of all the Liberall Sciences, for Grammar they know the Syntaxis, and the figure call'd Apollo P . . . for Retoricke, they know the Metonomia adiuncti, and Apostrophe' (pp. 53–54). Writers often draw attention to the use of a rhetorical figure by some preliminary or succeeding comment; Nashe adds at the end of Christ's long speech in *Christs Teares over Ierusalem:* 'Heere doe I confine our Sauiours collachrimate Oration, and putting off his borrowed person, restore him to the tryumphancie of his Passion' (*Works,* II, 60).

In *Nashes Lenten Stuffe* he parodies the high style in his story of the Pope and the herring-merchant by describing a bad smell in high-flown terms and then asking 'What needes there any more ambages?' (*Works,* III, 210). John Deacon in *Tobacco Tortuered* makes one of his characters say to the other, 'Forbeare (I beseech you) all such your further patheticall Prosopopoeias' (p. 76).

Discourses constructed in the manner recommended by the rhetoricians were often preceded by diagrammatic schemes, and accompanied by marginal glosses and elaborate headings. The chapter headings of such works indicated the author's efforts to produce a methodical arrangement, as this of William Heale's:

Chap. 1.
An introduction to the discourse following.

Chap. 2.
That it is not lawfull for a husband to beat his wife, is proved by reasons drawn from Nature.

Chap. 3.
The same confirmed by rules of morallitie or ciuill policie.

Chap. 4.
The same discussed by the Ciuill and Canon Lawes.

Chap. 5.
The same euinced by the law of God.

Chap. 6.
The Conclusion.

(*An Apologie for Women,* sig. A3)

Dekker's diagrammatic table of contents for *Lanthorne and Candle-light* (reproduced on p. 234) shows another example of methodical arrangement, less influenced by rhetoric. In pamphlets not subdivided into chapters the writers made sure that the niceties of arrangement, or disposition as the handbooks of rhetoric called it, were not overlooked. In *An Exhortation, To stirre up the mindes of all her Maiesties faithfull Subiects, to defend their Countrey* by Anthony Marten, the description of the Pope's procedures against Elizabeth is carefully ordered; Marten draws attention to his method at each stage:

Now let us see more at large by whom, against whome, and for what causes this warre, or rather cruel proscription, groweth (sig. A4).

A Table of all the matters, that are conteined in this Discourse.

Cap.1. { Of *Canting*.

Cap.2. { 1. What matters were tryed at a *Terme* that was in *Hell*.
2. The proceedings of that Court.
3. A councell held in Hell about the *Bell-man*.
4. A *Messenger* sent from thence, with instructions.

Cap.3. Of *Gull-groping*. { How *Gentlemen* are cheated at *Ordinaries*. To furnish which feast, these *Guests* are bidden, viz. { The Leaders. The *Fortune Hope*. The *Eagle*. The *Wood-pecker*. The *Gull*. The *Gull-groper*.

Cap.4. Of *Ferreting*. { How *Gentlemen* are vndone by taking vp *Commodities*. Which Tragædy hath these fiue Acts. viz. { A *Tumbler*. *Pursenetts*. A *Ferret*. *Rabbet-suckes*. A *Warren*.

Cap 5. Of *Hawking*. { How to catch *Birdes* by the *Booke*. Which is done with fiue *Netts*, viz. { A *Fawlconer*. A *Lure*. A *Tercell Gentle*. A *Byrd*. A *Mongrill*.

Cap.6. { Of *Iackes* of the *Clock-house*.

Cap.7. Of *Ranck-Riders*. { How *Inne-Keepers*, and *Hackney-men* are *Sadled*. To make whom goe a round pace, you must haue, { A *Colt*. A *Snaffle*. A *Ring*. *Prouander*.

Cap.8. { Of *Moone-men*.
Cap.9. { The Infection of the *Suburbes*.

Cap.10. Of *Jynglers*. { The Villany of *Horse-Coursers*. Who consist of { *Jynglers*. *Drouers*. *Goades*. *Skip-Iackes*.

Cap.11. { Of *Iack in a Box*: or a new kinde of *Cheating*, teaching how to change *Gold* into *Siluer*: vnto which is added a *Map*, by which a man may learne how to Trauell all ouer *England*, and haue his charges borne.

Cap.12. { The *Bell-mans* second Nights walke: In which he meetes with a number of Monsters that liue in *Darknesse*.

4. Table of contents for Dekker's *Lanthorne and Candle-light*.

> Now let us consider, against whome, this holy father and his adherents have raysed up so ungodly and so unnaturall a warre (sig. Bl^v).
>
> We see now by whome, and against whom this warre is made. It remaineth to declare breefly the causes thereof (sig. B4).

Even in news pamphlets and reports authors were anxious to show off the care they had taken in organizing their material. In Thomas Cooper's *The Cry and Reuenge of Blood* the account of a murder and its aftermath is set out in eight chapters, not so as to make it like a crime story, but rather to construct an anatomy of crime, centred on a particular event. The killing itself, not described until the third chapter, is presented in neat subdivisions:

> 1. Of the particular Murther at Halesworth. 2. Of the Actors and Accessories therein. 3. Of the parties that were Murthered. 4. Of the Manner and Circumstances how they were made away. 5. Of the Meanes to conceale the Murther beeing committed. 6. And diuerse obseruations considerable on either side.

Definition by reference to some of the Aristotelian categories or predicaments (substance, quantity, quality, relation, manner of doing, manner of suffering, when, where, situs, habitus) was used to give that sense of a subject being completely dealt with which Bacon rejected as spurious. Dekker in *Villanies Discouered* proves by citing certain of these categories that prison is an enchanted castle because 'it makes a wise man loose his Wits, a foole to know himselfe':

> Art thou sicke in Prison? Then Thou art sicke in health . . . Art Thou Olde and in Prison? . . . Art Thou young and in Prison? . . . Hast Thou gotten other mens goods into Thy hands, and so liuest on Them in prison? Imprisonment to Thee is a sāctuary, Thou art a robber borne out by Law . . . Art Thou in prison and full of wants, then art Thou a fielde of unripe corne, lodged by the winde and raine . . . Art Thou poore and in prison : then art Thou buried before Thou art dead (sigs. 14–14^v).

That such detail could be tedious was recognized by the formulation of a rhetorical device called paralepsis, whereby the writer would mention a technique only to state that he did not intend to employ it: 'This womans chastity nothwithstanding, he speedily attempts, and effectually, as it manifestly appeares, obtaines, the maner how? the times when? the places where, the meanes and causes by whom, were too intricate and tedious to expresse' (*A True Relation of the most Inhumane and bloody Murther, of Master Iames Minister and Preacher of the Word of God at Rockland in Norfolke*, sig. A3^v).

One particular form of rhetorical style which had a noticeable influence on pamphlet-writing in the 1580s and 1590s was Euphuism. It was a style which lent itself readily to the florid moralizing much in vogue in the early pamphlets. Some writers took up both Lyly's images from natural history as well as the predilection for certain figures of speech found to a less significant extent in the work of many other writers of the sixteenth century. These figures were *isocolon* (phrases or clauses of the same length), *parison* (syntactic correspondence between the words of each unit, noun corresponding to noun, verb to verb, and so on), and *paromoion* (similarity of sound.)[10] William Averell, for instance, opens his sententious tale of a proud wife in *A Dyall for dainty Darlings* with a Euphuistic fantasia on the theme of the leopard and his spots:

> But there is no arte can chaunge the spottes of the leoparde, no laboure washe off the colour of the Morian, nor force of the hammer breake the Adamant, nor no art nor strength resist a wicked woman, but if she once let loose the raines of pride and pleasure, shaking of the grace of God from of her careless shoulders: If the feare of her creator, can not reduce her from sinne, nor the worlds report conuert her to shame: it is neither wisdome nor pollicie, perswasion nor counsell, force nor fortitude, can alter the course of her corrupted nature (sig. B2).

He was the most slavishly Euphuistic of the early writers; the three simple tales in this pamphlet are spun out to amazing length by the use of figures of repetition and amplification, in particular similes in the 'but as . . . so . . .' construction—

> But as eche disease, if it be not taken in time creepeth by continuaunce into euerie part of the body, or as the water that breaketh out of his boundes, if it be not quicklie stopped, gathereth at length into a mightie flood: so this malladie of her minde, being let at lybertie, overflowed the bankes of reason (sig. B2^v);

hypozeuxis—

> Draw neere . . . you that have periwigs to curl your heaire, colours to paint your face, art to square your shoulders, bolsters to fashiō your wast (sig. B3);

and apostrophe—

O monstrous Pride, O unsatiable nature, O execrable furye (sig. B2)

O vanitie of vanitie, O fond and fickle beautye, nay, O stinking fleshly glory (sig. C1)

O myror of maidenhood, O glass of true virginitie, O mind endued with modesty, O hart fraught with true humility (sig. E4).

William Rankins, a close contemporary of Averell's, used Euphuistic devices in a more compact manner, but once again to expand on a theme and to use three words when one would have done, as for example in his description of actors as 'such as liue by others losse, laughes, at others languishing, florish by others fading, sing at others sorrow' (*A Mirrour of Monsters,* sig. B2). The proverbial wisdom that he was fond of citing—

> We see then that all is not golde that glistereth, nor euerie one to be esteemed a friend that speaketh faire, the deadest water hath the deepest chanell, from the finest Flower is gathered as well poison as Honye (*A Mirrour of Monsters,* sigs. D3^v–D4)—

was also a Euphuistic device, though common also to other kinds of writing that relied on truism and commonplace. Despite Greene's manifesto on behalf of plain writing in *The Second part of Connycatching* he never entirely abandoned his rhetorical style and in the moral exhortation to 'all the wanton youths of England' that prefaced his last pamphlet, *The Repentance of Robert Greene,* he made extensive use of the Euphuistic devices of cumulative analogy, repetition, and parison so characteristic of his earliest work:

> He forseeth not that such as clime hastely, fall sodainely: that Bees haue stings as well as honie: that vices haue ill endes as well as sweet beginnings: and whereof growes this heedles life, but of selfe conceit, thinking the good counsell of age is dotage: that the aduice of friends proceeds of enuie, and not of loue: that when their fathers correct them for their faults, they hate them: whereas when the Black Oxe hath trod on their feete, and the Crowes foote is seene in their eies, then toucht with the feeling & their owne follie, they sigh out had I wist, when repentance commeth too late (sig. A2^v).

Lodge was perhaps the last of the group of early pamphleteers to use Euphuistic techniques to any extent. There was a considerable development between his early pamphlet *An Alarum against Vsurers*

(1584) with its Ciceronian sentences, like the opening attack on merchants,

> But as among a tree of fruite there bee some withered fallings, and as among wholesome hearbes there growes some bitter *Colloquintida;* so it cannot be, but among such a number of Marchauntes, there shoulde bee some, that degenerate from the true name and nature of Merchaunts,

its use of apostrophe, exclamatio, and prosopopoeia, as well as alliteration and antithesis, and the vivid pseudo-conversational *Wits Miserie, and the Worlds Madnesse* of twelve years later. In the letter to the gentleman readers in *The Life and Death of William Longbeard* which came before *Wits Miserie* in 1593, Lodge stated, in a Baconian manner, that 'In the olde time menne studied to illustrate matter with words, now we striue for words beside matter'. But he still enjoyed the old florid style, and indulged in it for the speeches of his characters: 'The Cedar, though a tall tree, lets the little shrub prosper vnder him: the Eglantine flourisheth by the Oake: the Goldfinch feedeth by the Griffin: but the prouerbe is true among vs nowadaies. *Homo homini Demon*' (*The Life and Death of William Longbeard*, sig. B2). There was also another, apparently late, pamphlet, *The Divel coniured* (1596),[11] in which modified Euphuistic constructions, perhaps thought fitting on account of the medieval-style moralizing, continued to appear:

> Ah men, for whereas you neither respect age, nor regard deuotion, neither feare God, nor regard the lawes, wilde beasts assaile not vnprouoked, serpents sting not vntrod on, the harmlesse bird is no Harpies prey, shall then a Hermit in deuotion: an old man in yeares, a poore man in fortune, be subiect to your litannies? (sig. C1).

Nashe had rejected ornate writing and 'over-racked Rhetoricke' in his preface to *Menaphon* in 1589, and found several occasions to mock at Euphuism[12] and dissociate himself from it, particularly in *Strange Newes* in 1592: '*Euphues* I read when I was a little ape in Cambridge, and then I thought it was *Ipse ille:* it may be excellent good still, for ought I know, for I lookt not on it this ten yeere' (*Works*, I, 319). Harvey had earlier accused him (in the *Advertisement for Pap-hatchet*, written in 1589 but published as part of *Pierces Supererogation* in 1593) of writing 'nothing but pure Mammaday and a fewe morsels of flyblowne Euphuism, somewhat nicely minced for puling stomackes!'[13]

Middleton gave Euphuism a scornful mention in 1604, in the opening verses of *Father Hubburds Tales*, where the Nightingale advises the Ant on a suitable style for his tales:

> If thou Euphuize which once was rare,
> And of all English Phrase the life and blood,
> In those times for the fashion past compare,
> Ile say thou borrowest, and condemne thy stile.
>
> (sig. B3)

Ten years later Anthony Nixon, the plagiarist, recalled the style in his address to the readers of *A Straunge Foot-Post* (1613); by then it must have been a forgotten fashion:

> For eschewing the like enormities, I wish thee *(Reader)* instead of the *Persians* Picture of an *Epicure,* and the *Parthians* picture of an *Harlot* in thine house, to carry about thee this Packet in thy Pocket: Which being opened, with Present sufficient matter vnto thee that may both make thee weane thy selfe from wanton desires, and shun the misery that followes excessive superfluity (sig. A2).

Occasionally the pamphleteers showed some distrust of fine words and a sense that plain expression was to be preferred. One or two news writers, for instance, felt that their stories would seem more credible if worded simply: 'The playness of the Style wherein it is written, voide of *Ambages,* Amplifications, and all other Vaine flourishes... is to me no small argument of the verity thereof', wrote Edward Gresham in a letter to the reader at the beginning of *Strange fearful & true newes, which hapned at Carlstadt, in the Kingdome of Croatia,* an anonymous and highly improbable account of recent supernatural portents in Germany. Others thought that whereas educated readers liked an eloquent style, it did not appeal to the unlearned, though the evidence does not suggest this was the case. Simon Kellwaye wrote of his medical pamphlet, *A Defensative against the Plague,* that its style was 'not so exquisitly plotted with so orderly a method, or so finely polished with so filed an eloquence, thereby to breede a delight to the learned, which would be a loathing to the unlearned' (sig. A4). But John Taylor the Water-Poet, author, on his own reckoning, of sixty-three separate works of different kinds, knew that his readers enjoyed a display of style; although he began his pseudo-news pamphlet *The Great Eater of Kent, or Part of the Admirable Teeth and Stomack Exploits of Nicholas Wood* with the claim that he would 'write bare truth, bare and threed-bare, and almost starke naked truth', he then put in a plea for literary licence:

> Yet by your leaue, Master Criticke, you must give me licence to flourish my Phrases, to embellish my lines, to adorne my Oratory, to embroder my speeches, to enterlace my words, to draw out my sayings, and to bumbaste the whole suite of the businesse for the time of your wearing (*All the Workes*, p. 143).

There is here an implicit recognition that words and things are separate; Taylor did not distrust words, and he was proud to be doing what Bacon would have despised, inclining 'rather towards copie than weight'. It seems to have been what pamphlet readers really wanted.

ii

New stylistic influences arose alongside Euphuism, and superseded it, in particular those of Greene and Nashe. Greene's was the more circumscribed, being largely confined to pamphlets of the cony-catching genre which ceased to appear after about 1610;[14] the growing popularity of low-life subjects and of the plain style was part of a wider movement to which Greene's work gave considerable impetus, although it was not in itself an initiating factor. A number of pamphlets trading on Greene's name quickly appeared after his death[15]— 'what a coyle there is with pamphleting on him', wrote Nashe a few months later—and he had an influence on both Nashe and Dekker, although not essentially on their styles. Nashe indeed strongly denied the charge of imitating him:

> This I will proudly boast . . . that the vaine which I have . . . is of my owne begetting, and cals no man father in England but my selfe, neyther *Euphues*, nor *Tarlton*, nor *Greene* (*Works*, I, 319).

In fact, he even suggested that the boot was on the other foot:

> While he liu'd (as some Stationers can witness with me) hee subscribing to me in any thing but plotting plaies (*Works*, III, 132).[16]

Nashe's influence on his contemporaries was more diverse than Greene's; it worked through his style, through his fame, and through his creation of the character Piers Penniless. The pamphlet *Pierce Penilesse* inspired three sequels, Middleton's *The Blacke Booke*, Dekker's *Newes from Hell*, which had as its running title 'The Deuils Answere to Pierce Pennylesse' and the anonymous *Returne of the Knight of the Poste*. Nashe's ghost was employed as a mouthpiece for social and political satire in two late pamphlets, *Tom Nash his Ghost* (?1642) and John

Taylor's *Crop-Eare Curried, Or, Tom Nash his Ghost* (1644), and in the last decade of the sixteenth century and throughout the first half of the seventeenth there were literary allusions to him, recalling his connection with the Marprelate controversy[17] his taste for invective and his quarrel with the Harvey family,[18] and Piers' own fame.[19] Both his style and his views on the arts had their followers. Lodge called him 'true English Aretine' after the author whose style he professed most to admire, and imitated some of the vivid details of the Deadly Sins and sinners from *Pierce Penilesse* in his own *Wits Miserie*. Middleton and Dekker tried to imitate his colloquial prose, and the grotesquerie of Rowley's description of a woman weeping in *A Search for Money* may owe something to the exaggerated style of the Hero and Leander episode in *Nashes Lenten Stuffe:*

> Then twas full sea, and the water stretcht a little beyond her bounds, from forth the hollow caves of her eyes issued fountains, which walking downe the furrowed paths of her face, and venterouslie meaning (as it were) to passe the gulfe of her mouth in quietnesse, bound her tongue for a certaine space to peace, which afterward being releast, she went forwarde to tell us a strange Metamorphosis, and one indeede that *Ouid* had quite forgotten, how that all her Ale was transform'd into those fatall meteors, which was indeede Chalke (pp. 3–4).

It is always difficult with the pamphlets to be precise about the sources of stylistic habits or tricks in the absence of factual evidence about their derivation, but it is easy and not unreasonable to imagine, in an anonymous pamphlet ascribed to 'Philip Foulface', entitled *Bacchus Bountie*, published in 1593, that the combination of low language and classical allusions in a vigorously witty and alliterative style, owes something to the influence of Nashe:

> Nevertheless when my Braines fell to the Busines, and began to beate as though my Head had been ready to burst, disdaining withall the Help of Mother *Crackfart* the Midwife, *Iuno Lucina* was as deafe as a Dishclout, so that *Volens Nolens* I betooke myselfe to the Hearbe *Hellebore*, whose pleasant Operation produced so present a Purgation, that forthwith there followed a most speedie Deliuerance, excluding Cares, renuing Ioy (*The Harleian Miscellany*, ed. W. Oldys and T. Park, London, 1809, II, 300–10).

The author of *The Returne of the Knight of the Poste*, who claimed in his preface to have been an 'intimate and neare companion' of Nashe, lacked, as he admitted, both the 'wittie pleasentnes of his conceites ... and the gaulye bitternes of his pens sharpenes' (sig. A4); he paid tribute to his predecessor by echoing his views on the value of culture in a threnody on the decay of learning:

> Hence shall it come to passe that the loftie Poem wherein the soule of arte shalbe celestiallie infused and the rare amazing passions of life stirring tragedyes shalbe both neglected or vnrewarded . . . neither honour nor beauty shall haue any shieldes or defences against the piercing darts of ignorance and detraction (sigs. F4–F4^v).

Dekker, Nashe's closest disciple, was influenced by Nashe's attitude to learning as well as by his style. In *A Knights Coniuring* he lamented the decay of learning in an allegory which depicted the temple of the Muses falling into ruins, and showed how all those asked to help repair it—gentlemen, lawyers, soldiers, even scholars—refused; Nashe, newly arrived in Elysium, is described as being 'still haunted with the sharpe and *Satyricall spirit* that followed him heere vpon *earth*' on this account. In *Lanthorne and Candle-light*, writing of those pseudo-pamphleteers, he called 'faulconers', who patched up little books entirely out of snippets from other men's writing and then cozened rich men into becoming their patrons, Dekker took up the subject again: 'O sacred *Learning!* why doost thou suffer thy seauen leaued tree to be plucked by barbarous and most vnhallowed handes? Why is thy beatifull Mayden body, polluted like a strumpets and prostituted to beastly and slauish ignorance' (*Non-Dramatic Works*, III, 246).

Most of Dekker's allusions to Nashe occur, predictably, in *Newes from Hell*, where he praised his predecessor as 'ingenious, ingenuous, fluent, facetious, T. Nash', and copies his titles for the devil and several of his details about hell. His brief account of Orpheus and Eurydice (sig. C1^v), full of Nashean parentheses, may well have been inspired by Nashe's story of Hero and Leander.[20] His style derived vivacity from Nashe's speed and mocking way with literary allusions, both in *Newes from Hell* and elsewhere; this is particularly evident in what was probably Dekker's greatest literary success, *The Guls Horne-Booke*. The intimate, elbow-grabbing manner is especially Nashean, as in this witty panegyric on sleep:

> Can we drink too much of that whereof to tast too little, tumbles vs into a church-yard, and to vse it but indifferently, throwes us into Bedlam? No, no, looke vppon *Endymion*, the Moones Minion who slept threescore & fifteen yeares, and was not a haire the worse for it. Can lying abedde till noone then (being not the threescore and fifteenth thousand part of his nap) be hurtfull? (*Non-Dramatic Works*, II, 217).

Dekker sometimes shared Nashe's humour, and his bent for the mock-heroic or bathetic qualities which come to the fore in his anecdotes of plague-time. But his most characteristic stylistic effects, in particular his extensively developed conceits, were not Nashean, and he lacked Nashe's amazing verbal inventiveness and syntactical fluidity.

The influences of rhetoric, of Euphuism, of the style and trends initiated by Greene and Nashe, were explicitly acknowledged by many pamphleteers. The conventions of popular writing demanded that the authors show themselves aware of literary fashions, and many of the learned trappings of these pamphlets might well be ascribed, not to the reader's genuine interest in citations from Aristotle or Juvenal, but to the authors' desire to parade newly-acquired learning.[21] But the most significant influence on pamphlet style was unacknowledged by the pamphleteers, necessarily so, because it is only a historical understanding of the relationship between the prose of this period and what came before and after it that enables us to define this influence and give it a name: the oral tradition. Modern admirers of Elizabethan prose often isolate as one of its differences from modern prose the fact that it is closer to the spoken word, 'based on living idiomatic speech', as L. C. Knights puts it, 'richly colloquial' (I. A. Gordon), heavily reliant on customary usage, idioms and proverbs, punning and wordplay, requiring to be read aloud or at least 'interpreted' into sound (Ian Watt), for proper appreciation.[22] The quality of much Elizabethan prose that makes it come fully to life only when it is read aloud does not always endear it to the modern reader, who is used to absorbing printed prose rapidly and silently. It seems to require, as James Sutherland has said of Nashe,[23] the kind of attention we are willing to accord to poetry, which we expect to read carefully and, if necessary, over and over again, but not, of right, to prose. If we take into account the nature of the pamphleteers' audience, this requirement seems perfectly reasonable; they were, after all, more used to hearing than to reading, and in particular to hearing spoken poetry, or, at least, verse. And naturally enough they would bring some of their listening habits to bear when they read.

Elizabethan society in the late 1500s and early 1600s was in a state of transition between the values of a hierarchically based, largely feudal society, sustaining and sustained by the power of a hereditary aristocracy, and those of a commercial and competitive urban society in which the influence of a growing middle-class of professional men, merchants, lawyers, and financiers, was to become all-pervasive. The printed books and pamphlets of this period—the pamphlets especially, being less sophisticated both in presentation and in the nature of the readership for which they were designed—reflect another aspect of this transition. In their light, it is a transition between what has been characterized as the age of the ear, or the 'oral/aural'[24] culture of the middle ages, based for the small corpus of the literate on the manuscript and the spoken word, for the rest on the spoken word only, and the age of the eye, or the 'visual' culture and new attitudes and perceptions that developed in consequence of the invention of printing with moveable type. The impact made on society by the invention of printing is a vast subject, still largely unexplored;[25] but at least it is widely acknowledged now that printing, one of the three inventions which, along with gunpowder and the compass, Bacon had said 'changed the appearance and state of the whole world' (*Novum Organum,* Aphorism 129), was responsible for subtle and far-reaching transformations in thought and perception over a long period. It is one of the most significant aspects of the Elizabethan popular pamphlet that it appeared at a time of such importance in the history of the book, and that it was addressed, at least in part, to those who were not especially familiar with books. They were not, however, unfamiliar with words; and naturally, linguistic attitudes and usages derived from the experience of the oral tradition found their way into the language and form of the printed book.

It was not only the readers, but also the authors and the printers of pamphlets who were engaged in a kind of enterprise new to them, and there are many ways in which the fresh and unexplored aspects of the undertaking are evident. The new sense of the possibilities of the physical structure of a mass-produced book resulted in many typographical extravagances, and other devices calculated to appeal to the newly opened reading eye, such as indexes, tables of contents, elaborate chapter headings, marginal notes, and the significant uses of different sizes and kinds of type.[26] On the other hand, such characteristics of written language as consistent spelling and a punctuation system governed by rules, designed to appeal to the reader rather than the hearer, were slow to appear. From our point of view, the effects of the oral tradition were virtues as well as vices in written prose. It was in part responsible for both fluidity and formlessness, obscure shifts in tone and mood and unexpectedly fortunate variations. Formally, the influence is apparent in the wandering, digressive, non-organic structures of many pamphlets, the easy movement through a series of scarcely-connected devices reaching a conclusion in no way related to the beginning. The way that tirades against abuses and general social satires temporarily assume and presently abandon such traditional patterns as the Seven Deadly Sins or Estates satire, and the movement between personified abstractions and Character-portraits of conventional and contemporary types, were both features of this sort of writing, ordered like a speech to carry the audience along with it stage by stage rather than allowing them to go back and forth over it.

Barnaby Rich's pamphlets, for example, were almost all constructed with the sort of loose conversational flow and disregard for formal unity that can perplex and irritate a reader accustomed to closely organized structures. A typical example is *Faultes faults, And nothing else but Faultes,* of which a modern editor says, 'The book does not lack unity altogether, but it falls short of what it might have been and, indeed, started out to be'.[27] It does indeed start out in what appears to be an organized manner, with the proposition that all things are best in their proper time and season, and the deduction that the author's daring in taking upon himself to 'finde Faults in so daungerous a time, when there is no man willing to heare of his own misse' will not be approved. A second proposition that 'the world is growne to that passe that we can laugh at our owne imperfections in another, but we cannot see them in our selues' (sig. B3) opens the pamphlet proper. Rich begins by calling attention to the arbitrariness of his method:

> Amongst an infinite number of faults, I am not yet resolved with which of them I should beginne,

and then gives objective satirical portraits of two stock figures, the jestmonger and the parasite; the point of view changes, and the author becomes a narrator, interpreting for his audience the nature of a procession that passes in front of him: 'But see here a companie now presenting themselues . . .' (sig. C2). A scene evolves, with the narrator as part of it:

> Will you see how I am pestered with a finicall companie that comes in now all together (sig. C2).

He is individualized with a partiality for tobacco which gives Rich an opportunity for satire on one of his favourite subjects:

> But O for a Pipe of Tobacco! passion of me, how haue I forgotten my selfe, that haue vented so much idle breath without a pipe of Tobacco? (sig. D).

At this point the structure changes; tobacco makes Rich think of drinking, and in a trice he has embarked on a description of the Seven Deadly Sins, not as personalities but in terms of their social effects. He digresses briefly on the counterfeit soldier, another favourite topic, and then calls himself to order—'I haue almost lost my selfe in this intricate laborinth of abuses' (sig. D4^v)—and proceeds to describe Falsehood and Pride. He checks a movement towards abstraction and commonplace-book aphorisms with a sudden return to his persona as satirical observer:

> But Lorde, how haue I forgotten my self! I was bidden today to a dinner, where will be a great meeting of good company, I must frame my selfe to be sociable amongest them (sig. E4).

After some general satire on the inanity of social behaviour he introduces the next section with a story-teller's easy informality:

> I thinke it were best for mee now to take a little breath, but I haue yet a short iourney to make into the country, I must goe visite the seruantes of Christ those that liue by the plow and the cart (sig. F).

And so, with a succession of changes of viewpoint signalled by some such authorial intervention, the pamphlet moves through its leisurely survey of all the traditional abuses. The method is typical of anatomy style pamphlets like most of Rich's work, Nashe's *The Anatomie of Absurditie* and *Pierce Penilesse*, and many of Lodge's pamphlets. Fragmentary structures and devices punctuate the formless flow only briefly. Such interruptions by the author are very common; often he calls himself to order with some phrase such as 'Without further evasion, I will returne into the path of my intended purpose' (*This Worlds Folly*, sig. B3^v), or 'Tut preachers can better teach this (say you) return you to your deuils: I confesse it my friends, absolve me therefore' (Lodge, *Wits Miserie*, p. 25). They may signal confusion, but at the same time imply a kind of easy person-to-person relationship between writer and reader where a strictly regulated form is out of keeping. The illusion of a speaking voice, changing tone according to the speaker's changing relationship with his audience, is preserved.

The writer's intimate awareness of his reader sanctions the use of stylistic devices calculated to render their relationship as direct as possible. In particular, a modern reader is aware of the writers' efforts to work upon the emotions of their readers, which are often conspicuous in sensational prose, both moralizing and reportage. Nashe and Dekker use contrived figures of speech for this purpose.

In *Christs Teares* Nashe uses prosopopoeia, first having Christ speak a lamentation over the sins of Jerusalem, then giving Miriam a horrific speech as she decides to eat her son rather than allow him to die from famine. He prefaces Miriam's words with a direct appeal to the audience:

> Mothers of LONDON, (each one of you to your selues) doe but imagine that you were *Miriam,* wyth what hart (suppose you) could ye go about the cooquerie of your own chydren? Not hate, but hunger, taught Miriam to forgette mother-hood. To this purport conceite her discoursing with herselfe (*Works,* II, 71).

Dekker in *The Wonderfull Yeare* prepares for a description of the plague with an evocative account of his own fear: 'A stiffe and freezing horror sucks vp the riuers of my bloud: my haire stands on end with the panting of my braines: mine eye-balls are readie to start out, being beaten with the billowes of my teares' (*Plague Pamphlets,* p. 25). In another plague pamphlet, Thomas Brewen's *A Dialogue betwixt a Cittizen, and a poore Countrey-man* the author uses erotema (a series of rhetorical questions), one of Dekker's favourite devices, addressed to London which is personified, with the object of arousing fear by describing its effects: 'And yet, how art thou frighted? How pale are thy Cheekes? How does this one fit of a burning feauer, inflame all thy body?' (sig. C1). The author of *This Worlds Folly* uses apostrophe, metaphor, simile, and frequentatio in the grand *memento mori* where he appeals to different sections of his audience in turn:

> Remember, ô thou mighty man, that swelling titles of Honor are but *folia vanitatis,* the leaues of vanity, a Gnathonicall puffe, and a blast of the chaps: Remember, ô thou rich man, that terrene & transitory pleasures are like the Bee, though they yeeld hony, yet carry they a sting, and are but *Lilia Terrae,* more delectable in show, than durable in continuance: Remember o thou Extortioner, thou cruell man, thou murtherer, thou adulterer, thou deceitfull man, thou that vnconscionably detainest the hirelings wages, and thou that actest inexorable villanies secretly in the darke, imprisoned from the worldes dull eye; that if the Eagle can discerne, *Sub frutice Leporem, sub fluctibus piscem* (as one hath it), the Hare vnder the bush, and the Fish vnder the waues; much more can God, who is the Creator of creatures, penetrate the closet of thy hart with his all-seeing eye, and discerne thy clandestine sinnefull practises, before, and in their very conception, and for them he will bring thee to iudgement (sig. D2).

Writers of sensational news pamphlets resorted to all these devices in order to involve and move the readers. In the account of a child murder appended to *The Life and Death of Lewis Gaufredy* the author relates the passion that the tale has caused him to feel, he appeals to the murderers, he gives verbatim the mother's lament for her dead child, and finally he urges his readers to identify themselves with his protagonist: 'You mothers also which haue children, subiect in the like case, to the like perill and daunger as happned to this woman, would you not lament? ah would you not greeue for the violent death of your owne blood?' (sig. El^v).

Writers turn, as it were, away from the story and directly towards the audience to solicit a response: 'Now tell me, thou that readest; Didst thou ever read a thing more tragical?' (*The Bloudy booke, Or, The Tragicall and desperate end of Sir Iohn Fites (alias) Fitz*, 1605, sig. E3). The devices of apostrophe and exhortation, particularly at the end or at some climactic point where the writer addresses his readers as if he were a speaker making a final assault on their awareness, were conventional as a mode of conclusion, especially for moral anecdotes or criminal confessions. Averell in *A Dyall for dainty Darlings* exhorts his readers to follow the example of his matchless heroine with the finest flourish he can manage:

> O myror of maidenhood, O glasse of true virginitie, O mind endued with modesty, O hart fraught with true humility. See heere you gadding girles, that gape after euery gaude, and prease after ech peeuishe pastime, you that can daunce with the dantiest, smile with the smothest, & laugh with the leudest . . . Behold the exercise of this virgin, note her life, and follow her example (sig. E4).

This appealing to the audience, which functioned, crudely put, as a way of getting them into the mood of the passage, could be done on any level. Nashe's conversational asides show the device at its most intimate; Lodge with *Wits Miserie* introduces some of his sins in a quasi-melodramatic manner, with warnings and exclamations: 'Crosse your selues my maisters more Deuils are abroad, and MAMMONS sons begin to muster: what! a fiend in a square cap, a Schollers gowne! nay, more, in his hands a Testament! *Eho miraculum dicis;* by my sooth sir it is SIMONY' (p. 34). S. R, in *Martin Mark-All*, draws the reader into his confidence: 'Now Gentlemen (by my troth) I could finde it in my heart to haue spent a bottle of Ale, that you had beene there with me, to haue seene the concourse of these Caterpillers' (sig. E). Greene invites the readers' participation by suggesting, at the beginning of a story of crime, that they visit the site of the deed (*The Thirde and last Part of Conny-Catching*, p. 27).

Nashe's work is especially full of colloquially phrased interjections, but his insistence on their spontaneity feels like a cultivated device. He constantly recalls himself from digressions:

> A poyson light on it, how come I to disgresse . . .? (*Works*, I, 360).
>
> Come, come, I am entraunced from my Text (*Works*, I, 361).
>
> *Redeo ad vos, mei Auditores,* haue I not an indifferent prittye vayne in Spurgalling an Asse? if you know how extemporall it were at this instant, and with what hast it is writ, you would say so (*Works*, I, 199).
>
> Stay, let me looke about, where am I? in my text or out of it? (*Works*, III, 219).

At the end of the discourse on devils in *Pierce Penilesse* he appeals directly to the reader's patience:

> Gentle Reader, *tandem aliquando* I am at leasure to talke to thee. I dare say thou hast cald me a hundred times dolt for this senseless discourse: it is no matter, thou dost but as I haue doone by a number in my days (*Works*, I, 239).

Sentence structure is as fluid as form, and characterized by all manner of syntactical anomalies. Changes of structure in mid-sentence are very common. There are shifts from indirect to direct speech, as in *The Life and Death of Gamaliel Ratsey:*

> Then Ratsey. . . swore his man should neither carry it to hell nor heauen for abusing it so, for I bade him follow me (saith he) and he sure mistooke me (sig. Bl^v).

Greene in *A Disputation* changes person three times inside one sentence:

> Shordish wold complaine to dame Anne a Cleare, if wee of the sisterhood should not vphold her iollitie,—who is that Laurence comes in to heare our talke, Oh tis the boy Nan that tels vs supper is readie, why then Laurence what say you to me? (p. 39).

There are changes from past to present tense; the frequent use of the historic present heightens the sense of immediacy:

> Theyr dead bodies floate hourely aboue water, and are continuallye taken uppe: It cannot yet be knowne, howe manye haue fell in the Tempest of Gods fearful iudgement.[28]

> King *Iames* is proclaimed: now does fresh bloud leap into the cheekes of the Courtier: the Souldier now hangs vp his armor and is glad that he shall feede vpon the blessed fruits of peace (Dekker, *The Wonderfull Yeare*, in *Plague Pamphlets*, p. 23).

Some sentences contain more than one variation in tense:

> Words past betwixt Master Claxton and that Harlot *Besse of Canberry*, together those two goe, but who followeth them both, the poore Gentleman was altogether ignorant, and little suspected: After them both *Country Tom* hasteneth, with a short Trunchin, or Bastinado under his cloake, and findes accompanying together his Harlot with Master Claxton (H. Goodcole, *Heavens Speedie Hue and Crie sent after Lust and Murther*, sig. B2ᵛ).

In the following passage from *The Bloudy booke, Or, The Tragicall and desperate end of Sir Iohn Fites (alias) Fitz*, a vividly written and exceedingly gruesome account of murder and suicide, the fast-moving colloquial style of the narrative with its loosely coordinated syntax and changes of tense, contrasts strongly with the dramatic, rhetorical manner of the speech, which is like something out of a play. This sort of shift between styles is not at all unusual; again, perhaps, it is a feature of spoken rather than written story-telling where the speaker's change of tone and of voice is a recognized narrative technique:

> Yet rising againe, and pulling the blade out of his bodie again, he lookes vpon the place to view the wounde, and hauing with his eies looked therevpon, and with his fingers handled the same, as woondring at his owne courage, he grumbled out this speech, to this effect: Proude heart, Wilt thou not yeilde? Shall neyther the terror of Justice affright thee? The edge of this steele massacre thee? Nor death it selfe daunt thee? Split, split, and in this onely wound die: That I thy owner, may not liue, to heare the honour of my credite stayned, with these my odious actes (sig. E2ᵛ).

Another feature of oral style is the incorporation of rhyming phrases or verse rhythms within a sentence:

> Money, vengeance and Hell so soone as Money, he will not bide with mee, he answers not my loue with his company, he has promised me increase, but he returnes not himselfe... no honnie, no money, no honney... (W. Rowley, *A Search for Money*, p. 13).

> Surely they that abuse the world, that abuse their greatnesse, wealth, that abuse their wealth and wit, they lose a blessing of the world, of their greatnesse, wealth and wit. These things are theirs,

whilest well vsed: but being abvsed, they are not theirs (T. Tuke, *A Treatise Against Painting*, p. 20).

This syntactic freedom shows to its best effect in narratives, where the resultant prose has a quick-flowing vigour, as in this lively snippet from Greene's *A Notable Discouery*, which exactly captures the tone and rhythm of the speaking voice:

> But up goes he and his cros-biters with him, & seeing the Gentlemen in bed, out with his dagger and asked what base villain it was that there sought to dishonest his wife (p. 49).

The following passage, from *Two most vnnatural and bloodie Murthers* (1605), is less colloquially phrased; indeed, it aims, in its dramatically extended simile, at the high style. But once again, the free syntax of the main part of the sentence, breaking several grammatical rules at a blow, moves the story on at an extraordinary pace in the manner of an oral story-teller:

> And as the sea, beeing hurled into hideous billowes, by the fury of the winde, hideth both heauen and earth from the eye of man: so he being overwhelmed by the violence of his passion, all naturall loue was forgot in his remembrance, caught his childe up by the necke, and striking at him with his dagger, the childe lent him such a looke, would haue driuen a hand seauen yeares prentice unto murther to an ague (p. 13).

Fluid writing of this sort, combined with the devices of more conscious artifice, such as puns, alliteration, and various kinds of word-play, especially those involving some form of repetition, produced different effects. Sometimes the result was a very mannered style, heavily reliant on puns and the value of isolated inkhorn terms, such as this from the preface to *This Worlds Folly*:

> Let me thus far insinuate my selfe into thy favourable acceptance: that without squint-eye, thou wilt supravise this my hasty, and artlesse home-spun web (the rapted corrolarie of my more busie howers) and silently suspend the Cryticke censure: seeing it was (from th'Exordium to th'Exodium) warpt and wouen in some few sad minuts, softly stolne from the humide bosome of the silent Night (sig. A).

This is a use of language which sounds very sophisticated, but only because it relies on the reader's quickness of ear and the verbal awareness cultivated by a long habit of relying on memory. Another result was the complex and often syntactically confused sentence:

> *Lust,* the marrow-eater of the world, the canker of health, the azure complectioner of the eyes, the azure infeebler of the backe, the consumption of the braine: and lastly, thus seuerally the decay of the whole frame of man, and yet euery little world has his seuerall lights, and can Arithemetize and cast up this account (W. Parkes, *The Curtaine-Drawer,* p. 8).

But there was also the sort of rich prose alert to all the possibilities of language, much admired now at a time when the written and the spoken language are so distinct, as for instance, this sentence from Middleton's *The Blacke Booke:*

> I the blacke Constable commanded my white Guard, not onely to assist my Office with their brown Billes, but to raise vp the house extemporie: with that the dreadful watch men hauing authoritie, standing by them, thundred at the doore, whilst the Candle lightned in the Chamber, and so betweene thundring and lightning, the Bawde rizze, first putting the Snuffe to an vntimely death, a cruell and lamentable murther, and then with her fat-fag-chinne hanging down like a Cowes Udder, lay reeking out at the windowe, demaunding the reason why they did summon a Parly (sigs. B3–B3^v).

L. C. Knights compares a passage from Nashe's account of Hero and Leander (*Works,* III, 195) with one from a speech of Sir Winston Churchill, to the advantage of the former:

> Its language retained many of the more primitive functions of speech that are to be found after the seventeenth century. Not only was the relation of word and thing, of word and action, far more intimate than in a society that obtains most of its more permanent impressions from books and newspapers, a large number of Elizabethan words and phrases are the direct equivalent of action—gestures of sociability, contempt or abuse.[29]

The wordplay with 'black' (the colour of the devil), 'white' (presumably by contrast, innocent or harmless), and 'brown' (the colour of the watchmen's halberds), in the passage from *The Blacke Booke,* the punning on thunder and lightning, the joke about the extinction of the candle, and the brilliant description of the whore, evoked in the details of her udder-like chin and her 'reeking' presence, show Middleton using language with the colloquial and oral vividness that L. C. Knights admires in Nashe.

One of the most important characteristics of literature designed for oral reception is its adaptation of style, method, and subject matter, to suit the tastes of the audience. Bacon made this point in *The Advancement of Learning:*

> Aristotle doth wisely place rhetoric as between logic on the one side, and moral or civil knowledge on the other, as participating of both: for the proofs and demonstrations of logic are toward all men indifferent and the same; but the proofs and persuasions of rhetoric ought to differ according to the auditors:
> *Orpheus in sylvis, inter delphinas Arion.*
> Which application, in perfection of idea, ought to extend so far, that if a man should speak of the same thing to several persons, he should speak to them all respectively and several ways (Book II, XVIII, 5).

But the extent to which the pamphleteers moulded as well as followed the tastes of the audience is a nice point, for they borrowed both from the literature of earlier days already proven popular with mass audiences, such as sermons and jestbooks, as well as from more recent forms and writers with which the newly literate members of their audience could not have been so familiar. They were however distinctly aware of the three styles of writing, the *gravis,* the *mediocris,* and the *humilis,* and varied them according both to the dictates of fashion and of decorum. There was no question of the pamphlet audience requiring or preferring the low style, as could be said of readers of tabloid newspapers today; in fact, evidence suggests that they often preferred an ornate style. In genres which wholly or partially demanded the low style the authors made it very clear that they were eschewing ornamentation out of decorum, not inability. Greene was insistent on this point. His first cony-catching pamphlet, *A Notable Discouery of Coosnage* was by no means conspicuously free of artifice despite his rejection of Euphuism in *Menaphon* two years earlier. In *The Second part of Conny-catching* he explained the principle behind his style, in answer to criticism of the plainness of *A Notable Discouery:*

> But heere by the way, giue me leaue to answere an obiection, that some inferred against me, which was that I shewed no eloquent phrases, nor fine figurative conueiance in my first book as I had done in other of my workes: to which I reply that το πρεπον a certaine decorum is to bee kept in euerie thing, and not to applie a high stile in a base subiect beside the facultie is so odious, and the men so servile and slavish minded, that I should dishonor that high misterie of eloquence, and derogate from the dignitie of our English toonge, eyther to employ any figure or bestow one choyce English word vpon such disdained rakehels as those Conny-catchers (p. 7).

His predecessor, Thomas Harman, had also used two distinct styles, the 'formal-artificial' and the 'loose-colloquial',[30] according to his purposes. The ancedotes Harman tells follow the idiom and rhythms of speech:

> Tell me I pray the quoth I, who was the father of thy chylde she stodyed a whyle and sayde it hadde a father, but what was hee quoth I. Nowe by my trouthe, I knowe not quoth shee, you brynge me out of my matter so you do (sig. F2).

But he makes use also of rhetorical devices and ornate figurative expressions, not only, as might be expected, in his dedicatory epistle, but also in the actual framework of the tales and within the narrative, as in this passage, which contains some studied alliteration and word-play anticipating Sidney's Arcadian prose:

> This amerous man beholdinge with ardante eyes, thys glimmeringe glauncer, was presentlye pyteously persed to the hart, and lewdly longed to bee clothed under her lyuerye and . . . as a man mased, mused howe to attayne to his purpose, for he hadde no money (sigs. E2^v–E3).

Nashe, too, used both medium and low styles, and, on occasion, high style; he claimed in 1592, in *Strange Newes* that he had 'written in all sorts of humors privately . . . more than any yoong man of my age in England' (*Works*, I, 320). His version of the low style was more ornate than Greene's, attempting something quite different from Greene's extreme simplicity of diction. For both of them the publication of Greene's 'Arcadian *Menaphon*' marked a change of style; Nashe claimed that it entitled his friend 'to that *temperatum dicendi genus* which *Tully* in his Orator termeth true eloquence' (*Works*, III, 312), but neither was thereafter consistent in eschewing the high style and '*Ouids* and *Plutarchs* plumes'. If the style of *The Anatomie of Absurditie*, Nashe's earliest published work, written according to McKerrow in 1587–88, shows Nashe at his most Ciceronian, it is not hard to find examples of later prose just as ornate. In general, these tend to come in sections of works separable from the main body, such as epistles and dedications, or passages of burlesque or parody, with the exception of *Christs Teares over Ierusalem*. It is generally agreed that in this strange work Nashe was aiming at something quite different from his other writing, and that whatever he achieved, it was not successful. Much of this 'Treatise of Teares' was in the vein of 'tragicus Orator' which Nashe jestingly claimed as his own in his *Lenten Stuffe;* in the address to the reader in the second edition he found himself obliged to defend the decorum of his inflated style:

> My stile is no otherwise puft up then any mās should be which writes with any spirite; and whom would not such a deuine subiect put a high rauisht spirite into? For the prophaness of my eloquence, so they may tearme the eloquence of Sainct *Austen, Ierome, Chrysostome,* prophane, since none of them but takes vnto him farre more liberty of Tropes, Figures, and Metaphors (*Works*, II, 183).

Much more characteristic of Nashe was the low style in *Pierce Penilesse,* parts of *The Terrors of the Night,* the Harvey pamphlets, and *Nashes Lenten Stuffe,* which he carefully contrived to present the appearance of inventive spontaneity. He used all kinds of devices to capture an informal tone—direct address to the reader, frequent reference to himself as author, exclamations and interjections, questions and answers, ramblingly recounted personal experiences and opinions, asyntactic sentences with omitted verbs, ambiguous pronouns, and shifting constructions. He also included passages of sophisticated literary burlesque which mockingly define the pretensions of ornate style through the deflationary tactics of low style. The best known of these is the Hero and Leander story in *Nashes Lenten Stuffe,* a brilliant use of indecorum. Less familiar is the story at the climax of *The Terrors of the Night,* which also exhibits Nashe's skill in parody. Here 'an inueigling troupe of naked Virgins' appears in a vision to an old man; Nashe elaborates on their charms in high style, using several protic devices of sound and two witty comparisons, signposted for the reader's attention by a parenthetical 'as it were' to create an atmosphere of sensuous enchantment:

> Their haire they ware loose vnrowled about their shoulders, whose dangling amber trammels reaching downe beneath their knees, seemed to drop baulme on their delicious bodies; and euer as they moou'd too and fro, with their light windye wauings, wantonly to correct their exquisite mistresses.
> Their daintie feet in their tender birdlike trippings, enameld (as it were) the dustie ground; and their odiferous breath more perfumed the aire, than Ordinance would, that is charged with Amomum, Cyuet, and Amber-greece.

A brief dry comment introduces the next paragraph, focussing the reader's attention on the writer's art, and comically undercutting the carefully created mood: 'But to leave amplications and proceed'. Nashe does proceed, in a more direct, but still very ornamental style:

> Those sweet bewitching naked maides hauing maiestically paced about the chamber, to the end their naturall vnshelled mother pearle proportions might be more imprintingly apprehended, close to his bed-side modestly blushing they approached . . . He, obstinately bent to withstand these sinfull allurements no lesse than the former, bad them goe seek entertainment of hotter bloods, for he had not to satisfie them (*Works*, I, 380–81).

Then again, in a brief colloquial sentence, the mood is instantly changed and the tone deflated with masterly bathos: 'A cold comfort was this to poore wenches no better cloathed'. The lack of hot blood leads to cold comfort; so the metaphorical turns into the literal and the ridiculous in a phrase.

Nashe's conversational style reached its final variation, the humorous essay, in *Nashes Lenten Stuffe*. The style in this 'light friskin of my witte' was studiedly informal, its spontaneity artfully achieved. It was not the case here that the techniques of oral discourse and speech found their way into written prose, but rather that Nashe deliberately cultivated such techniques in order to create a kind of paradox: that of the airiest and most ephemeral display of verbal fireworks transfixed and made permanent in print. What Hibbard has to say of it is true:

> Kept aloft by sheer verbal dexterity, it never collapses or falls to earth. It is more like a circus turn, than anything else he wrote; but also, like a circus turn, there is nothing left when it is over. Only in the actual performance, the reading of it, does it exist as a thing in its own right (*Thomas Nashe*, p. 249).

While *Nashes Lenten Stuffe* represented a considerable literary achievement, it was the more conventionally written *Pierce Penilesse* that was Nashe's most popular work, both, it seems, with other writers and with the public. Three editions appears in 1592, and others in 1593 and 1595; three sequels at least were written to it, and the figure of Piers was mentioned in pamphlets and other works for many years after his creator's death.[31] But popularity with writers, popularity with the public, and literary achievement, then, as now, did not necessarily coincide. The best-selling pamphlets of the period, such as Greene's *Ciceronis Amor* with nine editions between 1589 and 1639, *A Disputation, Between a Hee Conny-Catcher and a Shee Conny-Catcher* with five between 1592 and 1637, Dekker's *Lanthorne and Candle-light* with at least eight versions in twenty years, and Swetnam's astonishing polemic, *The Araignment of Lewd, Idle, Froward and unconstant women* (1615) which had ten editions by 1635, represent neither their authors' best literary achievement nor a cultivation of low or conversational style. Throughout the period ornamentation, figures of speech, exempla, commonplaces, and the trappings of rhetorical discourse continued to be mandatory for popularity.

iii

In the same way that style was conceived of as an ornament to subject-matter, so forms were imposed on content, as a means of stimulating interest or providing variety. The sugared pill idea was conventionally applied to techniques intended to stimulate interest in hackneyed topics. Dekker gives a version of it in his address 'not to the Readers: but to the Vnderstanders' at the beginning of *A Strange Horse-Race:*

> Tart meates go easily downe, being strewd with sugar: as musicke in *Tauerns*, makes that wine go downe merily, till it confound us, which (if the *Fidlers* were not there) would hardly be tasted. So for the sake of the sawce which I haue tempered for this dish, you may (perhaps) eate the meat, which otherwise you would not touch (*Non-Dramatic Works*, III, 312).

One of the most common means of providing the sauce for a sour pamphlet was to put it into the form of a dialogue. The dialogue, long familiar as a didactic device, was used in all manner of pamphlets, even for conveying information and sometimes for news; John Balmford explains at the beginning of *A Short Dialogue Concerning the Plagues Infection* (1603), a pamphlet about measures to take against the plague, that he has 'contriued al in the form of a Dialogue, which is a more familiar maner of teaching; hoping that now yee will more readily both perceiue, and receiue the truth herein contained' (sig. A3). *The Great Frost. Cold doings in London* (1608), describes the various effects of the extreme cold of January 1608 in town and country in a dialogue between a citizen and a countryman who meet in London. Whetstone also uses the dialogue form for his account of the Babington conspiracy in *The Censure of a loyall Subiect* (1587), and so does John Deacon in *A Treatise, Intituled; Nobody is my name* (1585), a protest against dishonest business practices. It occurs also in satire, in pamphlets about women, marriage, the plague, tobacco, and cony-catchers, and in allegory. The speakers may be personifications, allegorical figures, or typical representatives of a social class, profession, or point of view. Often they are given significant names, such as Theophilus and Eumenides in Lupton's *A Dreame of the Devill and Dives* (1583), who represent the wise listener and the troubled speaker, Diogenes, Philoplutos, and Cosmophos in Lodge's *Catharos. Diogenes in his Singularitie* (1591), Metrodorus, Asterius, and Frumentarius in *The Diuel coniured* (1596), Captain Skill and Captain Pill in Rich's *The Fruites of Long Experience* (1604), Capnistus ('signifying a fierie perfumed fellow') and Hydrophorus ('betokening a water-bearer') in Deacon's *Tobacco Tortuered* (1616), and Hic Mulier and Haec Vir in *Haec-Vir* (1617).

Two patterns of dialogue prevail, the first where one speaker represents the norm and the rest divergent points of view, and the second where one speaker acts as guide or initiate, and the other as a novice. In Robert Snawsell's entertaining pamphlet *A Looking Glasse for Maried Folkes* (1610) the speakers debate the ideal marital relationship. Eulalie, the novice, asks for advice; she is given counsel by the pious Abigail, the scolding Xantippe, and the proud Margery who will not submit to her husband. In Deacon's *Nobody is my name* the four participants in the dialogue are described in the preface: 'The Ingroser he comprehends our principall merchants. The Pedler doth signifie the inferior sort of buiers and sellers. No-bodie stands for the state of our painfullest preachers. And Euerie-bodie puts upon him the person of the comminaltie' (sig. A5). The promise of satiric attack in this account of the *dramatis personae* is sadly not fulfilled.

The pattern of novice/informant is common in expository pamphlets as a device to present information entertainingly, in particular in rogue literature such as Gilbert Walker's *A manifest detection of Diceplay* (1552), Luke Hutton's *The Blacke Dogge of Newgate* (1596), and E.S.'s *The Discouerie of the Knights of the Poste* (1597). In Richard Johnson's *The Pleasant Walkes of Moore-fields* (1637) a citizen sings the praises of London to a visiting countryman, as the two walk round the city. In Thomas Powell's *The Art of Thriving* a man briefs his friend on the way to get on in the world. For all this talk and discussion there is rarely any genuine exchange of views or any attempt to make the characters respond to each other's arguments. In a few pamphlets different viewpoints and ideas are juxtaposed without authorial comment or arbitration, but even so the dialogue form is not used for any kind of real dialectic, where opposing views are modified by contact with each other. Some, like Nicholas Breton's dialogues, simply give two aspects of a subject in the tradition of rhetorical debate without interchange or give and take. For instance, in *A Dialogue full of pithe and pleasure* (1603) one speaker describes the misery of man's life compared with that of animals, a second refutes him, and the third synthesizes the two points of view concluding that it is in a man's own power to be god or devil as he chooses. In *The Court and the Country* a courtier and a countryman each praise their respective calling and denigrate that of the other in elegantly formal prose; the work is presented simply as a literary exercise: 'Matter of state is not here meddled with; scurrility here is none: no taxing of any person nor offence justly to any whatsoever: but passages of good wit, without the malice of any evil mind'.[32]

Averell's *A meruailous combat of contrarieties* uses parts of the body to represent in speeches the more important of the Seven Deadly Sins—the back is pride, the belly gluttony, and the tongue envy—as well as dissentient elements in the commonwealth. The structure is an extension of the medieval metaphor describing social in terms of physical disorder. Dekker, who experimented at least once with almost every formal device available to the pamphleteers, used the dialogue sparingly. In *The Meeting of Gallants at an Ordinarie* (1604), he begins with a verse dialogue between War, Famine, and the Pestilence, each boasting of his power to destroy; then, as a demonstration of the supremacy of Pestilence, he gives a prose dialogue set in a tavern during plague-time, between four gallants and the innkeeper, who tell anecdotes of the plague. The beery jocularity of the innkeeper is cleverly used to bring out the macabre comedy of his stories, and in this instance the dialogue form and dramatic setting contribute valuably to the pamphlet's total effect. *The Dead Tearme* (1609), however, is a dull debate between London and Westminster as to which of them is more sinful.

Greene's *A Disputation, Between a Hee Conny-Catcher and a Shee Conny-Catcher* begins promisingly as a dialogue between Nan, the whore, and Laurence, the cutpurse, 'whether a Whore or a Theefe is more preiuditiall' in the commonwealth, a subject on which genuine debate appears at first to be possible. But Greene is torn two ways with Nan; at the start she is defensive about her occupation, and belligerent in the face of opposition:

> Tis by wit that I liue and will liue, in despight of that peeuish scholler, that thought with his conny-catching bookes to haue crosbyt our trade (pp. 9–10).

But presently Green's didactic intent gets the better of his realism, and Nan abandons her professional pride to become his mouthpiece for a denunciation of prostitution:

What is the end of whoredom but consuming of goods and beggery, and besides perpetuall infamie, we bring yoong youthes to ruine and vtter destruction? (p. 35).

Nashe said that the dialogue form of *Haue with you to Saffron-Walden* was taken from William Bullein's *A Dialogue against the Feuer Pestilence* (1564) to which he refers in the preface to the reader, but his use of it was quite different from Bullein's. Nashe's five speakers 'clap up a *Colloquium*' on the subject of Gabriel Harvey, and they are differentiated according to their functions in the debate, an opponent, a moderator, a fault-finder, a judge, and the chief speaker Piers Penniless, or Nashe himself, called the Respondent, who defends himself against the charge of having failed to answer Harvey's last attack. Nashe said that his speakers were not feigned, like those in More's *Utopia*, but based on real friends of his; perhaps contemporary readers could have identified them. At all events, their functions are to add a variety and life to the invective, to highlight the almost novelistic sense of characterization in the absurd 'life' of Harvey, and through the debate form to create a quality of light-hearted, spontaneous wit that must indeed have provoked Nashe's more solid adversary.

One of the dialogue's chief functions, that of presenting the subject-matter from some viewpoint other than that of the author, was also partially fulfilled by some other forms and devices. That curious Elizabethan convention, whereby the author of a work would claim that he was only presenting someone else's material and therefore deny responsibility for it, might be seen in this light, as well as that of a device to avoid the 'stigma of print'.[33] Certainly the playful use of this convention in dream or visionary pamphlets where the author asserts that his material has been provided by the ghosts of dead writers serves as a means to vary the point of view, and perhaps allows a measure of authorial freedom. In Chettle's *Kind-Harts Dreame*, five apparitions appear to Kind-Hart as he sleeps in a tavern, leave him with 'seueral bills of invective against abuses raigning' and depart. One of the bills consists of a letter from Greene's ghost to Piers Penniless, urging him to awake and revenge the wrongs that envious adversaries have done him; it may be that the fictional framework gave the plea more weight.

Prosopopoeia, another means of varying the viewpoint which also allowed the author to display his command of various styles of writing, was used where an emotional effect was in order. In *Christs Teares over Ierusalem* where Nashe solicits inspiration from Christ himself to heighten his style suitably, this device is conspicuously utilized. 'The more to penetrate and inforce' Christ is given a lengthy oration lamenting Jerusalem's ungrateful treatment of the prophets, which ends with a short speech made by Jerusalem personified; Christ's style reaches the heights of figurative passion, but for grisly wit it cannot compare with the speech made by Miriam to her son as she prepares to eat him:

> Amongst the tablement shalt thou not miscarrie: Ile beare thee in my bosome to Paradise. Thy tombe shall be my stomack, with thy flesh will I feast mee. This shall be all the chyldes tribute I will require of thee, for the six yeeres lyfe I haue gyuen thee, to cherish me but six dayes, and rather then Famine should consume mee, to consume thy selfe in my sustenance (*Works*, II, 74).

Such strained 'endeauors of art' are peculiar to Nashe, although prosopopoeia is usually associated with heightened speech and effects of pathos. In plague pamphlets, the emotional temperature is raised by the device of presenting part or all of the work as a speech made by London, usually personified as a 'weeping lady' (Thomas Brewer, *The Weeping Lady*), or 'our Foster Mother' (Henry Petowe, *The Countrie Ague*), or 'poore, distressed reiected, diseased London, once the Phoenix, now the Owle' (Benjamin Spenser, *Vox Civitatis, or Londons Complaint*). In social pamphlets the invention of brief scenes with one or two characters and set speeches is a common way of varying the didactic emphasis. The reader is sometimes asked to visualize such a scene for himself, as in Deacon's *Tobacco Tortuered*, where the case against tobacco is reinforced by the provision of an extensive speech for a child whose father has wasted all the family fortune on smoking:

> Imagine thou shouldest here likewise behold before my face, a yong tender brat, a little pretie nest-cukkle . . . should cry out and say thus vnto him . . . Dad, hearke Dad in thine eare. Am I not thy best boy, am I not, Dad? And doest thou not loue me, thy best boy, Dad? Harke Dad, thou wert wont (whē thou wentest to the Faires) to buy thy best boy fine knacks, fine boxes, fine rattles, a fine feather, a fine gilden dagger, and a fine gilden hobbie-horse: wert thou not, Dad? And wilt thou now let thy white-headed boy runne barefoote and barelegged without hose and shooes? Why harke Dad, hath the fire of *Tobacco* filched thy purse? (p. 74).

In Lodge's *An Alarum against Vsurers* the speeches stand out less distinctly from the main body of the work which is narrative in form, but again their function is didactic rather than dramatic. Lodge gives first the lament of an old man, whose son has fallen into the hands of usurers in London:

> O my sonne, if thou knewest thy Fathers care, and wouldest aunswere it with thy well dooing, I might haue hope of the continuaunce of my progeny, & thou be a ioy to my aged yeres. But I feare me the eyes of thy reason are blinded, so that neither thy fathers teares maye perswade thee, nor thine owne follies laide open before thine eyes, reduce thee, but that my name shall cease in thee, and other couetous vnderminers shall inioye the fruites of my long laboures (*Works*, I, 20, sig. B4^v).

Then the youth has a parallel speech, repenting his folly from prison and emphasizing that his father was right: 'O that I had respected his vnfained teares, O that I had accepted his good aduice' (sig. D). The situation in Dekker's *Newes from Hell* has an interesting twist; here it is the prodigal son of a usurer speaking, who regrets both his wasted youth and also his father's lack of wisdom in bringing him up as an idle gentleman:

> Had he sett me to Grammer schoole, as I set myself to daunting schoole, instead of treading *Carontoes*, and making Fidlers fat with the rumps of Capons, I had by this time read *Homilyes*, and fedde upon Tithe-pigges of my owne vicaridge, whereas now, I am ready to get into the Prodigals seruice, and eate Iones nutes, that's to say, Acorns with swine: But men that are wisest for officers are commonly arrand woodcoks, for fathers (*Non-Dramatic Works*, II, 109).

In Parkes's *The Curtaine-Drawer* a miser exposes the true nature of his vice himself:

> My bagges are full, and now my coffers are cram'd with the white and red earth of the world, yet my body is diseased and my minde disquieted . . . yet cannot this God of the world assist me, nor lend me the least comfort against my extremity; neither can I find any reason why I should so Idolise the same (p. 26).

The relation of this sort of writing to the techniques of drama is obvious, and in a group of pamphlets where the narrative interest is stronger, that is, in news pamphlets describing sensational crimes, feigned speech or sometimes interior monologue is used much in the manner of a dramatic soliloquy to explain the motivation of the protagonists, as well as to involve the reader more intimately with the account. Where the speech style is, as often, depersonalized and full of literary contrivance, this technique can appear flat and lifeless. In repentance or confession speeches for example, the criminal is often made to utter something like the following before he goes to execution:

> Mine iniquitie is ever before me, and my sinne is euer in my sight. And which is more then all the rest, it is a fire, & a worme within the hart, a fire consuming, a worme gnawing, & fretting it: consuming, yet not consumed: gnawing, and neuer sufficed: an euer burning fire, a neuer dying worme, *Vermis eorum non morietur, & ignis eorum non extingueter* (*A True report of the horrible Murther, which was committed in the house of Sir Ierome Bowes,* 1607, sig. E2).

But some writers aim at a closer imitation of natural speech, with heightening, if necessary, and here the effect is much livelier. In *A True Relation of the most Inhumane and bloody Murther, of Master Iames* . . . (1609), the villainous curate Lowe, who has seduced the wife of the preacher James, soliloquizes as he prepares himself for the murder:

> Adultery is a sinne, and murther is no more, whithal, how much better it was to liue like a Master then a slaue, to command then to be commanded, with a number of such worldly intising Syllogismes, as intangled his poore and unarmd soule in the limetwigs and snares of perdition (sig. A).

This is an unskilful effort at blending direct and indirect speech certainly, but for a moment the author does search for insight into Lowe's mind. His effort is considerably improved upon by the author of *Two most vnnatural and bloodie Murthers* (1605), who deals competently with soliloquy, dialogue and characterization. In one of his stories Peter Golding, the wicked servant of old Mr Brown, plans his crime with dramatic duplicity:

> Yet I will seeme calme, shew dilligence, and creep againe into youre loue, but as a serpent in your bosome, that when I seeme most kind, I will be most subtile, and my reuenge most sodaine (p. 22).

In the other story, Walter Calverley, the villain, briefly reveals his better nature in a melancholy meditation on his failings as a brother or kinsman:

> O, I am the most wretched man that euer mother received the seede of, O would I had been slaine in my wombe, and that my mother hadde beene my sepulchre: I have begot my children to eate their bread in bitterness, made a wife to be nothing but lamentation, and a brother to die in care (p. 13).

In such cases the influence of techniques from different kinds of writing helps to blur the distinctions between history, legend, fact and fiction, and to produce the sort of heterogeneous blending so characteristic of these pamphlets.

A common device in satire to obscure or complicate the point of view is the adoption of a persona or literary mask. The satiric persona was a convention which in Elizabethan times blended elements from two diverse sources, classical satire, particularly of Juvenal, and medieval satire, or more properly complaint. Complaint is more impersonal than satire, and the medieval narrator, when his voice is distinct from the author's own, is broadly characterized as a blunt, honest truth-teller, often of peasant origin, and sometimes in comic writing as a fool or an innocent.[34] The influence of this tradition shows in the names given to the pamphlet speakers, such as Kind-Hart, Tell-Troth, Cock Watt, Robin Goodfellow, and Piers Penniless, and also in some of their characteristics, although it is here that the effects of Juvenalian satire, and especially of the etymological link between 'satire' and 'satyr' with its connotations of roughness, lechery, and burlesque, are felt.

Although it has been claimed that there are significant links between the satiric characters of prose and the malcontent commentators of the drama, not many of the pamphleteers' satiric personae are as extreme or introspective as those of drama. Perhaps the nearest to the malcontent are those satirizing characters whose function is to uncover disguise and reveal falsehood, such as Dekker's Bellman and Cock Watt, and the Curtain-drawer of the world in William Parkes' pamphlet of the same name. The diabolic visitant in *Lanthorne and Candle-light* (1608), though he does not serve in any sense as Dekker's mouthpiece, shares in an exaggerated form that cynical and somewhat salacious interest which all these characters have in secret and nocturnal vice; he prowls the London suburbs to spy out sin. The Juvenalian influence appears in the bitter wit of Piers Penniless and in the vivid contemporary detail of his supplication, and in the sexual obsessiveness of some of Dekker's pamphlets. But on the other hand many of the pamphlet personae are merely devices for variation, not sufficiently individualized to modify the overall nature of the pamphlets. McLuhan has rightly said that the 'I' of medieval narrative provides not 'a point of view so much as immediacy of effect'.[35] For instance, Kind-Hart, the tooth-drawer, in *Kind-Harts Dreame*, comments and elaborates upon the complaints made by the five other characters sometimes in the manner of a chorus; he adds, after Anthony Now-now's objections to ballad-singers and child actors, 'When

I had read this rabble, wherein I found little reason, I laide it by' (p. 23). But his remarks are not modified by any personal traits or attitudes. Tell-troth in *Tell-Trothes New-Yeares Gift* (1593) presents himself as the typical sharp-tongued satirist, 'Whoeuer haue been a sworne enemy to lasye lurdens, and a professed foe to Iacke No-body' (p. 3). In *Tom Tell Troath Or A free discourse touching the manners of the Tyme* (?1630) he is the honest but humble man who is bold enough to tell the King the truth when no-one else dare. In neither pamphlet is he clearly characterized, and the fact that Swetnam's *The Araignment* was originally put out under the authorship of 'Tho. Tel-troth'[36] was ignored by the many who opposed it. The controversy over women produced pamphlets written from a feminist standpoint under pseudonyms such as Jane Anger, Ester Sowernam, and Constantia Munda, but none of these writers has, or makes any pretensions to, individuality.

Piers Penniless is a different matter, although in Nashe's first pamphlet about him, with his name as its title, his voice is not consistently heard. It is the facetious quick-witted scholar who opens the work in the 'malcontent humour' of poverty, and begins the supplication to 'your impious excellence' and 'your honourable infernalship'; but in the sections attacking the Harveys and praising the theatre, the voice of Piers is not separable from the voice of Nashe who eulogizes *'Ioues Eagle-borne Ganimed,* thrice noble Amyntas' and 'heauenlie Spencer', and jibes at the 'most excrementorie dislikers of learning' at the end of the pamphlet. In *Haue with you* Piers and Nashe coalesce into the character under which Nashe has chosen to direct his attacks at Harvey. The speaker of *Strange Newes, The Terrors of the Night,* and *Nashes Lenten Stuffe* is not a named separable character but an 'I' who may or may not be identified with the Thomas Nashe that conjecture has constructed out of history, references, dedications, and such passages as the author has no excuse for in his own person. There is a sense in which this 'I' is only a mask; Hibbard suggests that Nashe adopted the role of jester because the literary organization of his day could offer him no other, and because he wanted to present his work in such a manner as to preclude critical comment.[37] McLuhan compares Nashe with Aretino, Erasmus and Swift, all writers 'led to adopt in varying degrees the only available soothsayer mask, that of the medieval clown.'[38]

It was not in general Dekker's method to present himself under a mask or guise; Cock Watt and the Bellman were basically narrative devices, though they were given some individual traits. In *The Guls Horne-booke* (1609), the subtly insidious voice of the nameless counsellor who urges the gull to extremes of inanity achieves a lightness of tone not commonly found in the pamphlets:

> I would desire you to draw your knife, and graue your name, (or, for want of a name, the marke, which you clap on your sheep) in great Characters vpon the leades [of St Pauls Church] by a number of your brethren... and so you shall be sure to haue your name lye in a coffin of lead, when yourselfe shall be wrapt in a winding-sheete (*Non-Dramatic Works*, II, 236).

This, however, is something of a variation from the original concept of a persona. Even if it was contemporary literary pressures that compelled Nashe to take up his jester's mask, his tensions were not felt in this form by many other writers, and in general the adoption of a mouthpiece was done in a more light-hearted spirit, to provide the diversification of an individualized satiric viewpoint.

Narrative devices such as the vision, the journey, the search, the coming of a novice to London and his initiation, and didactic forms such as the Seven Deadly Sins, the allegory, and Estates satire, have already been considered elsewhere. All of these constitute borrowings, in some form, from established literary genres, some of great antiquity. Certain techniques of comic writing, also the result of literary borrowing, still remain to be considered. Something has been said of the influence of jestbooks on the structure of rogue pamphlets.[39] The tendency that jestbooks always had to cluster groups of tales around a central figure who might be either fictional or real was carried on in the structure of rogue biographies, such as those of Ratsey the highwayman, Long Meg of Westminster, a female Robin Hood, William Longbeard, or Griffin Flood, where accounts of criminal activity originally intended as moral warnings, constantly would divagate into a series of humorous tales. *The Life and Death of Griffin Flood Informer* (1623), for instance, which sounds from its title-page likely to be a straightforward news pamphlet about a criminal recently executed, 'pressed to death the 18. day of *Ianuary* last past', is written entirely in the ancedotal manner of a jestbook, with almost no biographical information and little indication of time sequence, apart from the occasional phrase 'after this'. The separate sections are given headings such as

> Of the bad condition, foule speaches, and ill demeanor of Griffin Flood . . . Of the manner of his informations against Tapsters, Hostlers, Chamberlains, and such like . . . How he troubled an honest Ale-wife not farre from Cripplegate: and how finely she

requited him . . . How after all these his troublesome course of life, he was for a murther pressed to death.

There are other pamphlets influenced in their structure by the jest-book, which, though not described on the title-page as 'lives', make use of the name of some famous contemporary figure in order to get attention. Two such are *Tarltons Newes out of Purgatorie* (1590) and *Greenes Newes both from Heauen and Hell* (1593), both written in the form of other-worldly visions; in each case, the possibility of developing a narrative structure in its own right within the dream-vision framework has been set aside in favour of a simple series of tenuously connected tales. At the beginning of *Tarltons Newes* the ghost of Tarlton 'attired in russet' appears to the author in a dream and describes purgatory, from which he has just arisen:

> You come to a bridge, framed all of Needle points and ouer that must you passe bare footed . . . Then sir to haue a little ease after that sharp absolution, shall you come into a faire medow, and that is all ouer growne with *Ave Maries* and *Creeds*.

It describes purgatory as 'a very sumptuous hall, richelie hanged with tapistrie', then tells a series of comic stories, several of them taken from the *Decameron*, mostly with an anti-Catholic slant, about lascivious friars and hypocritical prelates. Tarlton himself is never mentioned again, and the author returns only briefly to his narrative context after the eighth story: 'With that I waked. . . and after supper tooke my pen, and as neere as I could set it downe, but not halfe so pleasantly as he spoake it' (p. 53).

The Cobler of Canterburie, quickly brought out in the same year as what the author called 'An Inuective against *Tarltons* Newes out of Purgatorie', though it was actually nothing more than a sequel, trading on the name of the earlier work, imitates, at a distance, the method of *The Canterbury Tales*.[40] It consists entirely of the tales told by passengers on a barge sailing from Billingsgate to Gravesend. The author of *Greenes Newes,* on the other hand, devotes attention to his satirical narrative, inserting tales only periodically and always with some relation to context. For instance when the main characters, Greene and his two creations Clothbreeches and Velvetbreeches meet a man who refuses to enter heaven because his wife is there, the man is given a long comic account of his marriage to an elderly cross-eyed shrew. A later tale of a cuckolded miller, a variant of Chaucer's *Reeve's Tale*, where the wife tricks her husband by sleeping in the guest room instead of the pretty visitor whom the miller had expected there, is fitted neatly into the context of anti-feminist satire and complaint about lechery.

The paradox and particularly the paradoxical encomium were devices borrowed from more aristocratic sources. The paradoxical encomium was extended to the length of a whole pamphlet by Nashe in *Nashes Lenten Stuffe,* influenced perhaps by Erasmus' *Encomium Moriae,* which he mentions elsewhere. In this case the praise of the red herring was only an excuse for a display of the sort of virtuosity that Nashe sometimes like to espouse, perhaps to flout the Renaissance belief that the function of art was to teach. In *Haue with you to Saffron-Walden* the technique of mocking praise was used satirically, in a letter supposedly from Gabriel Harvey's tutor, purporting to praise but in reality making him appear pedantic and vain. The paradox is commonly used with some sort of literary awareness, marked off, consciously, as a device for readers to take special note of, and by only a few of the better-known pamphleteers. Rich in *Opinion Diefied* refers scathingly to the contemporary proliferation of paradoxes:

> I might yet speak of some strange conceited books that hath been published by sundry authours, one amongst the rest *In the Contempt of Glory,* some others *In the prayse of the pestilence, In the prayse of the Quartans Ague, In the praise of Baldnes: In the praise of a Flie, in the praise of Nothing:* and that great Clarke *Erasmus* of *Roterdam,* writ a book *In the prayse of Folly:* & all these and diuerse others that might yet be named, the meere motiues of *Opinion* (p. 2)[41]

The paradox was mainly a technique of satire rather than an exhibition of learned wit. In Greene's *A Disputation,* Nan the whore puts to her companion a brief paradox in praise of prostitution:

> Sith tis almost supper time, and myrth is the friend to digestion, I meane a little to be pleasant, I praie you how many badde profittes again grow from whoores, Bridewell would haue verie few Tenants, the Hospitall would want Patientes, and the Surgians much woorke (pp. 38–39).

So too Fennor, in *The Compters Common-wealth,* sets down a paradox in praise of serjeants, and S.R. in *Martin Mark-all* shows how it is the criminals rather than their victims who suffer:

> We are daily persecuted by all sortes of Officers, as Marshals, Beadles, Sergeants, Bayliffes, Constables, and such other officers, lying continually as spyes to entrappe and catch us poore souls, as wee are following our callings in Markets, Faires, frayes, throngs, and assemblies (sig. C1).

Dekker uses paradox in a variety of ways. In *The Bel-man of London* he defines the peculiar life of the rogue by means of it:

> They are all freemen, yet scorne to liue in Citties: great travellers they are, and yet neuer from home, poore they are, and yet haue their dyet from the best mens tables. (*Non-Dramatic Works*, III, 80–81).

In *The Guls horne-Booke* it is an instrument of wit and a means to characterize his mocking narrator, who finds ways to recommend the idle life of the gallant with paradoxes in praise of sleeping late ('midday slumbers are golden; they make the body fat, the skin faire, the flesh plump, delicate and tender'), and of long hair. He fills out *The Dead Tearme* with three sections of paradox, in praise of litigation, of pen and ink, and of vacations from the Law Term. The section on pen and ink is more serious and two-edged than the others and from a light-hearted wonder at the power of the pen it moves on to a sombre conclusion, directly connecting writing with social change:

> How many thousandes (with that little Engyne along) do raise up houses to their posterity, whilest the Ignorant prodigall, drownes all the Acres of his Auncestors in the bottom of a Wine-celler, or buries them all in the belly of a Harlot? (*Non-Dramatic Works*, IV, 35).

In this case, the paradox, instead of representing a fanciful dalliance with wit and absurdity, becomes an instrument to convey the irony of truth. The paradox was a natural vehicle of thought for Dekker; his paradoxes were not usually subtle or deeply perceptive, but they were contrived with the kind of surface wit and delight in discovering unexpected truths that marks much of his work. He used them especially in his plague pamphlets: to express the suddenness of change—

> Vpon Thurseday it was treason to cry God saue King *Iames* King of England, and vpon Friday hye treason not to cry so. In the morning no voice heard but murmures and lamentation, at noone nothing but shoutes of gladnes & triumph (*The Wonderfull Yeare*, *Plague Pamphlets*, p. 21).

—to urge a kind of medieval scorn of life, telling his readers to see their plague-sores as 'GODS rich Ermines: to Inroabe thee like a King', and to comment, in the black comedy of his plague anecdotes on the unpredictability of human life.

The tendency towards burlesque and mockery crops up from time to time, although the conservative temper of the popular pamphleteers prevented it from being acceptable as an attitude towards many subjects. The Lucianic dialogue, for instance, in its original form was based on its mockery of the gods and heroes of ancient Greece, but its Elizabethan counterpart, the underworld vision treated only the devil in a comic spirit and not the concepts of heaven, hell or the life of the world to come. Nashe, sometimes an iconoclast, parodied the high style in several of his pamphlets, but in general neither stylistic nor formal parody is common in the pamphlets, except in one instance—mock almanacs and prognostications.

The small group of mock prognostications extant from this period is so homogeneous and closely related as to form a sub-genre, cross fertilized in the same way as the cony-catching pamphlets. Seriously intended prognostications had appeared in England at the end of the fifteenth century, and after about a hundred years exceeded all other categories of printed book or pamphlet in their annual sales.[42] The extraordinary popularity of these little works stimulated the development of the sub-genre, and mock almanacs were quick to appear; the earliest known comic prognostication of English origin was published in 1544.[43] Most of the Elizabethan ones were anonymous, with the exception of Anthony Nixon's *The Blacke yeare* (1606) and Dekker's *The Rauens Almanacke* (1609) and a late pamphlet, Wye Saltonstall's *A Description of Time* (1638), part essay, part mock prognostication; their literary quality varies from the wit and elegance of *The Rauens Almanacke*, the sharp parody of *The Owles Almanacke* (1618), the raciness of *Platoes Cap* (1604) which may have been written by an associate of Dekker and Nashe, to the dull and laboured jokes of *Fearefull and lamentable effects of two dangerous Comets* (1591) by 'Simon Smel-knave', and the heavy-witted plagiarisms of Nixon and *Vox Graculi, Or Jack Dawes Prognostication* (1623). The *Owles Almanacke* is the only one to follow in detail the serious almanac pattern,[44] with its tables of dates, tides, phases of the moon and historical events, its lists of kings, fairs, and Christian festivals, its astrological anatomies of the body, and so on; the most commonly preserved elements are the sections on comets and eclipses, the predictions for the four seasons, and the advice for the twelve months.

The basis of the satire was two-fold: the generality and obviousness of the serious prognostication, and the sense that the only predictions that can truly be made about human activities must be based on past experience and hence pessimistic and banal. The authors mingled their mockery of the astrologers' truisms with jibes at common satiric butts:

Mars being placed neere vnto the Sunne sheweth that there shalbe a great death among people: olde women that can liue no longer shall dye for age: and yong men that haue Usurers to their father shal this yeere haue great cause to laugh, for the Deuill hath made a decree that, after they are once in hell, they shall neuer rise againe to trouble their executors (*A Wonderfull, strange and miraculous, Astrologicall Prognostication for this yeer of our Lord God 1591 . . .* by Adam Fouleweather, printed in McKerrow, *The Works of Thomas Nashe*, III, 383).

The tone is often cynical in its implication that the perennial problems of mankind are never to be remedied; the returning seasons bring round the same responses. The authors' attitudes fluctuated between gloomy foreboding and the certainty, half-resigned, half-contented, that the affairs of the mass of people would go on as they always have. The form is based on commonplaces, parodied, mocked, repeated. Old puns and jokes recur continually, especially those on the subject of lechery. The connection between baldness and veneral disease is tirelessly reiterated, and there is the usual badinage about cuckoldry, widows, and the loss of virginity. The sense of division between social classes is very pronounced:

> Poore men shall be accounted knaves without occasion: those that flatter least, shall speede worst (*Fearefull and lamentable effects of two dangerous Comets*, 1591, sig. B1).

> Gentrye shall goe check mate with Iustice, and coyne out countenance oftimes equitie: the poor sitting on pennylesse benche shall sell their Coates to striue for a strawe, and Lawyers laugh such fooles to scorne as cannot keep their crownes in their purses (*A Wonderfull, strange and miraculous, Astrologicall Prognostication*, McKerrow, *Works*, III, 383).

Saltonstall's version of this theme treats social division from another angle: 'Let Taylers never cosen Gentlemen in their Sutes by the Custome of London, nor take vp more than will serue, conspiring with the Mercer to gull the Gentry' (sig. A4).

There are several verbal devices which give to this genre its characteristic flavour. Often the sentences are simply constructed out of a series of parallel clauses in the future tense:

> An ordinary cloth shal lose the nap within a month after it kist the backe, and a good showre of rain shall wash off the wooll of a new cloake. White frize will turne the warme fashion, because twill say well against the cold winde (*The Owles Almanacke*, p. 74).

Another common pattern is to list a number of subordinate temporal clauses preceding or following a single short main clause. Dekker in *The Rauens Almanacke* uses this technique often, and his anonymous imitator in *Vox Graculi* follows him. While the style is usually low and the construction simple, the authors do not eschew such figures as alliteration, parison, personification, and metaphor:

> Mine opinion is . . . That this Tatterdemalian *Autumne* . . . beginnes to shew his ill-fauoured face, when corne is ripe, and calls to be reaped . . .
> When the issue of the Earth are disroabed of all their Verdures, and the brood of man stript naked of all their Vertues:
> When greatnesse sits pruning her feathers (and those borrowed too) in the Sunne-shine of *Reputation,* and *Goodnesse* be faine to lie skulking in the shadow of *Contempt* . . .
> When Murther shall be held but manly reuenge . . .
> When the grass of *Grace* lie starke deaded in the hearts of men, and *Goodnesse* is excluded from humaine societie (*Vox Graculi*, sigs. ee 1–2).[45]

Instead of giving the traditional prophetic descriptions of plague, famine, and civil war, he inserts three long anecdotes, centred respectively on a garrulous wife, a Jewish usurer, and a young wife mistreated by an elderly husband, to which the three terms metaphorically apply. Twelve 'plagues' predicted for future occurrence consist of such everyday embarrassments as the plight of a marriageable girl without suitors (St Bridget's plague), and of a cuckolded husband who has no means of revenge (the Devil's plague). Storms take the form of brawls in taverns, marital quarrels, and cheating at cards; fire is to be found in ill-temper, a usurer's avarice, and unchastity. Illness is a fertile source for prediction, both vividly literal—

> All the Fidlers that play upon winde Instruments shall in cold nipping mornings have festulaes in their fingers (*The Owles Almanacke*, p. 68)

and metaphorical—

> Some shall haue a Palsey in their Teeth, in so much that they shall eat more in a week, then they wil be able to pay for in a twelue-moneth (*Platoes Cap*, sig. D1^v).

While these jokes, pleasantries, and satirical witticisms were not original, they had the great merit of being concise and well-constructed. Much of the satiric bite of these short pamphlets resulted from their being closely tied to a particular set of structures which precluded lengthy generalization.

The Owles Almanacke is closest in form to the genre it parodies, and it is in the precision of the parody that it is wittiest, as in the section headed 'a Memoriall of the time sithence some strange and remarkable Accidents, untill this year 1617', an imitation of the almanac convention of computing the years since events such as the Creation or the Flood:

> Since the first lye was told is (as I remember) 5565 yeares: and that was by all computation in Adams time, but now in these dayes men and women lye downe-right . . .
> Taylors haue bin troubled with stitches, euer since yards came up to measure womens petticoats, and that is at least agoe yeares 5000 . . .
> Since the German Fencer cudgelled most of our English Fencers now about a month past . . .
> Since close Caroaches were made running Bawdy-houses, Yesterday (pp. 33–35).

The genre had limited potentialities, and the vast amount of plagiarism involved in its use was symptomatic of its restricted scope. *The Penniles Parliament of Thread-bare Poets* (1604) was borrowed almost entirely but for verbal variants from Simon Smel-knave's *Fearefull and lamentable effects of two dangerous Comets*. *Platoes Cap* also borrows from the same source; Nixon in *The Blacke yeare* borrowed from Smel-knave, Lodge's *A Fig for Momus* (1593) and T. Wright's *The Passions of the Mind* (1604) among other works; *Vox Graculi* borrowed from Dekker and *A Wonderfull, strange and miraculous, Astrologicall Prognostication* (1591). Despite this lack of invention the little threadbare pamphlets were popular, though never of course as much as the form they imitated.[46]

iv

The innate conservatism of popular taste did not prevent certain changes taking place in the stylistic conventions of popular pamphlets. The form of the change was not that of a movement between extremes; Euphuism was rejected, but only as a kind of ornamentation old-fashioned in comparison with the more modern ones available. Greene and Nashe cast off artifice of a self-conscious kind, but both subsequently used it. Dekker's last pamphlet, *Penny-Wise Pound-Foolish* (1631), was distinctly simpler in style than his first, *The Wonderfull Yeare* (1603); *The Wonderfull Yeare* is rememberred for its ornate language and its witty exploitation of correspondences and paradoxes:

> Shee came in with the fall of the leafe, and went away in the Spring: her life (which was dedicated to Virginite,) both beginning & closing vp a miraculous Mayden circle: for she was borne vpon a Lady Eue, and died vpon a Lady Eue (*Plague Pamphlets*, p. 17).

But it also contains idiomatic and brilliantly expressive language in a colloquial idiom:

> Out of the house he wallowed presently, beeing followed with two or three doozen of napkins to drie vp the larde, that ranne so fast downe his heeles, that all the way hee went, was more greazie than a kitchin-stuffe-wifes basket: you woulde haue sworne, it had bene a barrell of Pitch on fire, if you had looked vpon him, for suche a smoakie clowde (by reason of his owne fattie hotte steeme) compassed him rounde, that but for his voice, he had quite bene lost in that stincking mist (*Plague Pamphlets*, p. 55).

And *Penny-Wise* in its turn has its passages of obvious artifice, a Greene-like meditation on inconstancy compared to faint sunshine, sandy foundations, and lightning-struck oak trees (sig. B2), a rhetorical head-to-foot description of a woman (sig. B2^v), and the justly famous image of the marriage bed as a music room (sigs. D–D1^v). The main contemporary movements in prose style, from the Ciceronian to the various kinds of anti-Ciceronian, were reflected to some extent in pamphlet-writing; but the tendency towards concision and aphorism was not always at one with the pamphleteers' habits of thought and their continued preference for amplification and exempla. It did however manifest itself in the development of a new genre, at once literary and popular, the Character.

Characters of the true Theophrastan type did not appear until after Joseph Hall's collection, *Characters of Vertues and Vices* in 1608, and the vogue of the genre extended for some time after 1640.[47] The form is not especially relevant to the study of moralistic pamphlets, since the Character-book itself really belongs to the realm of belles-lettres. Perhaps the chief distinction between pamphlets and belles-lettres is that the former rely much more on the appeal of their contemporaneity, and the Character is in essence concerned with the universal aspects of human nature. At any rate, Character-books mentioned here are included by virtue of their belonging as well to some other more relevant genre, as, for instance, Mynshul's *Characters and Essayes* (1618) to rogue and prison writing, and Lupton's *London and the Countrey Carbonadoed* (1632) to writing about London. Something has been said earlier of the relation of Character-writing to the Estates satire and the Seven Deadly Sins tradition, of the movement from allegory to description, and of the connection between such pamphlets as *Pierce Penilesse* and Lodge's *Wits Miserie* and the Character, as described by Benjamin Boyce. That Character-writing of a kind existed in English before 1608 is very clear; there were two important tendencies to encourage it, which had been active since medieval times—the preference in biography for the universal rather than the individual, which was supported by the desire among historians to provide clear-cut exempla of good and bad characters rather than complex portraits of historical personages, and the pleasure, sanctioned and encouraged by rhetorical precept, that medieval writers found in codifying and classifying. The relationship of the formal Characters to the pamphlets is not always straightforward; in the clearest cases it is a question of combined influences, but elsewhere the truth seems to be rather that the presence of the Character illuminated and defined certain elements of pamphlet-writing already present and perhaps derived from other sources.

In pamphlets such as the later work of Rich, Tuke's *A Treatise Against Painting and Tincturing*, Dekker's prison writing, Bernard's *The Isle of Man* and Braithwait's *Ar't asleepe Husband?*, the conception of the Character is behind the writing of several separate passages, along, of course, with other influences including medieval allegory, sermons and complaint, the Estates, and the Seven Deadly Sins. Rich specifically changed certain of his portraits from their original forms in *Faultes faults* to something much more akin to the Character in *My Ladies Looking Glasse;* he sometimes quoted, unacknowledged, from Overbury, and added new types such as the Temporiser (p. 50), the Formalist (p. 50), the Newsmonger (p. 51), and the Swaggerer (pp. 53–54). Tuke in *A Treatise* and Braithwait in *Ar't asleepe Husband?* appended Character portraits to the end of their work; Tuke's 'The Pictvr of a Pictvr, or, the Character of a Painted woman'[48] is intimately related to the rest of the pamphlet, an attack on the use of cosmetics. He writes in terse sentences constructed round pun, alliteration and antithesis:

> Her religion is not to liue wel, but *die* well. She loues confections better a great deale, then confessions, and delights in facing and feasting more, then fasting. Religion is not in so great request with her, as riches: nor wealth so much as worship (p. 58).

Brathwait gives an anatomy of a whore followed by a comparative study of the ideal *femme mariée;* the two are executed in contrasting descriptive methods, the whore by *effictio,* detailed head to foot description of externals, the married woman by *notatio,* a more general method, which describes nature rather than appearance. His style is less terse than Tuke's, and more allusive:

> To begin her anatomy at the head, the *haire* she weares came from *Naples;* and if any remaines, she dares not shew it, lest it should accuse her of the *Time past.* Her *Eyes* haue no other *browes* than those which a Pencill makes. Nor her *face* no other *colour* than that of painting (p. 313).[49]

The perfect married woman is described as a type:

> These will neuer spend, where discretion bids them spare; nor spare, where reputation bids them spend. These . . . though their care be great; yet so modest are they in arrogating aught to themselves, as they ascribe the good carriage and dispatch of all things to their Husbands wisdome and providence (p. 317).

Dekker, too, added character-sketches to a later edition of an early work, though never Characters as such. The third edition of *Lanthorne and Candle-light,* which came out as *O per se O* in 1612, had new descriptions, in the manner of Harman rather than Hall, of rogue types such as Abraham men, counterfeit soldiers, and 'clapperdogeons', with brief physical details, specimen speeches, and hints on how to recognize them in action. In *Villanies Discouered* (1616), the fourth edition, he inserted chapters entitled 'Certaine Discoueries of a Prison,' 'Of Prisoners,' 'Of Creditors', 'Of Visitants' and 'Of Iaylors', which combine description, exhortation, invective, and advice, thus entirely avoiding the objective and aphoristic style of the Character. As Boyce says, while character portraits in the informal sense had always been a feature of Dekker's writing, in, for example, the poems of *The Double PP* (1606), Politic Bankruptism in *The Seuen Deadly Sinnes,* the allegorical figures in *Worke for Armorours* and *A Strange Horse-Race,* and the sketch of a prison in *Iests to make you Merie,* he never wrote Characters proper, and even in the prison Characters added to the ninth impression of *The Overburian Characters* in 1616 his portraits differ from the rest in the quality of feeling, in that they are written not to entertain but to arouse indignation.[50] One of his closest approximations to the Character style, written too early to have been influenced by Hall, is the eulogy of William Epps in *Newes from Hell;*

the true Character deals, of course, with types and not individuals, but nonetheless the terse style and objective statements of this section could very easily be part of a 'Character of the temperate soldier':

> He was neuer ouer-maistered, but by his owne affections: against whom, whensoeuer he got the victorie, there was a whole man in him: he was of the sword, and knew better how to end quarrels, then to beginne them; yet was more apt to begin, then others (better bearded) were to answer ... Hee was married to the honour of a fielde in the morning, and died in the Armes of it the same day, before it was spoyled of the mayden-head: so that it went away chaste and vnblemishable (*Non-Dramatic Works*, II, 149–51).

Character-writing of a certain type was an element in rogue literature from its beginnings in the work of Awdeley and Harman. These early pamphlets have been said, like Greene's cony-catching pamphlets, to rely to a great extent on the Theophrastan method of Character-writing, as applied to personages of the underworld[51] but this is something of an exaggeration. Awdeley's sketches in the second half of *The Fraternitye of Vacabondes* (1560–61) were only the briefest of identifications, in many cases simply a definition of a name. In the first half the descriptions were longer, and sometimes included specimen speeches as an indication of character:

> A Curtesy man ... can behaue him selfe manerly, for he wyll desire him that he talketh withall, to take the vpper hand, and shew him much reuerence, and at last like his familier acquaintance will put on his cap, and walke syde by syde, and talke on in this fashion (*The Fraternitye of Vacabondes*. By John Awdeley, ed., E. Viles and F. J. Furnivall EETS, Extra Series no. 9, London, 1869, p. 6).

But they were entirely lacking in the individualizing detail and nicety of observation essential to the Character. Harman's *Caueat* included certain generalized character-sketches, but these consisted more of the visual details necessary for recognition, so that Harman's readers could be provided with a useful warning, than of moral estimates. In Greene's cony-catching pamphlets the detailed descriptions related rather to the methods used by thieves and cheats than to the criminals themselves: 'The nature of the Setter, is to draw any person familiarly to drinke with him, which person they call the Conie, & their methode is according to the man they aime at' (*A Notable Discouery*, p. 17).

With Mynshul, Lupton, and W. M.'s *The Man In the Moone* (1609) Character-writing was the major influence behind the construction of the whole pamphlet. Mynshul and Lupton called their work 'Characters', and did not contrive any framework for the series of portraits. W. M., however, set his within a simple narrative context; the narrator loses his way in a forest and comes upon the habitation of a fortune-teller and his assistants. After a couple of pages to set the scene, the pamphlet is given over to a demonstration of the fortune-teller's craft. The method combines elements from Estates satire and the Seven Deadly Sins tradition with Character-writing,[32] though the construction of the pamphlet, and the disconnected and arbitrary order in which the sketches are arranged, seem like evidence that the author's main intention was to write a Character-book.

The variegated structure of Parkes's *The Curtaine-Drawer Of the World* includes a section of individual type-portraits, influenced more by the Character-book format than by the concept or style of the Theophrastan Character. Each type is assessed in terms of his secular pursuits, his failure to live up to the ideal Christian standard, and the judgement due to him after his death:

> The *Country Gentleman*, though his life bee most secure and quyet of all other, free from the trouble and disturbance of the world . . . yet if through these most delicate contents, his unrelisht natur shall finde no true content . . . but that his backe shall engage him to the Mercers booke, and his belly pricke him on in delicasie of dyet . . . at the last comes this fellow, that comes first or last, taketh him prisoner by the throat, shackles him hand and foot, brings him to the barre of his answere, where these things, with many other, most largely, are layd to his charge (pp. 37–38).

The growing popularity of Character-writing was related also, both as cause and effect, to the movement away from Ciceronian prose style. The convention of the Character demanded brevity and a quantity of information which precluded stylistic flourish and ornament. The original Characters of Theophrastus were simply written, without much imagery or rhetorically constructed sentences; their length, on average only three hundred words, offered no opportunity for amplification. Hall's are about twice as long; his style in his Characters was strongly influenced by the vogue for Senecan prose, and while the sentences are by no means ornate they make use both of the more tightly constructed rhetorical figures such as antithesis, and, less often, of imagery. The overall effect, however, is of a terse elegance which had its effect on the Characters in the pamphlets. Dekker's prison Characters, in the later editions of *Lanthorne and Candle-light*, contain some of the most succinct and aphoristic of all his writing.

The whole vogue for Characters and this movement in prose style relates to changes taking place in other fields; it is a part of the trend away from authority and traditional wisdom, towards observation, experience, and new discoveries. It relates to the disappearance of certain kinds of writing and thought, such as Estates literature, the Seven Deadly Sins tradition, and attacks on abuses in terms of correspondences between body, state and heavens. It seems also to belong to what has been called the 'cultivation of social self-awareness'[55] which stems from that branch of satire devoted to the ridiculing of fashion, self-seeking, and aspiration. The Ciceronian style was the expression of a certain kind of sensibility, typified by that habit of mind which saw both the appearances and the reality of life in terms of the 'interrelation and interpenetration between divine, cosmic, and human affairs.'[54] Thought and expression move together, away from their medieval basis in analogy, authority and a fixed standard of reference. Stylistic generalizations over such a wide and varied field are invidious; yet it may be possible to define an early style, as exemplified in the pamphlets of Rankins, Whetstone, and Averell, and the early work of Rich which share a particular attention to verbal detail, a self-conscious use of rhetoric especially in elaborate figures of balance and antithesis, inkhorn vocabulary, reactionary attitudes, and a generalized complaint tone with frequent references to Doomsday and the Judgement. A succeeding phase is also discernible, though it overlaps with the first, including the work of Nashe, Greene and Lodge; here the satiric detail is more precise, the attacks sharper, more specifically directed, and the work of the early 1600s shows an intensification of these features. To some extent it can be said that Nashe takes Lyly's place as stylistic influence. The work of Middleton, Rowley, and the early Dekker is greatly indebted to him. But thereafter the tendencies are less clearly defined. The moralistic pamphlet as written by Nashe, Greene, Averell, Rankins, Rich, Lodge or Dekker grows rarer; instead appear the social and biographical tracts of Henry Goodcole, the moralistic news pamphlets, the leisurely compilations of Brathwait, the tracts of Puritan controversy. As the functions of the pamphlet genre grow more diversified and singly more specific, so styles develop to fit each purpose.

Notes

Key to abbreviations used in Notes and Bibliography

CHEL   *Cambridge History of English Literature*

HLQ   *Huntington Library Quarterly*

JEGP   *Journal of English and Germanic Philology*

NQ   *Notes and Queries*

OHEL   *Oxford History of English Literature*

PBSA   *Papers of the Bibliographical Society of America*

PMLA   *Publications of the Modern Language Association of America*

PQ   *Philological Quarterly*

RES   *Review of English Studies*

SB   *Studies in Bibliography*

SP   *Studies in Philosophy*

STC   Pollard, A. W. and Redgrave, G. R. et al., *A Short-title Catalogue of Books printed in England, Scotland and Ireland and of English Books printed Abroad, 1475–1640,* The Bibliographical Society (Oxford, 1926). Second edn revised and enlarged by W. A. Jackson, F. S. Ferguson, and K. F. Pantzer, vol. 2 (London, 1976).

PREFACE

1. This quotation is taken from *The Works of Thomas Nashe,* ed. R. B. McKerrow, reprinted from the original edition with corrections and supplementary notes, edited by F. P. Wilson, 5 vols. (Oxford, 1958), II, 138–39. This edition will henceforth be referred to as Nashe, *Works.*

2. *English Prose*, ed. H. Craik, 5 vols. (London, 1893–94), II, 583, 584.
3. *Thomas Dekker*, The Stratford-upon-Avon Library 4 (London, 1967), p. 17.
4. *Thomas Dekker* (New York, 1969), p. 118.

INTRODUCTION

1. For instance by J. H. Hexter, who was one of the first participants in the controversy in his attack on L. B. Wright, among others, in 'The Myth of the Middle Class in Tudor England', in *Reappraisals in History*, 2nd edn (University of Chicago Press, 1961).
2. As given by N. Z. Davis, *Society and Culture in Early Modern France* (London, 1975), p. 191: 'Popular books are not necessarily written by *petites gens*'. See also E. Eisenstein, *The Printing Press as an Agent of Change*, 2 vols. (Cambridge, 1979), I, 63. Contrast the view of H. S. Bennett, *English Books and Readers, 1603–1640* (Cambridge, 1970), who says of popular pamphlets that 'their nature and literary style show that their aim in the main was to interest people of the lower ranks of society' (p. 85).
3. E. L. Pearson, *Elizabethans at Home* (University of Stanford Press, 1957).
4. L. B. Wright, *Middle-Class Culture in Elizabethan England* (Chapel Hill, 1935).
5. E. H. Miller, *The Professional Writer in Elizabethan England* (Cambridge, Mass., 1959).
6. P. Sheavyn, *The Literary Profession in the Elizabethan Age*, 2nd edn, revised by J. W. Saunders (Manchester, 1967), p. 160.
7. The figures are taken from an unpublished lecture by the late Mr. J. Crow, entitled 'Popular Tastes in Reading in Shakespeare's Time'.
8. The latest book on the subject is by D. Cressy, *Literacy and the Social Order* (Cambridge, 1980).
9. See R. S. Schofield, 'The Measurement of Literacy in Pre-Industrial England', in *Literacy in Traditional Societies*, ed. J. Goody (Cambridge, 1968).
10. L. Stone, 'The Educational Revolution in England', *Past and Present*, 28 (1964), 68.
11. See W. R. Feyerham, 'The Status of the Schoolmaster and the Continuity of Education in Elizabethan East Anglia', *History of Education*, 5 (1976), 103–15, and W. K. Jordan, *Philanthropy in England, 1480–1660. A Study of the Changing Pattern of English Social Aspirations* (London, 1959), and *The Charities of Rural England 1480–1660. The Aspirations and Achievements of the Rural Society* (London, 1961).
12. See H. S. Bennett, *English Books and Readers, 1475–1577* (Cambridge, 1952), pp. 27–28.
13. J. W. Adamson, 'The Extent of Literacy in England in the Fifteenth and Sixteenth Centuries: Notes and Conjectures', *The Library*, Fourth Series, X (1929–30), 171.
14. G. B. Harrison tells the story in *The Elizabethan Journals*, new edn, 2 vols. (New York, 1965), I, 293–94.
15. Bannatyne Miscellany, II (1836), pp. 234 ff., cited in H. S. Bennett, *English Books and Readers 1603–1640* (Cambridge, 1965), p. 200.
16. See J. Jusserand, *English Wayfaring Life in the Middle Ages* (London, 1889), Chapter 2, and H. Chettle, *Kind-Harts Dreame* (1592), Bodley Head Quartos, ed. G. B. Harrison (London, 1923), p. 19. Autolycus in *The Winter's Tale* sells printed ballads to Mopsa and Dorcas in this way.
17. J. Saunders, 'The Stigma of Print', *Essays in Criticism*, 1, (1951), 139–64.
18. L. Lowenthal, *Literature, Popular Culture, and Society* (Boston, 1957).
19. J. W. Saunders, 'The Facade of Morality', in *That Soueraine Light*, ed. W. R. Mueller and D. C. Allen (Baltimore, 1952), p. 3.
20. Ibid., p. 5.
21. C. H. Conley, *The First English Translators of the Classics* (New Haven, 1927), pp. 82–101.

22. C. Mish, 'Best Sellers in Seventeenth-Century Fiction', *PBSA*, XLVII (1953), 356–73.

23. See R. B. McKerrow, *An Introduction to Bibliography* (Oxford, 1927), p. 123.

24. E. F. Bosanquet, 'English Seventeenth-Century Almanacs,' *The Library*, Fourth Series, X (1929–30), 366, says that the price was one penny a sheet, but from F. R. Johnson's list in 'Notes on English Retail Book Prices, 1550–1640', *The Library*, Fifth Series, V (1950), the price of a halfpenny a sheet seems more likely.

25. A. Pollard, *Shakespeare's Fight with the Pirates* (Cambridge, 1920), p. 24, notes the worst recorded payment made to an author as that to Richard Robinson, who received twenty-six copies of his book from the printer and no other payment.

26. See H. S. Bennett, *English Books and Readers 1558–1603*, p. 269. More than half as many books again were published between 1580 and 1603, as between 1558 and 1579.

27. For an account of Nashe's movements from 1592 see C. G. Harlow, 'Thomas Nashe, Robert Cotton the Antiquary, and The Terrors of the Night', *RES*, New Series, XII (1961), pp. 7–23, and 'Nashe's Visit to the Isle of Wight and his Publications of 1592–4', *RES*, New Series, XIV (1963), pp. 225–42.

28. On Nixon's plagiarism, see F. P. Wilson, 'Some English Mock-Prognostications', *The Library*, Fourth Series, XIX (1938), pp. 28–32, and L. Ennis, 'Anthony Nixon: Jacobean Plagiarist and Hack', *HLQ*, IV (1940), pp. 378–400.

29. Authors of *A Quest of Enquirie by women to know, whether the Tripe-Wife were trimmed by Doll yea or no* (1595), *A Wonderfull, strange and miraculous, Astrological Prognostication* (1591) (in Nashe, *Works*, III, 377–95), and *Fearefull and lamentable effects of two dangerous Comets* (1591) respectively.

30. Other such expressions occur in *The Wonderfull Yeare*, p. 4, *A Knights Coniuring* (1607), sig. A4, and *A Strange Horse-Race*, sig. A3.

31. See L. B. Wright, *Middle-Class Culture in Elizabethan England*, pp. 418–33, G. Wither, *The Schollers Purgatory* (1625) in *Miscellaneous Works of George Wither*, 6 vols. (1872), I, 29, and H. Chettle, *Kind-Harts Dreame* (1592).

32. M. Heinemann, *Puritanism and Theatre. Thomas Middleton and Opposition Drama under the Early Stuarts* (Cambridge, 1980), p. 4, gives this figure citing as its source the researches of Valerie Pearl.

33. E. Arber, ed., *A Transcript of the Registers of the Company of Stationers of London 1554–1640*, 5 vols. (London, 1875–94), III, 677.

34. E.g. R. H. Tawney, *Religion and the Rise of Capitalism* (London, 1926), M. M. Knappen, *Tudor Puritanism* (Chicago, 1939), B. M. Nelson, *The Idea of Usury* (Princeton, 1949).

35. See also Chapter 5.

36. See *English Prose* ed. H. Craik, II, 584. In the same introduction, Saintsbury said of Dekker's pamphlets that they belonged 'to a very curious division of English literature which has never since its own day been widely read'.

CHAPTER 1

1. R. Greene, *The Second and last part of Conny-catching* (1592), p. 7.

2. For instance, Beaumont and Fletcher, *Beggars Bush* (1612–14?), and Brome, *A Jovial Crew* (1641).

3. F. R. Aydelotte, *Elizabethan Rogues and Vagabonds*, Oxford Historical and Literary Studies, vol. I (Oxford, 1913), pp. 150–51.

4. Harrison states that 72,000 rogues were hanged in the reign of Henry VIII, and that in his own time 300 or 400 a year were hanged (*A Description of England*, ed. F. J. Furnivall, II, 231). An unsigned letter of 1569 estimates that in nationwide searches for vagabonds 13,000 were apprehended (cited in Aydelotte, op. cit., p. 65).

5. See F. R. Johnson, 'The Editions of Robert Greene's *Three Parts of Conny-catching*. A Bibliographical Analysis', *The Library*, Fifth Series, IX (1954), 17–24.

6. On the authorship of *The Defence* see D. Parker, 'Robert Greene and *The Defence of Cony-Catching*', *NQ* CCXIX (1974), 87–9, who shares the view of R. Pruvost, *Robert Greene et ses Romans (1588–1592)* (Paris, 1938), pp. 445–53, that it was Greene's work. E. H. Miller, in 'The Relationship of Robert Greene and Thomas Nashe (1588–1592)', *PQ* XXXIII (1954), thinks it may have been the result of a collaboration between Greene and Nashe.

7. For example, *The Groundworke of Conny-catching* (1592), largely plagiarized from Harman, *Mihil Mumchance his Discouerie of the Art of Cheating in false Dyce* (1597), based on *A manifest detection of . . . Diceplay*, S.R., *Greenes Ghost Haunting Conie-Catchers* (1602), and S.R., *The Art of Iugling, or Legerdemaine* (1612). Two articles dealing with plagiarism in these pamphlets are by E. D. McDonald, 'An Example of Plagiarism among Elizabethan Pamphleteers: Samuel Rowlands' *Greenes Ghost Haunting Conny-Catchers* (1602)', *Indiana University Studies*, I, (1913), 145–70, and J. L. Lievsay, 'Newgate Penitents: Further Aspects of Elizabethan Pamphlet Sensationalism', *HLQ* VII (1943), 49–69.

8. See the official report of the proceedings at Yorkshire Quarter Sessions on 8 May 1596 in which more than a hundred gipsies were tried and condemned to death. It is quoted in J.A.S. McPeek, *The Black Book of Knaves and Unthrifts* (University of Connecticut, 1969), pp. 264–65.

9. It has often been conjectured that there must have been an earlier edition of *Martin Mark-all*, now lost, which appeared between Dekker's *The Bel-man* and *Lanthorne and Candle-light*, since in the latter Dekker refers to 'an Vsurper, that of late hath taken ypon him the name of the Bel-man' which sounds like Martin. See F.R. Aydelotte, *Elizabethan Rogues and Vagabonds*, p. 136, H. O. White, *Plagiarism and Imitation during the English Renaissance* (Cambridge, Mass., 1935), p. 146, and A. V. Judges, *The Elizabethan Underworld. A Collection of Tudor and Early Stuart Tracts and Ballads* (London, 1930), p. 515.

10. The indictment of rogues here ascribed to the Bellman comes from Sir John Cheke, *The hurt of sedicion* (1549).

11. Dekker's authorship of the new material in this has been doubted, by Judges, op. cit., p. 514, who thinks it inferior to most of Dekker's prose, and by J. A. S. McPeek, *The Black Book of Knaves and Unthrifts*, p. 152, who thinks it much more vivid than anything else in Dekker except Chapter VII of *Lanthorne and Candle-light*. But given Dekker's authorship of all the other editions of *Lanthorne and Candle-light*, and the likelihood that he might want to re-establish himself after Martin Mark-all's attack, the general acceptance of his authorship of *O per se O* seems justified.

12. See Jonson, *The Alchemist*, I, i, 99, and Harvey, *Pierce's Supererogation*, in *The Works of Gabriel Harvey*, collected and edited by A. B. Grosart, 3 vols., The Huth Library (London, 1884–85).

13. For an account of the sources used, see J.J. O'Connor, 'On the Authorship of the Ratsey pamphlets', *PQ XXX* (1951), pp. 381–86.

14. E. Pendry, *Elizabethan Prisons and Prison Scenes*, 2 vols., Salzburg Studies in English Literature, Elizabethan and Renaissance Studies, ed., J. Hogg, 17 (Salzburg, 1974), Ch. 4 suggests identifications for the 'Black Dog' and for E.H. and N.S.

15. As also in Dekker's *Villanies Discouered*, in the chapters 'Of a prison' and 'of prisoners', and in the Character of a Prison in *The Overburian Collection*.

16. There are differences of opinion as to the extent of Dekker's authorship of this pamphlet. Grosart, in *The Non-Dramatic Works of Thomas Dekker*, 5 vols. (London, 1885), V. xxiii, thinks that 'probably Wilkins had little to do with the book'. M.L. Hunt, *Thomas Dekker. A Study* (New York, 1911), p. 135, ascribes the whole of the Cock Watt section to Dekker, and thinks he may also have had some part in the jests themselves. But the most convincing division seems to be that of M.T. Jones-Davies in *Un Peintre de la Vie Londonienne, Thomas Dekker*, 2 vols. (Paris, 1958), II, 377, who follows C. Dobb in his unpublished dissertation, *Life and Conditions in London Prisons, 1553–1643* (Oxford, 1952), in attributing to Dekker only the latter part of the pamphlet from 'The Miserie of a Prison, and a Prisoner' (sig. G3; Grosart, II, 337) to the end.

17. Although the prison chapters may have been included in an earlier edition of 1626, no longer extant. See E.D. Pendry, *Thomas Dekker*, The Stratford-upon-Avon Library 4 (London, 1967), pp. 325–27.
18. See Pendry, ibid., p. 6 for details of some of Dekker's debts.
19. See *The Overburian Characters*, ed. W.J. Paylor (Oxford, 1936), xxv-xxxi.
20. See Pendry, op. cit., p. 8.
21. P. Shaw, 'The Position of Thomas Dekker in Jacobean Prison Literature', *PMLA*, 62 (1947), pp. 366–91, credits Dekker with a part in several other prison pamphlets of the period, including T.M., *The Blacke Booke* (1604), Fennor's *The Compters Commonwealth*, and G. Mynshul, *Certaine Characters and Essays of Prison and Prisoners* (1618). These ascriptions have not been taken up elsewhere, and none of them seems to me particularly plausible.
22. See W.J. Paylor, ed., *The Overburian Characters* (Oxford, 1936), xxv-xxxi, B. Boyce, *The Theophrastan Character in England to 1642* (Cambridge, Mass., 1947), pp. 210–12, and Jones-Davies, op. cit., II, 395.
23. Boyce, op. cit., p. 212.
24. M.L. Hunt, 'Geffray Mynshul and Thomas Dekker', *JEGP* XV (1912), pp. 231–43, lists a number of identical or nearly identical passages in the two works.
25. G.R. Price, *Thomas Dekker* (New York, 1969), p. 175, has a very odd note in his bibliography on Dekker and Mynshul. 'Dekker's work is clearly evident in the last fourth of the book, three essays and three characters. In the earlier portions the Euphuistic style shows Mynshull's participation.' The 'earlier portions' must be those which M.L. Hunt has demonstrated to have been plagiarized from *Villanies Discouered* 'Geffray Mynshul and Thomas Dekker', *JEGP* XV (1912), 231–43; in any case it is hard to find much trace of Euphuism, a rare style by 1618. The 'last fourth' of the book is not clearly separable from the rest; the four final sections of the second edition are very much less Dekkerian than the others. Jones-Davies, op. cit., II, 289, rejects the notion that Mynshul's pamphlet was a collaboration between Dekker and Mynshul, and there certainly seems to be no good evidence for this idea.

CHAPTER 2

1. M. A. Shaaber, *Some Forerunners of the Newspaper in England 1476-1622* (Philadelphia, 1929), p. 3. Shaaber's book provides much essential historical background to this chapter, which I have not tried to summarize or repeat.
2. John Stow, *The Annales of England* (1600), pp. 1275–77.
3. Shaaber, op. cit., pp. 292–99.
4. *A True and plaine declaration of the horrible Treasons practised by William Parry the Traitor, against the Queenes Maiestie* (1584), p. 3.
5. *An Historical Account of the Life and Tryal of Nicholas Anthoine, burnt for Judaism at Geneva, in the year 1632*, in *The Harleian Miscellany*, ed. W. Oldys and T. Park (London, 1809), III, 213–20.
6. Shaaber, op. cit., p. 102, and H. S. Bennett, *English Books and Readers 1603-1640* (Cambridge, 1970), pp. 244–46 give several examples of extremely prompt publication. Lord John Burgh was murdered on 14 January 1591, and within two weeks three publications on the case had been entered in the *Stationers' Register*. The witches of Warboys were not found guilty until 4 April 1593, and on 9 April *The most strange and admirable discouerie of three Witches of Warboys* was entered in *The Stationers' Register*. These examples are typical.
7. Shaaber, op. cit., pp. 215–16 gives examples of pamphlets which use the word 'news' in the title as a bluff.
8. See D. A. Stauffer, *English Biography before 1700* (Cambridge, Mass., 1930), pp. 217–18 on the first uses of the word and its cognates.

9. A. M. Clark, *Thomas Heywood, Playwright and Miscellanist* (Oxford, 1931), pp. 173–74 gives convincing reasons for ascribing the authorship of this pamphlet, published anonymously, to Heywood.

10. E.g. Whetstone B3, on God's preservation of the innocent becomes Johnson's B1^v; Whetstone's example of Crassus' son, dumb from infancy, who speaks for the first time when his father's life is threatened (B3^v) appears in Johnson on B1^v; several of Whetstone's examples on D4^v appear almost *verbatim* in Johnson, B3^v.

11. J. P. Collier, in his edition of *A View of Sundry Examples* in *John a Kent and John a Cumber; A Comedy, by Anthony Munday*, printed for the Shakespeare Society (1857), writes concerning Munday's anecdotes of monstrous children, sigs. C3–C4:

> We have little doubt that Munday was himself the writer of some of the pieces (now lost) which came out on these occasions. On the 8th March, 1580, a ballad by him was entered by Charlwood; and although it was of a different character, it shows he was then an author of some popularity: he had commenced in 1577 (p. 102).

12. See Shaaber, op. cit., p. 292.

13. The Sabbatarian controversy took hold in the 1590s, with the publication of Nicholas Bownd's *The Doctrine of the Sabbath* (1595), and the sermons of his step-father, Richard Greenham. It was revived in 1633, when Charles I ordered the prosecution of Theophilus Bradburn for the publication of a Sabbatarian book. Charles' own *Declaration* of the same year was not well received by people or clergy, and Sabbatarian views became more popular. Burton, a staunch Puritan and anti-Episcopalian, was imprisoned for his views from 1637–40. At his release he led a triumphal procession into London, and was, at the time of the publication of *A Divine Tragedie*, in high popular favour (see J. Collier, *An Ecclesiastical History of Great Britain*, 9 vols. (London, 1832, vols. 7 and 8).

14. See the following pamphlets: John Denison, *The most Wonderfull and true storie, of a certaine Witch, named Alse Gooderige of Stapenhill* (1597), and John Darrell, *A True Narration of the strange and grevous Vexation by the Devil, of 7 persons in Lancashire, and William Somers of Nottingham* (1600).

15. For a sympathetic account of Darrell's career, see C. H. Rickert, *The Case of John Darrell*, University of Florida Monographs, Humanities no. 9 (University of Florida Press, Gainesville, 1962).

16. See also Chapter 5, p. 263.

17. See *A World of Wonders*, sig. E. The same anecdote is also found in Munday's *A View of Sundry Examples* (1580), sig. B3^v, and in Stow's *Annales* (1600), p. 1152.

18. The story is the source of George Lillo's play *Fatal Curiosity* (1736), although it is not likely that Lillo knew this pamphlet. See *Fatal Curiosity*, ed. W. H. McBurney, Regents Restoration Drama Series (London, 1967), Appendix B.

19. For an account of the historical facts of the case, see B. Maxwell, *Studies in the Shakespeare Apocrypha* (New York, 1956), Ch. 4.

20. No one has seriously questioned Dekker's authorship of all these pamphlets since F. P. Wilson first attributed to him *London Looke Backe* and *The Blacke Rod* in his edition of all six, *The Plague Pamphlets of Thomas Dekker* (Oxford, 1925). It is this edition I have used for the quotations. I am also much indebted to Wilson's companion study, *The Plague in Shakespeare's London* (Oxford, 1927).

21. For instance in Stephen Bradwell, *A Watch-man For the Pest*, p. 9, Simon Kellwaye, *A Defensative against the Plague* (1593), sig. B2^v, and Thomas Lodge, *A Treatise of the Plague*, sig. L3^v.

22. See F. P. Wilson, *The Plague in Shakespeare's London*, pp. 91–92, 104–5, 143–45.

23. This pamphlet is probably a reply to the more practical views of the Reverend James Balmford in *A Short Dialogue Concerning the Plagues Infection* (1603).

24. Dekker used a passage from *Three Miseries of Barbary*, sig. D4, in *The Blacke Rod*, pp. 202–4. See F. P. Wilson, *The Plague Pamphlets of Thomas Dekker* p. 252.

25. See F. P. Wilson, *The Plague in Shakespeare's London*, Ch. 11.

CHAPTER 3

1. Possibly by Tourneur and included, though for no good reason, by Allardyce Nicoll, in *The Works of Cyril Tourneur*, Fanfrolico Press (London, 1930).
2. See E. S. N. Thompson, *The Controversy Between the Puritans and the Stage*, Yale Studies in English (New York, 1903).
3. See. F. O. Waage, *Thomas Dekker's Career as a Pamphleteer, 1603–1609: Preliminary Studies of Five Major Works and their Background,* unpublished diss., Princeton University (1971).
4. E. H. Miller, 'Deletions in Robert Greene's *A Quip for an Upstart Courtier*', *HLQ* XV (1952), 277–82, and 'The Editions of Robert Greene's *A Quip for an Upstart Courtier*', *SB* VI (1953), 107–16.
5. R. B. Parker, *A Critical Edition of Robert Greene's 'A Quip for an Upstart Courtier',* unpublished diss., Shakespeare Institute, University of Birmingham (1959).
6. The authenticity of this pamphlet and of *Greenes Groats-Worth* has been doubted, but the case for them is well made by H. Jenkins, 'On the Authenticity of *Greene's Groatsworth of Wit* and *The Repentance of Robert Greene*,' *RES* XI (1935, 28–41. One recent view of the authorship of *Greene's Groatsworth* is that of W. A. Austin, *A Computer-Aided Technique for Stylistic Discrimination: The Authorship of Greenes Groatsworth of Witte* (Washington, 1969), who is convinced by computer-aided study of the language of this pamphlet that its author is Henry Chettle. See also Austin's article, 'The Technique of the Chettle-Greene Forgery: Supplementary Material on the Authorship of the *Groatsworth of Wit*', *Shakespeare News-Letter* 20 (December, 1970).
7. See *Thomas Dekker*, ed. E. D. Pendry, p. 317.
8. Waage, op. cit., p. 339.
9. See A. Walker, 'The Reading of an Elizabethan', *RES* VII (1932), 264–81 on Lodge's sources.
10. See M. W. Bloomfield, *Piers Plowman as a Fourteenth-Century Apocalypse*, Rutgers University Press (New Brunswick, 1963), for more on the medieval uses of the dream form.
11. There is some doubt about the relative dating of *Newes from Hell* and *The Returne*, both of 1606. McKerrow (Nashe, *Works,* IV, 85) and Jones-Davies, *(Un Peintre de la Vie Londonienne,* I, 105) both think *The Returne* to be the earlier. F. P. Wilson, in his unpublished thesis, *A Biography of Thomas Dekker,* (Oxford, M.A., 1913), suggests that '*Newes from Hell* was printed hurriedly perhaps in the endeavor to bring it out before *The Returne* . . . This attempt must have failed.'
12. A contemporary example of the form is Donne's *Ignatius his Conclave* (1611).
13. B. Boyce, 'News from Hell: Satiric Communications with the Nether World in English Writing of the Seventeenth and Eighteenth Centuries', *PMLA* LVIII (1948), 402–37, p. 404.
14. See Nashe, *Pierce Penilesse, Works* I, 207–8 and IV, 131. Day, *Peregrinatio Scholastica* (n.d.), in *The Works of John Day,* ed. Bullen (London, 1881), p. 52, gives five degrees of drunkenness. Shakespeare alludes to the idea in *Twelfth Night* I, v, 132–35 in relation to Sir Toby Belch.

CHAPTER 4

1. J. D. Peter, *Complaint and Satire in Early English Literature,* Ch. 1.
2. G. Mynshul, *Certaine Characters and Essayes of Prison and Prisoners* (1618), sig. C8.
3. The conventional expression to suggest a lawsuit foolishly undertaken. See Rowley, *A Search for Money* (1609) p. 19, *The Owles Almanacke,* ed. D. C. Allen (Baltimore, 1943), pp. 32–33, Nashe, *Works,* I, 189.
4. See W. Bullein, *A Dialogue . . . against the Feuer Pestilence* (1564), and T. Newton, *A Delectable Dialogue . . . Concerning Physick and Phisitions* (1580).

5. See L. Clarkson, *Death, Disease and Famine in Pre-Industrial England*, (Dublin, 1975), pp. 89–90, and P. H. Kocher, *Science and Religion in Elizabethan England* (repr. New York, 1969), p. 244.

6. Nashe may have had in mind Dr Burcot, a foreign physician, notorious in London in the 1570s. See *Works*, IV, 312, and P. H. Kocher, op. cit., p. 243.

7. See Greene, *A Quip*, sig. C4.

8. See C. T. Wright, 'Some Conventions Regarding the Usurer in Elizabethan Literature', *SP* XXXI (1934), 176–97, and 'The Usurer's Sin in Elizabethan Literature', *SP* XXXV (1938), 178–94.

9. Rowley, *A Search for Money*, p. 12.

10. W. M. *The Man in the Moone* (1609), sig. D4^v. The author puns on a contemporary meaning of 'to fox' as 'to intoxicate'.

11. J. Blaxton, *The English Vsurer* (1634), p. 42.

12. C. Courtney, *The Life, Apprehension, Arraignment, and Execution of Charles Courtney* (1612).

13. B. N. Nelson, *The Idea of Usury* (Princeton, 1949), p. 65.

14. See also Dekker, *The Deade Tearme, Non-Dramatic Works* IV, 50.

15. 'To rack' meaning 'to charge an excessive rent for land' or 'to oppress by extortions or exactions, especially of excessive rent' came into use at this time. The OED cites B. Rich, *Riche his farewell to militarie profession* (1581) and Lupton's *A Dreame of the Devill and Dives* (1581) respectively as the first users of the term in this sense.

16. See also Greene, *A Quip*, sig. Fl.

17. In Dekker's *A Strange Horse-Race* the tailor runs a race against pride, and is overthrown.

18. See G. R. Owst, *Literature and Pulpit in Medieval England* (Oxford, 2nd edn, 1961), p. 479.

19. Elizabethan attitudes to actors and acting have already been much discussed, and I have made no effort to deal fully with them here. For further detail, see E. N. S. Thompson, *The Controversy between the Puritans and the Stage* (Connecticut, 1903), J. D. Wilson in *CHEL* VI, 421–81, and E. K. Chambers, *The Elizabethan Stage* (Oxford, 1934), IV, 184–259.

20. In W. C. Hazlitt, *The English Drama and Stage* (London, 1879), p. 104.

21. See W. A. Armstrong, 'Shakespeare and the Acting of Edward Alleyn', *Shakespeare Survey* 7 (1954), pp. 82–89.

22. See also Introduction, p. 28 on ballads.

23. On the contemporary sense of the word 'pamphlet', see Introduction, pp. 23–24 'Pamphleteer' was not a familiar term at this time. The OED has no example before 1642, but Nashe in his *Preface to Greene's Menaphon, Works*, III, p. 324, predates it.

24. See Greene, *A Disputation*, p. 49, Nashe, *Works*, I, 9–10, 194, 239–40, III, 312, Dekker, *Lanthorne and Candle-light, Non Dramatic Works*, III, 177–78, and Rich, *Faultes faults*, pp. 39–40.

25. Detinue: an action at law to recover a personal chattel (or its value) wrongfully detained by the defendant (OED).

26. See C. Camden, *The Elizabethan Woman, A Panorama of English Womanhood* (London, 1952), pp. 178–81.

27. Quoted from E. P. Statham, *A Jacobean Letter-Writer: The Life and Times of John Chamberlain*, (London, 1920), p. 182. The quotation comes from a letter from Chamberlain to Sir Dudley Carleton, 25 January 1620, observing that James had commanded the clergy specially to preach against these things.

28. See W. Heale, *An Apologie for Women* (1608), p. 61, and R. Speght, *A Mouzell for Melastomus* (1617), p. 17.

29. J. D. Peter, *Complaint and Satire*, p. 99.

30. The term is from G. K. Hunter, 'Elizabethans and Foreigners', *Shakespeare Survey* 17 (1964), p. 45. See also C. N. Greenough, 'Characters of Nations', *Proceedings of the Massachusetts Historical Society*, LXV (1940), 224–25.

31. See. R. Ascham, *The Scholemaster* (1570), sig. J2, and T. Tuke, *A Treatise Against Painting*, p. 49, for two typical examples of the use of this proverb.

32. On Elizabethan attitudes to the Irish, see E. M. Hinton, *Ireland through Tudor Eyes*, University of Pennsylvania Press (Philadelphia, 1935) and D. B. Quinn, *The Elizabethans and the Irish*, Cornell University Press (1966).

33. Writing on Spenser and the popular imagination in *The Allegory of Love* (London, 1936), p. 311.

34. A version of the Second Story on the Fourth Day of the *Decameron* concerning Fra Alberto who seduces Lisetta by pretending to be the Angel Gabriel.

35. The ultimate source for such constructions, of which there are many in the pamphlets, where the features of the living being are enumerated in terms of their transformation after death, is probably Isaiah 3:18–24.

36. Vinegar was thought to assist in the cure of venereal disease.

37. See G. R. Owst, *Literature and Pulpit in Medieval England*, pp. 383–84.

38. See J. E. Brooks, *The Mighty Leaf: Tobacco through the Centuries*. (London, 1953), pp. 50–55, for an account of the rise in price of tobacco during the early years of the seventeenth century.

39. H. G. Hudson, in *Social Regulations in England under James I and Charles I: Drink and Tobacco* (Chicago, 1933), p. 22, suggests that tobacco was within the means of all classes because it could be bought in minute quantities, and also because it was often adulterated.

40. C. Bridenbaugh, *Vexed and Troubled Englishmen 1590–1642* (Oxford, 1968), pp. 363–66.

41. For examples of this popular formula see Nashe, *Works*, IV, 131, J. Day, *Peregrinatio Scholastica*, p. 52, T. Young, *Englands Bane*, sig. F3, and T. Heywood, *Philocothonista* (1635), pp. 2–6.

42. G. R. Owst, *Literature and Pulpit in Medieval England*, p. 431. Lodge echoes the idea in *Wits Miserie*, sig. N3, *(Works*, IV, 99).

43. A tabling house was a name for a public eating place.

44. Figures for London's population vary from 196,260 in 1605 (F. P. Wilson, *The Plague in Shakespeare's London*, Appendix 2), to 225,000 in 1603 (W. K. Jordan, *Philanthropy in England*, London, 1959, p. 27), to somewhere between 100,000 and 300,000 (M. St. Clare Byrne, *Elizabethan Life in Town and Country*, revised edn, London, 1961, p. 73. See also M. Heinemann, *Puritanism and Theatre: Thomas Middleton and Opposition Drama under the Early Stuarts*, p. 4. On the growth in importance of London as a social centre, see F. J. Fisher, 'The Development of London as a centre of conspicuous consumption in the sixteenth and seventeenth centuries', *Transactions of the Royal Historical Society*, 4th series, XXX (1948), 37–50, and L. Stone, *The Crisis of the Aristocracy 1558–1641* (Oxford, 1965), Ch. 8.

45. V. Pearl, *London and the Outbreak of the Puritan Revolution* (London, 1961; reprinted with corrections, 1964), p. 14.

46. P. Hentzner, quoted in *England as Seen by Foreigners*, ed. W. B. Rye (London, 1865), p. 283.

47. The precise nature of the social conflict in England in the sixteenth and seventeenth centuries continues to be a subject of controversy amongst historians. For a survey of the major positions taken, see L. Stone, *The Causes of the English Revolution 1529–1642* (London, 1972), Ch. 2, where a useful summary of the most recent theories about the social origins of the English revolution is given.

48. See W. H. Coates, 'An Analysis of Major Conflicts in Seventeenth-Century England' in *Conflict in Stuart England: Essays in honour of Wallace Notestein*, ed. W. A. Aiken and B. A. Henning (London, 1960), p. 19. Coates in fact offers a critique of this view as an explanation of the factors leading to the Civil War.

49. See V. Pearl, 'Puritans and Poor Relief: The London Workhouse, 1649–1660', in *Puritans and Revolutionaries: Essays presented to Christopher Hill*, ed. D. Pennington and K. Thomas (Oxford, 1978), pp. 107–8, on this controversy.

50. V. Pearl, ibid., p. 209, citing the views of Christopher Hill.
51. Chapter 3, pp. 137–42.
52. 'Soiled' is here used in the sense of overfed, satiated with rich feeding. See D. E. Blythe, 'Lear's Soiled Horse', *SQ* XXXI (1980), 87–88.
53. R. A. Foakes, in his note on *The Revenger's Tragedy*, II, i, 217–18, Revels Plays (London, 1966), p. 41, gives other examples of the image of ancestral estates transmuted into clothing, e.g. *King John*, II, i, 70, *Henry VIII*, I, i, 84, and Camden, *Remains* (1605), p. 221.
54. Chapter 2, pp. 98–99.
55. A. B. Grosart, ed., *Occasional Issues of Unique or Very Rare Books*, 17 vols. (London, 1881), XVI, vi.
56. G. Hibbard, *Thomas Nashe*, (London, 1962) p. 251.
57. By S. L. Thrupp, in the interesting introduction to her edition of *The Art of Drapery*, published by Harvard Graduate School of Business Administration (Boston, Mass., 1953).
58. S. L. Thrupp, ibid., pp. 12, 9.

CHAPTER 5

1. Cicero, *De Inventione*, (I, 7–9) trans. H. M. Hubbell, (The Loeb Classical Library, Cambridge, Mass. and London, 1949), p. 19.
2. J. M. Lechner, *Renaissance Concepts of the Commonplaces* (New York, 1962), p. 210.
3. This pamphlet is generally attributed to Anthony Gibson, who signs the dedication, but he himself claims it to be a translation of an original 'written in French by a Lord of great reckoning'. W. C. Hazlitt, *Handbook to the Popular, Poetical, and Dramatic Literature of Great Britain*, p. 674, says that it is translated from the Chevalier de L'Escale, *Le Champion des Femmes*. But the *Catalogue Générale des Livres Imprimés de la Bibliothèque Nationale* lists no edition of this work earlier than 1618.
4. In *Epicoene*, II, ii: 'Ther's Aristotle, a mere Common-place fellow'.
5. Other examples of pamphlets constructed in this way include John Lowin, *Conclusions Vpon Dances* (1607), William Heale, *An Apologie for Women* (1609), Thomas Tuke, *A Treatise Against Painting* (1616), William Prynne, *The Vnlouelinesse, of Love-Lockes* (1628), John Blaxton, *The English Vsurer* (1634), and many more.
6. See Nashe, *Works*, IV, 37–38.
7. R. W., *The Most horrible and tragicall murther of the right honorable, the vertuous and valerous Gentleman, . . . John Lord Bourgh, Baron of Castle Connell* (1591), sig. A2.
8. M. W. Croll, *Style, Rhetoric and Rhythm*, ed. J. M. Patrick and R. O. Evans, with J. M. Wallace and R. J. Schoeck (Princeton, 1966), p. 119.
9. W. S. Howell, *Logic and Rhetoric in England 1500–1700* (Princeton, 1956), an invaluable work on this subject.
10. This is the definition given by M. W. Croll in his introduction to *Euphues: The Anatomy of Wit*, eds. M. W. Croll and H. Clemens (London and New York, 1916), xvi.
11. It has been suggested by N. B. Paradise, *Thomas Lodge, The History of an Elizabethan* (New Haven and London, 1931), that Lodge actually wrote *The Divel coniured* at an earlier date, and handed it over to the printer with a batch of other work in his last year as a professional writer. But there is no evidence to prove this.
12. See *Works* I, 10, and III, 132 in particular.
13. G. G. Smith, ed., *Elizabethan Critical Essays*, II, 272.
14. See Chapter 1.
15. For example, *Greenes Newes both from Heauen and Hell* (1593), *Greenes Funeralls* (1594), *Greene in Coneeipt* (1598) by John Dickenson, and *Greenes Ghost Haunting Conie-Catchers* (1602).
16. For another aspect of Nashe's influence on Greene in the matter of the feud with the Harveys, see E. H. Miller, 'The Relationship of Robert Greene and Thomas Nashe (1588-1592)', *PQ* XXXIII (1954), pp. 353–67.

17. See W. Watson, *A Decacordon of Ten Quodlibeticall Questions concerning Religion and State* (1602), sig. S5^v.

18. See F. Meres, *Palladis Tamia* (1598), Sig. Oo3^v; T. Middleton, *Father Hubburds Tales* (1604), sig. B3^v; T. Dekker, *Newes From Hell* (1606).

19. See *Works*, V, 142-57 for a list of early allusions to Nashe.

20. On other aspects of Nashe's influence on Dekker, see J. Jusserand, *The English Novel in the Time of Shakespeare* (revised edn., London, 1908), pp. 334–36, and M. T. Jones-Davies, *Un Peintre de La Vie Londonienne: Thomas Dekker*, I, pp. 103-8.

21. There is evidence to show that an unlearned audience at this time did appreciate hearing and reading displays of learning. F. P. Wilson, *Seventeenth Century Prose* (Cambridge, 1960), in his chapter on the Sermon, p. 96, demonstrates the fondness of unlearned or illiterate sermon audiences for a learned style in their preacher. In the anonymous pamphlet, *An Alarme to Awake Church-sleepers* (1640), a list of hypothetical excuses given by people who do not regularly attend church includes objections to the preacher:

> Hee is no scholler; Hee is not read in humane Writers. Hee is no Logician, Historian, linguist. He is not acquainted with the Schoole-men. He citeth not the Testimonies of the Fathers, and Doctors of the Church (p. 104).

22. See L. C. Knights, 'Elizabethan Prose', *Scrutiny* II (1933); I. A. Gordon, *The Movement of English Prose* (London, 1966), Ch. 8; I. Watt, 'Elizabethan Light Reading', *The Pelican Guide to English Literature* (Harmondsworth, 1955), II, 119–30.

23. J. Sutherland, 'Apes and Peacocks', in *On English Prose*, Oxford University Press (London, 1957).

24. L. Febvre, *Le Problème de l'Incroyance au 16e Siecle: La Religion de Rabelais*, Evolution de l'Humanité LIII (Paris, 1947), pp. 461–73, argues that the sixteenth century was still the age of the ear, and that the age of the eye was yet to come. His theories about modes of perception in the pre-print era have been highly influential on later historians of print culture, including Father W. J. Ong, who uses the terms 'oral/aural' and 'visual' in *In the Human Grain* (London and New York, 1967), Ch. 1.

25. The most recent attempt to explore it has been made by E. Eisenstein, *The Printing Press as an Agent of Change*, 2 vols. (Cambridge, 1979).

26. For example, Nashe's *Strange Newes*, where the main text is in Roman type, quotations from Gabriel Harvey in Italic, and references to Richard Harvey's astrological work in the old-fashioned looking Blackletter. In the dedicatory epistle to *Haue with you to Saffron-Walden* he purposely leaves a framed blank space for readers' comments.

27. M. H. Wolf, ed., *Faultes faults, And nothing else but Faultes*, a facsimile reproduction, Scholars' Facsimiles and Reprints (Gainesville, Florida, 1965), Introduction, p. 65.

28. *A true report of certaine wonderfull overflowings of Waters, now lately in Summerset-shire* (1607), sig. B2^v.

29. L. C. Knights, 'Elizabethan Prose', p. 431.

30. So described by M. Schlauch, *Antecedents of the English Novel, 1400–1600. From Chaucer to Deloney* (Warsaw and London, 1963), p. 116.

31. See *Works*, V, 142–57.

32. In W. H. Dunham and S. M. Pargelis, *Complaint and Reform in England, 1436-1714* (New York, 1938), p. 457.

33. See J. W. Saunders, 'The Stigma of Print. A Note on the Social Bases of Tudor Poetry', *Essays in Criticism* I (1951), 139–64.

34. See J. D. Peter, *Complaint and Satire in Early English Literature*, Ch. 1 and 3, H. C. White, *Social Criticism in Popular Religious Literature* (New York, 1944), and H. Smith, *Elizabethan Poetry: A Study in Conventions, Meaning, and Expression*(University of Michigan Press, 1952), Ch. 4, on the Piers Plowman tradition in sixteenth-century literature.

35. H. M. McLuhan, *The Gutenberg Galaxy. The Making of Typographic Man* (Toronto, 1962), p. 136.

36. Only the first edition printed in 1615 by Edward Allde for Thomas Archer goes under this pseudonym.

37. G. R. Hibbard, *Thomas Nashe. A Critical Introduction*, pp. 250–53.
38. H. M. McLuhan, op. cit., p. 136.
39. See Chapter 1, pp. 67–68.
40. The artistry of this pamphlet is much admired by M. Schlauch, *Antecedents of the English Novel 1400–1600*, pp. 157–63.
41. Such lists of paradoxical praises were conventional in prefaces to books or pamphlets on light subjects, although Rich's is not one. See McKerrow's note on *Nashes Lenten Stuffe*, *Works*, III, 176–77, where Nashe himself provides such a list, longer and more ribald than Rich's.
42. See B. Capp, *Astrology and the Popular Press: English Almanacs 1500–1800* (London, 1979), Ch. 2.
43. F. P. Wilson, 'Some English Mock-Prognostications', *The Library*, Fourth Series, XIX (1938), 17–18.
44. D. C. Allen, ed., *The Owles Almanacke* (Baltimore, 1943), p. 8.
45. This passage is a close imitation of Dekker, *The Rauens Almanacke*, *Non-Dramatic Works*, IV, 208–9.
46. I am indebted to F. P. Wilson, 'Some English Mock-Prognostications', for many of these borrowings.
47. B. Boyce, *The Theophrastan Character in England to 1642* (1947), p. 53.
48. Originally published separately. See Boyce, op. cit., p. 216, and W. C. Hazlitt, *Handbook to the Popular, Poetical, and Dramatic Literature of Great Britain* (London, 1867), p. 616.
49. This section in Brathwait (pp. 313–15) is a translation from Quevedo, *Sueños y Discursos* (1627), pp. 76–77. The same passage can be found in Richard Croshawe's *Visions, Or, Hels Kingdome* (1640), the first complete version of the *Suenos* known in English.
50. See Boyce, op. cit., p. 212.
51. See Schlauch, op. cit., p. 113.
52. See Chapter 3, pp. 145–47.
53. The phrase is used by B. Harris, in 'Dissent and Satire', *Shakespeare Survey* XVII (1964), an article which discovers in some of the minor literature of the period, particularly verse satire, reflections of its changing sensibility.
54. Harris, ibid., p. 128.

Bibliography

A) PAMPHLETS AND CONTEMPORARY WORKS CITED IN THE TEXT

Anonymous pamphlets are listed either under a head-word from the title, as used in the *STC*, or under the name of the presumed author. The names of pseudonymous authors are put in inverted commas.

Adams, T., *Englands Sicknes, Comparatively Conferred with Israels*. (1615).

[Alarme] *An Alarme to Awake Church-Sleepers*. (1640).

[All] *All to Westminster*. (1641).

[Allott, R.] *Wits Theater of the Little World*. (1599).

[Almanacke] *The Owles Almanacke*. (1618). Ed. D.C. Allen, The Johns Hopkins Press (Baltimore, 1943).

'Anger, Jane', *Iane Anger her Protection for Women. To defend them against the Scandalous Reportes Of a late Surfeting Louer* . . . (1589).

[Anthoine, N.] *An Historical Account of the Life and Tryal of Nicholas Anthoine, burnt for Judaism at Geneva, in the year 1632*. In *The Harleian Miscellany*, ed. W. Oldys and T. Park, 10 vols. (London, 1809), III, 213–20.

Anton, R., *Moriomachia*. (1613).

Arthington, H., *Provision for the Poore, now in Penurie*. (1597).

———. *The Seduction of Arthington by Hackett especiallie, with some tokens of his vnfained repentance and Submission*. (1592).

Ascham, R., *The Scholemaster*. (1570).

Averell, W., *A Dyall for dainty Darlings, rockt in the cradle of Securitie*. (1584).

———. *A meruailous combat of contrarieties*. (1588).

Awdeley, J., *The Fraternitye of Vacabondes*. (1561). From the edition of 1575, ed. E. Viles and F.J. Furnivall, Early English Text Society, Extra Series, no. 9 (London, 1869).

Balmford, J., *A Short Dialogue Concerning the Plagues Infection*. (1603).

[Banquet] *The Batchelars Banquet* (1603), ed. F. P. Wilson (Oxford, 1929).

Barclay, A., *The Shyp of folys*. (1509). Trans. of *Narrenschiff* by Sebastian Brant. Reprinted with introduction by T.H. Jamieson, 2 vols. (Edinburgh, 1874).

Barclay, W., *Nepenthes, Or The Vertues of Tabacco*. (1614).

Beard, T., *The Theatre of Gods Judgments: or, a Collection of Histories*. (1597).

[Berkshire] *Looke up and see Wonders. A miraculous Apparition in the Ayre, seen in Barkeshire.* (1628).

Bernard, R., *The Isle of Man: Or, The Legall Proceeding in Man-Shire against Sinne.* (1627).

Blaxton, J., *The English Vsurer; Or Vsury Condemned . . .* (1634).

[Bloudy] *The Bloudy booke, Or, The Tragicall and desperate end of Sir Iohn Fites (alias) Fitz.* (1605).

[Bowes, Sir J.] *A True report of the horrible Murther, which was committed in the house of Sir Ierome Bowes.* (1607).

Bradwell, S., *A Watch-man For the Pest.* (1625).

Brathwait, R., *Ar't asleepe Husband? A Boulster Lecture . . . By Philogenes Panedonius.* (1640).

———. *The Smoaking Age, Or, The man in the Mist.* (1640).

Breton, N., *The Court and the Country. Or A Briefe Discourse between the Courtier and Country-man.* (1618).

———. *A Dialogue full of pithe and pleasure: between three phylosophers.* (1603).

[Breton, N.] *Choice, Chance, and Change: or, Conceits in the Colours.* (1606). In A.B. Grosart, ed. *Occasional Issues of Unique or Very Rare Books* (London, 1881), Vol. XVI.

Brewer, T. *Lord have Mercy vpon Vs. The World, A Sea, A Pest-House.* (1636).

———. *The Weeping Lady: Or, London Like Ninivie in Sack-Cloth.* (1625).

[Brewer, T.] *A Dialogue betwixt a Cittizen, and a poore Countrey-man and his Wife.* (1636).

Bullein, W., *A Dialogue bothe pleasaunt and pietiful against the Feuer Pestilence.* (1564).

Burton, H., *A Divine Tragedie Lately Acted, Or, A Collection of sundrie memorable examples of Gods judgements upon Sabbath-breakers.* (1641).

[Bush, M.] *A true Relation of the Trauels of M. Bush a Gentleman.* (1607).

[Canterbury] *The Cobler of Canterburie, Or An inuectiue against Tarltons Newes out of Purgatorie.* (1590).

[Carlstadt] *Strange fearful & true newes, which hapned at Carlstadt, in the Kingdome of Croatia.* (1606).

de Carthenay, J., *The Voyage of the Wandring Knight. Shewing al the course of mans life.* (1607).

Cartwright, F., *The Life, Confession, and Heartie Repentance of Francis Cartwright, Gentleman.* (1612).

[Cash, T.] *Two horrible and inhumane Murders done in Lincolneshire, by two Husbands upon their Wiues.* (1607).

[Chelmsford] *The Apprehension and Confession of three notorious Witches. Arreigned and by Justice condemned and executed at Chelmesforde.* (1589). In *Witchcraft*, ed. B. Rosen, The Stratford-upon-Avon Library (London, 1969).

Chettle, H., *Kind-Harts Dreame. Conteining fiue Apparitions, with their Inuectiues against abuses raigning.* (1592). Ed. G.B. Harrison, Bodley Head Quartos (London, 1923).

Churchyard, T., *The Wonders of the Ayre. The Trembling of the Earth, and the Warnings of the World before Iudgement Day.* (1602).

Clarke, T., *The Recantation of Thomas Clarke (sometime a Seminarie Priest of the English Colledge in Rhemes).* (1594).

'Cocke Lorell', *Cocke Lorelles Bote.* (1510?). Ed. H. Drury, The Roxburghe Club (London, 1817).

'Conny-Catcher, Cuthbert', *The Defence of Conny-Catching.* (1592). Ed. G.B. Harrison, Bodley Head Quartos (London, 1924).

Cooper, T., *The Cry and Reuenge of Blood.* (1620).

Copland, R., *The Hye Way to the Spyttel Hous.* (1536?).

Cottesford, S., *A Treatise Against Traitors.* (1591).

[Courtney, C.] *The Life, Apprehension, Arraignement, and Execution of Charles Courtney, alias Hollice, alias Worsley, and Clement Slie Fencer.* (1612).

Croshawe, R., *Visions, Or, Hels Kingdome, And the Worlds Follies and Abuses.* (1640).

Dando, J. and Runt, H., *Maroccus Extaticus. Or, Bankes Bay Horse in a Trance.* (1595).

Darrel, J., *A Detection of that Sinnful, Shamful, Lying, and Ridiculous Discours of Samuel Harshnet.* (1600).

———. *A True Narration of the strange and grevous Vexation by the Devil, of 7. persons in Lancashire, and William Somers of Nottingham.* (1600).

[Darrell, J.] *The Triall of Maist. Dorrell, Or, A Collection of Defences . . .* (1599).

'Dawe, Jack', *Vox Graculi, Or Jack Dawes Prognostication.* (1623).

Day, J., *Peregrinatio Scholastica Or Learneinges Pilgrimage.* (n.d.). In *The Works of John Day*, ed. A.H. Bullen (London, 1881).

Deacon, J., *Tobacco Tortuered, Or, The Filthie Fume of Tobacco Refined.* (1616).

———. *A Treatise, Intituled; Nobody is my name, which beareth euerie-bodies blame.* (1585).

[Death] *The Death of Usury, or, The Disgrace of Usurers.* (1594).

Dekker, T., *The Bel-man of London.* (1608).

———. *The Blacke Rod: and the White Rod.* (1630).

———. *The Dead Tearme Or, Westminsters Complaint for long Vacations and Short Termes.* (1608).

———. *Dekker his Dreame.* (1620).

———. *English Villanies Seven Several Times prest to Death by the Printers.* (1632).

———. *Foure Birds of Noahs Arke.* (1609). Ed. F.P. Wilson (Oxford, 1924).

———. *The Guls Horne-booke.* (1609).

———. *A Knights Coniuring. Done in earnest: Discouered in Iest.* (1607).

———. *Lanthorne and Candle-light. Or the Bell-mans second Nights walke.* (1608).

———. *London Looke Backe, At That Yeare of Yeares 1625.* (1630).

———. *The Meeting of Gallants at an Ordinarie.* (1604).

———. *Newes from Graues-end: Sent to Nobody.* (1604).

———. *Newes from Hell; Brought by the Diuells Carrier.* (1606).

———. *O per se O. Or A new Cryer of Lanthorne and Candle-light.* (1612).

Bibliography

———. *Penny-Wise Pound-Foolish Or, a Bristow Diamond, set in two Rings, and both Crack'd.* (1631).
———. *The Rauens Almanacke. Foretelling of a Plague, Famine, and Ciuill Warre.* (1609).
———. *A Rod for Run-awayes. Gods Tokens, Of his feareful Iudgements, sundry Wayes pronounced vpon this City.* (1625).
———. *The Seuen Deadly Sinnes of London.* (1606).
———. *A Strange Horse-Race.* (1613).
———. *Villanies Discouered by Lanthorne and Candle-light, and the helpe of a new Cryer called O per se O.* (1616).
———. *Warres, Warre(s), Warres.* (1628).
———. *The Wonderfull Yeare.* (1603).
———. *Worke for Armorours: Or, The peace is Broken.* (1609).

Dekker, T. and Wilkins, G., *Iests to make you merie: with The Coniuring vp of Cock Watt.* (1606).

[Dell, A.] *The Most Cruell and Bloody Murther committed by an Inkeepers Wife, called Annis Dell.* (1606).
———. *The Horrible Murther of a Young Boy of three yeres of age . . .* (1606).

D[enison], J., *The most Wonderfull and true storie, of a certaine Witch, named Alse Gooderige of Stapenhill.* (1597).

[Dichet] *A Miracle, of Miracles, As fearefull as euer was seene or heard of in the memorie of Man. Which lately happened at Dichet in Sommersetshire.* (1614).

Dickenson, J., *Greene in Conceipt. New raised from his graue to write the Tragique Historie of faire Valeria of London.* (1598). In *Occasional Issues of Unique or Very Rare Books,* ed. A. B. Grosart (London, 1878), Vol. VI.

[Discourse] *A Discourse of the Married And Single Life.* (1621).

Donne, J., *Ignatius his Conclaue: Or His Inthronisation in a late Election in Hell.* (1611).

[Dream] *A Dreame: or Newes from Hell.* (1641).

Dugdale, G., *A True Discourse Of The practises of Elizabeth Caldwell, Ma. Ieffrey Bownd, Isabell Hall Widdow, and George Ferneley.* (1604).

Earle, Sir T., *Micro-Cosmographie. Or, A Peece of the World Discovered.* (1628).

[Elwes, Sir G.] *The Lieutenant of the Tower his Speech and Repentance, at the time of his death.* (1615).

[England] *Gods Warning to his people of England.* (1606).
———. *A Looking Glasse for Englande.* (1590).

[Faustus, J.] *The Historie of the damnable life, and deserued death of Doctor Iohn Faustus.* (1592).

Fennor, W., *The Compters Common-wealth, or A Voiage Made To an Infernall Iland . . .* (1617).

Fetherstone, C., *A Dialogue agaynst light, lewde, and lasciuious dauncing.* (1582).

[Fian] *Newes from Scotland. Declaring the damnable life of Doctor Fian a notable sorcerer, who was burned at Edenbrough in Ianuarie last 1591.* (1591).

[Flood, Griffin] *The Life and Death of Griffin Flood Informer.* (1623).

'Fouleweather, Adam', *A Wonderfull, strange and miraculous, Astrologicall Prognostication.* (1591). In Nashe, *Works*, III, 377–95.

'Foulface, Philip', *Bacchus Bountie: Describing the debonaire Deitie of his bountifull Godhead, in the Royall Observance of his great Feast of Penticost.* (1593). In *The Harleian Miscellany*, ed. W. Oldys and T. Park (London, 1809), II, 300–310.

Foxe, J., *Actes and Monuments of these latter and perillous dayes . . .* (1563).

[Frost] *The Great Frost. Cold doings in London, except it be at the Lottery.* (1608). In *An English Garner*, ed. E. Arber (London, 1877), Vol. I.

Gardiner, E., *The Triall of Tabacco.* (1610).

Gascoigne, G., *The Steele Glas. A satyre, togither with the Complainte of Phylomene.* (1576).

[Gaufredy, L.] *The Life and Death of Lewis Gaufredy.* (1612).

Gibson, A., *A Womans Woorth, defended against all the men in the World.* (1599).

[God] *Gods Handy-Worke in Wonders. Miraculously shewen vpon two Women, lately deliuered of two monsters.* (1615).

Golding, A., *A discourse vpon the Earthquake that hapned throughe This Realme of England.* (1580).

Goodcole, H., *A True Declaration of the happy conuersion, contrition, and Christian preparation of Francis Robinson, Gentleman.* (1618).

———. *The wonderfull discouerie of Elizabeth Sawyer a Witch, late of Edmonton.* (1621).

G[oodcole], H., *Heavens Speedie Hue and Cry sent after Lust and Murther.* (1635).

Gosson, S., *The S[c]hool of Abuse, Conteining a pleasant inuective against Poets, Pipers, Plaiers, Iesters . . .* (1579). Reprinted for the Shakespeare Society (London, 1841).

Greene, R., *The Blacke Bookes Messenger. Laying open the Life and Death of Ned Browne.* (1592). Ed. G. B. Harrison, Bodley Head Quartos (London, 1924).

———. *Ciceronis Amor. Tullies Loue.* (1589).

———. *A Disputation, Between a Hee Conny-Catcher and a Shee Conny-Catcher.* (1592). Harrison (1923).

———. *Greenes farewell to Folly: sent to Courtiers and Schollers as a president to warn them . . .* (1591).

———. *Greenes Groats-Worth of witte, bought with a million of Repentance.* (1592). Harrison (1923).

———. *Greenes Mourning Garment: Given Him by Repentance at the Funerals of Love.* (1590).

———. *Greenes Never too late. Or, A Powder of Experience: Sent to all youthfull Gentlemen . . .* (1590).

———. *Greenes Vision: Written at the instant of his death.* (1592).

———. *Menaphon. Camillas Alarum to slumbering Euphues.* (1589).

———. *A Notable Discouery of Coosnage.* (1591). Harrison (1923).

———. *A Quip for an Upstart Courtier: Or, A quaint dispute between Velvet-breeches and Cloth-breeches.* (1592).

———. *The Repentance of Robert Greene Maister of Artes.* (1592). Harrison (1923).

———. *The Second and last part of Conny-catching.* (1592). Harrison (1923).

———. *The Spanish Masquerado.* (1589).

———. *The Thirde and last Part of Conny-catching.* (1592). Harrison (1923).

[Greene, R.] 'B. R.-R. B.', *Greenes Newes both from Heauen and Hell* (1593) and *Greenes Funeralls* (1594), ed. R. B. McKerrow (London, 1911).

[Groundworke] *The Groundworke of Conny-catching; the manner of their Pedlers-French, and the meanes to understand the same* . . . (1592).

Gurth, A., *Most true and More Admirable newes, Expressing the Miraculous Preservation of a Young Maiden of the towne of Glabbich in the Dukedome of Gulische.* (1597).

H., I., *This Worlds Folly. Or A Warning-Peece discharged vpon the Wickednesse Thereof.* (1615).

———. *Work for Chimny-sweepers: Or A warning for Tabacconists.* (1602).

[Haec Vir] *Haec-Vir: Or The Womanish-Man: Being an Answere to a late Booke intituled Hic-Mulier.* (1617).

Hall, J., *Characters of Vertues and Vices.* (1608).

Harman, T., *A Caueat or Warening, For Commen Cursetors vulgarely called Vagabones.* (1567).

Harris, A., *The Oeconomy of the Fleete: or an Apologeticall Answeare of Alexander Harris (late Warden there).* Ed. A. Jessop, Camden Society, New Series XXV (London, 1879).

Harrison, W., *Deaths Advantage Little Regarded, and the Soules solace against sorrow. Preached . . . at the buriall of Mistris Katherin Brettergh.* 2nd edn. (1602).

Harsnett, S., *A Declaration of Egregious Popishe Impostures.* (1603).

———. *A Discovery of the fraudulent practises of Iohn Darrel Bacheler of Artes.* (1599).

Harvey, G., *Foure Letters and certeine Sonnets: Especially touching Robert Greene, and other parties, by him abused.* (1592). Ed. G. B. Harrison, Bodley Head Quartos (London, 1922).

Hawkins, Sir Richard, *Observations of Sir R. Hawkins in his voiâge into the South Sea 1593.* (1622).

H[eale], W., *An Apologie for Women. Or An Opposition to Mr. Dr. G. his assertion.* (1608).

Heywood, T., *A Curtaine Lecture: As it is read By a Countrey Farmers Wife to her Good Man.* (1637).

———. *The Hierarchy of the Blessed Angels.* (1635).

———. *Philocothonista, or, The Drunkard.* (1635).

[Heywood, T.] *The Phoenix of these late times: or the life of Mr. Henry Welby Esq.* (1637).

[Hic Mulier] *Hic Mulier: Or, The Man-Woman.* (1617).

[Holdt] *Miraculous Newes, From the Cittie of Holdt, in the Lord-ship of Munster (in Germany) the twentieth of September last past.* (1616).

[Horsham] *True and Wonderfull. A discourse relating a Strange and Monstrous Serpent (or Dragon) lately discovered, and yet living . . . in Sussex, two Miles from Horsam.* (1614). In *The Harleian Miscellany*, ed. W. Oldys and T. Park (London, 1809), III, 110–12.

Hutton, L., *The Blacke Dogge of Newgate: both pithie and profitable for all Readers.* (1596).

I., T., *A World of Wonders. A masse of murthers. A couie of cosonages.* (1595).

James I, of England, *A Counter-blaste to Tobacco.* (1604).

[James] *A True Relation of the most Inhumane and bloody Murther, of Master Iames Minister and Preacher of the Word of God at Rockland in Norfolke.* (1609).

Johnson, R., *A Lanterne-light for Loyall Subiects. Or, A terrour for Traytours.* (1603).

———. *Looke on me London: I am an Honest English-man . . .* (1613).

———. *The Pleasant Walkes of Moore-fields. Being the guift of two Sisters . . .* (1607).

Kellwaye, S., *A Defensative against the Plague.* (1593).

Kemp, W., *Kemps nine daies wonder. Performed in a daunce from London to Norwich.* (1600). Ed. G. B. Harrison, Bodley Head Quartos (London, 1923).

King, H., *An Halfe-penny-worth of Wit, in a Penny-worth of Paper. Or, The Hermites Tale.* 3rd impression. (1613).

Kyd, T., *The trueth of the most wicked & secret murthering of Iohn Brewen, Goldsmith of London.* (1592).

[Lisbon] *Two Most S[t]range And notable examples, shewed at Lyshborne in Kent.* (1591).

Lodge, T., *An Alarum against Vsurers. Containing tryed experiences against worldly abuses.* (1584).

———. *Catharos. Diogenes in his Singularitie.* (1591).

———. *The Divèl coniured.* (1596).

———. *The Life and Death of William Longbeard, the most famous and witty English Traitor.* (1593).

———. *A Treatise of the Plague.* (1603).

———. *Wits Miserie, and the Worlds Madnesse: Discouering the Devills Incarnat of this Age.* (1596).

[Long Meg] *The Life and Pranks of Long Meg of Westminster.* (1582).

[Looking-Glass] *A Looking-Glasse for Drunkards: Or, The Hunting of drunkennesse.* (1627).

Lowin, J., *Conclusions Vpon Dances, Both Of This Age, And Of The Olde.* (1607).

Lupton, D., *London and the Countrey Carbonadoed and Quartred into seuerall Characters.* (1622).

Lupton, T., *A Dreame of the Devill and Dives.* (2nd edn., 1615).

Lyly, J., *Euphues: The Anatomy of Wit.* (1578). Ed. M. W. Croll and H. Clemens (London and New York, 1916).

M., I., *A Health to the Gentlemanly Profession of Seruingmen; or, The Seruingmans Comfort.* (1598).

M., W., *The Man In the Moone, Telling Strange Fortunes, or The English Fortuneteller.* (1609).

de Malynes, G., *Saint George for England, Allegorically described.* (1601).

Marbecke, R., *A Defence of Tabacco.* (1602).

'Mar-sixtus, Martin', *Martine Mar-sixtus. A second replie against the defensory and Apology of Sixtus the fift late Pope of Rome.* (1591).

Marten, A., *An Exhortation, To stirre up the mindes of all her Maiesties faithfull Subiects, to defend their Countrey . . .* (1588).

Meres, F., *Palladis Tamia. Wits Treasury being the second Part of Wits Commonwealth.* (1598). Ed. D. C. Allen, Scholars Facsimiles and Reprints (New York, 1958).

M[iddleton], T., *The Blacke Booke.* (1604).

——. *Father Hubburds Tales: Or The Ant, And the Nightingale.* (1604).

Milton, R., *Londons Miserie, The Countryes Crueltie: with Gods Mercie.* (1625).

[Mirror] *The Mirror for Magistrates.* Ed. . . . L. B. Campbell, Huntington Library Publications (Cambridge, 1938).

[Monmouthshire] *Lamentable newes out of Monmouthshire.* (1607).

[Muld Sacke] *Muld Sacke: Or The Apologie of Hic Mulier: To the late Declamation against her.* (1620).

'Munda, Constantia', *The Worming of a mad Dogge: Or, A Soppe for Cerberus The Iaylor of Hell.*(1617).

Munday, A., *A View of Sundry Examples Reporting Many Strange Murders.* (1580). In *John a Kent and John a Cumber, a Comedy,* ed. J. P. Collier, printed for the Shakespeare Society (London, 1857).

——. *A Watch-woord to Englande. To beware of traytours and tretcherous practises . . .* (1584).

[Murthers] *Sundrye strange and inhumaine Murthers, lately committed . . .* (1591).

——. *Two most vnnatural and bloodie Murthers: The one by Maister Cauerley, A Yorkeshire Gentleman . . .* (1605).

Mynshul, G., *Certaine Characters and Essayes of Prison and Prisoners.* (1618).

Nashe, T., *The Anatomie of Absurditie.* (1589).

——. *Christs Teares over Ierusalem.* (1593).

——. *Haue with you to Saffron-Walden. Or Gabriell Harueys Hunt is vp.* (1596).

——. *Nashes Lenten Stuffe.* (1599).

——. *Pierce Penilesse his Supplication to the Divell.* (1592).

——. *Strange Newes, Of the intercepting certaine Letters . . .* (1592).

——. *The Terrors of the Night. Or, A Discourse of Apparitions.* (1594).

[Nashe, T.] *Tom Nash his Ghost.* (?1642).

N[ewstead], C., *An Apology for Women: Or, Womens Defence.* (1620).

Niccholes, A., *A Discourse of Marriage and Wiving, and of the greatest Mystery therein contained.* (1615). In *The Harleian Miscellany,* ed. W. Oldys and T. Park (London, 1809), II, 156-82.

Nixon, A., *The Blacke yeare. Seria iocis.* (1606).

——. *The Scourge of Corruption. Or A Crafty Knave needs no Broker.* (1615).

——. *A Straunge Foot-Post, with A Packet full of Strange Petitions.* (1613).

'Oatmeale, Oliver', *A Quest of Enquirie by women to know, whether the Tripe-wife were trimmed by Doll yea or no.* (1595).

[Overbury, Sir T.] *The Bloody Downfall of Adultery, Murder, Ambition.* (1615).

The Overburian Characters. To which is added A Wife by Sir Thomas Overbury. Ed. W. J. Paylor (Oxford, 1936).

Parkes, W., *The Curtaine-Drawer Of the World.* (1612).

[Parliament] *The Penniles Parliament of Threed-bare Poets.* (1604).

[Parry, W.] *A True and plaine declaration of the horrible Treasons practised by William Parry the Traitor, against the Queenes Maiestie.* (1584).

Peacham, H. the elder, *The Garden of Eloquence.* (1593). Ed. W. G. Crane, Scholars Facsimiles and Reprints (Gainesville, Florida, 1954).

[Peele, G.] *Merrie Conceited Iests: Of George Peele Gentleman, sometimes a Student in Oxford.* (1627).

[Perin] *Newes from Perin in Cornwall: of A most Bloody and un-Exampled Murther.* (1618).

Petowe, H., *The Countrie Ague. Or, London her Welcome home to her retired Children.* (1625).

[Plato] *Platoes Cap. Cast at this yeare 1604, being leape-yeare.* (1604).

Potts, T., *The Wonderfull discouerie of Witches in the Countie of Lancaster.* (1612).

Powell, T., *The Art of Thriving, Or, The Plaine pathway to Preferment.* (1635).
———. *Wheresoeuer you see me, Trust vnto your selfe. Or, The Mysterie of Lending and Borrowing.* (1623).

Price, S., *Londons Warning by Laodiceas Luke-warmenesse.* (1613).

Prynne, W., *The Vnlouelinesse, of Love-Lockes.* (1628).

R., S., *The Art of Iugling or Legerdemaine.* (1614).
———. *Greenes Ghost Haunting Conie-Catchers.* (1602).
———. *Martin Mark-all, Beadle of Bridewell; His Defence and Answere to the Belman of London.* (1610).

[Raleigh, Sir W.] *A Declaration of the Demeanor and Cariage of Sir Walter Raleigh.* (1618).

R[ankins], W., *The English Ape, The Italian imitation, the Foot-steppes of Fraunce.* (1588).

Rankins, W., *A Mirrour of Monsters.* (1588).

[Ratsey, G.] *The Life and Death of Gamaliel Ratsey a famous thief, of England, Executed at Bedford the 26 of March last past* (1605) and *Ratseis Ghost. Or the Second Part of his madde Prankes and Robberies* (1605), ed. S. H. Atkins, Shakespeare Association Facsimiles, no. 10 (London, 1935).

[Ravilliack] *The Terrible and Deserved death of Francis Rauilliack.* (1610).

Rawlidge, R., *A Monster Late Found Out And Discovered. Or The scourging of Tiplers . . .* (1628).

[Retrait] *A Second and Third Blast of Retrait from Plaies and Theaters.* (1580). In W. C. Hazlitt, ed., *The English Drama and Stage under the Tudor and Stuart Princes. 1546-1664* (London, 1869).

[Returne] *The Returne of the Knight of the Poste from Hell, with the Diuels aunswere to the Supplication of Pierce Penilesse.* (1606).

Reynolds, J., *The Triumphs of Gods Revenge Against the Crying and Execrable Sinne of (Wilfull and Premeditated) Murther.* (1621).

Rich, B., *Allarme to England*. (1578).
———. *A Catholicke Conference* . . . (1611).
———. *The Excellency of good women*. (1613).
———. *Faultes faults, And nothing else but Faultes*. Facsimile reproduction, ed. M. H. Wolf (Gainesville, Florida, 1965).
———. *The Fruites of Long Experience*. (1604).
———. *The Honestie of This Age*. (1614).
———. *The Irish Hubbub Or, The English Hue and Crie*. (1617).
———. *My Ladies Looking Glasse. Wherein May Be Discerned A Wise Man From A Foole*. (1616).
———. *Opinion Diefied. Discouering the Ingins, Traps, and Traynes, that are set in this Age, whereby to catch Opinion*. (1613).
———. *Riche his farewell to militarie profession*. (1581).
———. *Roome for a Gentleman, Or The Second Part of Faultes* . . . (1609).
———. *The true report of a late practise enterprised by a Papist* . . . (1582).

Rowley, W., *A Search for Money*. (1609).

Rudierde, E., *The Thunderbolt of Gods Wrath Against Hard-Hearted and stiffe-necked sinners*. (1618).

S., E., *The Discouerie of the Knights of the Poste*. (1597).

Sanford, J., *Gods Arrowe of the Pestilence*. (1604).

Scott, T., *Robert Earle of Essex his Ghost, Sent from Elizian*. (1624).
———. *Sir Walter Rawleighs Ghost, Or Englands Forewarner*. (1626).

Scott, W., *An Essay of Drapery: Or, The Compleate Citizen. Trading Justly. Pleasingly. Profitably*. (1635). Ed. S. L. Thrupp (Boston, Mass., 1953).

Shakelton, F., *A blazing Starre or burnying Beacon . . . to call all sinners to earnest & speedie repentance*. (1580).

[Skinker, T.] *A certaine Relation of the Hog-faced Gentlewoman called Mistris Tannakin Skinker*. (1640).

'Smel-knave, Simon', *Fearefull and lamentable effects of two dangerous Comets, which shall appeare in the yeere of our Lord, 1591 the 25 of March*. (1591).

Smith, H., *The Examination of Vsury, in two Sermons*. (1591).

S[nawsell], R., *A Looking Glasse for Maried Folkes*. (1610).

[Somerset] *A true report of certaine wonderfull overflowings of Waters, now lately in Summerset-shire* . . . (1607).

'Sowernam, Esther', *Ester hath hang'd Haman: Or An Answere to a lewd Pamphlet, entituled The Arraignment of Women*. (1617).

'Speght, Rachel', *A Mouzell for Melastomus, The Cynicall Bayter of, and foule mouthed Barker against Evahs Sex*. (1617).

Spenser, B., *Vox Civitatis, or Londons Complaint against her Children in the Countrey*. (1625).
———. *Vox Ruris, Reverberating Vox Civitatis*. (1636).

Stow, J., *The Annales of England*. (London, 1600).

[Stubbe Peeter] *A true Discourse. Declaring the damnable life and death of one Stubbe Peeter, a most wicked Sorcerer* . . . (1590).

Stubbes, P., *The Anatomie of Abuses*. (1583).

―――. *A Christal Glasse for Christian Women. Contayning An Excellent Discourse, of the Godly life and Christian death of Mistresse Katherine Stubbes* . . . (1591).
―――. *The Intended Treason of Doctor Parrie: And His Complices, Against the Queenes most Excellent Maiestie.* (1584).
―――. *Two wunderful and rare Examples of the Vndeferred and present approching iudgement of the Lord our God.* (1581).

Swetnam, J., *The Araignment of Lewd, Idle, Froward, and unconstant women.* (1615).

T., C., *Laugh and lie downe: Or, The Worldes Folly.* (1605. In *The Works of Cyril Tourneur,* ed. A. Nicoll, Fanfrolico Press (London, 1930).

T., W., *A Casting Up of accounts of certain Errors.* (1603).

[Tarlton, R.] *Tarltons Newes out of Purgatorie.* (1590).

'Tattlewell, Mary', *The womens sharpe revenge: Or an answer to Sir Seldome Sober* . . . (1640).

Taylor, J., the Water-Poet, *Crop-Eare Curried, Or, Tom Nash His Ghost.* (1644).
―――. *The Fearefull Sommer: or Londons Calamitie.* (1625).
―――. *The Great Eater of Kent, or Part of the Admirable Teeth and Stomack Exploits of Nicholas Wood.* (1630).
―――. *The Vnnaturall Father: Or, The Cruell Murther committed by one Iohn Rowse of the Towne of Ewell.* (1621).
―――. *The World runnes on Wheeles: or Oddes betwixt Carts and Coaches.* (1623).

'Tel-troth, Tom', *Tell-Trothes New-Yeares Gift.* (1593). Ed. F. J. Furnivall. The New Shakespeare Society (London, 1876).
―――. *Tom Tell Troath Or A free discourse touching the manners of the Tyme.* (?1630).

[Treatise] *A Treatise of Daunses, wherin it is shewed, that they are accessories to whoredome: where also is proued, that playes are ioyned with them.* (1581).

Tuke, T., *A Treatise Against Painting and Tincturing of Men and Women.* (1616).

T[wyne], T., *A shorte and pithie Discourse, concerning the engendring, tokens, and effects of all Earthquakes in Generall.* (1580).

V., B., *The run-awyaes Answer, To a Booke called, A Rodde for Runne-awayes.* (1625).

Venner, T., *A Briefe and Accurate Treatise, Concerning The taking of the fume of Tobacco.* (1621).

[Vincent, M.] *A pitilesse Mother. That most vnnaturally at one time, murthered two of her owne Children.* (1616).

W., R., *The Most horrible and tragicall murther of the right honorable, the vertuous and valerous Gentleman,* . . . *John Lord Bourgh, Baron of Castle Connell.* (1591).

Walker, G., *A manifest detection of the most vyle and detestable use of Diceplay.* (1552). In A. V. Judges ed., *The Elizabethan Underworld* (London, 1930).

[Warboys] *The most strange and admirable discouerie of three Witches of Warboys.* (1593).

Ward, S., *Woe to Drunkards.* (1622).

Watson, W., *A Decacordon of Ten Quodlibeticall Questions concerning Religion and State.* (1602).

Whetstone, G., *The Censure of a loyall Subiect.* (1587).
——. *A Mirour for the Magestrates of Cyties.* (1584).
White, F., *Londons Warning, by Ierusalem.* (1619).
Wilkins, G., *Three Miseries of Barbary: Plague. Famine. Ciuill Warre.* (n.d. probably 1606/7).
Willymat, W., *A Loyal Subiects Looking-Glasse.* (1604).
[Windes] *The Last terrible Tempestious windes and weather. Truely Relating many Lamentable Ship-wracks* . . . (1613).
[Wine] *Wine, Beere, Ale, and Tobacco. Contending for Superiority. A Dialogue.* 2nd edn. (1630).
Wither, G., *The Schollers Purgatory, Discouered In the Stationers Common-wealth* . . . (1624).
[Wonders] *The Wonders of This Windie Winter. By terrible stormes and tempests* . . . (1613).
[Year] *The Windie Yeare. Shewing Many Strange Accidents that happened, both on the Land and at Sea, by reason of the winde and weather.* (1612).
Young, R., *The Drunkard's Character, or, A True Drunkard. Together with Compleat armour against evill society. By R. Junius.* (1638).
Young, T., *Englands Bane: Or, The Description of Drunkennesse.* (1617).

B) COLLECTIONS AND SELECTIONS OF ELIZABETHAN PROSE

Arber, E., ed., *An English Garner. Ingatherings from our history and literature*, 8 vols. (London, 1877–96).
Breton, N., *The Works in Verse and Prose of Nicholas Breton*, ed. A. B. Grosart, 2 vols. (Edinburgh, 1875–79).
Collier, J. P. ed., *Illustrations of Early English Popular Literature*, 2 vols. (London, 1863, reissued, New York, 1966).
Craik, Sir H. ed., *English Prose. Selections with Critical Introductions by Various Writers* . . . 5 vols. (London and New York, 1893–96).
Day, J., *The Works of John Day*, ed. A. H. Bullen (London, 1881).
Dekker, T., *The Non-Dramatic Works of Thomas Dekker*, ed. A. B. Grosart, 5 vols. (London, 1885, reissued, New York, 1963).
——. *The Plague Pamphlets of Thomas Dekker*, ed. F. P. Wilson (Oxford, 1925).
——. *Thomas Dekker. Selected Writings*, ed. E. D. Pendry, The Stratford-upon-Avon Library (London, 1967).
Dunham, W. H. and Pargelis, S. M. eds., *Complaint and Reform in England, 1436–1714* (New York, 1938).
Greene, R., *The Life and Complete Works in Prose and Verse of Robert Greene*, ed. A. B. Grosart, The Huth Library, 15 vols. (London, 1881–86).
Grosart, A. B. ed., *Occasional Issues of Unique or Very Rare Books*, 17 vols. (London, 1881).

[The Harleian Miscellany] *The Harleian Miscellany: A Collection of Scarce, Curious, and Entertaining Pamphlets and Tracts*, ed. W. Oldys, 8 vols. (London, 1744–46); ed. W. Oldys and T. Park, 10 vols. (London, 1808–13).

Harvey, G., *The Works of Gabriel Harvey*, collected and edited by A. B. Grosart, The Huth Library, 3 vols. (London, 1884–85).

Hazlitt, W. C. ed., *The English Drama and Stage under the Tudor and Stuart Princes, 1543–1664* (London, 1869).

Hibbard, G. R. ed., *Three Elizabethan Pamphlets*, (includes Greene, *The Third and Last Part of Conny-catching*, Nashe, *Pierce Penilesse*, and Dekker, *The Wonderfull Yeare*) (London, 1957).

Judges, A. V. ed., *The Elizabethan Underworld. A Collection of Tudor and Early Stuart Tracts and Ballads* (London, 1930).

Lodge, T., *The Complete Works of Thomas Lodge*, ed. E. W. Gosse, 4 vols. (London, 1883, reissued New York, 1963).

Middleton, T., *The Works of Thomas Middleton*, ed. A. H. Bullen, 8 vols. (London, 1885–86).

Muir, K. ed., *Elizabethan and Jacobean Prose 1550–1620*. The Pelican Book of English Prose, I (Harmondsworth, 1956).

Nashe, T., *The works of Thomas Nashe*, ed. R. B. McKerrow, reprinted with corrections by F. P. Wilson, 5 vols. (Oxford, 1958).

Roberts, M. ed., *Elizabethan Prose* (London, 1933).

Rosen, B., ed., *Witchcraft*, The Stratford-upon-Avon Library (London, 1969).

Rowlands, S., *The Complete Works of Samuel Rowlands, 1598–1628*, ed. S. J. H. Heritage and E. W. Gosse, 3 vols., The Hunterian Club (Glasgow, 1872–86).

Salgado, G. ed., *Cony-Catchers and Bawdy Baskets. An Anthology of Elizabethan Low Life* (Harmondsworth, 1972).

Smith, G. G. ed., *Elizabethan Critical Essays*, 2 vols. (London, 1904).

Taylor, J., the Water-Poet, *All the Workes of Iohn Taylor the Water-Poet*, London, 1630. Publ. in facsimile, Scolar Press (Menston and London 1973).

Tourneur, C., *The Works of Cyril Tourneur*. ed. A. Nicoll, Fanfrolico Press (London, 1930).

Wither, G., *Miscellaneous Works of George Wither*, printed for the Spenser Society, 6 vols. (London, 1872).

C) SELECTED SECONDARY SOURCES

Adamson, J. W., 'The Extent of Literacy in England in the Fifteenth and Sixteenth Centuries: Notes and Conjectures'. *The Library*, Fourth Series, X (1929–30), 163–93.

Arber, E. ed., *A Transcript of the Registers of the Company of Stationers of London 1554–1640*, 5 vols. (London, 1875–94).

Armstrong, W. A., 'Shakespeare and the Acting of Edward Alleyn'. *Shakespeare Survey*, 7 (1954), 82–89.

Austin, W. A., *A Computer-Aided Technique for Stylistic Discrimination: the Authorship of Greenes Groatsworth of Witte* (Washington, 1969).

———. 'The Technique of the Chettle-Greene Forgery: Supplementary Material on the Authorship of the *Groatsworth of Witte*'. *Shakespeare News-Letter*, 20 (December, 1970).

Aydelotte, F. R., *Elizabethan Rogues and Vagabonds*, Oxford Historical and Literary Studies, I (Oxford, 1913).

Baumgartner, P. R., 'From Medieval fool to Renaissance rogue: *Cocke Lorelles Bote* and the Literary Tradition'. *Annuale Medievale*, 4 (1963), 57–91.

Bennett, H. S., *English Books and Readers 1475–1557* (Cambridge, 1952).

———. *English Books and Readers 1558–1603* (Cambridge, 1965).

———. *English Books and Readers 1603–1640* (Cambridge, 1970).

Black, M. W. *Richard Brathwait: An Account of His Life and Works* (Philadelphia, 1928).

Bloomfield, M. W., *Piers Plowman as a Fourteenth-Century Apocalypse*, Rutgers University Press (New Brunswick, 1962).

Blythe, D. E., 'Lear's Soiled Horse', *Shakespeare Quarterly*, XXXI (1980), 87–88.

Bosanquet, E. F., 'English Seventeenth-Century Almanacs', *The Library*, Fourth Series, X (1929–30), 361–97.

Boyce, B., 'News from Hell: Satiric communications with the Nether World in English Writing of the Seventeenth and Eighteenth Centuries', *PMLA*, LVIII, (1948), 402–37.

———. *The Theophrastan Character in England to 1642* (Cambridge, Mass., 1947).

Bridenbaugh, C., *Vexed and Troubled Englishmen 1590–1642* (Oxford, 1968).

Brooks, J. E., *The Mighty Leaf: Tobacco through the Centuries* (London, 1953).

Byrne, M. St Clare, *Elizabethan Life in Town and Country* (London, 1925, revised edn. 1961).

Camden, C., *The Elizabethan Woman. A Panorama of English Womanhood* (London, 1952).

Capp, B., *Astrology and the Popular Press: English Almanacs 1500–1800* (London, 1979).

Chambers, E. K., *The Elizabethan Stage*, 4 vols. (Oxford, 1923).

Chandler, F. W., *The Literature of Roguery*. 2 vols. (London, Boston and New York, 1907).

Chaytor, H. J., *From Script to Print. An Introduction to Medieval Literature* (Cambridge, 1945).

Clark, A. M., *Thomas Heywood, Playwright and Miscellanist* (Oxford, 1931).

Clark, P., 'The Ownership of Books in England, 1560–1640: The Example of Some Kentish Townsfolk' in *Schooling and Society: Studies in the History of Education*, ed. L. Stone (Baltimore and London, 1976), 95–111.

Clarkson, L., *Death, Disease and Famine in Pre-Industrial England* (Dublin, 1975).

Coates, W. H., 'An Analysis of Major Conflicts in Seventeenth-Century England', in *Conflict in Stuart England: Essays in honour of Wallace Notestein*, ed. W. A. Aiken and B. D. Henning (London, 1960), 17–39.

Collier, J., *An Ecclesiastical History of Great Britain*, 9 vols. (London, 1832).

Collins, D. C., *A hand-list of news pamphlets, 1590–1610* (Walthamstowe, 1943).

Conley, C. H., *The First English Translators of the Classics* (New Haven, 1927).

Cranfill, T. M. and Bruce, D. H., *Barnaby Rich. A short biography* (Austin, Texas, and Edinburgh, 1953).

Cressy, D., *Literacy and the Social Order* (Cambridge, 1980).

Croll, M. W., *Style, rhetoric and rhythm. Essays by M. W. Croll*, ed. J. M. Patrick and R. O. Evans, with J. M. Wallace and R. J. Schoeck (Princeton, 1966).

Davenport, A., 'An Elizabethan Controversy: Harvey and Nashe', *NQ*, CLXXXII (1942), 116–19.

Davis, N. Z., *Society and Culture in Early Modern France* (London, 1975).

Dobb, C., 'Life and Conditions in London Prisons 1553–1643', unpublished diss., B.Litt., Oxford University (1952).

Eisenstein, E., *The Printing Press as an Agent of Change*, 2 vols. (Cambridge, 1979).

Ennis, L., 'Anthony Nixon: Jacobean Plagiarist and Hack'. *HLQ*, IV (1939–40), 378–400.

Febvre, L., *Le Problème de l'Incroyance au 16e Siecle: La Religion de Rabelais*. Evolution de l'Humanité LIII (Paris, 1947).

Feyerham, W. R., 'The Status of the Schoolmaster and the Continuity of Education in Elizabethan East Anglia', *History of Education*, 5 (1976), 103–15.

Fisher, F. J., 'The Development of London as a Centre of Conspicuous Consumption in the Sixteenth and Seventeenth Centuries', *Transactions of the Royal Historical Society*, Fourth Series, XXX (1948), 37–50.

Friedenreich, K., 'Nashe's *Strange Newes* and the Case for Professional Writers', *SP*, 71 (1974), 451–72.

Gordon, I. A., *The Movement of English Prose* (London, 1966).

Greenough, C. N., 'Characters of Nations', *Proceedings of the Massachusetts Historical Society*, LXV (1940), 224–45.

Handover, P. M., *Printing in London from 1476 to Modern Times* (London, 1960).

Harlow, C. G., 'Thomas Nashe, Robert Cotton the Antiquary, and *The Terrors of the Night*', *RES*, New Series, XII (1961), 7–23.

———. 'Nashe's Visit to the Isle of Wight and his Publications of 1592–4', *RES*, New Series, XIV (1963), 225–42.

———. 'A Source for Nashe's *Terrors of the Night* and the Authorship of *i Henry VI*', *Studies in English Literature*, V (1965), 31–47, 269–81.

Harner, J. L., *English Renaissance Prose Fiction 1500–1660, an annotated bibliography of criticism* (London and Boston, 1978).

Harris, B., 'Dissent and Satire', *Shakespeare Survey*, XVII (1964), 120–37.

Harrison, G. B., *The Elizabethan Journals*, 2 vols. new edn. (New York, 1955).

Harrison, W., *A Description of England*, ed. F. J. Furnivall, 2 vols. (London, 1877–81).

Hazlitt, W. C., *Handbook to the Popular, Poetical, and Dramatic Literature of Great Britain* (London, 1867).

Heinemann, M., *Puritanism and Theatre. Thomas Middleton and Opposition Drama under the Early Stuarts* (Cambridge, 1980).

Hexter, J. H., 'The Myth of the Middle Class in Tudor England', *Reappraisals in History*, 2nd edn., University of Chicago Press (1961), 71–116.

Hibbard, G., *Thomas Nashe. A Critical Introduction* (London, 1961).

Hinton, E. M., *Ireland through Tudor Eyes*, University of Pennsylvania Press (Philadelphia, 1935).

Hoppe, H. R., 'John Wolfe, Printer and Publisher, 1579–1601', *The Library*, Fourth Series, XIV (1933–4), 241–88.

Howell, W. S., *Logic and Rhetoric in England, 1500–1700*, Princeton University Press (Princeton, 1956).

Hudson, H. G., *Social Regulations in England under James I and Charles I: Drink and Tobacco* (Chicago, 1933).

Hunt, M. L., 'Geffray Mynshul and Thomas Dekker', *JEGP*, XV (1912), 231–43.

———. *Thomas Dekker, A Study* (New York, 1900).

Hunter, G. K., 'Elizabethans and Foreigners', *Shakespeare Survey*, 17 (1964), 37–52.

Hutton, C., 'Thomas Dekker's Indebtedness to Thomas Nash', unpublished diss., M.A., University of California (1902).

Jenkins, H., 'On the authenticity of Greene's *Groatsworth of Wit* and *The Repentance of Robert Greene*', *RES*, XI (1935), 28–41.

Johnson, F. R., 'Notes on English Retail Book-prices, 1550–1640', *The Library*, Fifth Series, V (1950), 83–112.

———. 'The Editions of Robert Greene's Three Parts of Conny-catching. A Bibliographical Analysis', *The Library*, Fifth Series, IX (1954), 17–24.

Jones-Davies, M. T., *Un Peintre de la vie Londonienne, Thomas Dekker, circa 1572–1632*, 2 vols. (Paris, 1958).

Jordan, W. K., *The Charities of Rural England. The Aspirations and Achievements of the Rural Society.* (London, 1961).

———. *Philanthropy in England, 1480–1660. A Study of the Changing Pattern of English Social Aspirations.* (London, 1959).

Jusserand, J. J., *The English Novel in the time of Shakespeare*, transl. E. Lee. (London, 1890, revised edn., 1908).

———. *English Wayfaring Life in the Middle Ages* (London, 1889).

Klotz, E. L., 'A Subject Analysis of English Imprints for Every Tenth Year from 1480 to 1640', *HLQ*, I (1937–8), 417–19.

Knappen, M. M., *Tudor Puritanism* (Chicago, 1939).

Knights, L. C., 'Elizabethan Prose', *Scrutiny*, II (1933), 427–38.

Kocher, P., *Science and Religion in Elizabethan England* (San Marino, California, 1953, reprinted, 1969).

Latham, A. M. C., 'Satire on Literary Themes and Modes in Nashe's Unfortunate Traveller', *English Studies* (1948), 85–100.

Lechner, J. M., *Renaissance Concepts of the Commonplaces* (New York, 1962).

Leishman, J. B. ed., *The Three Parnassus Plays* (London, 1949).

Lewis, C. S., *The Allegory of Love* (London, 1936).

———. *English Literature in the Sixteenth Century Excluding Drama*, OHEL, III (Oxford, 1954).

Lievsay, J. L., 'Newgate Penitents: Further Aspects of Elizabethan Pamphlet Sensationalism', *HLQ*, VII (1943), 47–69.

Lowenthal, L., *Literature, Popular Culture and Society* (Boston, 1957).

Mackerness, E. D., '*Christs Teares* and the Literature of Warning', *English Studies*, XXXIII (1952), 251–54.

Maclure, M., *The Paul's Cross Sermons 1534–1642*, University of Toronto Press (Toronto, 1958).

Marshburn, J. H., *Murder and Witchcraft in England, 1550–1640*, University of Oklahoma Press (1971).

Maxwell, B., *Studies in the Shakespeare Apocrypha* (New York, 1956).

McDonald, E. D., 'An Example of Plagiarism among Elizabethan Pamphleteers: Samuel Rowlands' *Greenes Ghost haunting Conny-Catchers* (1602)', *Indiana University Studies*, I (1913), 145–70.

McKerrow, R. B., *An Introduction to Bibliography* (Oxford, 1927).

McLuhan, H. M., *The Gutenberg Galaxy. The Making of Typographic Man* (Toronto, 1962).

McPeek, J. A. S., *The Black Book of Knaves and Unthrifts* (University of Connecticut, 1969).

Miller, E. H., 'Deletions in Robert Greene's *A Quip for an Upstart Courtier* 1592', *HLQ*, XIV (1951–2), 277–82.

———. 'The Editions of Robert Greene's *A Quip for an Upstart Courtier* (1592)', *SB*, VI (1954), 107–16.

———. *The Professional Writer in Elizabethan England, a Study of Nondramatic Literature* (Cambridge, Mass., 1959).

———. 'The Relationship of Robert Greene and Thomas Nashe (1588–1592)', *PQ*, XXXIII (1954), 353–67.

———. 'The Sources of Robert Greene's *A Quip for an Upstart Courtier* (1592)', *NQ*, CLXXXXIII (1953), 148–57, 187–91.

Mish, C., 'Best Sellers in Seventeenth-Century Fiction', *PBSA*, XLVII (1953), 356–73.

'Black Letter as a Social Discriminant in the Seventeenth-Century', *PMLA*, LXVIII (1953) 627–30.

Mohl, R., *The Three Estates in Medieval and Renaissance Literature* (New York, 1933).

Nelson, B. N., *The Idea of Usury* (Princeton, 1949).

O'Connor, J. J., 'On the Authorship of the Ratsey Pamphlets', *Philological Quarterly*, XXX (1951), 381–86.

Ong, W. J., *In the Human Grain* (London and New York, 1967).

Owst, G. R., *Literature and Pulpit in Medieval England* (Cambridge, 1933).

———. *Preaching in Medieval England* (Cambridge, 1926).

Paradise, N. B., *Thomas Lodge, The History of an Elizabethan* (New Haven and London, 1931).

Parker, D., 'Robert Greene and *The Defence of Cony-Catching*', *NQ*, CCXIX (1974), 87–89.

Parker, R. B., 'Alterations in the first edition of Robert Greene's *A Quip for an Upstart Courtier (1592)*', *HLQ*, XXIII (1959–60), 181–86.

———. 'A Critical Edition of Robert Greene's *A Quip for an Upstart Courtier*' (1592), unpublished diss., Shakespeare Institute, University of Birmingham (1959).

Pearl, V., *London and the outbreak of the Puritan Revolution: City Government and National Politics, 1625–43* (London, 1961, reprinted with corrections, 1964).

———. 'Puritans and Poor Relief: The London Workhouse, 1649–1660', in *Puritans and Revolutionaries: Essays in seventeenth-century History presented to Christopher Hill*, ed. D. Pennington and K. Thomas (Oxford, 1978).

Pearson, E. L. *Elizabethans at Home*, University of Stanford Press (1957).

Pendry, E., *Elizabethan Prisons and Prison Scenes*, 2 vols., Salzburg Studies in English Literature, Elizabethan and Renaissance Studies, ed. J. Hogg. (Salzburg, 1974).

Perkins, D., 'Issues and Motivation in the Nashe-Harvey Quarrel', *PQ*, XXXIX (1960), 224–33.

Peter, J. D., *Complaint and Satire in Early English Literature* (Oxford, 1956).

Pollard, A. W., *Shakespeare's Fight with the Pirates and the Problems of the Transmission of his Text* (Cambridge, 1920, 1967).

Pompen, Fr. A., *The English Versions of The Ship of Fools. A Contribution to the History of the Early French Renaissance in England* (London, 1925).

Price, G. R., *Thomas Dekker* (New York, 1969).

Pruvost, R., *Robert Greene et ses Romans (1558–1592)* (Paris, 1938).

Quinn, D. B., *The Elizabethans and the Irish*, Cornell University Press (1966).

Randolph, G. R., 'An Analysis of Form and Style in the Prose Works of Thomas Nashe', unpublished diss., Ph.D., Florida State University (1931).

Rickert, C. H., *The Case of John Darrell*, University of Florida Monographs, Humanities, no. 9 (Gainesville, 1962).

Routh, H. V., 'The Advent of Modern Thought in Popular Literature', *CHEL* VII (1911), 366–97.

———. 'London and the Development of Popular Literature', *CHEL* IV (1907), 316–63.

Rye, W. B. ed., *England as Seen by Foreigners* (London, 1865).

Saunders, J. W., 'The Façade of Morality', *That Soueraine Light. Essays in Honor of Edmund Spenser 1552–1952*, ed. W. R. Mueller and D. C. Allen (Baltimore, 1952), 1–34.
———. *The Profession of English Letters* (London and Toronto, 1964).
———. 'The Stigma of Print. A Note on the Social Bases of Tudor Poetry, *Essays in Criticism*, I (1951), 139–64.
Schofield, R. S., 'The Measurement of Literacy in Pre-Industrial England', *Literacy in Traditional Societies*, ed. J. Goody (Cambridge, 1968), 311–25.
Shaaber, M. A., *Some Forerunners of the Newspaper in England 1476–1622* (Philadelphia, 1929).
[Shakespeare's England] *An Account of the Life and Manners of Shakespeare's England*, 2 vols. (Oxford, 1917).
Shaw, P. 'The Position of Thomas Dekker in Jacobean Prison Literature', *PMLA*, LXII (1947), 366–91.
Sheavyn, P. A. B., *The Literary Profession in the Elizabethan Age*, revised by J. W. Saunders, second edn. (Manchester, 1967).
Smith, H., *Elizabethan Poetry: A Study in Conventions, Meaning, and Expression*, University of Michigan Press (1952).
Stauffer, D. A., *English Biography before 1700* (Cambridge, Mass., 1930).
Statham, E. P., *A Jacobean Letter-Writer: The Life and Times of John Chamberlain* (London, 1920).
Staton, W. F., 'The Characters of Style in Elizabethan Prose', *JEGP*, LVII (1958), 197–207.
Stone, L., *The Causes of the English Revolution 1529–1642* (London, 1972).
———. *The Crisis of the Aristocracy 1558–1641* (Oxford, 1965).
———. 'The Educational Revolution in England', *Past and Present*, 28 (1964), 41–80.
Sutherland, J. R., 'Apes and Peacocks', *On English Prose*, University of Toronto Press (Toronto, 1957), 31–56.
Tawney, R. H., *Religion and the Rise of Capitalism* (London, 1926).
Tawney, R. H. and Power, E., eds., *Tudor Economic Documents*, 3 vols. (London, 1924).
Thompson, E. S. N., *The Controversy between the Puritans and the Stage*, Yale Studies in English (New York, 1903).
Tilley, M. P., *A Dictionary of the Proverbs in England in the Sixteenth and Seventeenth Centuries* (Ann Arbor, Michigan, 1950).
Turner, C., (Wright), *Anthony Mundy, Elizabethan Man of Letters* (Berkeley, 1928).
Waage, F. O., 'Thomas Dekker's Career as a Pamphleteer, 1603–1609: Preliminary Studies of Five Major Works and their Background', unpublished diss., Princeton University (1971).
Walker, A., 'The Reading of an Elizabethan', *RES*, VII (1932), 264–81.
Watt, I., 'Elizabethan Light Reading', *The Pelican Guide to English Literature*, ed. B. Ford (Harmondsworth, 1955), II, 119–30.

White H. C., *Social Criticism in Popular Religious Literature of the Sixteenth Century* (New York, 1944).

White, H. O., *Plagiarism and Imitation during the English Renaissance* (Cambridge, Mass., 1935).

Whitworth, L., 'The Development, Scope, and Significance of Popular Satire in the Elizabethan Period', unpublished diss., Ph.D., University of London (1960).

Williamson, G., *The Senecan Amble. A Study in Prose Form from Bacon to Collier* (London, 1951).

Wilson, F. P., 'A Biography of Thomas Dekker, with a detailed Criticism of some of the Prose Pamphlets, and a Bibliography of his Complete Works', unpublished diss., M.A., Oxford University (1913).

———. 'The English Jest Books of the Sixteenth and Early Seventeenth Centuries', *HLQ*, II (1939), 121–58.

———. *The Plague in Shakespeare's London* (1927; revised edn., Oxford, 1963).

———. *Seventeenth Century Prose* (Cambridge, 1960).

———. 'Some English Mock-Prognostications', *The Library*, Fourth Series, XIX (1938), 6–43.

Wright, C. T., 'Some Conventions regarding the Usurer in Elizabethan Literature', *Studies in Philology*, XXXI (1934), 176–97.

———. 'The Usurer's Sin in Elizabethan Literature', *Studies in Philology*, XXXV (1938), 178–94.

Wright, L. G., *Middle-Class Culture in Elizabethan England* (Chapel Hill, 1935).

Index

Adams, Thomas: *Englands Sicknes, Comparatively Conferred with Israels*, 122
Adamson, J., 20, 281
Aesop: *Fables*, 226
Alarme to Awake Church-Sleepers, An, 160–61, 230, 290
All to Westminster, 149
Alleyn, Edward, 174, 287
Almanacs, 25, 270–73
Anthoine, Nicholas, 89, 284
Anton, Robert: *Moriomachia*, 124
Aretino, Pietro, 241, 265
Aristotle, 21, 37, 228, 231, 243, 253, 289
Armin, Robert, 28
Armstrong, W., 287
Arthington, Henry: *Provision for the Poore, now in Penurie*, 210; *The Seduction of Arthington, by Hackett especiallie, with some tokens of his vnfained repentance and Submission*, 88, 94
Ascham, Roger: *The Scholemaster*, 288
A True Relation of the most Inhumane and Bloody Murther, of Master Iames Minister, 102, 103, 235, 263
Atchelow, Thomas, 153
Austin, W. B., 286
Averell, William, 179, 221, 231, 279; *A Dyall for dainty Darlings*, 130, 136, 227, 231, 236, 248; *A meruailous combat of contrarieties*, 122, 123–24, 125, 142–43, 189, 219, 259
Awdeley, John: *The Fraternitye of Vacabondes*, 41, 42–43, 59, 63, 277
Aydelotte, F. R., 42, 45, 46, 282, 283

Bacon, Sir Frances, 235, 240; on biography as a form of history, 92; on printing, 244; on rhetoric, 224, 253
Ballads and ballad singers, 31, 154, 173, 175
Balmford, Rev. James: *A Short Dialogue Concerning the Plagues Infection*, 257, 285
Bancroft, Richard, Bishop of London, 31

Barclay, Alexander: *The Shyp of folys*, 40–41, 42
Barclay, William: *Nepenthes, Or The Vertues of Tabacco*, 196, 197
Batchelars Banquet, The, 178
Batman uppon Bartholome, 145
Beard, Thomas: *The Theatre of Gods Judgements*, 91, 97, 98
Beaumont, Francis, and Fletcher, John, 282
Bennett, H. S., 281, 284
Berkshire: *Looke up and see Wonders*, 105–6
Bernard, Richard: *The Isle of Man*, 125, 129–30, 275, 276;
Bible, The, 34, 148, 158, 191, 288
Blaxton, John: *The English Vsurer*, 161, 170, 287, 289
Bloody Downfall of Adultery, Murder, Ambition, The, 103
Bloomfield, M. W., 286
Bloudy booke, The, 106, 248, 250
Bosanquet, E. F., 282
Bowes, Sir Jerome: *A True report of the horrible Murther, which was committed in the house of Sir Ierome Bowes*, 101, 263
Bownd, Nicholas: *The Doctrine of the Sabbath*, 285
Boyce, B., 83, 145, 147, 157, 275, 284, 286, 291
Bradburn, Theophilus, 285
Bradwell, Stephen: *A Watch-man For the Pest*, 285
Braithwait, Richard, 10, 279, 291; *Ar't asleepe Husband?*, 32, 183, 195, 229, 275, 276; on poets, 175; *The Smoaking Age*, 124, 137, 196; *The Whimzies*, 81
Brant, Sebastian: *Narrenschiff*, 40
Breton, Nicholas, 10; *Choice, Chance, and Change*, 219–20; *The Court and the Countrey*, 229, 259; *A Dialogue full of pithe and pleasure*, 144–45, 258–59
Brettergh, Katherine: her pious death

312

Index 313

commemorated in W. Harrison, *Deaths Advantage Little Regarded*, 89
Brewer, Thomas: *A Dialogue betwixt a Cittizen, and a poore Countrey-man*, 177, 247; *Lord have Mercy upon Vs*, 119; *The Weeping Lady*, 261
Bridenbaugh, C., 288
Brome, Richard, 282
Brooks, J. E., 288
Bullein, William: *A Dialogue against the Feuer Pestilence*, 260, 286
Bunyan, John, 129
Burbage, Richard, 174
Burcot, Dr., 287
Burgh, John, Lord, 284, 289; *The most horrible and tragicall murther of . . . John Lord Bourgh*, 104, 105, 231–32
Burghley, Lord William Cecil, 46
Burton, Henry: *A Divine Tragedie Lately Acted*, 96, 97–98, 214, 285
Bush, M.: *A true Relation of the Travels of M. Bush*, 90
Byrne, M. St. Clare, 288

Calverley, Walter, 107–8
Camden, C., 287
Canterburie, The Cobler of, 21, 267–68
Capp, B., 291
Carey, Sir George, patron of Nashe, 27–28
Carthenay, Jean de: *The Voyage of the Wandering Knight*, 124, 129
Cartwright, Francis: *The Life, Confession, and Heartie Repentance of Francis Cartwright, Gentleman*, 93, 94
Censorship, 31, 87
Chamberlain, John, 287
Chambers, E. K., 287
Characters and Character books, 81–85, 145–47, 245, 274–79
Charles I, of England, 288: *Declaration for Sports and Pastimes*, 98
Chaucer, Geoffrey, 149, 153, 167; *The Canterbury Tales*, 200, 267
Cheke, Sir John: *The hurt of sedicion*, 283
Chelmsford, witches of: *The Apprehension and Confession of three notorious Witches, Arreigned and by Justice condemned and executed at Chelmesforde*, 109
Chettle, Henry, 17, 281, 286; Kind-Hart as a satiric persona, 264–65; *Kind-Harts Dreame*, 67, 148, 153, 168, 172, 174–75, 260; relations with Greene, 32, 153–54
Churchyard, Thomas, 29; *The Wonders of the Ayre*, 88, 95
Cicero, 289; and Ciceronian prose style,
37, 231–32, 254, 274, 278, 279; on rhetoric, 225
Clark, A. M., 285
Clarkson, L., 287
Clothes, extravagance of, 191–93, 212–14
Coates, W. H., 288
Cocke Lorelles Bote, 40
Cock Watt, satiric persona, 122, 216, 217, 264
Collier, J., 285
Collier, J. P., 285
Conley, C. H., 281
Conny-Catcher, Cuthbert, 25, 64; *The Defence of Conny-Catching*, 47, 50, 53, 54, 283
Cooper, Thomas: *The Cry and Reuenge of Blood*, 104–5, 235
Copland, Robert: *The Hye Way to the Spyttel Hous*, 40, 41
Cosmetics, 121, 179, 191–92, 212–13
Cottesford, Samuel: *A Treatise Against Traitors*, 205
Courtney, Charles: *The Life, Apprehension, Arraignement, and Execution of Charles Courtney*, 92–93, 94, 169, 287
Croll, M. W., 232, 289
Crop-Eare Curried, Or, Tom Nash His Ghost, 149, 150, 240
Croshawe, Richard, *Visions, Or, Hels Kingdome* (translation of Quevedo, *Suenõs y Discursos*) 173, 191, 291

Dancing, 159, 161, 193–94
Dando, John and Runt, Harrie, 21
Daniel, Samuel, 19, 30
Dante, Alighieri, 156
Danter, John, printer, 26, 28
Darrell, John, exorcist, 100, 285; *A Detection of that Sinnful, Shamful, Lying, and Ridiculous Discours of Samuel Harshoet*, 100; *The Triall of Maist. Dorrell, Or, A Collection of Defences* (anon.), 109; *A True Narration of the strange and grevous Vexation by the Devil, of 7 persons in Lancashire, and William Somers of Nottingham*, 285
Davies, John: *Epigrams*, 163
Davis, N. Z., 281
Daw, Jack: *Vox Graculi, Or Jack Daws Prognostication*, 270, 272, 273
Day, John: *Peregrinatio Scholastica*, 124, 141, 200, 202–3, 286, 288
Deacon, John: *Nobody is my Name*, 257, 258; *Tobacco Tortuered*, 131–32, 171, 186, 195–96, 214, 233, 258, 261
Death of Usury, The, 171

Decameron (Boccaccio), 267, 288
Dedications, 26–27, 30–31
Dekker, Thomas, 10, 12, 17, 18, 33, 38, 68, 69, 154, 173, 174, 175, 179, 206, 275, 279, 281, 282, 284, 285; *The Belman of London*, 20, 25, 58–60, 63, 66, 68, 74, 216–17, 264, 265, 269, 283; *The Blacke Rod*, 111, 120, 285; *The Dead Tearme*, 137, 188, 204, 218, 259, 269, 287; *Dekker his Dream*, 35, 77, 149, 156, 158; *The Double PP*, 276; *English Villanies*, 61, 76, 77, 78, 79, 80; *Foure Birds of Noahs Arke*, 77; *The Guls Horne-booke*, 136, 242, 265, 269; *Iests to make you merie* (with George Wilkins), 26, 71, 76, 77, 78, 80, 150–51, 174, 265, 276, 283; *If It Be Not Good*, 77; *A Knights Coniuring*, 150, 152, 215, 242, 282; *Lanthorne and Candle-light*, 17, 25, 29, 61–64, 66, 76, 77, 153, 156, 223, 233–34, 242, 256–57, 264, 276, 278, 283, 287; *London Looke Backe*, 111, 115, 285; *The Magnificent Entertainment*, 57; and Martin Markall, 23, 64–65, 283; *The Meeting of Gallants*, 111, 114, 259; and Nashe, 30, 112, 139, 152, 242–43, 290; *Newes from Grauesend*, 26, 30, 111; *Newes from Hell*, 30, 150, 151, 152–53, 155, 156, 158, 185, 195, 212, 240, 242, 262, 276–77, 286; *O per se O*, 61, 65–66, 276, 283; on pamphleteers, 17, 29, 30, 176–77; *Penny-Wise Pound Foolish*, 134–35, 183, 273, 274; *The Rauens Almanacke*, 270, 272, 273, 291; *A Rod for Run-awayes*, 32, 111, 114, 115, 205, 209; and rogue writing, 43, 57–64, 240; *The Seuen Deadly Sinnes*, 10, 30, 76, 78, 80, 138–39, 140, 174, 179, 187, 205, 276; *A Strange Horse-Race*, 77, 81, 123, 141, 155, 218–19, 257, 276, 282, 287; *Villanies Discouered*, 61, 71, 76, 79, 80, 81, 82, 83, 84, 235, 276, 284; *The Wonderfull yeare*, 22, 24, 25, 30, 111, 112–14, 167, 192, 213, 247, 250, 269, 273–74, 282; *Worke for Armorours*, 125–27, 170, 172, 276
Dell, Annis: *The Most Cruell and Bloody Murther*, 104
Deloney, Thomas, 11, 28, 68
Denison, John: *The Most Wonderfull and true storie, of a certaine Witch, named Alse Goodenge of Stapenhill*, 110, 285
Dialoges of Creatures Moralysed, The (source of Lodge's *Catharos Diogenes*), 146
Dialogue betwixt a Cittizen, and a poore Countrey-man, A. See Brewer, Thomas
Dickens, Charles: *Bleak House*, 166

Dickenson, John: *Greene in Conceipt*, 56, 149, 155, 289
Dobb, C., 283
Doctors and physicians, 155, 165, 167–68
Donne, John, 165: *Ignatius his Conclave*, 286
A Dreame: or Newes from Hell, 149
Dream visions, 29, 122, 148–50
Drunkenness, 121, 141, 145, 159–60, 198–202
Dugdale, Gilbert: *A True Discourse Of The Practises of Elizabeth Caldwell*, 99
Dunham, W. H., and Pargellis, S., 290

Earle, Sir John: *Micro-Cosmographie*, 81, 145, 231
Eisenstein, E., 281, 290
Elizabeth I, of England, 80, 88, 219, 229
Elwes, Sir Gervase: *The Lieutenant of the Tower, his Speech and Repentance, at the Time of his death*, 94
Englands Sicknes, Comparatively Conferred with Israels. See Adams, Thomas
Ennis, L., 282
Epps, William, 276–77
Erasmus, 265; *Apopthegms*, 226; *Colloquia*, 55, 226
Estates satire, 128, 137, 142–45, 211, 216, 245, 266, 275, 278–99
Euphuism, 36, 55, 130, 157, 231, 236–39, 243, 253, 273, 284

Faustus, Dr. John, 92; *The Historie of the damnable life, and deserued death of Doctor Iohn Faustus*, 94
Febvre, L., 290
Fennor, William: *The Compters Common-Wealth*, 20, 24, 68, 69–70, 71, 73–76, 82, 84, 165, 268, 284
Feyerham, W. R., 281
Fisher, F. J., 281
Fleetwood, William, 46
Foreigners, 125, 128, 186–89
Foulface, Philip: *Bacchus Bountie*, 241
Foulweather, Adam, 29; *A Wonderfull, strange and miraculous, Astrologicall Prognostication for this year of our Lord 1591*, 271, 273
Foxe, John: *Actes and Monuments*, 91, 97, 159

Gager, William, opponent of William Heale, 161
Gardiner, Edmund: *The Triall of Tabacco*, 197

Index

Gascoigne, George, 179
Gibson, Anthony: *A Womans Woorth*, 161, 228, 289
Golding, Arthur: *A discourse vpon the Earthquake that hapned throughe this Realme of England*, 89, 91, 101
Goodcole, Henry, chaplain to the prisoners at Newgate, 279; *Heavens Speedie Hue and Cry sent after Lust and Murther*, 100–1, 205, 250; *The wonderfull discouerie of Elizabeth Sawyer a Witch*, 88, 100, 110
Goodfellow, Robin, as a satiric persona, 151, 264
Gordon, I. A., 243, 290
Gosse, E., 12, 35
Gosson, Stephen, 17, 174; *The School of Abuse*, 176
Gower, John, 149
Great Frost, The, 228, 257
Greene, Robert, 12, 17, 18, 20, 26, 33, 60, 64, 153, 174, 176, 279, 283; *The Blacke Bookes Messenger*, 48, 49, 51, 55–56, 67, *Ciceronis Amor*, 256, *A Disputation*, 20, 47, 49, 50–51, 53, 54–55, 56, 249, 256, 259–60, 268; dissolute life of, 47–48, 132–34, 149, 177; *Greenes farewell to Folly*, 48, 50; *Greenes Groats-Worth of witte*, 38, 48, 94, 132, 133, 134, 286; *Greenes Mourning Garment*, 48, 56, 132, 134; *Greenes Never too late*, 48, 56, 132–33; *Greenes Vision*, 149; and Harvey, 32, 154, 289; and influence of his style on others, 240, 243; *Mamillia*, 132; *Menaphon*, 23, 229, 238, 253, 254; *Myrrour of Modestie*, 227; *A Notable Discouery of Coosnage*, 20, 48, 49, 51, 53, 251, 253, 277; *A Quip for an Upstart Courtier*, 25, 48, 49, 56, 125, 127–28, 166, 168, 172, 173, 175, 183–84, 187–88, 207, 282, 286, 287; *The Repentance of Robert Greene*, 38, 48, 93–94, ,132, 134, 237; and rogue writing, 40–41, 42, 43, 44, 46–56, 61, 74, 200, 223, 277; *The Second part of Conny-catching*, 48, 51–53, 68, 237, 253; *The Spanish Masquerado*, 229; style of, 55, 226–27, 231, 254, 273; *The Third and last Part of Conny-catching*, 48, 49, 50, 53, 248
Greenes Funeralls, 56, 289
Greenes Ghost Haunting Conie-catchers. See R., S.
Greenes Newes both from Heauen and Hell, 56, 150, 155, 190, 267, 289
Greenham, Richard, 285

Greenough, C. N., 287
Grosart, A. B., 10, 12, 35, 283, 289
Groundeworke of Conny-catching, The, 283
Gunpowder Plot, 138
Gurth, Alexander: *Most true and More Admirable news Expressing the Miraculous Preservation of a Young Maiden of the towne of Glabbich in the Duke dome of Gulīsche*, 99

Hackett, William, 88
Haec-Vir, 32, 179, 181, 182, 258
Hall, Joseph, 165; *Characters of Vertues and Vices*, 81, 145, 274, 278
Harlow, C. G., 282
Harman, Thomas, 59, 61, 63, 65, 66, 283; *A Caueat . . . for common Cursetors*, 41, 43–44; Characters in, 277; style of, 44–45, 254
Harris, B., 291
Harrison, G. B., 281
Harrison, William: *A Description of England*, 19–20, 22, 282
Harsnett, Samuel: *A Declaration of Egregious Popishe Impostures*, 100; *A Discovery of the fraudulent practises of Iohn Darrel Bachelor of Artes*, 100
Harvey, Gabriel, 23, 26, 260; feud with Nashe, 28, 31–32, 47, 154, 231, 238, 239; *Foure Letters*, 47, 56; *Pierce's Supererogation*, 238, 283
Harvey, Richard, 140; *Astrological Discourse*, 86, 290
Hawkins, Sir Richard: *Observations of Sir R. Hawkins*, 86
Hazlitt, W. C., 287, 289, 291
Heale, William: *An Apologie for Women*, 161–62, 229, 233, 287, 289
Health to the Gentlemanly Profession of Seruingmen, A (by I. M.), 122, 193
Heinemann, M., 282, 288
Henslowe, Philip, *Diary*, 57
Hentzner, P., 288
Herbert, George, 161
Herbert family, 30
Hexter, J. H., 281
Heywood, Thomas, 94, 285, 288; *A Curtaine Lecture*, 32; *The Hierarchy of the Blessed Angels*, 22; *Philocothonista*, 199; *The Phoenix of these late times: Or the life of Mr. Henry Welby Esq.*, 92, 94–95
Hibbard, G., 38, 221, 256, 265, 289, 291
Hic-Mulier, 32, 179, 180, 182
Hill, C., 289
Hinton, E. M., 288

Hooker, Richard: *Of Ecclesiastical Polity*, 34
Howard, Lady Frances, 87; and the Overbury case, 87, 103
Howell, W. S., 289
Hudson, H. G., 288
Hunt, M. L., 283, 284
Hunter, G. K., 287
Hutton, Luke, 32, 165, 283; *The Black Dog of Newgate*, 69, 72–73, 258

Iane Anger her Protection for Women, 177, 182, 229, 232, 265
Ireland, 188–89, 288

Jailors, 74–75, 80, 83, 165–66
James I, of England, 58, 69, 80, 179, 221, 230, 288; *A Counter-blaste to Tobacco*, 194, 195, 196
James, Reverend: *A True Relation of the most Inhumane and bloody Murther, of Master Iames Minister and Preacher of the Word of God at Rockland in Norfolke*, 102, 103, 235, 263
Jenkins, H., 286
Jestbooks, 266–68
Johnson, F. R., 282
Johnson, Richard, 29; *A Lanterne-light for Loyall Subiects*, 88, 96, 285; *Looke on Me London*, 170, 203; *The Pleasant Walkes of Moore-fields*, 204–5, 258
Jones-Davies, M. T., 283, 284
Jonson, Ben, 30, 32, 58, 147, 224; *The Alchemist*, 167, 283; *Epicene*, 289; *Volpone*, 50
Jordan, W. K., 281, 288
Judges, A. V., 41, 283
Jusserand, J., 281, 290
Juvenal, 243, 264

Kellwaye, Simon: *A Defensative against the Plague*, 239, 285
Kemp, Will: *Nine daies wonder*, 175
King, Humfrey, 29
Knappen, M. M., 282
Knights, L. C., 243, 252, 290
Kocher, P. H., 287
Kyd, Thomas, 17, 153; *The trueth of the most wicked & secret murthering of Iohn Brewen*, 108

Landlords, 125, 126, 171–72, 195
Last terrible Tempestious windes and weather, The, 90
Lawyers, 121, 165, 166–67, 170

Lechner, J. M., 226, 289
Lewis, C. S., 121, 189, 288
Lievsay, J. L., 283
Life and Death of Griffin Flood, The, 68, 266–67
Life and Death of Lewis Gaufredy, The, 102, 248
Life and Pranks of Long Meg of Westminster, The, 68, 266
Lillo, G.: *Fatal Curiosity*, 285
Literacy, extent of in Elizabethan times, 19–21
Lodge, Thomas, 12, 17, 24, 145, 241, 279, 289; *An Alarum against Vsurers*, 38, 130–31, 170, 206–7, 237–38, 261–62; *Catharos, Diogenes in his Singularitie*, 146, 258; *The Divel coniured*, 238, 299; *A Fig for Momus*, 273; *The Life and Death of William Longbeard*, 238, 266; *A Treatise of the Plague*, 21, 285; *Wits Miserie, and the Worlds Madnesse*, 137–38, 145, 169, 193, 214, 238, 241, 246, 248, 275, 288
London, 22, 33, 170, 221; beauty of, 203, 204; enmity with the countryside, 115, 116, 205–6; personified, 204, 218, 261; in plague time, 115–18, 205–6; population of, 31, 203, 288; taverns, 37, 200; wickedness of, 172, 201, 205
Londons Warning by Ierusalem. See White, Francis
Londons Warning by Laodiceas Lukewarmenesse. See Price, Sampson
Looke up and see Wonders. See Berkshire
Looking-glasse for Drunkards, A, 198–200, 202
Lowenthal, L., 281
Lowin, John: *Conclusions Vpon Dances*, 161, 193–94, 289
Lucian, of Samosata: *Dialogues of the Dead*, 148, 155, 157–58, 270
Lupton, Donald: *London and the Countrey Carbonadoes*, 81, 204, 232, 275, 277
Lupton, Thomas: *A Dreame of the Deuill and Dives*, 149, 158, 169, 171, 191, 258, 287
Lyly, John, 236, 279, 289

M., R.: *Micrologia*, 81
McDonald, E. D., 283
McKerrow, R. B., 254, 280, 282
McLuhan, H. M., 264, 265, 290, 291
McPeek, J. A. S., 283
Malynes, Gerard de: *Saint George for England*, 124, 169
Man in the Moone, The (by. W. M.), 146–47, 198, 277–78, 287

Index

Marbecke, Richard: *A Defence of Tabacco*, 196
Marlowe, Christopher, 32, 104, 153
Marprelate controversy, 18, 32, 241
Marriage, 139, 162, 177, 183
Mar-sixtus, Martine, 31
Marston, John, 165
Marten, Anthony: *An Exhortation*, 233–34
Maxwell, B., 285
Merchants, 165, 168, 170; and merchants' wives, 170–71, 178
Meres, Francis; *Palladis Tamia*, 57, 226, 290
Middleton, Thomas, 12, 17, 32, 279; *The Blacke Booke*, 135, 151–52, 153, 155, 169, 170, 195, 240, 252, 284; *Father Hubburds Tales*, 26, 32, 38, 135, 185, 195, 206, 239, 290; and Nashe, 241, plays of, 147, 212
Mihil Mumchance, 60, 283
Miller, E. H., 19, 281, 283, 286
Miracle, of Miracles, As fearefull as euer was seene or heard of in the memorie of Man, A; 96, 97
Miraculaus Newes From the Cittie of Holdt, 87
Mirror for Magistrates, 91, 95, 97
Mish, C., 282
More, Sir Thomas: *Utopia*, 260
Most Cruell and Bloody Murther, The, 104. See Dell, Annis
Muld Sacke, 32
'Munda, Constantia,' 32, 230, 265
Munday, Anthony, 17, 26, 29, 174, 285; *A view of Sundry Examples*, 88, 95, 96, 285; *A Watch-woord to Englande*, 190
Mynshul, Geoffrey: *Certaine Characters and Essays*, 69, 81, 82–85, 165, 274–75, 277–78, 284, 286

Nashe, Thomas, 12, 17, 18, 20, 24, 26, 27–28, 29, 33, 38, 47, 121, 145, 151–52, 153, 154, 187, 190–91, 279, 280, 282, 283, 287, 288, 289, 290, 291; *The anatomy of Abusrditie*, 20, 176, 190–91, 246, 254; attacks ballads, 20–31, 175; *Christs Teares over Ierusalme*, 9, 24, 27–28, 112, 119–20, 141, 157, 192, 213, 232–33, 247, 254, 260–61; defends theatre, 140, 174; on degeneracy, 172; on drunkards, 160, 198; feud with Harvey family, 28, 31–32, 47, 86, 140, 151, 231, 241, 265, 289; *Haue with You to Saffron Walden*, 24, 25, 28, 255, 260, 265, 268, 291; on lawyers, 166; on pamphleteers, 29, 30; *Pierce Penilesse*, 10, 28, 32, 57, 62, 139, 140–41, 145, 153, 155, 156–57, 171, 176–77; on poetry, 176; *Preface to Greene's Menaphon*, 23, 229, 238, 287; on poetry, 176; *Strange Newes*, 28, 70, 151, 238, 254, 265, 291; style of, 9, 139, 240–43, 249, 254–56, 270, 273; *The Terrors of the Night*, 20, 27–28, 167–68, 255–56, 265; *The Unfortunate Traveller*, 10, 11, 68; on women, 179
Nelson, B., 282, 287
Newstead, Christopher: *News from Perin in Cornwall*, 106; *An Apology for Women*, 229, 232
Newton, T.: *A Delectable Dialogue . . . Concerning Physik and Phisitions*, 286
Niccholes, Alexander: *A Discourse of Marriage and Wiving*, 38
Nicoll, A., 286
Nixon, Anthony, 29, 33; *The Blacke Yeare*, 270, 273; as plagiarist, 147, 273, 282; *The Scourge of Corruption*, 150; *A Straunge Foot-Post, with A Packet full of Strange Petitions*, 147
Nobility: enmity with citizens, 206–7
Norden, John, 34

Oatmeale, Oliver, 21, 29. 282
Ockland, Christopher: *The Fountaine and Welspring of all Variance*, 189
O'Connor, J. J., 283
Ong, Father W. J., 290
Overburian Characters, The, 20, 145, 165, 284; prison characters, 71, 77, 81, 82, 83, 84, 276, 283
Overbury, Sir Thomas: murder of, 87, 94, 103. See also *The Bloody Downfall of Adultery, Murder, Ambition*
Owles-Almanacke, The, 270, 271, 273, 286, 291
Owst, G. R., 37–38, 287, 288

Pamphlets: contemporary attitudes to, 26–27, 176–77; definition of, 18, 23–24, 38, 287; format and appearance of, 24–25, 244; readers of, 18, 20–22, 36, 86, 243; titles of, 90, 122
Paradise, N. B., 289
Parker, D., 283
Parker, R. B., 286
Parkes, William: *The Curtaine-Drawer Of the World*, 141–42, 143, 168, 208, 216, 217, 252, 262, 278
Parry, William: *True and plaine declaration*

of the horrible Treasons practised by William Parry the Traitor, against the Queenes Maiestie, 88–89, 284
Peacham, Henry, the Elder: *The Garden of Eloquence*, 225
Pearle, V., 282, 288, 289
Pearson, E. L., 18–19, 281
Peele, George, 153
Pendry, E. D., 10, 79, 81, 283, 284, 286
Penniles Parliament of Thread-bare Poets, The, 273
Peter, J. D., 164–65, 186, 286, 287, 290
Petowe, Henry: *The Countrie Ague*, 115, 118, 205, 206, 261
Piers Penniless, as a satiric persona, 62, 122, 135, 151–52, 154, 195, 240, 241, 260, 264, 265
Piers Plowman (Landland), 169
Plagiarism, 33, 60, 65, 84, 96, 147, 273, 285
Plague, 29; pamphlets dealing with, 32, 87, 110–20 passim, 205–6, 211
Platoes Cap, 270, 272, 273
Politeuphuia (by Nicholas Ling), 226
Pollard, A., 282
Potts, Thomas, *The Wonderfull discouerie of witches in the Countie of Lancashire*, 100
Powell, Thomas: *The Art of Thriving, Or, the Plaine pathway to Preferment (Tom of all Trades)*, 221–22, 258
Price, G. R., 10, 284
Price, Sampson: *Londons Warning by Laodiceas Luke-warmenesse*, 122
Prison, 68–85 passim, 165–66
Pruvost, R., 283
Prynne, William, 174; *The Vnlouelinesse, of Love-Lockes*, 193, 203, 289
Puritans, 163, 193, 221; attacks on, 190–91, impetus to education, 35; opposition to classical learning, 23

Quevedo, Francisco de: *Sueños y Discursos*, 291. See also Croshawe, Richard
Quinn, D. B., 288

R., S.: *The Art of Iugling*, 29, 33; *Greenes Ghost Haunting Conie-Catchers*, 29, 33, 56, 60, 74, 283, 289; *Martin Mark-All*, 23, 64–65, 66, 210, 216, 268, 283
Raleigh, Sir Walter: *A Declaration of the Demeanor*, 86–87
Ramus (Pierre de la Ramée), 21, 37, 231
Rankins, William, 174, 279; *The English Ape*, 187, 215; *A Mirrour of Monsters*, 124–25, 141, 174, 237

Ratsey, Gamaliel, highwayman, 67, 266, 283; *The Life and Death of Gamaliel Ratsey*, 66–68, 249; *Ratseis Ghost*, 66–68, 148–49, 166
Rawlidge, Richard, *A Monster Late Found Out And Discovered. Or The scourging of Tiplers*, 200–2, 204, 211
Recantation of Thomas Clarke, The, 227–28
Returne of the Knight of the Poste from Hell, The (by E. S.), 151, 152, 155, 215; and Nashe, 151, 240–42; relation to Dekker, *Newes from Hell*, 286
Reynolds, John: *The Triumphs of Gods Revenge Against the Crying, And Execrable Sinne of Murther*, 91, 97, 98
Rhetoric, 158–59, 224–40 passim
Rhodes, N., 12
Rich, Barnaby, 10, 12, 17, 27, 28, 29, 145, 175, 179, 208–9, 275, 279, 291; *Allarme to England*, 188, 202; *The Excellency of good women*, 178; *Faultes, faults*, 141, 146, 176, 245–46, 275, 290; *The Fruites of Long Experience*, 162, 188–89, 258; *The Honestie of This Age*, 143–44, 193; *The Irish Hubbut*, 166, 188, 190; *My Ladies Looking Glasse*, 144, 146, 187, 275; *A New Description of Ireland*, 188; *Opinion Diefield*, 268; on pamphleteers, 177; *Riche his farewell to militarie profession*, 287; *Roome for a Gentleman*, 144, 166, 184, 189; style of, 245–46
Rickert, C. H., 285
Roman Catholics, 143, 150, 187, 189–90
Rowlands, Samuel, 17, 223, 283. See also R., S.
Rowley, William, 279; *A Search for Money*, 124, 135, 171, 173, 241, 250, 286, 287
Rudierde, Edmund: *The Thunderbolt of Gods Wrath*, 96
Run-awyaes Answer, The (by B. V.), 32, 115, 116, 118, 206

S., E.: *The Discouerie of the Knightes of the Poste*, 56–57, 73, 258
Sabbatarian controversy, 98, 285
Saintsbury, George, 10, 38, 282
Saltonstall, Wye: *A Description of Time*, 270; *Picturae Loquentes*, 81
Sanford, Rev. John, *Gods Arrowe of the Pestilence*, 118
Saunders, J., 281, 291
Schlauch, M., 290, 291
Schofield, R., 281
Scott, Thomas, 150; *Robert Earle of Essex his Ghost*, 153; *Sir Walter Rawleighs Ghost, Or Englands Forewarner*, 153

Scott, William: *An Essay of Drapery*, 221, 222–23
Second and Third Blast of Retrait from Plaies and Theaters, A, 174
Senecan prose, 278
Sermons, 37, 164–65, 172, 201, 230
Seven deadly sins, 122, 137, 139, 141–42, 173, 176, 195, 198, 203, 211, 216, 245, 246, 259, 266, 275, 278–79
Shaber, M. A., 91, 284, 285
Shakelton, Francis; *A blazing Starre or burnying Beacon . . . to call all sinners to earnest & speedie repentance*, 101
Shakespeare, William, 17, 32, 47, 57; *Coriolanus*, 142; *Hamlet*, 67; *Henry VIII*, 289; *King John*, 289; *King Lear*, 60, 171, 212, 217; *1 Henry IV*, 86; *Richard II*, 221; *Timon of Athens*, 212; *Twelfth Night*, 286; *2 Henry VI*, 166–67; *The Winters Tale*, 281
Shaw, P., 284
Sheavyn, P., 19, 281
Sidney, Sir Philip, 19, 254; the Sidney family, 30
Skinker, Tannakin: *A certaine Relation of the Hog-faced Gentlewoman called Mistris Tannakin Skinker*, 101
Smel-knave, Simon, 29, 283; *Fearefull and lamentable effects of the two dangerous Comets*, 270, 273
Smith, G. G., 289
Smith, Hallett, 291
Smith, Henry: *The Examination of Vsury*, 161, 169
Snawsell, Robert: *A Looking Glasse for Maried Folkes*, 258
'Sowernam, Ester', 32, 266
'Speght, Rachel': *A Mouzell for Melastomus*, 32, 230–31, 287
Spenser, Benjamin: *Lachrymae Londinenses*, 114; *Vox Civitatis*, 115, 117, 205, 206, 209, 261; *Vox Ruris*, 115, 117, 209–10
Spenser, Edmund, 19, 64, 124, 138, 140, 153, 265, 288; on allegory, 123; *The Faerie Queene*, 123, 196
Spufford, M., 12–13
Stage: attacks on, 174; attacks on actors, 173–74; defences of, 140, 174–75
Statham, E. P., 287
Stationers' Company, 25, 26
Stauffer, D. A., 284
Stephens, John: *Satyrical Essayes Characters and Others*, 81
Sternhold-Hopkins Psalter, The, 34

Stone, L., 281, 288
Stow, John: *The Annales of England*, 87, 284, 285
Strange fearful & true newes, which hapned at Carlstadt, in the Kingdom of Croatia, 239
Stubbe, Peeter: *A true Discourse. Declaring the damnable life and death of one Stubbe Peeter*, 92, 95
Stubbes, Katherine: her pious death commemorated in *A Christal Glasse for Christian Women*, 89
Stubbes, Philip, 28, 34, 179; *The Anatomie of Abuses*, 172, 190; *A Christal Glasse for Christian Women*, 89; *The Intended Treason of Doctor Parrie*, 103; *Two wunderful and rare Examples of the Vndeferred and present approaching iudgement of the Lord our God*, 102
Sundrye strange and inhumaine Murthers, 89, 104
Sutherland, J., 243, 290
Swetnam, Joseph: *The Araignment of Lewd, Idle, Froward and unconstant Women*, 24, 32, 178, 179, 230, 257, 265
Swift, Johathan, 10, 265

T., C.: *Laugh and lie downe*, 124
T., W.: *A Casting Up of accounts of certain Errors*, 118
Tailors, 135, 155, 173, 215
Tarlton, Richard: in Chettle, *Kind-Harts Dreame*, 149
Tarltons Newes out of Purgatorie, 149, 190, 267
Tawney, R. H., 282; and E. Power, 46
Taylor, John, the Water Poet, 26, 29, 73, 206; *Crop-Eare Curried*, 149, 241; *The Fearfull Sommer*, 116; *The Great Eater of Kent*, 95, 239–40; *The Vnnatural Father: Or, The Cruell Murther committed by one Iohn Rowse of the Towne of Ewell*, 101; *The World runnes on Wheeles, or Oddes betwixt Carts and Coaches*, 122–23
Tell-Trothes New-Yeares Gift, 151: Telltroth as a satiric persona, 254–65
This Worlds Folly (by I. H.), 142, 174, 176, 208, 246, 247, 251
Thompson, E. S. N., 286, 287
Three Parnassus Plays, The, 26, 28
Thrupp, S. L., 289
Thynne, Francis, *Debate between Pride and Lowliness* as a source of Greene's *A Quip*, 127–28
Tobacco, 121, 194–97, 245, 261
Tofte, Robert, *Of Mariage and Wiving*, 179

Tom Tell Troath Or A free discourse touching the manners of the Tyme, 265
Tourneur, Cyril, 286; *The Revengers Tragedy*, 212–13, 214, 289
Treatise of Daunces, A, 193
True and most Dreadull discourse of a woman possessed with the Devill, A, 97
True and Wonderfull. A discourse relating a Strange and Monstrous Serpent . . . discovered . . . in . . . Horsham, 90, 101–102
Trundle, John, Printer, 96, 97
Tuke, Thomas, *A Treatise Against Painting and Tincturing of Men and Women*, 145, 178, 179, 192, 213, 250–51, 275, 288, 289
Two Most S[t]range And notable examples, shewed at Lysborne (Lisbon), 190
Two most unnatural and bloodie Murthers (the Calverley case), 103–4, 107–8, 251, 263
Twyne, Thomas, *A shorte and pithie Discourse*, 91

Upstarts, 143, 177, 183–86
Usurers, 35, 121, 126, 131, 165, 168–70, 195, 287

Venner, Tobias, *A Briefe and Accurate Treatise*, 194, 196
Vincent, Margaret, *A pitilesse Mother*, 108
Vives, Joannes Ludovicus, 193

Waage, F. O., 286
Walker, A., 286
Walker, Gilbert: *A manifest detection of Diceplay*, 41–42, 45, 60, 258, 283
Warboyds, witches of: *The most strange and admirable discouerie of three Witches of Warboys*, 284
Ward, Samuel: *Woe to Drunkards*, 197, 198
Watson, Thomas, 153
Watson, William: *A Decacordon of Ten Quodlibeticall Questions*, 290

Watt, I., 243, 290
Webster, John, 212
Welby, Henry: *The Phoenix of these late times: Or the life of Mr. Henry Welby Esq. See* Heywood, Thomas
Whetstone, George, 221, 231, 279: *The Censure of a loyall Subiect*, 96, 229, 257; *A Mirour for the Magestrates of Cyties*, 141, 173, 185–86, 200, 215, 285
White, Francis: *Londons Warning by Ierusalem*, 122
White, H. C., 291
White, H. O., 283
Whitgift, John, Archbishop of Canterbury, 31, 154
Wilkins, George: collaboration with Dekker, 283; *The Miseries of Enforced Marriage*, 107; *Three Miseries of Barbary*, 120, 285
Willymat, William: *A Loyall Subiects Looking-Glasse*, 210, 230
Wilson, F. P., 282, 285, 286, 288, 290, 291
Wilson, J.D., 287
Windie Yeace, The, 89
Wine, Beere, Ale, and Tobacco, 194
Wither, George, 282
Wits Theater of the little World (by R. Allot), 226
Wolfe, John, 26
Women, 38, 161–62, 177–83
Wonders, of This Windie Winter, 40
Work for Chimny-sweepers (by I. H.), 194, 196
World of Wonders, A, 96, 99, 202, 285
Wright, C. T., 287
Wright, L. B., 19, 23, 281, 282
Wright, T.: *The Passions of the Mind*, 273

Yorkshire Tragedy, A, 107
Young, Richard (R. Junius): *The Drunkard's Character*, 145, 197, 198, 200, 220
Young, Thomas: *Englands Bane: Or, The Description of Drunkennesse*, 159–60, 230–238